CHAMPAGNE
& SPARKLING WINE GUIDE
2001

CHAMPAGNE
& SPARKLING WINE GUIDE
2001

TOM STEVENSON

A Dorling Kindersley Book

Dorling **DK** Kindersley

LONDON, NEW YORK, SYDNEY, DELHI,
PARIS, MUNICH AND JOHANNESBURG

Dedication

This third edition is dedicated to Jerry
Mead, a crusty, crotchety, cantankerous
American wine hack who had strong
opinions on most things and lived his life
his way. This probably meant that in March
2000 he departed this earth a few years
early, but he did so in good spirits and he
would have been miserable had he hung on
by following every bit of medical advice.
I have no doubt that they are beginning to
wonder who's running the place up top.
Give 'em hell Jerry!

Senior Editor Edward Bunting

Senior Art Editor Kevin Ryan

Editor Sally Somers

DTP Designer Sonia Charbonnier

Managing Editor Sharon Lucas

Managing Art Editor Derek Coombes

Production Sarah Coltman, Marie Ingledew

This completely revised edition first
published in Great Britain in 2000 by
Dorling Kindersley Limited,
9 Henrietta Street, London WC2E 8PS

First edition published in 1998

2 4 6 8 10 9 7 5 3 1

A CIP catalogue record is available from
the British Library.

ISBN 0-7513-3346-8

Reproduced by Colourscan
Text film output by Graphical Innovations
Printed and bound in Spain by AGT (Artes
Gráficas Toledo S.A.U.) D.L. TO: 1607-2000

See our complete
catalogue at

www.dk.com

CONTENTS

Street name in Hautvillers.

THE WORLD'S BEST PRODUCERS

Poster for Veuve Clicquot.

UK STOCKISTS

THIS YEAR'S TASTINGS

Vineyard planted for sparkling wine in the Marlborough region of New Zealand.

FOREWORD

This is the third annual edition of *The Champagne & Sparkling Wine Guide* and as the now defunct British Rail once famously said – we're getting there. They never did, of course, and frankly neither will this Guide. Its ultimate destination can never be reached. To do so would require the inclusion of every single Champagne and sparkling wine worthy of recommendation. That's a dream and I'll keep chasing it, but although I taste a minimum of 3,000 such wines a year at my private facility and at least 1,000 during my travels and at centralized tastings, I'm hardly scratching the surface. When it comes to fizz, I know of no one else who tastes as widely or as deeply as this, but to put this into perspective there are 12,599 brands of Champagne alone and with an average of four *cuvées* per brand: that's well over 50,000 different Champagne labels on the shelf every year. Some expert, eh?

Champagne is just one of the sparkling wines. The best and most exciting, maybe, but just one place of origin. There are 38 other French fizz appellations and beyond that there is, literally, a world of sparkling wine to choose from. Okay, so I'm just scratching the

surface, but that's where the cream is. Most of the stuff underneath isn't worth contemplating, let alone tasting. I am acquainted with all of the greatest producers and know, or know of, most of the best of the rest. Furthermore, I'm usually one of the first to hear about any exciting new fizzmaker on the block. If there is anyone serious I am unaware of, then they will certainly know who I am and with more than enough contact notices throughout this Guide, all submissions welcome and absolutely no charge applicable, there is no reason why they should not to get in touch.

In addition to the wines that are submitted directly to me and the centralized tastings that are arranged especially for this guide by various generic organizations, I also travel to Champagne on a regular basis and every year select various other areas to visit. This year, for example, I made trips specifically for this guide to Germany, Franciacorta, Asti, New York, Michigan, New Zealand and Australia. My aim when visiting such areas is to taste the current and future vintage of every serious sparkling wine produced. So although the dream I'm chasing is a mission most impossible, readers can at least be assured that I'm tasting virtually everything worth tasting every year.

Tom Stevenson

Champagne Vilmart looks to the Third Millennium with its 1990 Cuvée Création.

July 2000

INTRODUCTION

A brief history of sparkling wine, how it
is made, how to store and serve it, and
what style to choose.

A Brief History

Wines have accidentally effervesced since biblical times, as shown by "wine…when it moveth itself" (Proverbs) and "neither do men put new wine into old bottles, else the bottles break" (Matthew). But as a deliberate style, sparkling wine dates only from the 17th century.

The **Champagne Riots** of 1911 were all about protecting the quality of this frothy, frivolous wine *(see p20)*.

AN ENGLISH INVENTION

Until the end of the 17th century the wine made in the Champagne region of France was a murky *rosé* colour, and it was still, not sparkling *(see p18)*. The first French document that mentions sparkling Champagne, dated 1718, refers to the emergence of this style "more than 20 years earlier". As French glass was too weak for fizzy wine before about 1695, and an efficient seal such as a cork was not available, sparkling Champagne's debut in France must have been between about 1695 and 1698.

The English, by contrast, already had the technology – their glass was coal-fired and strong, and they had cork – and there is proof that they used it to make still wines sparkle at least 30 years before the French. At the Royal Society in 1662, a Dr Merret stated that "our wine-coopers of recent times use vast quantities of sugar and molasses to all sorts of wines to make them drink brisk and sparkling". There is also evidence that the English deliberately put a sparkle into the imported still wines of Champagne. In 1676 the dramatist Sir George Etherege wrote that "sparkling Champaign…makes us frolic and gay, and drowns all sorrow".

GROWTH OF AN INDUSTRY

Even if the Champenois did not invent sparkling wine, they began to capitalize on their *terroir's* unique suitability *(see p16)* to the style in the 18th century. Markets were

The Joy of Fizz

No other drink has developed such a hedonistic image as Champagne. Winners, lovers and revellers of all kinds have been drenching themselves with it throughout the 20th century as well as imbibing it. And aficionados happily spend small fortunes to savour a great *cuvée*.

found across Europe, and Americans took to it soon after George Washington served it in 1790. In the 19th century sparkling Champagne was exported under the *marques* (names) of famous houses, and most of the civilized world began to drink it in quantity.

The secret of sparkling wine-making leaked out to other wine regions in France and Germany by the 1820s, as far as America by the 1840s, and all the way to Australia by the 1850s. At the turn of the 20th century Champagne was enjoying its Golden Era, turning over 30 million bottles a year compared to 600,000 a hundred years earlier. The technology to produce sparkling wine on a vast commercial scale was available to all wine-producing countries, and the world was awash with bubbles.

Champagne is so extraordinary a wine that its greatest role has become one in which it is not drunk at all, but dashed against the side of a ship about to be launched.

CHAMPAGNE
JOSEPH PERRIER

Sparkling wine's most powerful image has long been that it is a drink for the exuberant and extrovert.

Ideas have changed over the years of how best to enjoy your fizz – taking it through a straw was in vogue a century ago.

Some brand names have become world famous.

Cordon Rouge

G. H. MUMM & C⁰· REIMS
SOCIÉTÉ VINICOLE DE CHAMPAGNE SUCCESSEUR

Louis Roederer, whose monogram this is, was the favoured *grande marque* of those famous hedonists, the Russian tsars. That some of their Communist usurpers also drank Champagne is not so well known.

HOW IT IS MADE

The theory behind sparkling wine is simple. Fermentation converts sugar into alcohol and carbonic gas – if the gas is set free the wine is still, if not, it is sparkling. To capture the gas, the wine undergoes a second fermentation in a sealed container. The gas gushes out in the form of tiny bubbles when the container is opened.

THE GRAPES
Various grapes are used, but Chardonnay and Pinot Noir are best for premium quality sparkling wine – they are relatively neutral, with a good balance of sugar and acidity when ripe.

CUVE CLOSE METHOD
Most cheap fizz is produced by *cuve close* (or "Charmat" or "tank" method). Both fermentations take place in large vats, then the wine is bottled under pressure. As *cuve close* is a bulk-production method it attracts low-calibre base wines, but the speed and minimum yeast contact makes it perfect for sweet, aromatic fizz such as Asti *(see pp50–51)*.

MÉTHODE CHAMPENOISE
The greatest *brut*-style (dry) sparkling wines are made by *méthode champenoise*. As in *cuve close*, the first fermentation takes place en masse, sometimes in oak *barriques*, but the second takes place in the actual bottle in which the wine is sold.

In the European Union the term *méthode champenoise* is reserved for Champagne. However, the terms below are all synonymous with *méthode champenoise*:

ENGLISH-LANGUAGE COUNTRIES

Traditional Method

FRANCE

Méthode Traditionnelle
Méthode Classique
"Crémant" appellations

SPAIN

The "Cava" appellation

ITALY

Metodo Classico
Metodo Tradizionale
Talento

GERMANY

Flaschengärung nach dem Traditionellen Verfahren
Klassische Flaschengärung
Traditionelle Flaschengärung

SOUTH AFRICA

Cap Classique

CHOCOLAT GUÉRIN-BOUTRON
LES DIFFÉRENTES INDUSTRIES
72 Sujets

FABRICATION DU CHAMPAGNE · REMUEUR · DÉGORGEUR · MÉLANGEUR

There are 250 million bubbles waiting to gush out of the average bottle of sparkling wine.

Three winemakers capture the sparkle of twice-fermented grape juice.

MALOLACTIC CONVERSION

Most fizz undergoes "malolactic", a natural process of fermentation that converts hard malic acid into soft lactic acid and adds creaminess to the wine. Of the few producers who prevent the malolactic, Bollinger, Alfred Gratien, Krug and Lanson are the most famous. In the New World the malolactic is often overworked because grapes are picked early, and have higher levels of malic acid.

BLENDING AND THE PRISE DE MOUSSE

The blending *(assemblage)* of the base wine is undertaken after the first fermentation. The Champenois are the masters of this, and may create a non-vintage *cuvée* from as many as 70 base wines. Sugar, selected yeasts, yeast nutrients and a clarifying agent are then added to induce the mousse. The second fermentation is often referred to as the *prise de mousse*, or "capturing the sparkle", and it can take months to complete. In contrast to the first fermentation, which should be relatively fast and warm, the second is slow and cool.

AUTOLYSIS

When the second fermentation is complete, the yeast cells undergo an enzymatic breakdown called autolysis, which is epitomized by an acacia-like flowery finesse. Good autolysis adds complexity.

REMUAGE AND DISORGEMENT

In *méthode champenoise* only, the yeast deposit created during the second fermentation is encouraged down the neck of the inverted bottle into a small plastic pot held in place by a crown-cap. *Remuage* (or riddling), as this is called, takes eight weeks by hand, or eight days by machine. The sediment is removed (disgorged) by immersing the bottle in freezing brine, and ejecting the semi-frozen pot without losing too much wine or gas.

THE DOSAGE

Before corking, the *liqueur d'expédition* is added. In all cases except *extra brut* (very dry), this will include some sugar. The younger the wine, the greater the dosage of sugar required.

THE MAIN STAGES OF MÉTHODE CHAMPENOISE

First fermentation en masse in oak or stainless steel.

Bottled with sugar and yeast for second fermentation.

Sediment collected by the *remuage* method.

Disgorging the sediment for a crystal-clear wine.

---

*T*he internal pressure in a bottle of sparkling wine is equivalent to the pressure of a double-decker bus tyre.

STORING AND SERVING

Most fizz is best drunk within a year or so. Only a few *cuvées* are capable of developing truly complex aromas and flavours after disgorgement.

WHY STORE?
Typically, Chardonnay turns "toasty" and Pinot Noir "biscuity", although the reverse is possible and even a whiff of clean sulphur can contribute to the toastiness of a wine. Some first-class Chardonnays develop specific, complex aromas such as flowery hazelnuts, creamy brazil nuts, and mellow walnuts. The greatest Champagnes can age gracefully for decades, to create rich nuances of macaroons, coconut, cocoa and coffee.

HOW TO STORE
Fizz is more sensitive to temperature and light than other wines, but there should be no problem keeping it for a year or two at any fairly constant temperature between 12 and 18°C (40–60°F). Higher temperatures increase the rate of oxidation; erratic temperatures can seriously damage the wine. If you do not have a cellar, keep it in a cool place inside a box. Very long-term storage should be at 9–11°C (48–52°F) in total darkness. There is no reason why bottles should be stored horizontally apart from to save space: the CO_2 in the bottle neck keeps the cork moist and swollen even when upright. Some Champagnes have retained their sparkle for a century under ideal conditions.

A wide, shallow glass is not the ideal vessel for drinking sparkling wine – the mousse goes flat too quickly. However it is perfect for those special occasions when you want to stack them high and watch them froth.

Some Champagnes, such as Roederer Cristal, are shipped with a yellow, anti-UV wrapping, which you should leave on while storing. Brown-glass bottles offer better protection against ultraviolet than green-glass, and dead-leaf or dark green is better than light or bright green.

Champagne *cuvées*, boxed up and ready for shipment.

Chilling

Temperature determines the rate at which bubbles in a sparkling wine are released. Bubbly should not be opened at room temperature – the wine will quickly froth up and go flat. Chill it, ideally down to 4.5–7°C (40–45°F), the lower temperature for parties and receptions where the room temperature is likely to rise.

It is okay to chill wine in a refrigerator for a couple of hours, but try not to leave it longer than a day because the cork might stick or shrink. Emergency chilling of a sparkling wine by putting it in the coldest part of a deep-freeze for 15 minutes is fine.

A bucket of ice and water (never just ice) is still one of the quickest ways to chill a bottle of fizz, but faster still are the gel-filled jackets that are kept in the deep freeze and slip over the bottle for about six minutes. Invert the bottle gently a couple of times before opening to help chill the wine in the neck.

Gel-filled jacket for efficient, fast chilling.

Opening

Remember that the secret of success is to try and prevent the cork from actually coming out.

Remove the foil to begin, or simply score around the base of the wire cage. Then gently untwist the wire and loosen the bottom of the cage, but don't remove it. Hold the bottle with a cloth if you are a novice, and completely enclose the cork and cage in one hand (the right, if you are right-handed). Holding the base of the bottle with your other hand, twist both ends in opposite directions, backwards and forwards.

As soon as you feel pressure forcing the cork out, try to push it back in, but continue the opening operation ever more gently until the cork is re-leased from the bottle with a sigh, not a bang.

The "Champagne Star", made by Screwpull. Designed specially to open a bottle of fizz, it is the best bet for a stubborn cork.

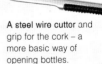

Pouring

Pour a little into each glass first to allow for the foam, then go back and top up each one to between two-thirds and three-quarters of the vessel. Do not tilt the glass and pour gently down the inside, it is not lager!

A steel wire cutter and grip for the cork – a more basic way of opening bottles.

Untwist the wire and loosen the cage.

Twist cork and bottle in opposite directions.

Allow the cork to be released with a sigh.

STYLES

Dry *(brut)* is a classic style of bubbly, while *sec* and *doux* indicate a rising scale of sweetness. Other categories of style include the basic division of vintage and non-vintage, grape variety, colour and degree of mousse.

WHAT'S IN A VINTAGE?

A Champagne vintage implies that the harvest was exceptional, while for most other fizz "vintage" is best regarded as a statement of age, not quality. Vintage Champagne must be 100 per cent from the year, but elsewhere it varies (95 per cent in California; 85 in Australia). Store vintage Champagne for 8–10 years from the date of harvest. The term non-vintage (NV) sounds derogatory to many people, but wines from various years can be skilfully blended to create some of the finest *cuvées* available.

Prestige cuvées are particular wines that producers feel best epitomize their style. Examples are Dom Pérignon (made by Moët & Chandon), Cristal (by Louis Roederer) and

COLOUR

Pure Chardonnay *blanc de blancs* (white wine made from white grapes) make good *brut*-style sparkling wines, and the best come from the Côte des Blancs in Champagne. In the New World, *blanc de noirs* (white wine made from black grapes) can be various shades, but in Champagne the skill is to produce as white a wine as possible from Pinot Noir or Meunier, and the most famous is Bollinger's Vielles Vignes Françaises. Champagne *rosé* can be made by blending white wine with a little red. Sparkling red wines are also available, such as Australian Sparkling Shiraz.

Belle Epoque (by Perrier-Jouët). They are produced in tiny quantities, and it is their rarity value that determines the high price. The selection of base wines is the most significant defining factor in any prestige *cuvée*.

CRÉMANT

The *crémant* style has a soft mousse, and few producers outside France have a reputation for it. Normal fizz has a pressure of 5–6 atmospheres, while *crémant* has 3.6. To be a true *crémant*, the mousse must unfold slowly, leaving a creamy cordon in the glass. Mumm de Cramant (sic) is the best known.

THE WORLD'S BEST PRODUCERS

An overview of Champagne, other parts
of France, and Spain, Germany, Italy,
the USA, Australia, New Zealand
and South Africa.

FRANCE
THE CHAMPAGNE REGION

The world's finest *brut*-style sparkling wine is created from Chardonnay, Pinot Noir and Meunier grapes grown on the pure chalk hillsides of the Champagne region in northern France. A fizz from anywhere else, including other parts of France – no matter how good – is simply not Champagne.

Chardonnay, whose acidity is well suited to Champagne, is cultivated across about a quarter of the AOC area.

A UNIQUE VITICULTURAL REGION

Elsewhere in the world sparkling wine producers have to work hard to produce decent fizz, but the Champenois can make it almost without trying. The region is in a viticultural twilight zone where the vine struggles to ripen each year. Grapes eventually ripen at a relatively low alcoholic strength, ideal for a second fermentation, and have a very high level of ripe acidity, which is necessary for the wine to age well in bottle.

It is true that Chardonnay and Pinot Noir can be grown almost anywhere, and vines thrive on chalk hillsides in many places, but only in the Atlantic-influenced north of France (the country's northernmost winemaking region) do these and other factors come together, albeit precariously, with a climate that is barely on the right side of the knife-edge between success and failure. Yet the risks are deemed worth taking because, when all goes well, the result is undoubtedly the world's finest sparkling wine.

The harvest brings Champagne to life in the autumn. Even grapes from lesser years can make good Champagnes.

Veuve Clicquot *(see p34)* is one of the largest and best-loved houses, exporting its top-notch fizz to scores of countries.

AOC DISTRICTS

Five main Champagne districts, encompassing some 32,000 hectares of vineyards, lie within the AOC (Appellation d'Origine Contrôlée) delimited region. Reims and Épernay are the area's main towns.

Remuage performed by a cellar worker at Charles Heidsieck *(see p25)*. This involves the gradual rotation of bottles so any sediment is loosened and can be removed.

Paris

FRANCE

• REIMS

VALLÉE DE LA MARNE

MONTAGNE DE REIMS

ÉPERNAY •

CÔTE DES BLANCS

Châlons-en-Champagne

• Montmirail

• Sézanne

Vitry-le-François

CÔTE DE SÉZANNE

Brienne-le-Château

Troyes

AUBE

☐ Vallée de la Marne
☐ Montagne de Reims
☐ Côte des Blancs
☐ Côte de Sézanne
▨ Aube
☐ Other areas of AOC Champagne

| 0 KILOMETRES | 20 |
| 0 MILES | 10 |

CHAMPAGNE – A STILL WINE?

It may seem strange to us now, but the wine of Champagne was originally still, not sparkling. It was introduced in this form to the French Court – traditionally the domain of Burgundy – in the 15th century. Merchants from around Europe took this still wine to other parts of France, Spain, Italy, England and the Low Countries.

The English are known to have put a sparkle into imported Champagnes in the 17th century *(see p8)*. Dom Pérignon (1639–1715), a monk at Hautvillers Abbey, near Reims, is widely thought to have invented sparkling Champagne, but there is little hard evidence to support this. Most French gourmands despised the idea of fizzy Champagne at the time. However, in the 18th century the habit of drinking sparkling as well as still Champagne spread across Europe and as far as Russia.

Iron sign in Hautvillers, Vallée de la Marne.

Ruinart, in Reims, was the first Champagne house.

THE FIRST CHAMPAGNE HOUSES

Ruinart *(see p30)*, the first proper Champagne house, was founded in 1729. Others soon followed, though the vast majority of Champagne produced was still, and this remained the situation up to the end of the 18th century. Several houses started out as textile firms, offering gifts of Champagne to customers, until demand for the gifts outstripped that for the textiles.

Many firms hired German salesmen, renowned for their linguistic and commercial skills, some of whom later set up their own firms in the Champagne region (such as Krug and Bollinger).

Heidsieck & Co Monopole was founded in 1834 by Henri-Louis Walbaum, a member of the famous Heidsieck family.

Best Houses
1. Billecart-Salmon p22
   Mareuil-sur-Aÿ
2. Bollinger p23
   Aÿ-Champagne
3. Gosset p24
   Aÿ-Champagne
4. Charles Heidsieck p25
   Reims
5. Jacquesson p26
   Dizy
6. Krug p27 *Reims*
7. Laurent-Perrier p28
   Tours-sur-Marne
8. Moët & Chandon p29
   Épernay
9. Pol Roger p30
   Épernay
10. Louis Roederer p31
    Reims
11. Ruinart p32 *Reims*
12. Salon p33
    Le Mesnil-sur-Oger
13. Veuve Clicquot p34
    Reims
14. Vilmart p35
    Rilly-la-Montagne

GRAND CRU AREA

The *crus* of Champagne are 300 or so villages whose vineyards are rated according to a percentile system called the Échelle des Crus. Of the villages surrounding Épernay and Reims, 17 have *grand cru* status – the quality of their grapes is rated 100 per cent.

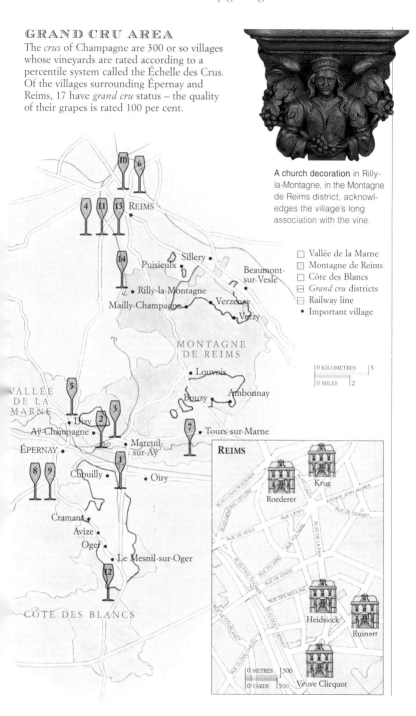

A church decoration in Rilly-la-Montagne, in the Montagne de Reims district, acknowledges the village's long association with the vine.

- ☐ Vallée de la Marne
- ☐ Montagne de Reims
- ☐ Côte des Blancs
- ⊟ *Grand cru* districts
- ⊟ Railway line
- • Important village

Sillery
Puisieulx
Beaumont-sur-Vesle
Rilly-la-Montagne
Mailly-Champagne
Verzenay
Verzy

MONTAGNE DE REIMS

Louvois
Bouzy
Ambonnay
Dizy
Aÿ-Champagne
Tours-sur-Marne
ÉPERNAY
Mareuil-sur-Aÿ
Chouilly
Oiry
Cramant
Avize
Oger
Le Mesnil-sur-Oger

VALLÉE DE LA MARNE

CÔTE DES BLANCS

REIMS

0 KILOMETRES 5
0 MILES 2

REIMS

Roederer
Krug
Heidsieck
Ruinart
Veuve Clicquot

0 METRES 500
0 YARDS 500

BLVD LOUIS ROEDERER
BLVD LUNDY
BLVD GÉNÉRAL LECLERC
AVENUE JEAN JAURÈS
RUE DE CERNAY
RUE LADIES
RUE DE VESLE
BLVD VICTOR HUGO
BLVD DE LA PAIX
RUE DU LAND
RUE DES MOULINS
RUE PAUL DOUMER
RUE DE VENISE
BLVD DOCT DUCHÉ
RUE DE COURANCY
RUE CLOVIS CHEZEL
HENROT

Moët & Chandon produces more than 13 per cent of all *négociant-manipulant* (house) Champagne.

CHAMPAGNE TAKES ON THE WORLD

It was not until the early 19th century, when the entrepreneurs of the most famous houses hawked their brands to all four corners of the globe, that the production and therefore name of the Champagne region became synonymous with sparkling wine. The English and Americans, especially, took to Champagne's natural appeal as a wine to celebrate with, and were drinking themselves under the table by the mid-19th century. Surprisingly to us now, it was a sweet wine that they were imbibing. At the turn of the century one in ten bottles was as sweet as the dessert wine Sauternes.

In the early 20th century, as increasingly more land in the Champagne region was given over to viticulture, and the quality of the wine grew ever higher, the Champenois started to quarrel over the Champagne name. Not only were other nations calling their own sparklers "Champagne" but some houses were using grapes from other parts of France. The Champagne Riots of 1911 brought the issue to a head, with growers from the Marne and Aube fighting in the streets of Aÿ. Worse still, the vineyards were the scene of trench warfare a few years later as German forces swept into Champagne.

Exports suffered after World War I, as the Russian market collapsed and Prohibition took America *(see p54)* and parts of

*S*ince the Americans christened Charles-Camille Heidsieck *(see p25)* "Champagne Charlie" and George Leybourne hit the boards with his celebrated song *(see p29)*, Champagne has been affectionately referred to by some slang-name or other. In England, the Victorians were the first to call it fizz. The Edwardians knew it as bubbly, in the 1960s and '70s it was champers, and in the '80s it became known as shampoo.

The world's most prestigious wine has long been associated with celebration, romance and general *joie de vivre.*

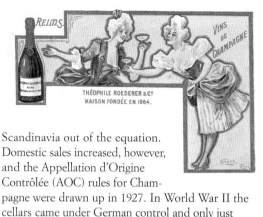

Théophile Roederer was once a separate company from Louis Roederer *(see p31)*, but was purchased by the latter in 1907.

Scandinavia out of the equation. Domestic sales increased, however, and the Appellation d'Origine Contrôlée (AOC) rules for Champagne were drawn up in 1927. In World War II the cellars came under German control and only just escaped being blown up as the Germans retreated.

Many new markets have developed since the 1950s, but at the Millennium France is drinking almost twice as much Champagne as the rest of the world put together.

There are over 9,000 brands of Champagne marketed by 2,500 houses, growers and cooperatives. Also, there are 3,000 buyers'-own-brands, making a total of more than 12,000 seemingly different brands. With each offering an average of four *cuvées*, there are thus about 50,000 "different" Champagnes!

THE CHAMPAGNE QUALITY

The Champagne name is considered such a guarantee of quality that it is the only AOC wine not obliged to mention AOC on the label. The Champenois are not only blessed with perfect growing conditions for sparkling wine, but they have also spent centuries perfecting their art. It is they who developed the *méthode champenoise* and who take the *assemblage* more seriously than other producers.

WHO ARE THE PRODUCERS?

A Champagne "house" is a *négociant-manipulant* (NM on labels) – it makes and sells Champagne using its own vineyards and buying extra grapes from small growers. There are over 250 houses, producing about 70 per cent of the wines and nearly all exports. The biggest house is Moët & Chandon. Some small growers and cooperatives, collectively known as the *vignoble*, also make their own wines, mostly for the domestic market. On pages 22–35 we take a closer look at the best houses.

Gosset *(see p24)* started to make Champagne in the 16th century, though it was a still wine at the time.

BILLECART-SALMON

A SMALL, family-owned house that produces Champagne of great finesse, Billecart-Salmon is famous for its delicate *rosé*, which represents one-fifth of all it sells.

Founded in 1818, the firm says its wine "crosses the centuries...".

Nicolas-François Billecart established the house in 1818 with the help of his brother-in-law Louis Salmon, in Mareuil-sur-Aÿ, where his family has lived since the 1500s.

Billecart-Salmon's entire range will delight those who enjoy a purity and ripeness of fruit in their Champagnes, yet also want them to be able to age well. Billecart-Salmon was exceptional 20 years ago, but due to the acquisition of another ten hectares of vineyards and a constant upgrade in grapes, the wines are even better today.

Billecart-Salmon quickly gained a world-wide reputation but nearly went bust just 12 years after being founded, when an American agent lost the company a staggering 100,000 golden francs.

The essence of the Billecart-Salmon style has always been its meticulous production, from the double *débourbage,* or cleansing of the must, through the use of its own cultured yeast (from natural yeasts of Avize, Cramant and Verzenay), to its long, slow, very cool fermentation. This regime was formulated by James Coffinet, the *chef de caves* under Jean Roland-Billecart until the mid-1980s. That Coffinet was head-hunted by Pol Roger *(see p30)* is a testament to his winemaking skill and reputation. The fact that his successor, François Domi, has made even better wines under François Roland-Billecart should reassure aficionados of this house.

The Billecart house has an attractive English-style garden and the only Chasselas vine in Champagne.

Building on its reputation for *rosé*, Billecart-Salmon introduced a superb new wine with its 1988 vintage Cuvée Elizabeth Salmon.

BOLLINGER

The Bollinger house in the village of Aÿ was spared from destruction during the Champagne Riots of 1911. A growers' uprising had started when the government tried to bring in strict laws to control the Champagne name.

THE KEY TO "Bolly's" success is its 140 hectares of top-rated vineyards, providing some 70 per cent of its needs compared with 12 per cent for the average house. The keys to its style are judicious selection of grape juice, the use of oak *barriques*, minimal malolactic and extraordinary reserve wines.

Who drinks Bolly? James Bond, Prince Charles; and Joanna Lumley's Patsy thinks it's Absolutely Fabulous.

Jacques Bollinger first sold wines in 1822 for Müller-Ruinart (now Henri Abelé) and seven years later formed a company with Paul Renaudin, using the vineyards of the Comte de Villermont. The house was called Renaudin Bollinger until 1984.

Bollinger's vintage Champagnes are all 100 per cent barrel-fermented, whereas its non-vintage Special Cuvée is 50 per cent. Reserve wines are bottled in magnums with a tiny dosage of sugar and yeast, which helps to keep them fresh, or *pétillant* (lightly sparkling). There are some amazing Bollinger reserves up to 80 years old, although 15 years is usually the limit set for commercial use.

Reserve wines are bottled in magnums, and some are left undisturbed literally for decades.

Lily Bollinger (1899–1977) was responsible for Champagne's most famous quote. When asked how she enjoyed a glass of Bolly she replied: "I drink it when I'm happy and when I'm sad. Sometimes I drink it when I'm alone. When I have company I consider it obligatory. I trifle with it when I'm not hungry and drink it when I am. Otherwise I never touch it – unless I'm thirsty of course."

GOSSET

JEAN GOSSET was Seigneur d'Aÿ in 1531, and his son Claude was a vigneron in 1555, but there is no proof that they traded wine, thus the honour of founding the house goes to Pierre Gosset in 1584.

As mayor of Aÿ between 1584 and 1592, Pierre had the privilege of receiving Henri IV, who in all probability drank Gosset's wine, though it was still, not sparkling, at the time. (Ruinart was the first Champagne house on record to produce sparkling wine.)

In 1992 Gosset became the first new *grande marque* (literally "famous name") for more than 30 years, though ironically the Syndicat des Grandes Marques de Champagne was disbanded in 1997.

In 1994, after 410 years of family ownership, Gosset was sold. While this was very sad, at least it was not taken over by one of the large groups. It is owned by the Cointreau family, under the direct control of Béatrice Cointreau. The *chef de caves* and oenologist remain the same at Gosset, as do the winemaking techniques, which involve the use of some wood and an avoidance of malolactic fermentation . The production level is also unchanged, at just over 500,000 bottles (similar in size to Krug). Small is indeed beautiful at Gosset, where the Grande Réserve, Grand Millésimé, Grand Millésimé Rosé and Celebris consistently rank among the best wines made in Champagne.

The **temperature** inside stainless steel fermenting tanks is checked by Jean-Pierre Marson of Gosset.

*A*n extremely large bottle of Champagne was produced by Gosset in 1986 to celebrate the 100th Anniversary of the Statue of Liberty. Called a "Salomon" and made of pure crystal, it held the equivalent of 24 bottles of Champagne, and was 20 per cent larger than a Nebuchadnezzar size of bottle.

Béatrice Cointreau, who has breathed some fresh air into the Champagne trade, enjoying Gosset.

CHARLES HEIDSIECK

THERE ARE THREE Heid-
siecks in Champagne:
Charles Heidsieck, Piper-
Heidsieck and Heidsieck & Co
Monopole, and all three claim
roots back to the Heidsieck
firm established by Florens-
Louis Heidsieck in 1785.

Daniel Thibault justly won
the award of Sparkling
Winemaker of the Year in
1994 for his contribution to
non-vintage Champagne.

The first two belong to Rémy-
Cointreau, a French family-
owned group that includes Krug. The best of the
three is Charles Heidsieck, established in 1851 by
Charles-Camille Heidsieck, a grand-nephew of
Florens-Louis. He was known as "Champagne
Charlie" in America in the late 1850s through his
flamboyant and daring lifestyle, which landed him
in prison in 1861 for smuggling French company
contracts through enemy lines to the Confederates.

Charles Heidsieck Reserve has been the most
consistent and best-value non-vintage Champagne
since the late 1980s, when master blender Daniel
Thibault transformed the brand. Its rich, complex
flavour is tinged with oak-like vanilla,
though the stainless-steel fermented
cuvée has never seen so much as a
stave of oak.

Much is made of Thibault's
extensive use of reserve wines,
but it is his philosophy of Champagne's *crus* (Champagne-pro-
ducing villages) that has had the
greatest influence. Thibault insists
on emphasizing the individual
characteristics of each village, by
allowing the fermentation to progress as naturally as possible. He
wants a palate of the purest colours
when he paints his blend on the canvas of a *cuvée*.
To his mind, he cannot possibly produce an
expressive Champagne blend if each component
part has not been allowed to express itself.

*C*harles-Camille Heid-
sieck inspired George
Leybourne's famous

1860s music-hall song
"Champagne Charlie".
For a shilling, however,
Leybourne would insert
the name of any other
Champagne firm in his
song. The most quoted
version is for Moet and
Shandon (sic), so Moët
must have had more
shillings than anyone
else, even then.

JACQUESSON & FILS

The label of the 1985 Dégorgement Tardive ("late disgorgement") depicts the gold medal awarded by Napoleon after he visited the cellars in 1810.

I T WAS NOT UNTIL 1974, when Jacquesson was purchased by the Chiquet family of Dizy, that the foundations of the superb quality we know today were laid down.

The firm was established in 1798 by Claude Jacquesson and his son Memmie. They built ten kilometres of magnificent cellars in Châlons-sur-Marne (now called Châlons-en-Champagne). The "richness and beauty" of these cellars prompted Napoleon to award the house a special medal.

In 1834 Jacquesson employed a young German by the name of Joseph Krug, who later left the company to set up his own house. By 1867 Jacquesson was selling in excess of one million bottles, but after Adolphe Jacquesson died in 1875, his family chose other careers and sales dwindled. In the 1920s Jacquesson was bought by a broker called Léon de Tassigny, who moved the firm to Reims. The Chiquet family, who have owned it since 1974, have been growers for generations (their cousins, in Dizy, sell under the *récoltant-manipulant* Champagne Gaston Chiquet label).

Some of Jacquesson's base wines are vinified in large oak *foudres* (large wooden casks or vats), which are also used to store the reserve wines. This factor contributes to the great complexity that these Champagnes can have.

*O*n 4 July 1849, the *Niantic* dropped anchor in San Francisco Bay, and her crew deserted to join the gold rush. The abandoned, beached ship was used as a warehouse then hotel for a few years. When the hotel was demolished in the 1870s some 35 baskets of wine labelled Jacquesson were found. Newspaper clippings report this wine was "so completely covered as to be almost excluded from the air, and some of the wine effervesced slightly on uncorking, and was of a very fair flavour".

The Chiquet family's vineyards in Aÿ, Dizy, Hautvillers and Avize provide the heart and soul of the Jacquesson style.

KRUG

AS FAR AS wine investors are concerned, Krug is the only blue-chip Champagne on the market: it never fails to attract bidders at auction.

Ever since the house was founded in 1843 by the Mainz-born Joseph Krug, the family has put quality first, regardless of popular taste or production costs. No better example exists of the extraordinary lengths Krug goes to than Krug Grande Cuvée, which is fermented in small oak *barriques*, receives 35 to 50 per cent of reserve wines from six to ten different vintages, and spends about five to seven years on its yeast. With the possible exception of the tiny house of Salon (*see p33*), this sort of quality is not equalled by any other producer, although it could be if others were willing to sell tiny quantities at extremely high prices.

Not everyone appreciates the Krug style, but that merely makes Krug drinkers more elitist. The problem is that it is the world's most famous yet least-consumed Champagne, so it gets deified on the one hand, and vilified on the other.

Krug's house in Reims *(top)* was used as a hospital during World War I. Jeanne Krug was one of the last women to evacuate the heavily shelled city. The family has its own philosophy for making wine, such as using small oak *barriques (bottom)*.

Most regular wine drinkers have never drunk Krug, and even the wine trade and wine writers rarely have a chance to taste it. Happily I have tasted Krug countless times and can honestly say that I have detected a drop in quality just twice in over 20 years: namely Clos du Mesnil 1980, and a very green Grande Cuvée that was circulating in 1988, and in the twilight zone of Champagne that is as close to perfection as you can get.

*K*rug is served at some of the most fashionable social events in England. Guests at the annual bash of novelist and politician Jeffrey Archer are greeted with a plate of shepherd's pie and a glass of the bubbly.

LAURENT-PERRIER

Bernard de Nonancourt's Château de Louvois was built in 1680 by Louis XIV's Secretary of State for War, on the site of a ruined castle. It is said to be haunted.

THE LAURENT FAMILY were coopers in the village of Chigny-les-Roses, when in 1812 they tired of seeing other people's wines in their own casks, and set up a house in the remains of an abbey at Tours-sur-Marne.

Eugène Laurent married Mathilde Émile Perrier, but they died without heirs. Marie-Louise de Nonancourt, one of the Lanson family (*see A–Z listing*), bought the firm in 1938, keeping the name Laurent-Perrier. It became really successful under her son Bernard and is now ranked in the top six houses. The Laurent-Perrier group also includes De Castellane, Delamotte, Lemoine, Joseph Perrier and Salon (*see p33*).

The general house style leans towards light and elegant, but the vintage is fuller, while the prestige *cuvée* Grand Siècle can be almost sumptuous in its richness, attaining great complexity and finesse with age. Laurent-Perrier is also famous for its *rosé*, and it is one of the few houses to make it by the *saignée* method, whereby surplus liquid is drawn off from the fermenting vat. The non-vintage *rosé* with the salmon pink label is the best known, but the vintaged Grand Siècle Cuvée Alexandre is a class apart. Bernard de Nonancourt named it after his daughter, and no doubt his winemaker, Alain Terrier, did not dare produce anything but the best.

In the 1980s there was a trend for non-dosage (extremely dry) Champagnes, which died a quick death, to the relief of many. But few people knew that Laurent-Perrier had sold a "Grand Vin Sans Sucre" a century earlier. In 1893 the firm described it as: "The natural highest class Champagne of remarkably fine flavour, taste and bouquet, without any added sugar or alcohol, shipped by Laurent-Perrier & Co. A wine of marvellously clean taste, invigorating and exhilarating properties, superior to all Champagnes containing sugar."

MOËT & CHANDON

WHILE Napoleon's patronage laid the foundations for Moët's early success, what has sealed this firm's fortune is a marketing vision that keeps it several steps ahead of the rest of the pack.

Jean-Rémy (1758–1841), grandson of the founder, Claude Moët, had one great claim to fame: his friendship with Napoleon, which had begun when the young Bonaparte was still at military school in Brienne. The Emperor would stop off at his old friend's cellars on his way to war with Prussia.

After Jean-Rémy retired in 1832, control of the house went to his son-in-law Pierre Gabriel Chandon. Later, the firm started to associate itself with another historical figure, Dom Pérignon, the 17th-century Benedictine monk from the Abbey of Hautvillers, who is credited (wrongly) with inventing Champagne *(see p18)*. Moët had the foresight to purchase the Abbey back in 1823 and happily fostered the legend. The crowning glory of this association was the use of Dom Pérignon's name for the very first prestige *cuvée*. The name had already been registered by Mercier, but had never been used. Moët purchased it in 1930 and used it in 1936 to launch their 1921 vintage (a 15-year-old wine speaks volumes of the sort of maturity expected of Champagne in those days). So successful was it that Moët was able to return to Mercier in 1970 and purchase the entire company. Moët & Chandon is now part of the LVMH (Louis Vuitton-Moët Hennessy) group.

That Moët & Chandon is Champagne's largest and best-known producer is due to ceaseless

marketing strategies. From making ephemera, such as this 1920s fan, to sponsoring international sporting events, Moët has made itself a household name in the wine-drinking world (though few people realise they should pronounce the "t" of Moët!).

By 1900 Moët & Chandon's small army of workers was enjoying company rights and benefits, such as sick pay, that at the Millennium are still denied in many industries around the world.

POL ROGER

Churchill said of Champagne that "In victory we deserve it, in defeat we need it". His favourite Pol Roger vintages were 1928, 1934 and 1947. At the launch of the firm's Cuvée Sir Winston Churchill in 1984, Lady Soames said

of her father's passion for Pol Roger, "I saw him many times the better for it, but never the worse".

POL ROGER was only 19 when he founded the house in 1849. His son Maurice took control in 1899 and built up the firm's reputation, particularly between the two wars in England, where it became the top-selling brand.

Maurice changed the family name from Roger to Pol-Roger. He was Mayor when the Germans occupied Épernay for seven days in September 1914, during which time he withstood German threats to shoot him and burn the town to the ground. His grateful fellow townsmen voted him Mayor at every subsequent opportunity.

The most famous admirer of Pol Roger was Winston Churchill, and he proved to be the firm's greatest promoter. In November 1944, just three months after the liberation of Paris, he met Odette Pol-Roger at a luncheon party and was so captivated by her wit, charm and intelligence that he named one of his racehorses Odette Pol-Roger (although it always ran simply as Pol-Roger). He even ordered his supply of Pol Roger to be bottled in imperial pints, so that he could drink it even when alone.

This family-owned house continues to produce the classic quality and style that Churchill adored. These Champagnes nearly always last longer and remain fresher than those of any other house.

Churchill once dubbed this château "the most famous address in Europe". It is still owned by the Pol-Roger family.

LOUIS ROEDERER

THIS IS THE MOST profitable house in Champagne, and as such should be an object lesson for those houses that count success in the number of bottles they sell rather than the money they make.

Jean-Claude Rouzaud knows not to exceed 2.5 million bottles a year, lest the brand's quality and exclusivity are compromised.

The Roederer house style is typified by a creamy-biscuity complexity, which is usually apparent in its non-vintage Brut Premier but can take two to three years after disgorgement to evolve in the vintage *cuvées*. The house is famous for its Cristal prestige *cuvée*, which sells like hot-cakes in the US, while its least-known gem is its Blanc de Blancs. Cristal was originally produced exclusively for the Russian Imperial Court, until the Revolution of 1917 left the firm in dire straits. Unlike today, Cristal was made very sweet to suit the palate of the tsars. The first commercial vintage of Cristal was in 1945.

Nowadays, the key to true success in Champagne, as owner Jean-Claude Rouzaud demonstrates, is an impeccable reputation to secure a premium price, enough vineyards to guarantee quality for a production that is sufficient to rake in the money, yet the self-discipline not to go beyond this turnover. Rouzaud does not, however, like to see his capital lie idle, which is why he took over Deutz *(see A–Z listing)*. That Roederer is not in hock to the bank, when most Champagne houses have overdraft facilities, also helps. Rouzaud's biggest financial worry has been deciding when the exchange rate might be best to transfer 15 million dollars from California to France. A problem others would love to have.

This diploma of the Tsar of Russia was issued to Louis Roederer in 1908.

*L*ouis Roederer also owns the lesser-known Théophile Roederer, which has always been a good value Champagne brand; Château Haut-Beauséjour in St-Estèphe; Roederer Estate in California; and the Port house of Ramos-Pinto in Spain.

A Methuselah of Cristal 2000 is opened by one of Roederer's winemakers.

RUINART

THIS HOUSE WAS founded by Nicolas Ruinart on 1 September 1729 and is the oldest house to trade in sparkling, rather than still, Champagne. Nicolas's uncle, Dom Thierry Ruinart, was a contemporary of Dom Pérignon *(see p18)*.

Ruinart actually started trading in linen goods, rewarding loyal customers with bottles of his Champagne, but the wine was so good that he had more orders for it than the linen, and gradually it took over his business. Nicolas's grandson Jean-Irénée was active in selling Ruinart Champagne to such famous customers as Joseph Bonaparte, King of Spain, Joachim Murat, King of Naples, and Talleyrand. He also sold wine to the Empress Josephine, but she refused to pay her bills after the divorce. Jean-Irénée was ennobled as Vicomte de Brimont by the decree of Louis XVIII, and, as Deputy of the Marne and Mayor of Épernay, he received the Empress Marie-Louise and, later, Charles X.

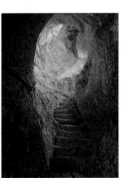

This high-quality Champagne has never been produced in large amounts. Even though sales quadrupled just before its purchase by Moët & Chandon in 1963, and have almost trebled since, Ruinart's turnover is still below two million bottles, which positions it between Bollinger and Louis Roederer in size. Ruinart is known for its stunning Dom Ruinart in both *blanc de blancs* and *rosé* styles, but its basic "R" de Ruinart range is all too often overlooked, and amazing value.

Rheims, the old-fashioned English spelling of Reims, is sometimes still used by Ruinart on its labels.

*T*he firm's cellars *(left)*, a series of Gallo-Roman chalk pits, are officially classified as a historical monument. You must write for an appointment to visit Ruinart, but it is worth the effort to see the magnificent *crayères*.

SALON

Maxim's Restaurant in Paris chose Salon's vintage *blanc de blancs* – the only style of Champagne that Salon has ever produced – as its house wine in the 1920s.

*P*aul Bergeot was so impatient to relaunch Salon in a new, fatter bottle, he ordered what remained of the 1971 and 1973 vintages to be decanted, mixed with a light *liqueur de tirage* and re-bottled. This caused a third fermentation and was illegal, but no one realised at the time. Thus it is possible to find "old" and "new" versions of these two vintages.

SALON SHOT TO FAME during the 1920s and '30s, when it was the house wine at Maxim's in Paris, but after the death of its founder in 1943 it declined into obscurity.

Eugène-Aimé Salon (1867–1943) spent much of his boyhood assisting his brother-in-law Marcel Guillaume, the *chef de caves* of a small firm producing a single vineyard Champagne called Clos Tarin. Later he purchased five hectares of vines at Le Mesnil-sur-Oger where, in his spare time, he set about realising a youthful ambition: to create a perfectly balanced Champagne from a single growth and from just one grape variety, Chardonnay. He used only the best fruit and exclusively the *vin de cuvée* or first pressing, selling off the rest. Furthermore, he produced only vintage Champagne. Through such strict measures, Salon mastered *blanc de blancs* and appears to have been the first to exploit this style commercially, founding the House of Salon in 1921.

Salon was taken over by Besserat de Bellefon in 1963, but its existence remained low-key until Besserat was in turn purchased by Pernod-Ricard. Paul Bergeot, the new chairman, took an active interest in Salon, relaunching it as Salon Cuvée S in 1976. Salon was acquired by Laurent-Perrier in 1989, and run for eight years by Bertrand de Fleurian, who did all he could to assure the ascendancy of this minute, yet extraordinary Champagne house.

Salon, relaunched in 1976, is one of the few Champagnes that does not undergo malolactic.

VEUVE CLICQUOT PONSARDIN

The Hôtel du Marc, Veuve Clicquot's house in Reims, was bequeathed by Madame Clicquot to her business partner, Édouard Werlé.

THE NAME AND IMAGE of Veuve Clicquot Ponsardin are still identified with its illustrious 19th-century owner, the Grande Dame of Champagne, and quality is still surprisingly high for such a large operation.

It is true that a satisfying quality is simpler to achieve in a full-bodied and characterful wine like Clicquot's than it is in a lighter one (because the lighter the style, the easier it is to discern the slightest flaw). It is much harder, however, to achieve finesse in a full-bodied style. Nonetheless, what comes across about Clicquot is that it is not just big but also beautiful.

The house was founded in 1772 by Philippe Clicquot-Muiron, but it was his daughter-in-law, who took over in 1805, who really established Clicquot as one of the truly great houses. She was aided by a man named Bohne, who at first criticized the mousse of the Champagne, notably claiming "this is a terrible thing that gets up and goes to bed with me: toad's eyes!" Heeding this, she employed winemaker Antoine Müller. It was through the pair's enterprise that *remuage*, a process that draws out sediment, became widespread.

*W*hat did Pushkin, Chekhov, Ian Fleming, Alfred Hitchcock, Jules Verne, the Bourbons, Romanovs, Hapsburgs, Bonapartes and every British monarch after Edward VII have in common? They all drank Veuve Clicquot.

Widowed at the age of 27 ("Veuve" means widow), Nicole-Barbe Clicquot-Ponsardin had become the Grande Dame of Champagne by the time of her death, over 60 years later.

VILMART

Bottles of Champagne undergo *remuage (see p11)* while resting at a 45° angle in V-shaped *pupitres* in Vilmart's cellars at Rilly-la-Montagne.

*R*ené Champs is an exceptionally talented man who has designed and built his own home as well as creating a first-class Champagne. The stained-glass window showing the traditional way to crush Chardonnay grapes is just one of the building's many delightful flourishes.

*V*ILMART DATES BACK to 1890, but its breakthrough as one of the great houses of Champagne was very recent – it was only in the late 1980s that the owner, René Champs, started to make a brilliant wine.

The Champs family have always owned Vilmart, and René's son Laurent now assists his father. The location of the firm's vineyards in Rilly-la-Montagne is responsible for the fullness and complexity of its Pinot-driven style. But Vilmart's quality is less due to the vineyards' location than their low yield, which means the wine is rich and balanced by abundant ripe acidity.

Oak is another major factor. Most of the wines are fermented in large wooden ovals more reminiscent of Alsace than Champagne, but the top *cuvées* are all fermented in small oak *barriques*.

This and other panes each took René Champs about 200 hours of patient and meticulous work to create.

Indeed, Vilmart has spearheaded a mini-trend in Champagne to return to fermenting in new oak *barriques*. The policy has been implemented with too much zeal at times – the 1991 Coeur de Cuvée and the 1990 Cuvée du Nouveau Monde are too oaky.

The Champs have learned from such experiences, however, and had they not been aiming so ambitiously high in the first place, Vilmart's wines would not be as great as they are today.

FRANCE
SPARKLING
WINE REGIONS

Best Producers

1 Aigle (Domaine)
 Roquetaillade
2 Baumard
 Rochefort-sur-Loire
3 Bouvet
 St-Florent
4 Deliance
 Dracy-le-Fort
5 Die (Cave
 Coopérative)
 Die
6 Dopff Au Moulin
 Riquewihr
7 Gratien & Meyer
 Saumur
8 Picamelot
 Rully
9 Sieur d'Arques
 Limoux
10 Wolfberger
 Eguisheim

Sparkling wines have been produced in parts of France outside of the Champagne region since at least 1820. There is a tendency to overlook French fizz alternatives, yet, of the two billion bottles of bubbly produced globally each year, the rest of France accounts for about an eighth.

APPELLATIONS
There are 50 French sparkling wine appellations. Of these, Saumur, in the Loire, is the most important and Limoux the most intriguing, but the Burgundy and Alsace appellations are more rewarding for quality and range. From the tiny region of Die comes Clairette de Die Méthode Dioise Ancestrale, one of the world's finest sweet fizzes.

ALSACE
Crémant d'Alsace, the sparkling wine appellation of the Alsace region, is dominated by the producers Wolfberger, Laugel and Dopff Au Moulin. Dopff effectively established the sparkling wine business in Alsace in 1900. Early-picked Pinot Blanc is the most popular style. Pinot Gris makes a more superior *cuvée*, but the higher price of this grape has prevented its widespread use. Riesling is also sometimes used. *Crémant rosé* is the region's most underrated fizz: an elegant, pure Pinot Noir wine with soft strawberry or cherry fruit. Note that these wines seldom improve beyond 18 months.

CRÉMANT

Crémant d'Alsace was the first French sparkling wine appellation to adopt the term *crémant* in 1976.

Some producers in the wine villages of Alsace make use of the extra richness and higher acidity of Pinot Gris, but the grape costs 40 per cent more than Pinot Blanc.

SPARKLING WINE APPELLATIONS

Most of France's sparkling wines come from the north and central part of the country – southern regions such as Provence are not known for fizz, although Limoux is interesting. There are appellations for sparkling wine in regions such as Bordeaux, but the best ones are in Alsace, Burgundy and the Loire.

☐ Major sparkling wine appellations
☐ Champagne *(see pp16–21)*

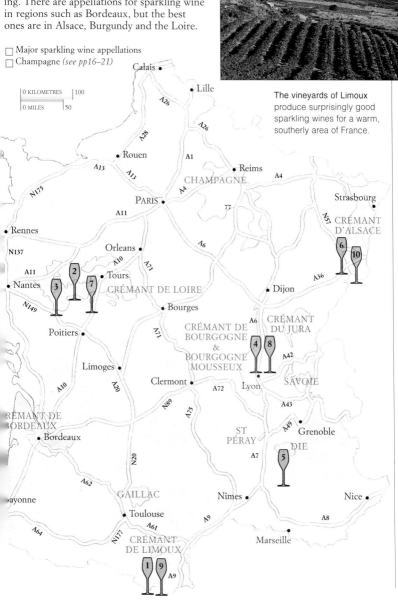

The vineyards of Limoux produce surprisingly good sparkling wines for a warm, southerly area of France.

0 KILOMETRES 100
0 MILES 50

Calais

Lille

A26

A28

A26

Rouen

A1

A13

A13

Reims

CHAMPAGNE

A4

N175

PARIS

A11

77

Strasbourg

N57

CRÉMANT D'ALSACE

Rennes

Orleans

A6

A36

6 10

N137

A10

A71

2

A11

Tours

7

Dijon

Nantes

3

CRÉMANT DE LOIRE

N149

Bourges

A6

CRÉMANT DU JURA

A71

Poitiers

CRÉMANT DE BOURGOGNE & BOURGOGNE MOUSSEUX

4 8

A42

Limoges

A10

A20

Clermont

A72

Lyon

SAVOIE

N89

A75

A43

ℝÉMANT DE ℝORDEAUX

A49

Grenoble

Bordeaux

ST PÉRAY

DIE

A7

5

N20

A62

GAILLAC

Nîmes

Nice

ayonne

A64

Toulouse

A61

A9

A8

N177

CRÉMANT DE LIMOUX

Marseille

1 9

A9

BURGUNDY (BOURGOGNE)

There are three major production centres of sparkling wine in Burgundy: the Yonne or Chablis district, the Région de Mercurey or Chalonnaise district, and the Mâconnais. The appellation for sparkling Burgundy is Crémant de Bourgogne, which has now superseded the term Bourgogne Mousseux for all but fizzy red Burgundy.

There are some very good Crémant de Bourgogne wines, but the average quality is not as good as it should be because too many producers rely on buying grapes that are sold off cheaply after being rejected for still Burgundy. Such wines suffer from excessive sulphur levels. The sparkling wine industry in Burgundy has yet to understand that grapes must be cultivated specifically for sparkling wines if serious progress is to be made across the board.

However, when Crémant de Bourgogne is good it is usually very good and almost always a bargain. The best are invariably made purely from Chardonnay grapes. Styles range from full and toasty (often from Yonne), through rich and smooth (usually from the Chalonnaise) to fresh, light and vivacious (mainly Mâconnais). *Crémant rosé* from Burgundy is not usually interesting, unless made from 100 per cent Pinot Noir grapes. Most good quality Crémant de Bourgogne is best consumed within three years of purchase.

The best producers include Caves de Bailly, André Bonhomme, Deliance, Picamelot, Roux Père, Simonnet-Febvre and Caves de Viré.

The thrill of effervescing sweet wine was such a vogue in France in the 1870s that the production of another wine – sweet, still Sauternes – was under threat from the bubbly bandwagon. In *A History of Champagne* (1882), Henry Vizetelly records vast quantities of Sauternes being transported by rail to Messers Normandin Sparkling Sauternes Manufactory near Angoulême, where it was turned into award-winning sparkling wine.

Burgundy, one of France's oldest wine regions, vied with the Champagne region for royal favour in the 17th century, when both wines were still. Later, as sparkling Champagne took off, most Burgundy resolutely remained still.

LIMOUX

This small region near Carcassonne claims to have made sparkling wine more than 160 years before Dom Pérignon *(see p18)*, but this has not yet been proved. What is true, however, is that Limoux makes exceptionally fine sparkling wines for such a sunny southern location, and winemaking techniques have improved by leaps and bounds over the last decade. The style of Crémant de Limoux and Blanquette de Limoux has moved away from the distinctive character of fresh-cut grass to a much finer aroma. The best producers include Domaine de l'Aigle, Antech, Robert, Sieur d'Arques and Héritiers Valent.

Winemaking is shown in this detail of a medieval painting from the Loire.

THE LOIRE

If you are used to good-quality Champagne, you might find Loire sparklers difficult to appreciate. This is because the main grape used, Chenin Blanc, is too aromatic for a classic *brut* style.

Saumur is the largest French sparkling wine appellation outside of Champagne, and were it restricted to Chardonnay and Pinot Noir it would be the best. Saumur Mousseux *Rosé* can be made from several varieties, but many are pure Cabernet Franc, and the best are some of the most thrilling raspberry-flavoured fizzes in the world. Some pure Cabernet Sauvignon *rosés* can also be very good, in a smoother, less overt way.

Sparkling Vouvray and, particularly, Montlouis are hard to find, but can be delightfully fresh, smooth and elegant, especially when *pétillant*. Touraine and Crémant de Loire can be good value, but too many poorly made, cheap fizzes have debased those appellations. However, there are numerous good producers throughout the Loire – too many to name here.

The appellation Blanquette Méthode Ancestrale, from Limoux, is made by *méthode rurale*. There is no second fermentation, which most other sparkling wines undergo. Instead, the wine is bottled before the first alcoholic fermentation is over. In the 19th century, all Blanquette de Limoux was produced in this fashion.

Bouvet, one of the best Saumur producers, associates itself with the sport of motor-racing.

SPAIN

C ava has been widely exported since the mid-1970s and is now the world's second largest bottle-fermented sparkling wine appellation. The industry is dominated by two houses: Codorníu, the oldest, largest and most innovative firm, and Freixenet, which is probably the best known.

Freixenet (pronounced roughly "freh-zhe-net") delights in a fun-loving image for its Cava.

WHAT IS CAVA?

Cava is the generic name for bottle-fermented Spanish sparkling wine; it simply means "cellar". It was devised in 1970 for all Spanish sparkling wines made by the *méthode champenoise*, regardless of where in Spain they are made. However, when Spain joined the Common Market in 1986, Cava became subject to the EC wine regime, which is based on the integrity of origin. The EC made the Spanish choose between confining the Cava name to a geographical appellation or dropping it altogether.

This demand was cruelly ironic because at the same time the EC was failing to protect the integrity of the name "sherry" – the world's oldest geographical appellation. But Spain managed to extract its revenge simply by pinpointing every known Cava producer and drawing boundaries around individual municipalities. Cava was thus transformed overnight into a "geographical" appellation scattered across half of Spain. In practice, though, most Cava comes from the Penedés region and always has done, with the area around Sant Sadurní d'Anoia producing much of the best.

CAVA COUNTRY

Penedés is Cava Country, but there are pockets of Cava production in Rioja, Navarra, Aragón and elsewhere. Thus the Cava appellation is geographical only in a loose sense.

SPAIN

· Madrid

☐ Main Cava districts

Codorníu began to win gold medals for its Cava in 1888.

The Art Nouveau winery of Codorníu was designed in the late 19th century by Josep Maria Puig i Cadafalch and declared a National Historical Monument in 1976.

Most famous for its Cava, the Freixenet group also includes Gloria Ferrer in California, Castellblanch and the Champagne house of Henri Abelé.

Best Producers

1 Codorníu
   Sant Sadurní d'Anoia
2 Freixenet
   Sant Sadurní d'Anoia
3 Gramona
   Sant Sadurní d'Anoia
4 Mascaró
   Vilafranca del Penedès
5 Raimat
   Costers del Segre
6 Raventós Rosell
   Masquefa

THE CAVA INDUSTRY

It was long widely believed that the first Spanish sparkling wine was made in 1872 by José Raventós, the head of Codorníu (a winery dating back to the 16th century), but recent research has revealed that it was "invented" much earlier by Luis Justo Vilanueva, and first produced in 1862 by Antoni Gili. This date coincides with the migration of French Champagne producers to the region. However, there was no Cava industry as such until after World War II, and until 1974 production was so small that export statistics were not even recorded.

Gramona was founded in 1881 and started to produce Cava in 1921. The wines, shown here being corked, spend five years in darkness in Gramona's cellars before being sold.

A SOFT ACIDITY

Cava is an obvious choice for buyers who find the acidity of even the best Champagnes too aggressive. For many drinkers, however, Cava suffers from being too soft. Not that softness is itself a shortcoming, but in a sparkling wine if the acidity is softer than the mousse, the dosage *(see p177)* will be minimal, making the wine short and hollow, with no potential for long-term maturation. Cavas that best manage to overcome these drawbacks include Codorníu, Freixenet, Gramona, Mascaró, Raimat and Raventós Rosell.

THE GRAPES OF CAVA

The three grapes used most in Cava are Parellada, Macabéo and Xarello, which were all growing locally when Cava was first made. According to the Cava gospel, Macabéo, which is usually the base of a Cava *cuvée*, provides the fruit, Xarello the strength and body, and Parellada the softness and aroma. However, each of these grapes is problematic in sparkling wine.

*S*ome of the Spanish *méthode champenoise* wines started production after the Cava boundaries were drawn up and therefore do not come under the Cava appellation. They include Xamprada (León), Oriella (Madrid), Juan de Arges (Valencia), Montsec and Ibón (Zaragoza), El Grifo (Lanzarote) and Cantares and Mantolán (Ciudad Real).

The best Parellada grapes come from the highest vineyards, where they take longer to ripen.

Macabéo is not bad as a base wine, having good fruit and decent acidity, and Xarello is useful in small amounts, but Parellada has very little acidity and is prone to an internal rot that is hard to detect.

Freixenet's headquarters are at Sant Sadurní d'Anoia, the most important Cava town in Spain, in the heart of the Penedés region.

IN SEARCH OF BETTER GRAPES

Given that it took the Champenois 250 years to settle on the best three grapes for Champagne, the Cava industry has been surprisingly reluctant to try other varieties until recently. Codorníu realised the problem in the 1970s, and started cultivating Chardonnay as a quality booster. Freixenet opposed this, fearing that foreign grapes would erode Cava's Spanish character (a fair point), and this stance sparked a rift between the houses.

The Spanish terms *Fermentación en Botella*, *Vino Espumoso Natural* and *Método Transfer* indicate the transfer method *(see p178)*. Sparkling wines stating *Vino Gasificado* or *Granvás* are carbonated in the same way as lemonade or cola.

However, this author believes that Cava can be improved through using different native grapes, especially black grapes in a white wine blend. Codorníu was the first house to try this style, and even went to the extreme of making a *blanc de noirs*, albeit with the foreign Pinot Noir, producing the most sumptuous of Spanish sparkling wines. Freixenet is now experimenting with the native black Monastrell in a white *cuvée*, which is starting to show promise.

Trepat and Garnacha have been used in experiments with

rosé Cava. The producer Mont Marcal has used Tempranillo, the greatest of all Catalan grapes, and Can Ràfols dels Caus has even tried Merlot, both of them for pink Cava.

Manuel Raventós, who took over Codorníu in 1885, commissioned posters from Catalan artists such as Ramón Casas (1866–1932).

GERMANY

Sekt, the German fizz, is now the largest sparkling wine industry in the world. In some years, production tops half-a-billion bottles, which is almost twice that of Champagne. However, very little Sekt has so far been exported, making this wine practically unknown outside Germany.

A GERMAN TASTE
For most of the 20th century, the Germans have essentially made Sekt for themselves. The wine is off-dry with an unusual youthful tartness, which most sparkling wine drinkers elsewhere do not comprehend, let alone enjoy. Exports average barely eight per cent of total Sekt sales, and have dropped to as low as four per cent. Yet the Germans are drinking more and more Sekt, with per capita consumption currently running at five litres, compared with less than one litre in 1960.

EARLY ATTEMPTS
German salesmen were widely employed by the earliest Champagne houses (*see p18*). The first attempts to make sparkling wine in Germany date back to 1783, but because the process took a while to master, the oldest commercial producer, Kessler, was not founded until 1826. Ten years later, when it became possible to measure the amount of sugar left in a wine after the first fermentation, the number of producers significantly increased.

Sign for the town of Durbach in the southern wine region of Baden.

Best Producers
1 Deis
   Mosel-Saar-Ruwer
2 Durbach
   Baden
3 Kassner-Simon
   Pfalz
4 Kirsten
   Mosel-Saar-Ruwer
5 Knyphausen
   Rheingau
6 Ratzenberger
   Mittelrhein
7 Ress
   Rheingau
8 Winzersekt
   Sprendlingen
   Rheinhessen
9 Wilhelmshof
   Pfalz
10 Zähringer
   Baden

Bremm is beautifully located by the Mosel in the Mosel-Saar-Ruwer wine region.

SOUTHERN WINE DISTRICTS

Most of Germany's QbA delimited wine districts (Qualitätswein bestimmter Anbaugebiete) are based around the Mosel and Rhein (Rhine) river valleys in the south of the country. Sparkling wine is produced in most of these regions.

☐ QbA regions

GERMANY

• Berlin

• Frankfurt

An advertisement for Söhnlein "Champagne" from 1901.

KÖLN • (COLOGNE)

A1
A4
A3
A45
A5

Rhein

AHR   MITTELRHEIN

Koblenz • **6**   **5** **7**

A5   A66   A7

1 **4**   *Mosel*

MOSEL-
SAAR-RUWER   RHEINGAU   **FRANKFURT**

• Mainz   A3   A70

NAHE   **8**   FRANKEN

RHEINHESSEN   *Main*

HESSISCHE
BERGSTRASSE   A81   • Würzburg

A3

A1   A62

A8   **3** **9**

A6

• Saarbrücken   • Heidelberg

PFALZ   A6

0 KILOMETRES   25

0 MILES   10

Karlsruhe   WÜRTTEMBERG   A7

2 **10**

A8   • Stuttgart

BADEN

A81

Rhein   A5   Ulm •   A8

A7

• Freiburg   *Donau*

A96

"Sekt" is Born

A boom in sales came in the 1850s, coinciding with when the peculiar term "Sekt" is thought to have first been used. The classical German actor Ludwig Devrient was in the Berlin restaurant Lutter & Wegener one November night in 1852 and ordered a glass of

Wine presses in a museum owned by State Domaine Kloster Eberbach, in the Rheingau region.

sherry. In jocular mood, he quoted a line from Falstaff in Shakespeare's *Henry IV* to the waiter: "Give me a cup of sack, rogue. Is there no virtue extant?" Not understanding that Shakespeare's "*sack*" meant sherry (in turn deriving from the Spanish *sacar*: to take away or, less favourably, to loot – i.e. exported sherry!), the waiter brought him a glass of his usual German sparkling wine. After going the rounds of Berlin restaurants, it is thought that "*sack*" became "*sekt*" and by 1900 was widely used to refer to German sparkling wine (also known as "Champagne" at the time).

Many of the Sekt houses that sprang up from the 1850s soon disappeared, but by 1872 production had risen to four million bottles, and no fewer than 12 Sekt houses were of sufficient size and repute to exhibit at the World Exhibition in Vienna.

The sack (shorry) of Falstaff is thought to have given its name to Sekt, in a convoluted manner.

Deutscher Sekt means the wine is made only with German grapes.

Rheinhessen is one of the delimited QbA wine regions.

Klassische Flaschengärung is the equivalent of the French *méthode champenoise.*

The language on German wine labels is notoriously complex, and Sekt is no exception. To start, Sekt is synonymous with Schaumwein. If either term is used without qualification, the wine is probably a blend of grapes from various countries. Deutscher Sekt tells you that only German grapes have been used, and Deutscher Sekt bA and Deutscher Qualitätsschaumwein both mean that the grapes come from a specified QbA region *(see p45)*.

Moving up the quality scale, Flaschengärung means bottle-fermented, while Flaschengärung nach dem traditionellen Verfahren, Klassische Flaschengärung and Traditionelle Flaschengärung are all equivalents of *méthode champenoise*. Handgerüttelt means hand-riddled, and Jahrgangssekt is vintage Sekt. At the opposite end of the scale, Perlwein is cheap, semi-sparkling wine made by carbonation.

ORDINARY SEKT

Although it started as a bottle-fermented product, virtually all Sekt is now produced by *cuve close* or tank method, and over 85 per cent is made from imported foreign base wines. Most Deutscher Sekt (sparkling wines made exclusively from German grapes) are also *cuve close* and thus little better than the ordinary Sekt of no fixed abode.

SEKT AT THE MILLENNIUM

Germany's Sekt industry underwent its largest expansion in very recent times, increasing from 200 producers in the late 1980s to more than 1,300 today. Although this represents a 650 per cent increase, total production has increased by just 25 per cent, and therein lies the clue to the radical change that has occurred at the very top of Sekt's quality scale. A small but growing band of quality-conscious estates has been crafting some truly excellent sparkling wines since the early 1990s. Most of these are small, go-ahead wine estates, rather than large, old-established Sekt factories.

The most obvious development is pure Riesling Sekt, whereas the most unlikely style evolving is pure Pinot Noir *rosé*, the quality of which should bowl over the most ardent Sekt-hater. It will not be long before specialist importers on major export markets pick up on this emerging new breed of Sekt. But although their numbers are increasing, the wines are by nature produced in such small quantities that they will remain in short supply.

Germans make merry with Sekt in this engraving from the journal *Jugend* in 1897.

𝒯he best Sekt this author has ever tasted is the rare Wegeler-Deinhard Bernkasteler Doktor. Just two vintages were produced, 1978 and 1984, and, like Champagne, they were aged for three years, but in a special vat fitted with a paddle to stir the lees.

Riesling, the greatest German grape, is increasingly being used on its own to make Sekt.

ITALY

No other country has as many sparkling wine appellations as Italy, with its optional "may be *spumante*" (sparkling) clauses cluttering up more than 100 of the country's Denominazione di Origine Controllata (DOC) appellations. Yet Italy had no appellation specifically for classic *brut* sparkling wine until Franciacorta was elevated to the higher rung of Garantita (DOCG) in 1995.

A MYRIAD OF HALF-FORGOTTEN WINES

Italy's little-known sparkling wine appellations are nearly all *cuve close* (undergoing a second fermentation in a vat or tank rather than in a bottle). This is the best method for sweet sparkling wines like Asti, which has DOCG status and is Italy's best contribution to the sparkling wine world. However, *cuve close* is the worst possible method for classic *brut*. This is not because it is an intrinsically inferior method; in theory it should be able to produce *brut* sparkling wines that are every bit as good as those made in bottle, but in practice it does not. It is a bulk-production process and consequently attracts the cheapest base wines. To remedy the situation, the Italian Wine Law should require all *brut*-style DOC sparkling wines to be produced by the *metodo classico*, the Italian equivalent of *méthode champenoise*.

Ferrari, one of the few firms to use *metodo classico*, says that it delights in "conserving the original excellence of the *spumante*".

The view over Bellavista's aptly named vineyards in Lombardy.

NORTHERN ITALY

Sparkling wines are made throughout Italy, but the most interesting ones are made in the north. The best appellations are Asti, for sweet fizz, and Franciacorta, for *brut*-style sparkling wine.

☐ Main wine regions

Sophia Loren drinking classic Italian *brut* at the Venice Biennale.

0 KILOMETRES | 50

0 MILES | 25

Best Producers

1 Banfi *Tuscany*
2 Bellavista *Franciacorta*
3 Berlucchi *Franciacorta*
4 Ca'del Bosco *Franciacorta*
5 Equipe Trentino *Trentino*
6 Ferrari *Trentino*
7 Gancia *Asti*

FRANCIACORTA

The Franciacorta appellation covers various producers with vineyards on the hills around Lake Iseo northeast of Milan. The wines are made from Chardonnay, Pinot Bianco (Pinot Blanc), and up to 15 per cent Pinot Nero (Pinot Noir). Franciacorta is still the only Italian classic *brut* appellation – the only wine that must be made by *metodo classico*.

Until September 1995, Franciacorta, like most Italian DOCs, was allowed to be still or sparkling. The still reds were, in fact, quite impressive. However, in a rare decision by the Italian Wine Law to put quality first, the most successful sparkling style was elevated to a super-appellation, its production restricted to the finest areas, its yield lowered, and its production method tightened up.

The *Festa dell'uva* (Grape Harvest Festival) celebrates the wines of Northeast Italy.

The still wines retain their DOC status, re-named Terre di Franciacorta. Only the sparkling wines may claim the Franciacorta DOCG. Were this uncompromising attitude applied to every appellation in the country, Italy would not only be the largest wine-producing nation in the world, as it is now, but also the greatest. With 25 months ageing on its lees (if the label says *riserva* then it is 37 months), Franciacorta has the potential for producing fine, biscuity *brut*, and lightly rich *rosé* sparkling wines. The best brands include Bellavista, Berlucchi, Ca'del Bosco, and Faccoli.

*T*he most ubiquitous cheap Italian sparkling wine is probably sparkling Lambrusco, which comes in pretty shades of red, white, and *rosé*, but much the same effect for the tastebuds can be had by putting a shot of Vodka into a soft fizzy drink.

ASTI – THE SWEET FIZZ

The town of Asti in Piedmont gives its name to the local sweet fizz made by *cuve close*. The finest Asti are the greatest sweet sparkling wines in the world – a fraction of the price of *demi-sec* Champagne, but ten times the quality. It was formerly sold as Asti Spumante, but *spumante*, which like *mousseux* in France merely means "sparkling", had become tarnished by the cheap products that also use the term, thus was dropped when Asti was promoted to the status of DOCG in 1993.

Bernhard Langer is given a silver cup filled with Berlucchi after winning the Vincitore Open d'Italia golf competition in 1997.

Asti is made entirely from Moscato (Muscat) grapes, which come from 52 communes throughout the provinces of Asti, Cuneo, and Alessandria. The *cuve close* method of production is well suited to an aromatic, sweet sparkling wine like Asti because its most vital quality – the freshness of its fruit – gains nothing from the extended yeast contact of *metodo classico*.

AC Milan shower themselves with the locally produced Ca'del Bosco after another historic win.

The best Asti has a fine mousse of tiny bubbles, a fresh, grapey aroma, a luscious sweetness, and a light yet rich flowery-fruitiness that should be vivacious and mouthwatering. The greatest examples are reminiscent of peaches, and may even have a hint of orange. One of the most important compounds in the Moscato aroma is geraniol, which is wonderful when fresh, but with bottle-age assumes an unpleasantly pungent geranium odor. Asti is not, therefore, a wine that should be kept.

Good Asti producers include Araldica, Fontanafredda, Gancia, Giuseppe Contratto, and Tosti. Gancia's special selection *cuvée*, Camilo Gancia, is a class apart.

OTHER FIZZ

After Franciacorta, Tuscany and Northeast Italy are the leading areas for *brut* sparkling wines, although the grapes may be sourced from far and wide. Equipe Trentino (Trentino), Ferrari (Trentino), and Villa Banfi (Tuscany) are among the best. Of the rest, Prosecco is one of Italy's most widely available bubblies but often boringly amylic. Soldati la Scola is based in Gavi and makes various sparkling wines.

*W*hile Asti is a pure Moscato sparkling wine, Moscato d'Asti is an entirely different product, which is not supposed to be fully sparkling, just *frizzantino* (very lightly sparkling), or even still. A Moscato d'Asti is easily recognized by its normal cork, which is fully inserted into the neck, with no mushroom top. If a wine simply states Moscato, it will be an inexpensive, fizzy blend of Moscato grapes from anywhere in Italy. Such wines rarely have the scintillating freshness of Asti, but even an average Moscato is preferable to an Asti that is too old.

Ferrari has recently diversified its image with a range of label designs inspired by Pop Art *(left)*.

THE UNITED STATES

Americans were among the first to appreciate Champagne, and have been producing their own fizz since the mid-19th century. The sparkling wines of California have come of age, but the states of Washington and Oregon possibly possess as much potential as their southern counterpart. A number of producers are the US arms of French Champagne and Spanish Cava houses.

CATAWBA AND OTHER EARLY SUCCESSES

The first American sparkling wine was made in 1842 by Nicholas Longworth, using Catawba grapes planted along the Ohio River near Cincinnati. Catawba is a native American variety with an exotic, cloying taste often described as "foxy".

The first of New York's fabled "champagnes" was made in 1865 by Joseph Masson. Five years later the Great Western Champagne brand was launched, which became the first American sparkling wine to win a gold medal in Europe. Great Western Champagnes claimed to be made in "Rheims, New York" – the winery's postroom was cunningly named Rheims for this purpose. This so-called champagne became the most important brand of sparkling wine in the country for a staggering 50 years, until Prohibition intervened.

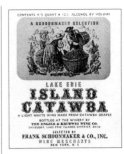

Catawba, a native American grape used for both still and sparkling wines, was so famous by the 1850s that the *Illustrated London News* reported that "sparkling Catawba ... transcends the Champagne of France".

Hollywood, ever keen to associate itself with romance and the high life, strategically places a bottle of Mumm by Bogart and Bergman.

NAPA, SONOMA AND MENDOCINO

California, Washington and Oregon are the main sparkling wine states, with the Napa Valley, Sonoma and Mendocino districts north of San Francisco taking the lion's share.

☐ Major wine districts

Best Producers

1 Argyle
  Willamette Valley
2 Carneros (Domaine)
  Napa Valley
3 Chandon (Domaine)
  Napa Valley
4 Handley
  Mendocino
5 Iron Horse
  Sonoma Green Valley
6 J Wine *Sonoma*
7 Mumm *Napa Valley*
8 Roederer *Mendocino*
9 Scharffenberger
  Mendocino
10 Schramsberg
  Napa Valley

Carneros in Sonoma County is one of California's premier districts for sparkling wine.

CALIFORNIA

The first California sparkling wine was made in about 1855 at the San Gabriel Winery, and various producers were making it by the turn of the century. The industry was going reasonably well until virtually all alcohol production came to a grinding halt in 1920. After Prohibition was re-pealed, in 1933, California's wine industry was painfully slow to re-establish itself. The only sparkling wine was cheap, bulk-produced and had little to commend it.

Schramsberg was eventually the first quality California fizz. A boost came in 1973, when Moët & Chandon chose the Napa Valley to locate its first premium quality winery

The end of Prohibition (1933) was celebrated in the most appropriate way.

outside Champagne. These companies converted a sporadic production into California's fully-fledged industry today. A flood of French-owned and Franco-American fizz ventures appeared on the scene in the 1980s, and the two giant Spanish Cava houses, Frei-xenet and Codorníu, also began to invest in California at this time. Technologically, California fizz came of age in the early 1990s, when the acidity became less "ribby" and more in tune with the fruit, giving the wines greater elegance than before. This was a surprising development because, as with many other New World sparkling wine areas, the climate is less than ideal. California producers are faced with two basic choices: pick ripe grapes that have too much sugar and insufficient acidity, or harvest earlier, when acidity levels are much higher and the grapes have an almost ideal sugar level. Unsurprisingly, most winemakers have chosen to harvest early, but they have to expend much effort overcoming numerous problems posed by grapes that have too much hard malic acid.

*T*he clergy, of all people, demanded wine during Prohibition (for sacramental use, of course!), so a few wine-ries had permits for still, but not sparkling, wine for this purpose. Not satisfied with this, the Pleasant Valley Wine Company filed a suit for the right to sell bubbly to the clergy. Amazingly, it was granted. The company enjoyed a monopoly on fizz for two years until several other wineries won the same right. The end of Prohibition closed this most peculiar chapter of American Law.

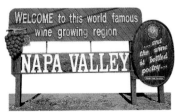

The best California sparkling wine areas already proven are Mendocino, Carneros and Sonoma, but perhaps the most exciting potential for the future is the Santa Maria Valley, which was first planted for sparkling wines in the 1960s and 1970s, long before its potential for silky Pinot Noir red wines was known.

"Who drinks well, sleeps well, Who sleeps well, thinks well, Who thinks well, aets well, Who aets well, avoids Hell. Therefore, drink only *Golden State Champagne* and you will go straight to Heaven."

An advert for Golden State Champagne claims that those who drink it will go "straight to heaven".

"MAD HARRY"

A few producers, like "Mad Harry" Osborne of Kristone, have decided to go the opposite route to other California sparkling winemakers and pick ripe grapes. Osborne challenges critics with such logic as "why harvest unripe grapes when they have no flavour and the wrong acidity, when you can harvest a larger crop of ripe grapes and simply add the acidity?" It is not as simple as that, of course, because they invariably contain too much sugar, but "Mad Harry" has managed to create a first-class product from truly ripe grapes (*see* Kristone in A–Z listing), and has helped New Zealanders to improve their bubbly too (*see p59*).

It is legal in the USA to sell domestically produced sparkling wine as "Champagne", because the term has been used to describe American sparkling wine from very early days, and is thus defined as a generic name under Federal Law. However, most serious sparkling wine producers have stopped using the term.

WASHINGTON AND OREGON

These two states are slow developers in the field of sparkling wine production, yet they may have as much potential as California. In Washington, Château Ste. Michelle's sparkling wines showed great promise in the late 1970s, but they have been disappointing ever since. Dr Michael Manz is currently making this state's most serious fizz at the Mountain Dome winery in Spokane.

Given Oregon's reputation for Pinot Noir, it is perhaps surprising that the Champenois have not shown more interest. Laurent-Perrier purchased land there in the early 1990s, but made nothing of it. Another French Champagne house, Bollinger, has a financial-only interest in Argyle, in the Red Hills of Dundee, which is owned by Croser in Australia and is Oregon's best fizz by far.

Pinot Noir is picked by a vineyard worker for sparkling wine in the Willamette Valley in Oregon.

AUSTRALIA AND NEW ZEALAND

The climate and geography of New Zealand are very suited to sparkling wine production – maybe more so than anywhere else outside the Champagne region. By contrast, a vast expanse of Outback makes Australia one of the least obvious countries associated with the industry. Yet Australia's winemaking history is almost as old as its colonial history, and there are many areas where excellent sparkling wine grapes can be grown.

FLYING WINEMAKERS AND OTHER FIRSTS

The concept of the flying winemaker was born in Australia: owing to the size of this continent and the staggered picking dates, consultant winemakers hop by plane from harvest to harvest. Domaine Chandon Australia (aka Green Point) has zoomed ahead of its sister company in California mainly because flying winemakers like Tony Jordan and his former partner Brian Croser have quickly identified numerous suitable vineyard areas.

Australia's first so-called Sparkling Burgundy was produced by Auldana in 1881. This was the precursor to the country's famed Sparkling Shiraz, a generic style that includes wines made from Cabernet Sauvignon, Merlot and other grapes.

Australian cricketers celebrate victory over England.

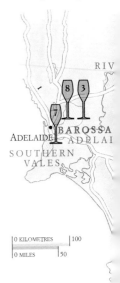

Victoria's stunning mountain scenery is the setting for Great Western's vineyards.

SOUTHEASTERN AUSTRALIA

Sparkling wine production is burgeoning in the Marlborough region of New Zealand and in most winemaking areas of Australia. The best Australian producers are located near Melbourne and Adelaide.

☐ Main wine regions

Best Producers

1 Brun (Daniel Le)
   Marlborough
2 Chandon (Domaine)
   Yarra Valley
3 Croser
   Barossa Eden
4 Hunter's
   Marlborough
5 Jackson Estate
   Marlborough
6 Pelorus
   Marlborough
7 Seaview/Seppelt
   Southern Vales
8 Yalumba
   Barossa Eden
9 Yellowglen
   Ballarat

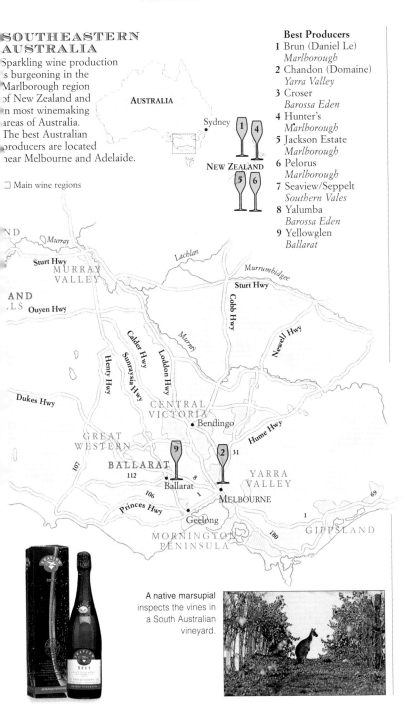

A native marsupial inspects the vines in a South Australian vineyard.

AUSTRALIAN PIONEERS

In 1843, about 50 years after the first vines were planted in Australia, the first Australian sparkling wine was made at Irrawing in the Hunter Valley, New South Wales, by James King, a free settler originally from Hertfordshire.

The Yalumba winery, founded 1849, lies in the verdant Barossa Valley.

From the late 1840s onwards, South Australian winemakers, including Patrick Auld (Auldana), Thomas Hardy, Samuel Smith (Yalumba) and Joseph Ernest Seppelt (B. Seppelt & Sons; Seppeltsfield; and Chateau Tanunda), experimented with fizz. Some of these firms are still going strong.

The main development in Australia's emerging sparkling wine industry came in the 1890s when Hans Irvine purchased Great Western. He installed specialist equipment for sparkling wine and employed Charles Pierlot, who had trained at Pommery. Irvine's friend Benno Seppelt bought the company in 1918, thus creating Seppelt Great Western, which soon dominated the Australian fizz industry.

A year later, a French cook, Edmund Mazure, left Auldana to make his own fizz under the La Perouse label. This was taken over by Wynns, and in 1975 became the famous Seaview label.

Minchinbury was the first Australian winery to utilize the transfer method, whereby wines are filtered from one bottle to another after fermenting. Many famous Australian sparkling wines are now produced in this manner rather than strictly by *méthode champenoise*, according to which the wine must be fermented in the same bottle in which it is sold.

*K*een to be acknowledged by Europe as a cultured people rather than a nation of outcasts, in 1855 James King and other Australian winemakers sent their wines sailing halfway round the world to the Paris Exposition. This was at a time before settlers had crossed Australia overland from south to north.

In their official report on the wines of New South Wales, the French judges magnanimously described the "bouquet, body and flavour" of King's sparkling wine as "equal to the finest champagnes". It was chosen as one of only two wines to be served to Napoleon III at the final banquet.

Benno Seppelt owned a wine merchant's in Broken Hill, New South Wales, before buying Great Western in 1918.

SPARKLING SHIRAZ

Sparkling Shiraz has an appealing deep purple-red colour and is made in two basic styles, oaky or fruity. When tasting a sparkling Shiraz for the first time, drinkers often complain that it tastes like a full-bodied red wine that just happens to be fizzy. However, for most people, the more sparkling Shiraz encountered, the more seriously the style will be taken. Sparkling Shiraz certainly has its place at the dinner table, particularly when partnering strong flavours such as Stilton sauce.

Pinot Noir grapes are harvested in the Brancott Valley of Marlborough for the New Zealand producer Cloudy Bay.

NEW ZEALAND'S LATE START

Sparkling wine did not became serious business in New Zealand until 1981, when industry giant Montana put its muscle behind the launch of Lindauer. One factor for such a late development was that few classic grape varieties had been planted. The collaboration between Montana and Champagne Deutz in 1988 then put this country on the bottle-fermented sparkling wine map. Also in that year, Cloudy Bay produced its first vintage of Pelorus under the wandering eye of "Mad Harry" Osborne (*see p55*). It took one year longer for an expatriate Champenois, Daniel Le Brun, to demonstrate the Marlborough region's true potential for sparkling wine.

In the 1990s Domaine Chandon has produced a New Zealand *cuvée* using the facilities at Hunter's, which makes its own fizz too. This came of age in 1997 when Jane Hunter launched her compelling Miru Miru wine. Hopefully we will see more individually crafted sparkling wines from New Zealand, particularly Marlborough, which is capable of competing with Champagne in terms of quality as well as value.

*M*ate Selak made New Zealand's first fizz in 1956, although he was unable to market it at the time. The Chasselas grape he used did not work well, and, most alarmingly, many of the bottles exploded. It took 15 years of experimentation before Mate could launch his bubbly. He died in 1991, and there is now a top-of-the-range Blanc de Blancs named after him.

Jackson Estate takes its distinctive 50-ft high inflatable bottle and tent to wine festivals.

SOUTH AFRICA

Nelson Mandela drinks to the post-apartheid era.

The ostracism of South Africa during the final phase of its apartheid period stifled developments in the wine industry. However, in the 1990s, after the country finally embraced a multiracial democracy, world markets suddenly opened up, and a fledgling sparkling wine industry gained strength.

THE FINE FRUIT OF THE CAPE

Wineries are concentrated in the delimited Wine of Origin (WO) districts around Cape Town. Many produce sparkling wine, though at the moment much of it is merely fruity fizz. However, there is a fine structure and a certain delicacy of fruit about Cape grapes that promise an interesting future. The best sparkling wine brands include Graham Beck, Krone Borealis (made by Twee Jongegezellen), Jacques Bruère (made by Bon Courage), Pierre Jourdan (made by Clos Cabrière), Oak Village (made by Vinfruco) and Villiera.

FIRST PRODUCERS

The first South African sparkling wine was made by the Stellenbosch Farmers' Winery in 1929.

Called Grand Mousseux Vin Doux, it was simply a still wine that had been carbonated like a fizzy soft drink. Made from the grape varieties Chenin Blanc and Clairette Blanche, Grand Mousseux Vin Doux was the market leader for 60 years, and is still a big success today, particularly in neighbouring Namibia. Nederburg Première Cuvée, a *cuve close* fizz, was launched in 1945.

Vredendal

Olifantsrivier

OLIFANTS-
RIVIER

PIKETBERG

Velddrif   *Bergsrivier*

SWARTLAND
Moorreesburg •
TULBAG
Malmesbury •   6

PAAI
CAPE TOWN •
STELLEN-
BOSCH

Main map
☐ Wine of Origin
(Wyn van Oorsprong) distric

CAPE WINE DISTRICTS

Although wine is also made in areas between Cape Town and Pretoria, sparkling wine production is confined to the main swathe of wine regions within 100 miles of Cape Town. Terminology on labels is increasingly in English, or both English and Afrikaans. A few have just the Afrikaans terms.

SOUTH AFRICA

LESOTHO

Cape Town

Best Houses
1 Beck
   Robertson
2 Bon Courage
   Robertson
3 Clos Cabrière *Paarl*
4 Oak Village
   Stellenbosch
5 Twee Jongegezellen
   Tulbagh
6 Villiera *Paarl*

| 0 KILOMETRES | 50 |
| 0 MILES | 25 |

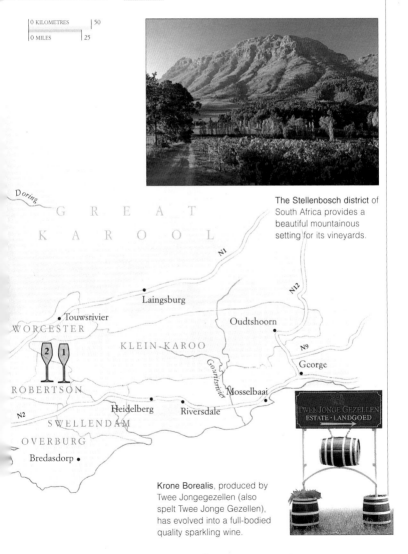

The Stellenbosch district of South Africa provides a beautiful mountainous setting for its vineyards.

Doring

GREAT KAROO

N1

N12

Laingsburg

Touwsrivier

WORCESTER

Oudtshoorn

KLEIN-KAROO

N9

2 1

Gouritsrivier

George

ROBERTSON

Mosselbaai

N2

Heidelberg   Riversdale

SWELLENDAM

OVERBURG

Bredasdorp

TWEE JONGE GEZELLEN
ESTATE · LANDGOED

Krone Borealis, produced by Twee Jongegezellen (also spelt Twee Jonge Gezellen), has evolved into a full-bodied quality sparkling wine.

Labels of South African wines sometimes mention a night harvest – a wise way to overcome the problems of a hot climate on newly picked grapes. Grapes harvested at night tend to produce fresher, more aromatic and livelier wines compared with those picked in the day.

FIRST HINTS OF QUALITY

The first South African *méthode champenoise* sparkling wine was made by Frans Malan at Simonsig in 1979. This was called Kaapse Vonkel and was originally made primarily from Chenin Blanc, though it is now made from Pinot Noir and Chardonnay. Such was the grip of low-priced wines on the domestic market that this remained the only bottle-fermented South African wine until Boschendal produced its first *cuvée* in 1979.

The international sanctions imposed on South Africa during the 1980s affected wine exports. However, in 1984 Jeff Grier of Villiera entered into a fruitful ten-year partnership with the French winemaker Jean-Louis Denois, originally from Cumières (where his family still makes Champagne), but now one of the most innovative producers in Limoux. Since the end of apartheid, Champagne Mumm has collaborated with Nicky Krone of Twee Jongegezellen, producer of Krone Borealis, one of South Africa's best sparkling wines.

*M*ost South African fizz is made by the *cuve close* (tank) method, and some is even made by carbonation, including virtually all those described as *perlé* or *perlant*. For higher quality fizz, look out for the words Cap Classique on the label: this has been the South African term for *méthode champenoise* since 1992.

The Cabrière Estate in the Paarl region is run by Achim von Arnim, and it owns the phenomenally successful Pierre Jourdan brand of sparkling wine.

THE CAPE COMES OUT OF ISOLATION

In the early 1990s, as a new South Africa began quickly to re-establish and forge new export links with other countries, it became clear that the Cape's vineyards were in a rather poor state after lengthy international isolation, and the country's viticultural knowledge was lagging ten years behind the rest of the winemaking world. The Cape wine industry, however, was eager to learn, and started this process in the winery, where

fairly instantaneous results could be achieved simply through a stricter selection of grapes and also a massive investment in new wood and better winemaking equipment. More importantly, a visionary scheme called the Vineyard Improvement Programme (or VIP for short) was set up soon after sanctions were lifted, and this is being funded by a substantial proportion of South Africa's growing export income from wine.

THE FUTURE

Phase One of VIP, involving clonal selection and rootstock improvement, is underway. Nevertheless, a vine needs three years before it yields a crop, and five years before its true potential is known, thus the earliest effects of Phase One are only just now being seen.

Phase Two of the programme, which is to test the suitability of Phase One clones and rootstock in the different *terroirs* of the Cape, is a very long-term project.

Thus, although a number of South African still wines have already noticeably improved through the better winery practices, the real expected leap in quality will not start to show for a decade or so. Moreover, the learning curve for sparkling wine vinification is taking longer than for still wine. A winemaker can see the result of his or her work on a still wine within a year of its harvest, but it takes at least two years, often three, and sometimes even longer, before a serious-quality sparkling wine can be taken off its yeast lees.

The Cape winelands generally have a Mediterranean climate, which lends itself more to still wines than sparkling wines, but the idea that South Africa is simply too hot for sparkling wine is an exaggeration. Coastal regions have a much higher rainfall and are chilled by the icy Benguela current from Antarctica. In some places it is impossible for grapes to ripen properly, which is ideal for sparkling wine production, and the South African fizz industry will eventually gravitate towards such areas rather than rely on the inappropriate balance of early-harvested grapes.

Villiera has gone from strength to strength in the 1990s and now exports around the world as well as selling from the cellar door.

OTHER COUNTRIES

Fizz is made in several other countries. None has the sophistication of the industries already covered, but some have great potential.

Countries such as Switzerland and Austria produce surprisingly little fizz given the potential of their *terroirs*, but Nyetimber has recently emerged as the UK's first world-class sparkling wine. All East European countries produce some bubbly, usually the disappointingly bland product of the Russian Continuous system. Hopefully, the same miracle that transformed Portuguese table wines will soon occur with Portuguese sparkling wines.

Harvesting Chardonnay in Argentina, a country that is likely to produce much better fizz in the next millennium.

In Canada, the Brights-Cartier group has produced top-scoring wines and now has the pioneering Inniskillin winery. British Columbia's bottle-fermented Blue Mountain is world-class, and Colio's *cuve close* Chardonnay Lily is worth trying.

South American potential is barely tapped. In Chile, Mumm's new fizz shows promise, and Miguel Torres has recently returned to form. Moët & Chandon makes a reasonable quality fizz in Brazil, but less so in Argentina, although huge new plantations of Chardonnay and a change of emphasis from *cuve close* to *méthode champenoise* will transform this firm's South American sparkling wines over the next decade.

On the other side of the world, the best Asian fizz, Omar Khayyam, has been made in the Sahyadri Mountains, east of Bombay, for more than ten years.

Good bottle-fermented fizz includes Nyetimber and Omar Khayyam, from England and India respectively.

Cricova in Moldova is the most intriguing sparkling wine facility in Eastern Europe. An underground "city" with 40 miles (65 km) of roads and enough cellars to store a billion bottles, it was clearly built for more than just the two million bottles of fizz that it now produces. Who might have installed such opulent reception halls and marble-clad men's rooms, and a series of steel doors that could withstand a nuclear blast? Who but the now defunct Politburo!

THIS YEAR'S TASTINGS

Performance tables and an alphabetical
listing of recommended producers,
with notes on over 1,000 individual
Champagnes and sparkling wines.

THE 100-POINT SCORING SYSTEM

Almost all the wines in this guide are recommended by me; those without a score are in an unusual developmental phase and cannot be fully judged yet, but are likely to be good when ready. Most wines were tasted blind (with labels covered) at my own professionally equipped facility, where producers submit samples. Others were tasted at events specially organized for the purpose of this guide by various trade bodies.

In addition to regular trips to Champagne, I travel to different sparkling wine regions each year to carry out in-depth tastings *in situ*. Champagnes had to score 80 or above (on a scale of 100) to qualify for this guide; other sparkling wines had to score 70 or above.

HOW WINES ARE JUDGED

All wines are chilled and tasted against others of a similar style and category. Tasting sparkling wines chilled is crucial because temperature affects the release of carbonic gas, which affects the tactile impression of the mousse and the balance of the wine. Most wines are tasted in my own facility because I do not wish to be influenced by other people's comments. This also allows me to devote as much time as I like to each wine, to search out finesse, rather than size (which is all too obvious and thus the bane of blind tastings). I compare and contrast as many different permutations within a category as possible because the positioning of a wine in a line-up can dramatically influence its perception.

Obviously, I open the back-up for any faulty wine, but so many faults are not easily discernible (subliminal cork or TCA, for example). Therefore I have devised a system whereby a second chilled sample can be on the table within four minutes. Last, but by no means least, some wines that do not shine in the cold, analytical setting of a blind tasting can hint at their usefulness at the table, so they are lugged home, where supper is swamped in a sea of covered-up bottles and a different insight can be gleaned.

HOW WINES ARE DESCRIBED

It is harder to describe a wine with a few words than it is to use many, and a quick flick through this Guide will indicate how dismally I have failed in this respect! But I do try to be specific because it is much easier for readers to distinguish between one wine that is reminiscent of, say, strawberries and another that tastes of, perhaps, pineapple. If, however, I list a dozen different fruits, flowers and spices for both wines, it is difficult to imagine what either tastes like, let alone what makes them different from each other. Should a wine have these characteristics, I will list them, but if they're not there, I won't invent them. Many *cuvées* smell and taste like a very fine Champagne without having the slightest hint of pineapple, lemon, peach, apple blossom, walnut, or anything else that specific. In truth, few wines reveal more than one or two specific aromas or flavours, be they flowers, fruits, nuts, or whatever. As far as colour and mousse are concerned, an absence of comment can be taken to mean that they are at least satisfactory. Only extremes are worthy of note.

How to Read the Tasting Notes and Scores

KEY
☐ Real Champagne
☐ Sparkling wine
◐ Overall score given by the author
⊖ Overall score impossible to judge yet
❗ Ready to drink now until year indicated
◤ Preferably store until years indicated

PRICE BANDS
The publishers have provided price bands in the *Tasting Notes* because it is impossible to indicate exact prices for different outlets in numerous markets for an international publication. Price-banding relates to 75 cl bottle.
£ Up to £9.99
££ £10–£19.99
£££ £20–£34.99
££££ £35 and above

PRICES IN LOCAL CURRENCIES
⚘ The price in local currency at the cellar door or, where this does not exist, for retail sales in the country of origin (applicable to the time of tasting and not updated prior to publication).

A NOTE ON CRITERIA
When tasting for this Guide, I try to maintain the same yard-stick, whatever the origin or style of the wine; but I taste by category, and to be absolutely honest I sometimes worry whether an 85-point rated California fizz is indeed the equiv-alent of, say, an 85-point rated Champagne tasted two or three weeks apart. Hopefully it is – or at least, more often than not.

However, what confuses the concept of the universal score is that the intrinsic qualities of each style or region must be resp-ected. Some critics believe that this dilutes the universal yardstick; but if it does, then no-one could say that a 90-point Bordeaux is the same quality as a 90-point Burgundy, and that would be sheer poppycock.

WHAT THE SCORES TELL US
The 100-point scale, by which a critic makes an overall judge-ment on a wine, is now globally recognized.

70 The point at which any sparkling wine other than Champagne becomes interesting as far as I'm concerned.

75 Any sparkling wine other than Champagne that receives this score is not just interesting, but good enough to grace the table of a self-confessed Champagne addict.

80 Because Champagne has such intrinsic advantages over sparkling wines produced in less favourable *terroirs*, this is the level at which I start to take interest in an inexpensive BOB or secondary brand.

85 The sort of quality that Champagne has to be to warrant inclusion in my cellar. If a non-Champagne sparkling wine scores this high, it is of exceptional quality indeed.

90 A top quality Champagne, probably vintage or prestige *cuvée*. Any wine scoring this high deserves to demand a premium over the competition and will probably repay 3–5 years' additional cellarage to reveal its true potential.

95 The greatest Champagnes. Rare even from the top houses. A very special and memorable experience. Most could be left forgotten in a cellar for 10 years without any worry at all.

100 Perfection – impossible!

Notes The scores for the same wine can fluctuate from year to year because different disgorgements produce wines of a different potential. (This also applies to the "when to drink" timescales.) Scores can also vary because although I take into account both actual and potential quality, the emphasis in any annual guide has to be on the former rather than latter.

When unexpected factors have come into play, causing a wine to show less well than had been predicted the year before, I give the wine a ⊖ symbol and try to explain what has happened.

HOW THE WINES PERFORMED

Some winemakers have tried too hard to maximize complexity and end up losing fruit or finesse. Often both. The result is invariably coarse, unappealing, too oxidative, and too aldehydic (primarily the sherry-like aroma of acetaldehyde). These wines are to be found in every region and appellation from Champagne through Cava to one-off sparkling wine producers in the back of beyond. Such wines have been eliminated from the Guide. Should any producers wonder why their "most complex" Champagne or sparkling wine has not been recommended, yet their cheaper *cuvées* have, they now know. If they are selling these wines so fast that they have difficulty meeting demand, then they can afford to ignore my comments, but if they are slow to move, then I suggest they concentrate on retaining finesse by allowing the fruit to express itself and allowing any complexity to come naturally and, above all, slowly.

CHAMPAGNE

The world's greatest sparkling wine comes first. If and when any other area produces a greater volume of higher quality sparkling wine, then I will happily place that first.

REMEMBER!
85 Points: "The sort of quality Champagne has to be to warrant inclusion in my cellar"
–TOM STEVENSON
Don't restrict your choice to 90-point wines – I don't!

CHAMPAGNE, BRUT NON-VINTAGE
This category is supposed to be restricted to basic Brut non-vintage and to this end I have tried to weed out all the non-vintage *cuvées* that sell at a premium (*see* next performance table). A Brut style must have between 0 and 15 grams per litre of residual sugar (added as the dosage after disgorgement). This sugar should not be noticeable, even at the top end of the range, if properly balanced with the acidity. A true Brut should thus taste dry, but this does not mean austere, as young *cuvées* should possess fruit, while mature ones will have a mellowed richness.

90	£££	Charles Heidsieck NV Brut Réserve, Mis en Cave en 1996
89	£££	Charles Heidsieck NV Brut Réserve, Mis en Cave en 1995
89	£££	Pommery NV Brut Royal (*magnum*)
88	££	Gatinois NV Grand Cru Brut
88	£££	Charles Heidsieck NV Brut Réserve Privée, Mis en Cave en 1990
88	£££	Charles Heidsieck NV Brut Réserve, Mis en Cave en 1993
88	£££	Serge Mathieu NV Tête de Cuvée Select Brut

88	££	Louis Roederer NV Brut Premier
88	££	de Venoge NV Brut Sélect, Cordon Bleu
88	££	Veuve Clicquot Ponsardin NV Brut
87	££	Canard-Duchêne NV Brut
87	££	Charles de Cazanove NV Brut Azur, Premier Cru
87	££	Alfred Gratien NV Brut
87	££	Jacquart NV Brut Mosaïque (magnum)
87	££	Lanson NV Black Label Brut
86	££	Alexandre Bonnet NV Cuvée

Tradition Brut

86 ££ Deutz NV Brut Classic

86 ££ Paul-Louis Martin NV Grand Cru Bouzy

86 ££ Pannier NV Brut Sélection

86 ££ R de Ruinart NV Brut

86 ££ Michel Arnould & Fils NV Brut Grand Cru

85 ££ Gaston Chiquet NV Tradition, Brut Premier Cru

85 ££ Veuve A. Devaux NV Grande Réserve Brut

85 ££ Drappier NV Carte d'Or Brut

85 ££ Fleur de Champagne NV Brut, Duval-Leroy

85 ££ Paul Déthune NV Brut Grand Cru

85 ££ Henri Goutorbe NV Cuvée Traditionnelle Brut

85 ££ Michel Guilleminot NV Brut

85 ££ Henriot NV Brut Sovereign

85 ££ Jacquesson & Fils NV Perfection Brut

85 ££ Laurent-Perrier NV Brut L.P.

85 ££ AR Lenoble NV Brut Réserve

85 ££ Henri Mandois NV Cuvée de Réserve Brut

85 ££ Marguet-Bonnerave NV Brut Tradition Grand Cru

85 ££ Mercier NV Brut

85 ££ Bruno Paillard NV Brut Première Cuvée

85 ££ Palmer NV Brut

85 ££ Perrier-Jouët NV Grand Brut

85 ££ Pommery NV Brut Royal

85 ££ Louis de Sacy NV Brut Grand Cru

85 ££ Taittinger NV Brut Réserve

85 ££ Claude Renoux NV Brut

85 ££ Bernard Tornay NV Brut Carte d'Or

85 ££ Georges Vesselle NV Brut Grand Cru

84 ££ Baron-Fuenté NV Brut Tradition

84 ££ Canard-Duchêne NV Brut *(magnum)*

84 ££ Château de Boursault NV Brut Tradition

84 ££ Forget-Chemin NV Brut Carte Blanche

84 ££ Lanson NV Black Label Brut

84 £££ Moët & Chandon NV Brut Premier Cru

84 ££ Pol Roger NV Brut White Foil, Extra Cuvée de Reserve

84 ££ Alain Thienot NV Brut

83 ££ Philippe Brugnon NV Brut

83 ££ Michel Gonet NV Brut Réserve

83 ££ M. Hostomme NV Cuvée Tradition Brut

83 ££ Mumm Cordon Rouge NV Brut

83 ££ A. Soutiran-Pelletier NV Grand Cru Brut

83 ££ Jean-Paul Suss NV Brut Réserve

83 ££ Pierre Vaudon NV Brut Premier Cru

82 ££ Chanoine NV Grande Reserve Brut

82 ££ Cheurlin-Dangin NV Brut

82 ££ Raoul Collet NV Carte Rouge Brut

82 ££ Delouvin Nowack NV Brut

82 ££ Fleury NV Brut

82 ££ Georges Gardet NV Brut Spécial

82 ££ Jean Louis Malard NV Brut Grand Cru Pinot Noir-Chardonnay

82 ££ Jean-Michel Pelletier NV Brut Selection

82 ££ De Saint Gall NV Brut Premier Cru

81 ££ H. Blin & Co NV Brut Tradition

81 ££ Guy Charbaut NV Cuvée de Réserve Brut

80 ££ Bardoux Père & Fils NV Brut Premier Cru

80 ££ Baron Albert NV Brut Carte d'Or

80 ££ Th. Blondel NV Carte Or Brut, Premier Cru

80 ££ Raymond Boulard NV Réserve Brut

80 ££ Jacquart NV Brut Mosaïque

80 ££ Jean-Pierre Marniquet NV Brut Tradition

80 ££ Mathieu-Gosztyla NV Brut Tradition

80 ££ Moutard NV Brut Réserve

80 ££ Moët & Chandon NV Brut Impérial

80 ££ Oudinot NV Cuvée Brut

80 ££ Piper-Heidsieck NV Brut

80 ££ Roger Pouillon NV Le Brut Vigneron, Premier Cru

80 ££ Pierre Vaudon NV Premier Cru Brut

CHAMPAGNE, PREMIUM BRUT NON-VINTAGE

This category includes every recommended Brut non-vintage sold for a premium above the price of the basic non-vintage. These *cuvées* are often labelled as Réserve instead of tradition (or Grande Réserve when the basic Brut claims to be a Réserve), Carte d'Or or Carte Or instead of Carte Blanche or, perhaps, Cuvée Prestige, Tête de Cuvée et al. While large differences in price occur from brand to brand, the small premium asked for the step up in quality for most of these *cuvées* is usually well worth it. This category also includes special one-off non-vintage *cuvées* for the millennium, although it has become increasingly difficult to distinguish between real one-offs and regular lines that just happen to have the magical 2000 splashed over the bottle this year. True prestige or luxury *cuvées* of the Krug, Cristal and Dom Pérignon ilk are listed separately.

94 ⓔⓔⓔ Gosset NV Grande Réserve Brut

90 ⓔⓔ Charles de Cazanove NV Grande Réserve An 2000 Brut

90 ⓔⓔ Vilmart NV Cuvée Cellier Brut

89 ⓔⓔⓔ Billecart-Salmon NV 2000 Brut Réserve

89 ⓔⓔ Roger Pouillon, 50ème Anniversaire NV Fleur de Mareuil

88 ⓔⓔ Beaumont des Crayères, Nuit d'Or NV Cuvée 2000 Millénaire

88 ⓔⓔ Brice NV Aÿ Grand Cru Brut

88 ⓔⓔⓔⓔ André Clouet NV Un Jour de 1911, Brut Grand Cru Classé

88 ⓔⓔ Serge Mathieu NV Cuvée Prestige Brut

88 ⓔⓔⓔ Pommery NV Brut Royal Apanage

86 ⓔⓔ Michel Arnould & Fils NV Brut, Réserve Grand Cru

86 ⓔⓔⓔ Vve A. Devaux 2000 NV D de Devaux Brut

86 ⓔⓔ Princesse des Thunes NV Cuvée Prestige Brut, Ambonnay Grand Cru

86 ⓔⓔ Forget-Brimont NV Cuvée An 2000 Brut

86 ⓔⓔⓔ Perrier-Jouët NV Blason de France Brut

86 ⓔⓔⓔ Philipponnat NV Le Reflet du Millénaire An 2000 Brut

85 ⓔⓔ E. Barnaut NV Grande Réserve, Brut Grand Cru

85 ⓔⓔ Brice NV Bouzy Grand Cru Brut

85 ⓔⓔ Tsarine NV Tête de Cuvée Brut, Chanoine

85 ⓔⓔ J. Dumangin NV Grande Réserve, Brut Premier Cru

85 ⓔⓔ Daniel Dumont NV Grande Réserve Brut

85 ⓔⓔ Gallimard Père & Fils NV Cuvée An 2000 Brut

85 ⓔⓔ J.M. Gobillard NV Grande Réserve, Brut Premier Cru

85 ⓔⓔ Goutorbe NV Cuvée Prestige, Brut Premier Cru

85 ⓔⓔ J. Lassalle NV Cuvée Impérial Préférence, Premier Cru

85 ⓔⓔ Cuvée Compagnie des Wagons-Lits NV Pullman Orient-Express

85 ⓔⓔ Moutard NV Brut Grande Réserve

85 ⓔⓔ Moutard NV Cuvée Prestige Brut

85 ⓔⓔ Moët & Chandon NV Cuvée Claude Moët

85 ⓔⓔ Georges Vesselle NV Cuvée Juline Grand Cru Brut

85 ⓔⓔ Vilmart NV Grand Cellier, Brut Premiers Crus

84 ⓔⓔ Princesse de Baudry NV Brut, Patricia Baudry

84 ⓔⓔ Bauget-Jouette NV Grande Réserve Brut

84 ⓔⓔ Alexandre Bonnet NV Cuvée Prestige Brut

84 ⓔⓔ Brice NV Cramant Grand Cru Brut

84 ⓔⓔ Fleur de Champagne NV Brut Premier Cru, Duval-Leroy

84 ⓔⓔ Andrew Garrett & Nicolas Feuillatte NV Signé, Brut, CVC

83 ⓔⓔ Charles de Cazanove NV Brut Classique

83 ⓔⓔ Eugène Mercier NV Cuvée du Fondateur Brut

82 ⓔⓔ Beaumont des Crayères NV Grand Prestige Brut

82 ⓔⓔ Raymond Boulard NV Brut

		Grand Cru Mailly-Champagne			René Geoffroy NV Cuvée Prestige, Brut Premier Cru
82	££	Brice NV Verzenay Grand Cru Brut	82	£££	
82	££	Cheurlin-Dangin NV Cuvée Spéciale Brut	80	£££	Besserat de Bellefon NV Cuvée des Moines Brut
			80	££	J. Bourgeois NV Cuvée An 2000, Carte Or Brut

EXTRA-BRUT, VINTAGE AND NON-VINTAGE

Due to the severe selection process, I have been forced to mix vintage and non-vintage Champagnes for this category. Although I am not a great fan of non-dosage Champagnes, this has less to do with its style than the quality. Such wines do not improve with age for the simple reason that sugar is required to develop post-disgorgement aromas of any finesse, but should a non-dosage Champagne be fresh and young, with enough ripeness of fruit to excel without the need for any sugar, then I will certainly enjoy the wine, even if I cannot recommend cellaring it.

95	££££	Veuve Pommery 1979 Flacon d'Excellence Nature *(magnum)*			Oenophile, Blanc de Blancs, Maxi-Brut
90	££££	Bollinger 1985 R.D. Extra Brut	85	£££	Fleur de Champagne 1990 Extra Brut Millésimé, Duval-Leroy
88	££	de Bruyne NV Cuvée Absolue Brut, Sézanne	85	£££	Mailly NV Cassiopee, Brut Nature, Grand Cru
88	£££	Fleur de Champagne 1992 Extra Brut Millésimé, Duval-Leroy	83	££	Larmandier-Bernier NV Né d'Une Terre de Vertus, Brut Nature
88	££	Lamiable NV Extra Brut, Grand Cru	82	££	Jean Vesselle NV Brut Prestige Extra Brut
88	£££	Larmandier-Bernier 1995 Vieilles Vignes de Cramant Extra Brut	80	££	André et Michel Drappier NV Brut Nature, Pinot Noir Zero Dosage
86	£££	Pierre Gimonnet & Fils NV	80	££	Tarlant NV Brut Zero

CHAMPAGNE SEC AND DEMI-SEC, VINTAGE & NON-VINTAGE

For many years this sweet style, which must have between 35 and 50 grams of residual sugar, has been debased by the vast majority of Champagne producers who have pandered to an unsophisticated sector of French supermarket customers who like to drink sweet. By this I do not mean that sweetness in Champagne or indeed any wine is debasing or that to enjoy sweetness is a sign of poor taste, but there are vast numbers who can only enjoy sweet drinks and cannot taste beyond that sweetness, thus Champagne producers have been able to hide their inferior wines behind a mask of sugar. However, we are gradually seeing a rise in the number of high quality *demi-sec* produced.

88	££	Billecart-Salmon NV Demi-Sec Réserve			1995 Rich Reserve
88	££	Gatinois NV Demi-Sec	82	££	Aubeline de Vauversin NV Blanc de Blancs, Grand Cru, Sec
88	££	Lanson NV Ivory Label Demi-Sec	82	££	Jacquart NV Demi-Sec
88	£££	Moët & Chandon NV Nectar Impérial	80	£££	Veuve Clicquot Ponsardin NV Demi-Sec
88	£££	Pol Roger NV Rich Special Demi-Sec			
88	£££	Louis Roederer NV Rich			
85	£££	Veuve Clicquot Ponsardin			

VINTAGE CHAMPAGNE: 1996

This vintage is possibly greater than 1990, but legally the earliest its wines could be commercially disgorged was January 2000 and because most producers bottle in May or June, the earliest in practical terms was in fact spring 2000. On top of this there will be a 3–6 month resting period after disgorgement before the wines are ready for shipping, plus six weeks to distribute, thus it really is stretching things to expect to find this vintage on the shelves before the last quarter of 2000. Indeed, many of the 1996s I tasted were preview samples. The best wines from this vintage will not be released for another two or three years, so there was little point in submitting them for this edition. The following therefore represents the best of the earliest releases.

90 ©©© Taittinger 1996 Brut Millésimé

89 ©© Fluteau 1996 Brut Blanc de Blancs

88 ©© René Geoffroy 1996 Cuvée Sélectionnée, Brut Premier Cru

88 ©©© Mumm Cordon Rouge 1996 Brut

88 ©©© Joseph Perrier 1996 Brut

Cuvée Royal

87 ©© Doyard 1996 Collection de l'An I, Oeil de Perdrix Rosé Brut

86 ©©© Michel Gonet 1996 Prestige 2000, Brut Grand Cru

83 ©©© Nicolas Feuillatte 1996 Rosé Millésime, Brut Premier Cru

---

VINTAGE CHAMPAGNE: 1995

The first true vintage after 1990, but the extra maturity of 1993 and 1992 can make those Champagnes seem even better, and this situation will continue for another couple of years at least.

95 ©©©© Taittinger Comtes de Champagne 1995 Blanc de Blancs

90 ©©© Cuvée Charles Gardet 1995 Brut

90 ©©© Pierre Gimonnet & Fils 1995 Premier Cru Chardonnay

90 ©©© Pierre Gimonnet & Fils 1995 Fleuron

90 ©©© Pierre Gimonnet & Fils 1995 Brut Gastronome

90 ©©© Larmandier 1995 Grand Cru Chardonnay Brut

90 ©©© Henri Mandois 1995 Cuvée Victor Mandois Brut

90 ©©©© Perrier-Jouët 1995 Belle Epoque Brut

90 ©©© Veuve Clicquot Ponsardin 1995 Rosé Reserve Brut

89 ©©© Le Mesnil 1995 Réserve Sélection, Blanc de Blancs Brut

89 ©©© Bruno Paillard 1995 Brut

88 ©©© Cattier 1995 Brut Premier Cru

88 ©©© Drappier 1995 Grande Sendrée Brut

88 ©©© Fleur de Champagne 1995

Blanc de Chardonnay Brut, Duval-Leroy

88 ©©© Larmandier-Bernier 1995 Vieilles Vignes de Cramant Blanc de Blancs

88 ©© Henri Mandois 1995 Brut Millésimé, Brut Premier Cru

88 ©©© Henri Mandois 1995 Chardonnay, Brut Premier Cru

88 ©©© GH Martel 1995 Cuvée Victoire

87 ©© Beaumont des Crayères 1995 Fleur de Prestige Brut

87 ©©© Mumm Cordon Rouge 1995 Brut Millésimé

87 ©©© Joseph Perrier 1995 Brut Cuvée Royal

87 ©©© R de Ruinart 1995 Brut

87 ©©© De Saint Gall 1995 Blanc de Blancs, Brut Premier Cru

86 ©© Philippe Brugnon 1995 Brut

86 ©©© Gaston Chiquet 1995 Brut, Club de Viticulteurs Champenois

86 ©©© Nicolas Feuillatte 1995 Blanc de Blancs Millésimé, Brut Premier Cru

86 ⓔⓔⓔ Jacquesson & Fils 1995 Blanc de Blancs, Brut Grand Cru

86 ⓔⓔ Mercier 1995 Vendange Brut

86 ⓔⓔⓔ Pommery 1995 Brut, Grand Cru

85 ⓔⓔ Beaumont des Crayères 1995 Fleur de Rosé Brut

85 ⓔⓔ H. Blin & Co 1995 Brut

85 ⓔⓔ Th. Blondel 1995 Brut Millésime, Premier Cru Blanc de Blancs

85 ⓔⓔⓔ Tsarine 1995 Brut Millésime, Chanoine

85 ⓔⓔⓔ Guy Charbaut 1995 Memory Blanc de Blanc

85 ⓔⓔⓔ Deutz 1995 Blanc de Blancs Brut

85 ⓔⓔⓔ Drappier 1995 Carte d'Or Brut

85 ⓔⓔⓔ Nicolas Feuillatte 1995 Cuvée Spéciale, Brut 1er Cru

85 ⓔⓔⓔ Heidsieck Monopole 1995 Brut

85 ⓔⓔⓔ Lagache 1995 Prestige de Consorts Grand Cru

85 ⓔⓔ Palmer 1995 Blanc de Blancs Brut

85 ⓔⓔ Pierrel Cuvée 1995

85 ⓔⓔ Piper-Heidsieck 1995 Brut

85 ⓔⓔⓔ Taittinger 1995 Brut Millésimé

85 ⓔⓔⓔ Georges Vesselle 1995 Brut Millésimé Grand Cru

85 ⓔⓔⓔ Veuve Clicquot Ponsardin 1995 Rich Reserve

84 ⓔⓔⓔ Chartogne-Taillet 1995 Cuvée Sainte-Anne Brut

84 ⓔⓔⓔ Doyard 1995 Collection de l'An I, Blanc de Blancs Brut

84 ⓔⓔⓔ Serge Mathieu 1995 Brut Millésime

83 ⓔⓔ Vve. A. Devaux 1995 Brut

83 ⓔⓔⓔ Lemaire-Rasselet 1995 An 2000 Brut

83 ⓔⓔⓔ Mailly 1995 Brut Grand Cru Millésime

82 ⓔⓔ Forget-Chemin 1995 Brut

82 ⓔⓔⓔ Henriot 1995 Brut Millésimé

80 ⓔⓔⓔ Egérie de Pannier 1995 Brut

REMEMBER!

85 Points: "The sort of quality Champagne has to be to warrant inclusion in my cellar"
–TOM STEVENSON
Don't restrict your choice to 90-point wines – I don't!

VINTAGE CHAMPAGNE: 1994

The worst of the lesser vintages between the great 1990 and the excellent 1995, all four of which were spoiled by rain at harvest time. However, whilst there are a number of very good to excellent 1993s, 1992s and to a lesser extent 1991s, most of the 1994s would have been better off in the non-vintage blends.

92 ⓔⓔⓔⓔ Louis Roederer Cristal 1994 Brut

89 ⓔⓔⓔⓔ Taittinger Comtes de Champagne 1994 Blanc de Blancs

87 ⓔⓔⓔⓔ Louis Roederer 1994 Vintage Rosé Brut

85 ⓔⓔⓔ Beaumont des Crayères 1994 Grande Prestige Millésime

84 ⓔⓔ La Préférence de Baron Albert 1994 Brut Millésime

84 ⓔⓔ Cuvée Jean De La Fontaine 1994 Brut, Baron Albert

84 ⓔⓔ J.Dumangin 1994 Brut Millésimé, Premier Cru

84 ⓔⓔⓔⓔ Blanc de Blancs de Lanson 1994 Brut

82 ⓔⓔⓔⓔ Louis Roederer 1994 Brut

80 ⓔⓔⓔ Lanson 1994 Gold Label Brut

VINTAGE CHAMPAGNE: 1993

On paper the ripeness and acidity levels achieved during this vintage are less favourable than those of 1992, but what matters is in the bottle and for the second year running the number of higher scoring 1993s has definitely edged ahead of the 1992s.

93	££££	Vilmart 1993 Coeur de Cuvée, Brut Premiers Crus
89	£££	Henri Mandois 1993 Cuvée des Trois Générations Brut
89	££££	Perrier-Jouët 1993 Belle Epoque Blanc de Blancs
89	£££	Pol Roger 1993 Brut
88	££££	Gosset 1993 Grand Millésime Brut
88	£££	Lanson 1993 Gold Label Brut
88	£££	Laurent-Perrier 1993 Vintage Brut
88	£££	Moët & Chandon 1993 Brut Impérial
88	££££	Pol Roger 1993 Brut Chardonnay
87	££	Alexandre Bonnet 1993 Blanc de Blancs Brut
87	££	Gauthier 1993 Brut Millésime
87	£££	Moët & Chandon 1993 Brut Impérial Rosé
87	££££	Pol Roger 1993 Brut Rosé
87	£££	R de Ruinart 1993 Brut
86	£££	Veuve Clicquot Ponsardin 1993 Brut Vintage Reserve
85	££	Raoul Collet 1993 Carte d'Or Brut
85	££	Alain Thienot 1993 Brut
84	££	F. Vauversin 1993 Blanc de Blancs, Brut Grand Cru
81	££	Madrigal 1993 Brut, Alexandre Bonnet
80	££	Vollereaux 1993 Cuvée Marguerite Brut

VINTAGE CHAMPAGNE: 1992

Theoretically the only vintage quality year between 1990 and 1995, and although it has provided some excellent Champagnes, 1993 has the edge.

89	££££	Moët et Chandon 1992 Cuvée Dom Pérignon Brut
89	£££	Pommery 1992 Brut, Grand Cru *(magnum)*
88	£££	Fleur de Champagne 1992 Extra Brut Millésimé, Duval-Leroy
88	£££	Jacquart 1992 Cuvée Mosaïque, Blanc de Blancs Brut
88	£££	Perrier-Jouët 1992 Grand Brut
88	£££	Pommery 1992 Brut, Grand Cru
87	££	Autreau-Lasnot 1992 Brut Prestige
86	£££	Jacquart 1992 Mosaïque Millésimé Brut
86	££	Palmer 1992 Brut
85	££	Dumont Grande Réserve 1992 Cuvée d'Excellence Brut
85	£££	Fleur de Champagne 1992 Brut, Duval-Leroy
85	£££	Fleur de Champagne, LeRoy Neiman 1992 Brut, Duval-Leroy
85	££	A.R. Lenoble 1992 Blanc de Noirs Premier Cru
85	£££	Moët & Chandon 1992 Brut Impérial
85	£££	Taittinger 1992 Brut Millésimé
84	££	Nicolas Feuillatte 1992 Brut
84	££	D. Henriet-Bazin 1992 Carte d'Or Brut Premier Cru
82	££	Charles de Cazanove 1992 Brut Azur, Premier Cru

REMEMBER!

85 Points: "The sort of quality Champagne has to be to warrant inclusion in my cellar"
–TOM STEVENSON
Don't restrict your choice to 90-point wines – I don't!

VINTAGE CHAMPAGNE: 1991

Although fewer houses declared this vintage and the ripeness/acidity levels were less impressive than either 1992 or 1993, some producers evidently got it right.

89 ⓔⓔⓔ Boizel 1991 Joyau de France Brut

88 ⓔⓔⓔ Pierre Moncuit, Cuvée Nicole Moncuit 1991 Vieille Vigne

88 ⓔⓔⓔ Veuve Clicquot Ponsardin 1991 Brut Vintage Reserve

85 ⓔⓔ Alfred Gratien 1991 Brut

85 ⓔⓔ Palmer 1991 Brut

85 ⓔⓔⓔ Philipponnat 1991 Grand Blanc Brut

84 ⓔⓔ Raoul Collet 1991 Carte d'Or Brut

80 ⓔⓔ Forget-Brimont 1991 Cuvée Prestige, Brut Premier Cru

VINTAGE CHAMPAGNE: 1990

This is not only a true vintage, it is one of the 18 greatest Champagne vintages of the century. The grapes were riper in 1990 than they were in the drought year of 1976, but the acidity levels were surprisingly high, with a much greater proportion of ripe tartaric to unripe malic than any other top vintage on record. About the only thing I can think of to dampen my enthusiasm for this exceptional vintage is that 1996 threatens to be even better!

98 ⓔⓔⓔⓔ Pol Roger 1990 Cuvée Sir Winston Churchill Brut

96 ⓔⓔⓔⓔ Billecart-Salmon 1990 Grande Cuvée

96 ⓔⓔⓔ Pol Roger 1990 Brut

95 ⓔⓔⓔⓔ Jacquesson & Fils 1990 Grand Vin Signature Brut *(magnum)*

95 ⓔⓔⓔⓔ Veuve Clicquot Ponsardin 1990 La Grande Dame Brut

94 ⓔⓔⓔⓔ Veuve Clicquot Ponsardin 1990 La Grande Dame Rosé Brut

92 ⓔⓔⓔ Pierre Gimonnet & Fils 1990 Millésime de Collection *(magnum)*

92 ⓔⓔⓔⓔ Pommery 1990 Louise Rosé Brut

91 ⓔⓔⓔⓔ Jacquesson & Fils 1990 Grand Vin Signature Brut

91 ⓔⓔⓔ Laurent-Perrier 1990 Vintage Brut

90 ⓔⓔⓔⓔ Gosset Celebris 1990 Brut

90 ⓔⓔⓔⓔ Jacquesson & Fils 1990 Grand Vin Signature, Brut Rosé

90 ⓔⓔⓔⓔ Moët et Chandon 1990 Cuvée Dom Pérignon Rosé Brut

90 ⓔⓔⓔ Mumm Cordon Rouge 1990 Cuvée Limitée, Brut Millésime

90 ⓔⓔⓔⓔ Louis Roederer 1990 Brut Vintage

89 ⓔⓔⓔ Drappier 1990 Grande Sendrée Brut

89 ⓔⓔⓔ Cuvée des Roys 1990 Brut, Duval-Leroy *(magnum)*

89 ⓔⓔⓔ de Venoge 1990 Brut Blanc de Noirs

88 ⓔⓔⓔ Boizel 1990 Cuvée Sous Bois Brut

88 ⓔⓔⓔ Drappier 1990 Grande Sendrée Rosé Brut

88 ⓔⓔⓔ Cuvée des Roys 1990 Brut, Duval-Leroy

88 ⓔⓔⓔⓔ Laurent-Perrier Grand Siècle 1990 Alexandra Rosé Brut

87 ⓔⓔⓔ Georges Vesselle 1990 Brut Millésime Grand Cru

86 ⓔⓔⓔ Delamotte 1990 Blanc de Blancs Brut

85 ⓔⓔⓔ Canard-Duchêne 1990 Brut

85 ⓔⓔ Doquet-Jeanmaire 1990 Blanc de Blancs, Brut Premier Cru

85 ⓔⓔⓔ Fleur de Champagne 1990 Extra Brut Millésimé, Duval-Leroy

85 ⓔⓔ A.R. Lenoble 1990 Gentilhomme, Brut Grand Cru

85 ⓔⓔⓔⓔ Bruno Paillard 1990 N.P.U. Neo Plus Ultra Brut

84 ⓔⓔⓔ Fleur de Champagne, LeRoy Neiman 1990 Brut, Duval-Leroy

VINTAGE CHAMPAGNE: 1989

The middle year of the great trio of exceptional successive vintages, 1989 initially caused confusion amongst Champagne drinkers because after an extraordinary degree of hype during the harvest itself, many of the first *cuvées* to be released were disappointing. However, this was because of a physiological problem with the Pinot Noir that plagued the cheaper, earlier-released Champagnes. As the better 1989s entered the market, so the exciting quality of this vintage has at last been realized. The style is generally fatter than either the 1988s or the 1990s.

91 £££ Pierre Gimonnet & Fils 1989 Premier Cru Chardonnay Brut

91 ££££ Gosset 1989 Grand Millésime Brut

90 ££££ Perrier-Jouët 1989 Belle Epoque Rosé Brut

89 £££ Boizel 1989 Joyau de Chardonnay Brut

88 £££ Drappier 1989 Grande Sendrée Brut

87 ££££ Billecart-Salmon 1989 Grande Cuvée

86 ££££ Pommery 1989 Louise Brut

85 ££ Charles Ellner 1989 Brut

85 £££ J. Lassalle 1989 Blanc de Blancs, Premier Cru

VINTAGE CHAMPAGNE: 1988

The best Champagnes from this vintage still require a few years before they will be drinking as well as the 1989s and 1990s, or even the 1992s and 1993s. The problem is that due to the maturity of this vintage, very little remains available, so buy it if you can.

97 ££££ Krug 1988 Brut

95 ££££ Pol Roger 1988 Cuvée Sir Winston Churchill Brut

90 ££££ Bollinger 1988 R.D. Extra Brut

88 ££££ Henriot 1988 Cuvée des Enchanteleurs Brut

88 ££££ Laurent-Perrier Grand Siècle 1988 Alexandra Rosé Brut

87 £££ Mailly 1988 Cuvée Les Echansons, Brut Grand Cru

VINTAGE CHAMPAGNE: 1985 AND OLDER

As part of the ongoing millennium celebrations, a number of houses have decided to release old vintages from their library collection (Dom Pérignon did so too late for inclusion in this year's Guide). There are, however, huge variations in quality, which resulted in relatively few of these wines surviving my tasting.

The champenois are, after all, French, and it must be remembered that the French generally prefer their Champagnes young, thus it is not uncommon to find that they are the last to understand the qualities that make a mature Champagne great. Often they think that because a Champagne is old, a certain maderized or oxidized character is acceptable, but it's not, of course.

In addition to complexity and finesse, the greatest mature Champagnes are those that remain the freshest and youngest for the longest period of time. It's that simple.

98 ££££ Krug Collection 1979 Brut

95 ££££ Veuve Pommery 1979 Flacon d'Excellence Nature *(magnum)*

90 ££££ Bollinger 1985 R.D. Extra Brut

88 ££££ Jacquesson & Fils 1985 Brut, Dégorgement Tardif

86 £££ Pierre Vaudon 1985 Premier Cru Brut

85 £££ Cuvée des Roys 1986 Brut, Duval-Leroy *(magnum)*

CHAMPAGNE BLANC DE BLANCS: VINTAGE & NON-VINTAGE

Without doubt, *blanc de blancs* are more expressive from a single vintage, but as a style of wine I think it fair to compare the performance of both vintage and non-vintage.

(95) ££££ Taittinger Comtes de Champagne 1995 Blanc de Blancs

(92) £££ Pierre Gimonnet & Fils 1990 Millésime de Collection (*magnum*)

(91) £££ Pierre Gimonnet & Fils 1989 Premier Cru Chardonnay

(90) ££ Gaston Chiquet NV Blanc de Blancs d'Aÿ, Brut Grand Cru

(90) £££ Pierre Gimonnet & Fils 1995 Premier Cru-Chardonnay

(90) £££ Pierre Gimonnet & Fils 1995 Fleuron

(90) £££ Pierre Gimonnet & Fils 1995 Brut Gastronome

(90) £££ Larmandier 1995 Grand Cru Chardonnay Brut

(89) £££ Boizel 1989 Joyau de Chardonnay Brut

(89) ££ Fluteau 1996 Brut Blanc de Blancs

(89) £££ Le Mesnil 1995 Réserve Sélection, Blanc de Blancs Brut

(89) ££££ Perrier-Jouët 1993 Belle Epoque Blanc de Blancs

(89) ££££ Taittinger Comtes de Champagne 1994 Blanc de Blancs Brut

(88) £££ Fleur de Champagne 1995 Blanc de Chardonnay Brut, Duval-Leroy

(88) £££ Pierre Gimonnet & Fils NV Blanc de Blancs Brut, 1er Cru

(88) £££ Jacquart 1992 Cuvée Mosaïque, Blanc de Blancs Brut

(88) £££ Larmandier-Bernier, Vieilles Vignes de Cramant 1995 Blanc de Blancs, Extra Brut Grand Cru

(88) £££ Henri Mandois 1995 Chardonnay, Brut Premier Cru

(88) £££ Pierre Moncuit, Cuvée Nicole Moncuit 1991 Vieille Vigne, Blanc de Blancs, Brut Grand Cru

(88) ££££ Pol Roger 1993 Brut Chardonnay

(87) ££ Alexandre Bonnet 1993 Blanc de Blancs Brut

(87) £££ De Saint Gall 1995 Blanc de Blancs, Brut Premier Cru

(86) ££ Delamotte 1990 Blanc de Blancs Brut

(86) £££ Nicolas Feuillatte 1995 Blanc de Blancs Millésimé, Brut Premier Cru

(86) £££ Pierre Gimonnet & Fils NV Oenophile, Blanc de Blancs, Maxi-Brut

(86) £££ Jacquesson & Fils 1995 Blanc de Blancs, Brut Grand Cru

(86) ££ Launois Père & Fils NV Blanc de Blancs Cuvée Réserve Grand Cru Brut

(86) £££ Joseph Perrier NV Cuvée Royal Blanc de Blancs

(86) £££ Pommery NV Summertime, Blanc de Blancs Brut

(85) ££ Th. Blondel 1995 Brut Millésime, Premier Cru Blanc de Blancs

(85) £££ Boizel NV Chardonnay Brut Blanc de Blancs

(85) £££ Guy Charbaut 1995 Memory Blanc de Blanc

(85) ££ Delamotte NV Blanc de Blancs Brut

(85) £££ Deutz 1995 Blanc de Blancs Brut

(85) ££ Doquet-Jeanmaire NV Blanc de Blancs, Carte Or Brut Premier Cru

(85) ££ Doquet-Jeanmaire 1990 Blanc de Blancs, Brut Premier Cru

(85) ££ Michel Gonet NV Blanc de Blancs, Brut Grand Cru

(85) ££ Henriot NV Blanc de Blancs Chardonnay Brut

(85) ££ Larmandier-Bernier NV Blanc de Blancs Brut, Premier Cru

(85) £££ J. Lassalle 1989 Blanc de Blancs, Premier Cru

(85) ££ Jean-Louis Malard NV Grand Cru Chardonnay

(85) £££ Mumm de Cramant NV Chardonnay, Brut Grand Cru

85	£££	Bruno Paillard NV Chardonnay Réserve Privée Brut
85	££	Palmer 1995 Blanc de Blancs Brut
85	£££	Philipponnat 1991 Grand Blanc Brut
85	££	Royer Père et Fils NV Cuvée Prestige, Blanc de Blancs Brut
84	££	Raymond Boulard NV Blanc de Blancs Brut
84	£££	Doyard 1995 Collection de l'An I, Blanc de Blancs Brut
84	££££	Blanc de Blancs de Lanson 1994 Brut
84	££	F. Vauversin 1993 Blanc de Blancs, Brut Grand Cru
83	££	Larmandier-Bernier NV Né d'Une Terre de Vertus, Brut Nature
82	££	M. Hostomme NV Brut Grand Cru, Blanc de Blancs
82	££	Jean Milan, An 2000 NV Blancs de Blancs, Brut Spécial, Grand Cru
82	££	Aubeline de Vauversin NV Blanc de Blancs, Grand Cru, Sec
80	££	Amyot NV Blanc de Blancs
80	£££	Besserat de Bellefon NV Cuvée des Moines, Blanc de Blancs Brut
80	££	Philippe Gonet NV Blanc de Blancs Brut
80	££	M. Hostomme, Grande Réserve NV Blanc de Blancs, Brut Grand Cru
80	££	Larmandier NV Blanc de Blancs, Brut 1er Cru
80	££	Jean Charles Milan, Cuvée de Réserve NV Blanc de Blancs, Brut Grand Cru
80	££	F. Vauversin NV Blanc de Blancs, Brut Grand Cru

Remember!
85 Points: "The sort of quality Champagne has to be to warrant inclusion in my cellar."
–Tom Stevenson
Don't restrict your choice to 90-point wines – I don't!

Champagne Blanc de Noirs: Vintage & Non-vintage

The idea that a *blanc de noirs* is a big, rich, meaty Champagne evolved because Bollinger set the yardstick with its Vieilles Vignes Françaises, but that is made from overripe grapes grown on ungrafted vines, thus the size and body of this wine are an anomaly. Some *blanc de noirs* can have such finesse that it is hard to imagine that they do not contain a substantial amount of Chardonnay. Although many Champagnes have always been made from exclusively black grapes, particularly in the Marne Valley, few producers marketed them as *blanc de noirs* until fairly recently. There is also the notion that these wines are pure Pinot Noir, whereas many *blanc de noirs* are blends of Pinot Noir and Meunier. The following recommendations are all classic *blanc de noirs*, which is to say that they contain only black grapes and the aim is to produce as colourless a wine as possible. These are not New World *blanc de noirs*, which often contain a small percentage of white grapes and vary in colour from copper-tinged to full rosé.

90	£££	de Venoge NV Brut Blanc de Noirs
89	£££	de Venoge 1990 Brut Blanc de Noirs
88	££	Veuve A. Devaux NV Blanc de Noirs Brut
86	£££	Canard-Duchêne NV Charles VII Grande Cuvée, Blanc de Noirs Brut
85	££	A.R. Lenoble 1992 Blanc de Noirs Premier Cru, Brut Millésime
85	££	Serge Mathieu NV Cuvée Tradition, Blanc de Noirs Brut
83	££	E. Barnaut NV Blanc de Noirs, Brut Grand Cru
80	££	André et Michel Drappier NV Brut Nature, Pinot Noir Zero Dosage
80	££	Mailly NV Blanc de Noirs, Brut Grand Cru

CHAMPAGNE ROSÉ, VINTAGE & NON-VINTAGE

With so many producers not taking Champagne rosé seriously and most of even those who do tending to consider it a style best drunk young and fresh, the widespread habit of making vintage rosé has to be viewed as rather odd. After all, a vintage infers a wine that should be aged. Occasionally a rosé that will improve with age is made, but usually this will be unintentionally.

96 ££££ Krug Rosé NV Brut

94 ££££ Veuve Clicquot Ponsardin 1990 La Grande Dame Rosé Brut

92 ££££ Pommery 1990 Louise Rosé Brut

90 ££££ Jacquesson & Fils 1990 Grand Vin Signature, Brut Rosé

90 ££££ Moët et Chandon 1990 Cuvée Dom Pérignon Rosé Brut

90 ££££ Perrier-Jouët 1989 Belle Epoque Rosé Brut

90 £££ Veuve Clicquot Ponsardin 1995 Rosé Reserve Brut

89 £££ Perrier-Jouët NV Blason de France Rosé Brut

88 £££ Billecart-Salmon NV Brut Rosé

88 £££ Drappier 1990 Grande Sendrée Rosé Brut

88 £££ Fleur de Champagne NV Rosé de Saignée Brut, Duval-Leroy

88 ££ Paul Déthune NV Brut Rosé, Grand Cru

88 £££ Gosset NV Grand Rosé Brut

88 ££ Henri Goutorbe NV Brut Rosé

88 ££££ Laurent-Perrier Grand Siècle 1990 Alexandra Rosé Brut

88 ££££ Laurent-Perrier Grand Siècle 1988 Alexandra Rosé Brut

88 £££ R de Ruinart NV Brut Rosé

87 ££ Michel Arnould & Fils NV Brut Rosé, Grand Cru

87 £££ Canard-Duchêne NV Charles VII Grande Cuvée, Rosé Brut

87 ££ Doyard 1996 Collection de l'An I, Oeil de Perdrix Rosé Brut

87 ££ René Geoffroy NV Brut Rosé

87 £££ Moët & Chandon 1993 Brut Impérial Rosé

87 ££££ Pol Roger 1993 Brut Rosé

87 ££££ Louis Roederer 1994 Vintage Rosé Brut

86 £££ Lanson NV Rose Label Brut Rosé

86 ££ Henri Mandois NV Brut Rosé, Premier Cru

86 ££ Serge Mathieu NV Rosé Brut

86 ££ Moutard NV Brut Rosé

85 ££ Amyot NV Brut Rosé, Carte Rubis

85 ££ Baron Albert NV Brut Rosé

85 ££ Beaumont des Crayères 1995 Fleur de Rosé Brut

85 ££ Raymond Boulard NV Cuvée Rose Brut

85 ££ Canard-Duchêne NV Brut Rosé

85 ££ Guy Charbaut NV Brut Rosé

85 ££ Drappier NV Val des Demoiselle, Rosé Brut

85 ££ Forget-Brimont NV Brut Rosé, Premier Cru

85 ££ Gatinois NV Brut Rosé

85 ££ René James Lallier NV Brut Rosé

85 ££ Larmandier-Bernier NV Brut Rosé, Premier Cru

85 £££ Mumm Cordon Rosé NV Brut

85 £££ Bruno Paillard NV Brut Rosé Première Cuvée

85 ££ Pannier NV Cuvée Louis Eugène, Rosé Brut

85 ££ Taittinger NV Brut Prestige Rosé

85 ££ Alain Thienot NV Brut Rosé

85 ££ Pierre Vaudon NV Premier Cru Brut Rosé

85 £££ de Venoge NV Princesse Rosé Brut

85 ££ Georges Vesselle NV Brut Rosé Grand Cru

85 ££ Vilmart NV Cuvée Rubis Brut

84 ££ Cattier NV Brut Rosé

84 ££ Charles de Cazanove NV Brut Rosé

84 ££ Raoul Collet NV Brut Rosé

84 ££ Forget-Chemin NV Brut Rosé

84 £££ Jacquesson & Fils NV

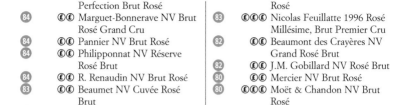

Perfection Brut Rosé

84 ££ Marguet-Bonnerave NV Brut
Rosé Grand Cru

84 ££ Pannier NV Brut Rosé

84 ££ Philipponnat NV Réserve
Rosé Brut

84 ££ R. Renaudin NV Brut Rosé

83 ££ Beaumet NV Cuvée Rosé
Brut

83 ££ Alexandre Bonnet NV Brut

Rosé

83 £££ Nicolas Feuillatte 1996 Rosé
Millésime, Brut Premier Cru

82 ££ Beaumont des Crayères NV
Grand Rosé Brut

82 ££ J.M. Gobillard NV Rosé Brut

80 ££ Mercier NV Brut Rosé

80 £££ Moët & Chandon NV Brut
Rosé

TRUE PRESTIGE OR DELUXE CUVÉES – WHITE

There is no doubt about it: when a true prestige *cuvée* works well, it works very well indeed. However, despite a fairly long list, a number of prestige *cuvées* did not make it into the book, including some of the most famous names.

98 ££££ Pol Roger 1990 Cuvée Sir
Winston Churchill Brut

98 ££££ Krug Collection 1979 Brut

97 ££££ Krug 1988 Brut

95 ££££ Jacquesson & Fils 1990
Grand Vin Signature Brut
(magnum)

95 ££££ Pol Roger 1988 Cuvée Sir
Winston Churchill Brut

95 ££££ Taittinger Comtes de
Champagne 1995 Blanc de
Blancs

95 ££££ Veuve Clicquot Ponsardin
1990 La Grande Dame Brut

93 ££££ Vilmart 1993 Coeur de
Cuvée, Brut Premiers Crus

92 ££££ Louis Roederer Cristal 1994
Brut

91 ££££ Jacquesson & Fils 1990
Grand Vin Signature Brut

90 ££££ Bollinger 1988 R.D. Extra
Brut

90 ££££ Bollinger 1985 R.D. Extra
Brut

90 ££££ Gosset Celebris 1990 Brut

89 £££ Boizel 1991 Joyau de France
Brut

89 £££ Boizel 1989 Joyau de
Chardonnay Brut

89 £££ Cuvée des Roys 1990 Brut,
Duval-Leroy *(magnum)*

89 ££££ Perrier-Jouët 1993 Belle
Epoque Blanc de Blancs

89 ££££ Taittinger Comtes de
Champagne 1994 Blanc de
Blancs

88 £££ Cuvée des Roys 1990 Brut,
Duval-Leroy

88 £££ Drappier 1989 Grande
Sendrée Brut

88 ££££ Henriot 1988 Cuvée des
Enchanteleurs Brut

87 £££ Mailly 1988 Cuvée Les
Echansons, Brut Grand Cru

86 ££££ Pommery 1989 Louise Brut

80 £££ Egérie de Pannier 1995
Brut

TRUE PRESTIGE OR DELUXE CUVÉES – ROSÉ

This category includes some of the most sublime wines produced in Champagne, but the prices charged cannot be justified even in terms of a deluxe *cuvée*. The difference between the same vintage of a Grande Dame and a Grande Dame Rosé or a Dom Pérignon and a Dom Pérignon Rosé is a splash of red wine, yet the rosé version usually costs more than twice as much. It does not worry me, however, since most of the people buying these wines have so much money that they would not notice the difference.

94 ££££ Veuve Clicquot
Ponsardin 1990 La
Grande Dame Rosé Brut

92 ££££ Pommery 1990 Louise
Rosé Brut

90 ££££ Jacquesson & Fils
1990 Grand Vin
Signature, Brut Rosé

90 ££££ Moët et Chandon 1990
Cuvée Dom Pérignon

90 ℰℰℰℰ Rosé Brut
Perrier-Jouët 1989 Belle
Epoque Rosé Brut

88 ℰℰℰ Drappier 1990 Grande
Sendrée Rosé Brut

88 ℰℰℰℰ Laurent-Perrier Grand
Siècle 1990 Alexandra Rosé
Brut

88 ℰℰℰℰ Laurent-Perrier Grand
Siècle 1988 Alexandra
Rosé Brut

CHAMPAGNE CELLAR DOOR SALES: SCORE ORDER

Most Champagne producers sell from the cellar door, but many are reluctant to supply prices to this Guide, particularly the larger houses. Apparently they were worried that this would encourage readers to buy Champagne from them rather than through their importers. I doubt it, but what certainly will happen is that those readers who visit Champagne and intend taking home a few cases will not be buying from them, but from their neighbours below.

96 580FF Billecart-Salmon 1990 Grande Cuvée

95 620FF Taittinger Comtes de Champagne 1995 Blanc de Blancs

94 800FF Veuve Clicquot Ponsardin 1990 La Grande Dame Rosé

93 205FF Vilmart 1993 Coeur de Cuvée, Brut Premiers Crus

92 650FF Louis Roederer Cristal 1994 Brut

92 700FF Pommery 1990 Louise Rosé Brut

91 350FF Jacquesson & Fils 1990 Grand Vin Signature

90 100.50FF Henri Mandois 1995 Cuvée Victor Mandois

90 100FF Charles de Cazanove NV Grande Réserve An 2000 Brut

90 140FF Vilmart NV Cuvée Cellier

90 180FF Charles Heidsieck NV Brut Réserve, Mis en Cave en 1996

90 180FF Taittinger 1996 Brut Millésimé

90 250FF Veuve Clicquot Ponsardin 1995 Rosé Reserve

90 390FF Jacquesson & Fils 1990 Grand Vin Signature, Brut Rosé

89 120FF Roger Pouillon, 50ème Anniversaire NV Fleur de Mareuil

89 170FF Billecart-Salmon NV 2000 Brut Réserve

89 180FF Drappier 1990 Grande Sendrée

89 450FF Pommery 1992 Brut, Grand Cru *(magnum)*

89 620FF Taittinger Comtes de Champagne 1994 Blanc de Blancs

89 88FF Fluteau 1996 Brut Blanc de Blancs

89 90.50FF Henri Mandois 1993 Cuvée des Trois Générations

89 900FF Pommery NV Brut Royal *(magnum)*

88 110FF Veuve A. Devaux NV Blanc de Noirs

88 110FF Larmandier-Bernier 1995 Vieilles Vignes de Cramant

88 160FF Veuve Clicquot Ponsardin NV Brut

88 170FF Billecart-Salmon NV Demi-Sec Réserve

88 180FF Drappier 1995 Grande Sendrée

88 180FF Louis Roederer NV Brut Premier

88 185FF Pommery NV Brut Royal Apanage

88 195FF Drappier 1989 Grande Sendrée

88 220FF Pommery 1992 Brut, Grand Cru

88 230FF Drappier 1990 Grande Sendrée Rosé

88 255FF Billecart-Salmon NV Brut Rosé

88 300FF Charles Heidsieck NV Brut Réserve Privée, Mis en Cave en 1990

88 350FF André Clouet NV Un Jour

de 1911, Brut Grand Cru
Classé .

88 550FF Jacquesson & Fils 1985
Brut, Dégorgement Tardif

88 75.50FF Henri Mandois 1995 Brut
Millésimé, Brut Premier
Cru

88 77FF Henri Mandois 1995
Chardonnay, Brut Premier
Cru

88 85FF Lamiable NV Extra Brut,
Grand Cru

88 89FF Henri Goutorbe NV Brut
Rosé

88 95FF Paul Déthune NV Brut
Rosé, Grand Cru

87 121.50FF De Saint Gall 1995 Blanc
de Blancs, Brut Premier
Cru

87 130FF Charles de Cazanove NV
Brut Azur, Premier Cru

87 130FF Doyard 1996 Collection de
l'An I, Oeil de Perdrix
Rosé Brut

87 150FF Gauthier 1993 Brut
Millésime

87 160FF Lanson NV Black Label

87 275FF Louis Roederer 1994
Vintage Rosé

87 305FF Mailly 1988 Cuvée Les
Echansons, Brut Grand Cru

87 580FF Billecart-Salmon 1989
Grande Cuvée

86 130FF Princesse des Thunes NV
Cuvée Prestige Brut,
Ambonnay Grand Cru

86 140FF Palmer 1992 Brut

86 160FF Jacquart 1992 Mosaïque
Millésimé Brut

86 170FF Philipponnat NV Le Reflet
du Millénaire An 2000

86 180FF Lanson NV Rose Label
Brut Rosé

86 180FF Pommery NV Summertime,
Blanc de Blancs Brut

86 220FF Pommery 1995 Brut,
Grand Cru

86 250FF Vve A. Devaux 2000 NV D
de Devaux

86 260FF Jacquesson & Fils 1995
Blanc de Blancs, Brut
Grand Cru

86 550FF Pommery 1989 Louise

86 73FF Henri Mandois NV Brut
Rosé, Premier Cru

86 74FF Moutard NV Brut Rosé

86 86FF Pannier NV Brut Sélection

85 100FF Th. Blondel 1995 Brut
Millésime, Premier Cru
Blanc de Blancs

85 102FF Doquet-Jeanmaire 1990
Blanc de Blancs, Brut
Premier Cru

85 105FF René James Lallier NV
Brut Rosé

85 108FF Georges Vesselle NV Brut
Grand Cru

85 109FF Jean Louis Malard NV Brut
Grand Cru Chardonnay

85 109FF Jean-Louis Malard NV
Grand Cru Chardonnay

85 110FF Veuve A. Devaux NV
Grande Réserve

85 113FF Vilmart NV Grand Cellier,
Brut Premiers Crus

85 115FF Raymond Boulard NV
Cuvée Rose

85 115FF Charles Ellner 1989 Brut

85 118FF Drappier NV Carte d'Or
Brut

85 120FF Pannier NV Cuvée Louis
Eugène, Rosé Brut

85 128FF Georges Vesselle 1995 Brut
Millésimé Grand Cru

85 129FF Tsarine NV Tête de Cuvée
Brut, Chanoine

85 129FF Cuvée Compagnie des
Wagons-Lits NV Pullman
Orient-Express

85 130FF Drappier NV Val des
Demoiselle, Rosé Brut

85 133FF Palmer 1995 Blanc de
Blancs Brut

85 135FF Drappier 1995 Carte
d'Or Brut

85 149FF Tsarine 1995 Brut
Millésime, Chanoine

85 160FF Jacquesson & Fils NV
Perfection Brut

85 160FF Pommery NV Brut Royal

85 162FF Georges Vesselle NV Cuvée
Juline Grand Cru Brut

85 180FF Taittinger 1995 Brut
Millésimé

85 215FF Mailly NV Cassiopee, Brut
Nature, Grand Cru

85 236FF Philipponnat 1991 Grand
Blanc

85 250FF Veuve Clicquot Ponsardin
1995 Rich Reserve

85 68FF Michel Guilleminot
NV Brut

REMEMBER!

85 Points: "The sort of quality Champagne has to be to warrant inclusion in my cellar"
–TOM STEVENSON

Don't restrict your choice to 90-point wines – I don't!

⑧⑤	68FF	Henri Mandois NV Cuvée de Réserve Brut
⑧⑤	77FF	Henri Goutorbe NV Cuvée Traditionnelle
⑧⑤	78FF	Baron Albert NV Brut Rosé
⑧⑤	79FF	Doquet-Jeanmaire NV Blanc de Blancs, Carte Or Brut
⑧⑤	80FF	Moutard NV Brut Grande Réserve
⑧⑤	87FF	E. Barnaut NV Grande Réserve, Brut Grand Cru
⑧⑤	88FF	Paul Déthune NV Brut Grand Cru
⑧⑤	93FF	Vilmart NV Cuvée Rubis
⑧⑤	95FF	Moutard NV Cuvée Prestige
⑧⑤	98FF	Larmandier-Bernier NV Brut Rosé, Premier Cru
⑧⑤	98FF	Larmandier-Bernier NV Blanc de Blancs Brut, Premier Cru
⑧⑤	98FF	Palmer NV Brut
⑧⑤	98FF	Louis de Sacy NV Brut Grand Cru
⑧④	107FF	F. Vauversin 1993 Blanc de Blancs, Brut Grand Cru
⑧④	112FF	Raymond Boulard NV Blanc de Blancs Brut
⑧④	120FF	Charles de Cazanove NV Brut Rosé
⑧④	155FF	Doyard 1995 Collection de l'An I, Blanc de Blancs Brut
⑧④	160FF	Lanson NV Black Label Brut
⑧④	167FF	Philipponnat NV Réserve Rosé
⑧④	180FF	Jacquesson & Fils NV Perfection Brut Rosé
⑧④	91FF	Pannier NV Brut Rosé
⑧③	100FF	Beaumet NV Cuvée Rosé Brut
⑧③	100FF	Charles de Cazanove NV Brut Classique
⑧③	101FF	Larmandier-Bernier NV Né d'Une Terre de Vertus, Brut Nature
⑧③	153FF	Mailly 1995 Brut Grand Cru Millésime
⑧③	87FF	E. Barnaut NV Blanc de Noirs, Brut Grand Cru
⑧②	109FF	Jean Louis Malard NV Brut Grand Cru Pinot Noir-Chardonnay
⑧②	119FF	Raymond Boulard NV Brut Grand Cru Mailly-Champagne
⑧②	125FF	Jacquart NV Demi-Sec
⑧②	150FF	Charles de Cazanove 1992 Brut Azur, Premier Cru
⑧②	275FF	Louis Roederer 1994 Brut
⑧②	65FF	Cheurlin-Dangin NV Brut
⑧②	71FF	Jean-Michel Pelletier NV Brut Selection
⑧②	74FF	Domaine de Corrigot NV Extra-Dry, Vollereaux
⑧②	79FF	Delouvin Nowack NV Brut
⑧②	82FF	Aubeline de Vauversin NV Blanc de Blancs, Grand Cru Sec
⑧②	86FF	Jean Milan, An 2000 NV Blancs de Blancs, Brut Spécial
⑧②	88FF	Cheurlin-Dangin NV Cuvée Spéciale
⑧②	99.50FF	De Saint Gall NV Brut Premier Cru
⑧⓪	110FF	Raymond Boulard NV Réserve Brut
⑧⓪	115FF	Vollereaux 1993 Cuvée Marguerite Brut
⑧⓪	125FF	André et Michel Drappier NV Brut Nature, Pinot Noir Zero Dosage
⑧⓪	125FF	Jacquart NV Brut Mosaïque
⑧⓪	142FF	Egérie de Pannier 1995 Brut
⑧⓪	144FF	Mailly NV Blanc de Noirs, Brut Grand Cru
⑧⓪	160FF	Besserat de Bellefon NV Cuvée des Moines
⑧⓪	160FF	Veuve Clicquot Ponsardin NV Demi-Sec
⑧⓪	190FF	Lanson 1994 Gold Label Brut
⑧⓪	200FF	Besserat de Bellefon NV Cuvée des Moines Blanc de Blancs
⑧⓪	71FF	Mathieu-Gosztyla NV Brut Tradition

(80) 72FF Moutard NV Brut Réserve
(80) 77FF Baron Albert NV Brut
Carte d'Or
(80) 80FF Th. Blondel NV Carte Or
Brut, Premier Cru
(80) 80FF F. Vauversin NV Blanc de
Blancs, Brut Grand Cru

(80) 88FF Bardoux Père & Fils NV
Brut Premier Cru
(80) 90FF Oudinot NV Cuvée Brut
(80) 90FF Roger Pouillon NV Le Brut
Vigneron, Premier Cru
(80) 92FF Philippe Gonet NV Blanc
de Blancs Brut

CHAMPAGNE CELLAR DOOR SALES: PRICE ORDER

If you are heading for Champagne and looking for a Champagne within a specific price category, then this should help you. **Note:** Prices were correct at the time of tasting. You should expect some to change, but this should be within reason, and this guide should at least help you to spot any outrageous increases.

(82) 65FF Cheurlin-Dangin NV Brut
(85) 68FF Michel Guilleminot NV
Brut
(85) 68FF Henri Mandois NV Cuvée
de Réserve Brut
(80) 71FF Mathieu-Gosztyla NV Brut
Tradition
(82) 71FF Jean-Michel Pelletier NV
Brut Selection
(80) 72FF Moutard NV Brut Réserve
(86) 73FF Henri Mandois NV Brut
Rosé, Premier Cru
(86) 74FF Moutard NV Brut Rosé
(82) 74FF Domaine de Corrigot NV
Extra-Dry, Vollereaux
(88) 75.50FF Henri Mandois 1995 Brut
Millésimé, Brut Premier
Cru
(80) 77FF Baron Albert NV Brut
Carte d'Or
(85) 77FF Henri Goutorbe NV
Cuvée Traditionnelle
(88) 77FF Henri Mandois 1995
Chardonnay, Brut
Premier Cru
(85) 78FF Baron Albert NV Brut
Rosé
(82) 79FF Delouvin Nowack NV
Brut
(85) 79FF Doquet-Jeanmaire NV
Blanc de Blancs, Carte Or
Brut
(80) 80FF Th. Blondel NV Carte Or
Brut, Premier Cru
(85) 80FF Moutard NV Brut Grande
Réserve
(80) 80FF F. Vauversin NV Blanc de
Blancs, Brut Grand Cru
(82) 82FF Aubeline de Vauversin NV
Blanc de Blancs, Grand
Cru, Sec

(88) 85FF Lamiable NV Extra Brut,
Grand Cru
(82) 86FF Jean Milan, An 2000 NV
Blancs de Blancs, Brut
Spécial
(86) 86FF Pannier NV Brut Sélection
(85) 87FF E. Barnaut NV Grande
Réserve, Brut Grand Cru
(83) 87FF E. Barnaut NV Blanc
de Noirs, Brut Grand Cru
(80) 88FF Bardoux Père & Fils NV
Brut Premier Cru
(82) 88FF Cheurlin-Dangin NV
Cuvée Spéciale
(85) 88FF Paul Déthune NV Brut
Grand Cru
(89) 88FF Fluteau 1996 Brut Blanc
de Blancs
(88) 89FF Henri Goutorbe NV Brut
Rosé
(89) 90.50FF Henri Mandois 1993
Cuvée des Trois
Générations
(80) 90FF Oudinot NV Cuvée Brut
(80) 90FF Roger Pouillon NV Le Brut
Vigneron, Premier Cru
(84) 91FF Pannier NV Brut Rosé
(80) 92FF Philippe Gonet NV Blanc de
Blancs Brut
(85) 93FF Vilmart NV Cuvée
Rubis
(88) 95FF Paul Déthune NV Brut Rosé,
Grand Cru
(85) 95FF Moutard NV Cuvée
Prestige
(85) 98FF Larmandier-Bernier NV Brut
Rosé, Premier Cru
(85) 98FF Larmandier-Bernier NV
Blanc de Blancs Brut,
Premier Cru
(85) 98FF Palmer NV Brut

85   98FF Louis de Sacy NV Brut Grand Cru

82   99.50FF De Saint Gall NV Brut Premier Cru

90 100.50FF Henri Mandois 1995 Cuvée Victor Mandois, Brut

83 100FF Beaumet NV Cuvée Rosé Brut

85 100FF Th. Blondel 1995 Brut Millésime, Premier Cru Blanc de Blancs

90 100FF Charles de Cazanove NV Grande Réserve An 2000 Brut

83 100FF Charles de Cazanove NV Brut Classique

83 101FF Larmandier-Bernier NV Né d'Une Terre de Vertus, Brut Nature

85 102FF Doquet-Jeanmaire 1990 Blanc de Blancs, Brut Premier Cru

85 105FF René James Lallier NV Brut Rosé

84 107FF F. Vauversin 1993 Blanc de Blancs, Brut Grand Cru

85 108FF Georges Vesselle NV Brut Grand Cru

85 109FF Jean Louis Malard NV Brut Grand Cru Chardonnay

85 109FF Jean-Louis Malard NV Grand Cru Chardonnay

82 109FF Jean Louis Malard NV Brut Grand Cru Pinot Noir-Chardonnay

80 110FF Raymond Boulard NV Réserve Brut

88 110FF Veuve A. Devaux NV Blanc de Noirs, Brut

85 110FF Veuve A. Devaux NV Grande Réserve, Brut

88 110FF Larmandier-Bernier 1995 Vieilles Vignes de Cramant

84 112FF Raymond Boulard NV Blanc de Blancs Brut

85 113FF Vilmart NV Grand Cellier, Brut Premiers Crus

85 115FF Raymond Boulard NV Cuvée Rose

85 115FF Charles Ellner 1989 Brut

80 115FF Vollereaux 1993 Cuvée Marguerite Brut

85 118FF Drappier NV Carte d'Or Brut

82 119FF Raymond Boulard NV

    Brut Grand Cru Mailly-Champagne

84 120FF Charles de Cazanove NV Brut Rosé

85 120FF Pannier NV Cuvée Louis Eugène, Rosé Brut

89 120FF Roger Pouillon, 50 ème Anniversaire NV Fleur de Mareuil, Brut Premier Cru

87 121.50FF De Saint Gall 1995 Blanc de Blancs, Brut Premier Cru

80 125FF André et Michel Drappier NV Brut Nature, Pinot Noir Zero Dosage

80 125FF Jacquart NV Demi-Sec

80 125FF Jacquart NV Brut Mosaïque

85 128FF Georges Vesselle 1995 Brut Millésimé Grand Cru

85 129FF Tsarine NV Tête de Cuvée Brut, Chanoine

85 129FF Cuvée Compagnie des Wagons-Lits NV Pullman Orient-Express

98 130FF Moët & Chandon NV Esprit du Siècle

87 130FF Charles de Cazanove NV Brut Azur, Premier Cru

87 130FF Doyard 1996 Collection de l'An I, Oeil de Perdrix Rosé Brut

85 130FF Drappier NV Val des Demoiselle, Rosé Brut

86 130FF Princesse des Thunes NV Cuvée Prestige Brut, Ambonnay Grand Cru

85 133FF Palmer 1995 Blanc de Blancs Brut

85 135FF Drappier 1995 Carte d'Or Brut

86 140FF Palmer 1992 Brut

90 140FF Vilmart NV Cuvée Cellier

80 142FF Egérie de Pannier 1995 Brut

80 144FF Mailly NV Blanc de Noirs, Brut Grand Cru

85 149FF Tsarine 1995 Brut Millésime, Chanoine

82 150FF Charles de Cazanove 1992 Brut Azur, Premier Cru

87 150FF Gauthier 1993 Brut Millésime

83 153FF Mailly 1995 Brut Grand Cru Millésime

(84) 155FF Doyard 1995 Collection de l'An I, Blanc de Blancs Brut

(80) 160FF Besserat de Bellefon NV Cuvée des Moines

(86) 160FF Jacquart 1992 Mosaïque Millésimé Brut

(85) 160FF Jacquesson & Fils NV Perfection Brut

(87) 160FF Lanson NV Black Label

(84) 160FF Lanson NV Black Label Brut

(85) 160FF Pommery NV Brut Royal

(88) 160FF Veuve Clicquot Ponsardin NV Brut

(80) 160FF Veuve Clicquot Ponsardin NV Demi-Sec

(85) 162FF Georges Vesselle NV Cuvée Juline Grand Cru Brut

(84) 167FF Philipponnat NV Réserve Rosé

(89) 170FF Billecart-Salmon NV 2000 Brut Réserve

(88) 170FF Billecart-Salmon NV Demi-Sec Réserve

(86) 170FF Philipponnat NV Le Reflet du Millénaire An 2000

(89) 180FF Drappier 1990 Grande Sendrée

(88) 180FF Drappier 1995 Grande Sendrée

(90) 180FF Charles Heidsieck NV Brut Réserve, Mis en Cave en 1996

(84) 180FF Jacquesson & Fils NV Perfection Brut Rosé

(86) 180FF Lanson NV Rose Label Brut Rosé

(86) 180FF Pommery NV Summertime, Blanc de Blancs Brut

(88) 180FF Louis Roederer NV Brut Premier

(90) 180FF Taittinger 1996 Brut Millésimé

(85) 180FF Taittinger 1995 Brut Millésimé

(88) 185FF Pommery NV Brut Royal Apanage

(80) 190FF Lanson 1994 Gold Label Brut

(88) 195FF Drappier 1989 Grande Sendrée

(80) 200FF Besserat de Bellefon NV Cuvée des Moines, Blanc de Blancs Brut

(93) 205FF Vilmart 1993 Coeur de Cuvée, Brut Premiers Crus

(85) 215FF Mailly NV Cassiopee, Brut Nature, Grand Cru

(88) 220FF Pommery 1992 Brut, Grand Cru

(86) 220FF Pommery 1995 Brut, Grand Cru

(88) 230FF Drappier 1990 Grande Sendrée Rosé

(85) 236FF Philipponnat 1991 Grand Blanc

(86) 250FF Vve A. Devaux 2000 NV D de Devaux

(90) 250FF Veuve Clicquot Ponsardin 1995 Rosé Reserve

(85) 250FF Veuve Clicquot Ponsardin 1995 Rich Reserve

(88) 255FF Billecart-Salmon NV Brut Rosé

(86) 260FF Jacquesson & Fils 1995 Blanc de Blancs, Brut Grand Cru

(87) 275FF Louis Roederer 1994 Vintage Rosé

(82) 275FF Louis Roederer 1994 Brut

(88) 300FF Charles Heidsieck NV Brut Réserve Privée, Mis en Cave en 1990

(87) 305FF Mailly 1988 Cuvée Les Echansons, Brut Grand Cru

(88) 350FF André Clouet NV Un Jour de 1911, Brut Grand Cru Classé

(91) 350FF Jacquesson & Fils 1990 Grand Vin Signature

(90) 390FF Jacquesson & Fils 1990 Grand Vin Signature, Brut Rosé

(89) 450FF Pommery 1992 Brut, Grand Cru *(magnum)*

(88) 550FF Jacquesson & Fils 1985 Brut, Dégorgement Tardif

(86) 550FF Pommery 1989 Louise

(96) 580FF Billecart-Salmon 1990 Grande Cuvée

(87) 580FF Billecart-Salmon 1989 Grande Cuvée

(95) 620FF Taittinger Comtes de Champagne 1995 Blanc de Blancs

(89) 620FF Taittinger Comtes de

Champagne 1994 Blanc
de Blancs

92   650FF   Louis Roederer Cristal
1994 Brut

92   700FF   Pommery 1990 Louise
Rosé Brut

84   800FF   Veuve Clicquot Ponsardin
1990 La Grande Dame
Rosé

89   900FF   Pommery NV Brut Royal
(*magnum*)

REMEMBER!

75 Points: "Any sparkling wine other than Champagne that receives this score is not just
interesting, but good enough to grace the table of a self-confessed Champagne addict."

–TOM STEVENSON

Don't restrict your choice to 90-point wines – I don't!

OTHER FRENCH
SPARKLING WINES

This year it was the producers of Crémant d'Alsace who submitted the
most samples, although the number of Loire was once again very high.
There was also a very good showing from Limoux, Jura and Clairette de
Die, but only a handful from Burgundy, and hardly any from Bordeaux.
An entire shipment from Gaillac apparently went astray!

Although I have been surprised by the number of Alsace that I could
recommend for this edition and I have to admit that even the Loire wines
were generally cleaner this year, there were still a lot of shockers from all
regions, including Alsace and Loire. The problem as I explained in *The
Champagne & Sparkling Wine Guide 2000* is that very few French wine
areas outside of Champagne have built their reputations on sparkling
wines, hence there is a tendency to use their best grapes for their more
famous wines and fizz-up the substandard leftovers. Anyone who
understands sparkling wine and knows anything about Burgundy will
realize that Crémant de Bourgogne should be world-class, but no wines
from that appellation qualified for recommendation this year and I've
never ever tasted anything remotely close to the stunning quality that
these wines could and should be.

In May 2000 the producers of Crémant de Bourgogne proposed
the creation of vineyards assigned specifically for the production of
sparkling wine. In other words a geographic appellation from which
only Crémant de Bourgogne may be produced. This, you would think,
can only be for the good of this wine, and it may be, but if so it will be
unintentional because the reason given for this initiative is "to ensure a
regular supply of grapes". No mention of targeting the best areas for
this style of wine, which would not conflict with keeping the best areas
for still versions of Chardonnay and Pinot Noir. No mention of planting
with the most suitable clones, which are totally different to those used
for still wine. And no mention of enforcing the different methods of
training and pruning required to achieve a vineyard balance that is more
suited to sparkling than still Burgundy. Hopefully the producers of

Crémant de Bourgogne will take advantage of a new geographically based appellation to institute these much needed disciplines, otherwise the only thing that this delimitation will achieve is even more undrinkable dross.

ALSACE, ALL STYLES

This region impressed this year, with its strong representation performing extremely well. Crémant d'Alsace has overtaken Saumur as the largest-producing and largest-selling French sparkling wine outside of Champagne.

(80) Ⓔ Wolfberger, Cuvée de l'An 2000 NV Crémant d'Alsace, Prestige Brut

(78) Ⓔ Heimberger NV Blanc de Blancs, Crémant d'Alsace Brut

(78) Ⓔ Rieflé NV Crémant d'Alsace Brut

(78) Ⓔ Wolfberger NV Crémant d'Alsace Demi-Sec

(77) Ⓔ Willm NV Crémant d'Alsace Brut

(77) Ⓔ Wolfberger NV Blanc de Noirs, Crémant d'Alsace Brut

(76) Ⓔ B de Becker 1998 Blanc de Blancs, Crémant d'Alsace Brut

(76) Ⓔ Bestheim NV Crémant d'Alsace Brut

(76) Ⓔ Bestheim NV An 2000 Prestige, Crémant d'Alsace Brut

(75) Ⓔ Jean-Baptiste Adam NV Crémant d'Alsace Brut

(75) Ⓔ Charles Baur 1996 Crémant d'Alsace Brut

(75) Ⓔ Dopff & Irion 1997 Crémant d'Alsace Brut

(75) Ⓔ Muller-Koeberle NV Cuvée Marianne, Crémant d'Alsace Brut Rosé

(75) Ⓔ Pierre Sparr NV Crémant d'Alsace, Brut Réserve

(75) Ⓔ Wolfberger NV Crémant d'Alsace Brut

(75) Ⓔ Wolfberger NV Crémant d'Alsace Rosé

(74) Ⓔ Château d'Orschwihr NV Cuvée 2000, Crémant d'Alsace Brut

(74) Ⓔ Dopff & Irion NV Crémant d'Alsace Brut

(74) Ⓔ Jean Geiler, Cuvée An 2000 NV Crémant d'Alsace, Brut Prestige

(74) Ⓔ Baron de Schiele NV Crémant d'Alsace Brut

(74) Ⓔ Baron de Schiele NV Riesling, Crémant d'Alsace Brut

(73) Ⓔ Baron de Hoen NV Blanc de Noirs, Crémant d'Alsace Brut

(73) Ⓔ Blanck 1997 Crémant d'Alsace, Extra Brut

(73) Ⓔ Clérotstein NV Crémant d'Alsace Brut

(73) Ⓔ Gruss NV Crémant d'Alsace, Brut Prestige

(72) Ⓔ Cuvée Madame Sans-Gêne 1996 Blanc de Blancs, Crémant d'Alsace

(72) Ⓔ Joseph Gruss & Fils NV Crémant d'Alsace Brut

(72) Ⓔ René Muré NV Crémant d'Alsace, Brut Cuvée Prestige

(72) Ⓔ Sipp Mack NV Crémant d'Alsace Brut

(72) Ⓔ Pierre Sparr 1995 Dynastie, Crémant d'Alsace, Brut Millésimé

(72) Ⓔ Pierre Sparr 1995 Glorius 2000, Crémant d'Alsace, Brut R.D.

(72) Ⓔ Ch. Wantz NV Carte Noire Brut Tradition, Crémant d'Alsace

(72) Ⓔ Wolfberger NV Riesling, Crémant d'Alsace Brut

(71) Ⓔ Brut de Becker 1996 Blanc de Blancs, Crémant d'Alsace

(71) Ⓔ Jean Geiler NV Riesling Brut, Crémant d'Alsace, Prestige

(70) Ⓔ Seppi Landmann NV Crémant d'Alsace, Brut de Brut

(70) Ⓔ Seppi Landmann 1987

Crémant d'Alsace, Brut de
Brut *(magnum)*
70 Ⓔ Baron de Castex NV
Crémant d'Alsace Brut
70 Ⓔ Wolfberger NV Tokay Pinot
Gris, Crémant

d'Alsace Brut
70 Ⓔ Wolfberger NV Chardonnay,
Crémant d'Alsace Extra Brut
70 Ⓔ Wolfberger 1995 Crémant
d'Alsace

JURA, ALL STYLES

Now this really did surprise me. Although there are vague claims that sparkling wines were produced in the Jura in the 18th century, I have been unable to substantiate this, but I can confirm that I encountered more interesting Jura fizz this year than I have in the previous 10 years.

76 Ⓔ Jacques Tissot NV 2000,
Crémant du Jura Brut
75 Ⓔ Marcel Cabelier 1997
Crémant du Jura Brut
74 Ⓔ André & Mireille Tissot NV
Crémant du Jura Brut
73 Ⓔ Grand Frères NV Crémant
du Jura, Brut Prestige
73 Ⓔ Rolet 1996 Crémant du
Jura Brut
71 Ⓔ Domaine Berthet-Bondet NV

Crémant du Jura
71 Ⓔ Domaine Martin Faudot NV
Crémant du Jura Brut
71 Ⓔ Michel Geneletti et Fils NV
Crémant du Jura Brut
71 Ⓔ Désiré Petit NV Cuvée de
l'An 2000, Crémant du Jura
Brut
70 Ⓔ Château de l'Etoile NV
Crémant du Jura Brut

LIMOUX, ALL STYLES

In contrast to the Jura, and without wishing to detract from the good examples listed below, I have to confess that I'm seeing less exciting Limoux, whether Blanquette or Crémant, as each year goes by. Is it because premium quality sparkling wines elsewhere have moved on and Limoux now seems old hat? Or simply that the producers can't be bothered to show off their wines? Time I think for an in-depth tasting at source. In the meantime, however, I have been impressed by the small but increasing number of succulently sweet Méthode Ancestrale wines that have started to appear.

82 Ⓔ Domaine de l'Aigle NV
Crémant de Limoux Brut
78 Ⓔ Sieur d'Arques 1997
Crémant de Limoux Brut
76 Ⓔ Grande Cuvée 1531 de
Aimery NV Crémant de
Limoux, Tête de Cuvée
75 ⒺⒺ Les Vignobles Vergnes de

Martinolles NV Méthode
Ancestrale
74 Ⓔ Guinot NV Impérial,
Crémant de Limoux, Brut-
Tendre
72 Ⓔ Aimery Sieur d'Arques NV
St-Hilaire

LOIRE, ALL STYLES

This year Crémant de Loire produced most of the best quality sparkling Loire wines, although Saumur and Vouvray both did well, with Saumur actually pipping Crémant de Loire by one wine in terms of the number qualifying for recommendation.

80 Ⓔ Bouvet 1998 Saphir Brut
Vintage, Saumur
77 Ⓔ Cray 1993 Crémant de Loire
Brut
76 ⒺⒺ Bouvet-Ladubay 1997 Tresor

Brut, Saumur
75 Ⓔ Baumard NV Carte Corail,
Crémant de Loire Brut
75 Ⓔ Domaine Bourillon-Dorléans
1996 Cuvée Hélène

	Dorléans, Vouvray		Loire, Brut Rosé
75	ⓔ Bouvet NV Crémant Excellence Brut	72	ⓔ Caves des Producteurs de Montlouis NV Cuvée Réservée Sec
75	ⓔ Gratien & Meyer NV Cuvée Royale Brut	72	ⓔ Blanc Foussy NV Brut Touraine, Grandes Caves Saint-Roch
75	ⓔ Langlois NV Crémant de Loire Brut	72	ⓔ Veuve Amiot NV Club Demi-Sec, Vouvray
75	ⓔ Langlois 1995 Crémant de Loire, Brut Réserve	71	ⓔ Laisement Jean-Pierre NV Méthode Traditionnelle Brut, Vouvray
74	ⓔ Bouvet-Ladubay 1998 Saphir, Saumur	70	ⓔ Les Caves Louis de Grenelle NV Brut Grande Cuvée 2000, Saumur
74	ⓔ Domaine Dutertre NV Cuvée Saint Gilles, Crémant de Loire Brut	70	ⓔ Château de Montgueret 1997 Tête de Cuvée, Saumur
74	ⓔ Domaine du Clos de l'Epinay 1997 Tête de Cuvée Brut, Vouvray	70	ⓔ Cave des Vignerons de Saumur 1997 Cuvée de la Chevalerie
74	ⓔ Caves des Producteurs de Vouvray 1997 Tête de Cuvée	70	ⓔ Veuve Amiot NV Cuvée Réservée Brut, Saumur
72	ⓔ Baumard 1997 Crémant de Loire Brut	70	ⓔ Veuve Amiot NV Club Brut, Vouvray
72	ⓔ Gratien Meyer Seydoux NV Cuvée Flamme Brut, Saumur		
72	ⓔ Langlois NV Crémant de		

FRENCH: NO FIXED ABODE

Plus one wine from Savoie and one from Die! The rest of the wines might in fact be from a specific area, sometimes even a famous appellation, but when this is so they will always be from declassified grapes and the label must make no mention of their origin. They can be blended from grapes grown anywhere in France, not just known regions, but most non-AOC sparkling wine is in fact produced from the unwanted dregs of more famous areas. The mention of any pure varietal content increases the price of these sparkling wines, and the use of classic grapes adds a further premium. However, many of the sparkling wines made from classic grapes are often worse than those made from supposedly inferior varieties. The reason for this is that fizz producers can buy pretty good quality Ugni Blanc or Colombard for the same price they have to pay for the cheapest Chardonnay or Chenin Blanc, and my tastings have borne this out.

75	ⓔ Carod 1995 Crémant de Die Brut		Grands Vins NV L. Palais Blanc de Blanc
74	ⓔ Domaine de l'Aigle NV Tradition	70	ⓔ Compagnie Française des Grands Vins NV Veuve Valmante
74	ⓔ Les Rocailles Pierre Boniface NV Brut	70	ⓔ Les Caves de Landiras NV Kraemer Blanc de Blancs
74	ⓔ Tête de Cuvée Rosé Demi-Sec NV Prestige, Vin Pétillant, Pellin	70	ⓔ Veuve Ambal NV Méthode Traditionnelle Tradition
70	ⓔ Compagnie Française des		

REMEMBER!

75 Points: "Any sparkling wine other than Champagne that receives this score is not just interesting, but good enough to grace the table of a self-confessed Champagne addict."
–TOM STEVENSON
Don't restrict your choice to 90-point wines – I don't!

REST OF THE WORLD

France leads because no one can dispute Champagne's position as the king of sparkling wine. The other countries are listed in alphabetical order.

AUSTRALIA, VINTAGE & NON-VINTAGE

Last year's centralized tasting of Australian fizz was the most inconsistent and disappointing I had experienced, so I headed downunder for this year's edition and I'm glad to say that I found the quality is back to what we've become accustomed to. A vintaged wine, as far as Australian fizz is concerned, definitely represents a step up in terms of quality, although this is usually due to stricter selection rather than any specific vintage characteristics, and any variation between the years is more likely to be attributed to a learning curve.

91	££	Pirie 1996 Pipers Brook
91	££	Pirie 1995 Pipers Brook
90	££	Croser 1994 Petaluma
88	££	Croser 1998 Petaluma
88	££	Croser 1995 Petaluma
88	££	Croser 1998 Petaluma
88	££	Yarrabank 1994 Tibault and Gillet Cuvée
87	££	Croser 1992 Petaluma
87	££	Croser 1993 Petaluma
87	£	The Rothbury Wine Society 1996 Chardonnay Pinot Noir
86	££	Croser 1991 Petaluma
86	££	Green Point by Chandon 1993 Brut
85	££	Croser 1996 Petaluma
85	£	Domaine Chandon NV Brut Premium Chardonnay Pinot Noir
85	££	Green Point by Chandon 1997 Brut
85	££	Green Point by Chandon 1991 Brut
85	££	Rosemount Kirri Billi 1997 Vintage Brut
85	££	Taltarni Clover Hill 1996
85	££	Wirra Wirra 1996 The Cousins, Pinot Noir Chardonnay
85	££	Yalumba D 1997 Cuvée 97-1
85	££	Yarrabank 1995 Tibault and Gillet Cuvée
85	£	Yellowglen Vintage 1997
84	££	Croser 1997 Petaluma
83	££	Blue Pyrenees Estate NV Midnight Cuvée
83	££	Green Point by Chandon 1992 Brut
83	££	Jansz 1996 Tasmania Brut Cuvée
83	£	Seaview 1997 Chardonnay

82	£	Brown Brothers NV Pinot Noir Chardonnay, King Valley
82	££	Croser 1997 Petaluma
80	££	Plunkett Wines 1997 Strathbogie Ranges Chardonnay Pinot Noir
80	££	Red Hill Estate 1997 Mornington Peninsula Pinot Noir Chardonnay
80	££	Wirra Wirra 1991 Limited Edition The Cousins
79	£	Pipers Brook 1996 Delamere Cuvée
78	£	Blue Pyrenees Estate Reserve NV Brut
78	£	Stefano Lubiana 1995
78	£	Wolf Blass 1996 Vintage Pinot Noir Chardonnay
78	£	Yarra Burn 1997 Pinot Noir Chardonnay
77	£	Sir James Brut de Brut NV Pinot Noir Chardonnay
76	£	Seaview 1995 Chardonnay Blanc de Blanc
76	£	Yellowglen Yellow NV Brut
75	££	95er Cleveland Macedon Brut
75	£	Andrew Garrett 1996 Chardonnay Pinot Noir
75	££	Domaine Chandon 1995 Victoria Cuvée
75	££	Grant Burge NV Barossa Pinot Noir Chardonnay
75	££	Green Point by Chandon 1997 Brut Rosé
75	£	McLarens on the Lake Sparkling NV Brut Cuvée
75	£	Orlando Trilogy Cuvée NV Brut
75	£	Yellowglen NV Pinot Noir

Chardonnay
73 ⓔⓔ Delatite Demelza NV
72 ⓔ Conniston Australian Sparkling Wine NV Brut Reserve
72 ⓔ Haselgrove NV-2 Mt. Gambier Chardonnay Pinot Noir
72 ⓔ Heathfield Ridge 1999 Wonambi Limestone Coast
72 ⓔⓔ Jansz NV Australia Premium Non Vintage Cuvée

72 ⓔ Tatachilla NV Brut McLaren Vale
72 ⓔ Yaldara NV Cuvée Reserve, Brut Rosé
71 ⓔ Deakin Estate Brut NV Australian Sparkling Wine
71 ⓔ Yaldara NV Cuvée Reserve Brut
70 ⓔ Miranda Brut NV Blanc de Blanc
70 ⓔ Wolf Blass Wines NV Blass Brut

AUSTRALIA: SPARKLING RED

This style vies with Liqueur Muscat as the most distinctively Australian style of wine. Red fizz was first produced in Burgundy and initially the Australians opted for Pinot Noir and the lighter Burgundian style that grape produces. However, Shiraz soon became the dominant variety and the style much darker, deeper and sweeter, characteristics that also apply to most other fizzy reds, whether made from Cabernet, Merlot or indeed more obscure varieties such as Chambourcin (Cassegrain). Most of these wines fall into two basic categories, oaked and fruit driven, although there are inevitably some that fall between these two stools, just as there is a minority that attempt to be dry or at least drier. Over and above this there is the Show Reserve style or, more specifically, Seppelt Show Reserve, although others have adopted it. This is a very mature Shiraz with concentrated blackcurrant liqueur fruit and in addition to the cult following for fizzy Australian reds in general, there is a sub-cultural following for the Show Reserve style. Moving beyond these two fan clubs there is general acceptance amongst the base of wine drinkers in Australia for the bulk of red fizz as an unpretentious barbecue fodder.

90 ⓔⓔ Charles Melton NV Barossa Valley Sparkling Red
88 ⓔⓔ Joseph NV Sparkling Red
85 ⓔⓔ Irvine Merlot NV Brut
85 ⓔ Killawarra K Series NV Sparkling Shiraz Cabernet
85 ⓔ Leasingham Classic Clare Sparkling Shiraz 1992
85 ⓔⓔ Seppelt 1987 Show Reserve Shiraz Sparkling
85 ⓔⓔ St Leonards Carlyle 1997 Sparkling Shiraz
85 ⓔⓔ Tatachilla Sparkling Malbec Padthaway NV
85 ⓔ Trentham Estate Ruby Sparkling Red 1998
85 ⓔⓔ Yalumba D 1996 Black 96-1
84 ⓔⓔ The Wilson Vineyard Hippocrene NV Sparkling Red
82 ⓔⓔ Fox Creek Vixen NV Sparkling Shiraz Cabernet Franc
80 ⓔ Haselgrove NV McLaren Vale Garnet SG-6
80 ⓔ Morris Sparkling Shiraz

Durif NV
80 ⓔ Seppelt Original Sparkling Shiraz 1995
78 ⓔⓔ Sir James Shiraz NV
77 ⓔ Andrew Garrett NV Sparkling Burgundy
77 ⓔⓔ Miranda 1994 Sparkling Shiraz Barossa Old Vine
76 ⓔ Rumball NV Sparkling Shiraz
75 ⓔ Brewery Hill NV Premium Sparkling Shiraz
75 ⓔⓔ Cofield Wines 1997 Sparkling Shiraz
75 ⓔⓔ Garden Gully 1998 Sparkling Shiraz
75 ⓔ McLarens on the Lake NV Sparkling Red Shiraz
75 ⓔⓔ Mitchell NV Clare Valley Sparkling Peppertree
75 ⓔⓔ Scarpantoni Black Tempest NV
75 ⓔ Yellowglen Y Sparkling Burgundy NV
70 ⓔ Yellowglen Red NV

ENGLAND & WALES

The UK's climate is every bit as variable as Champagne's and the White Cliffs of Dover are part of the same chalk basin that extends under the Channel and Paris to emerge in the famous region itself as the Côte des Blancs. Furthermore, the English deliberately put the bubbles into wine long before the French did, as documented by Christopher Merret in 1662, six years before Dom Pérignon set foot in Hautvillers. Consequently sparkling Champagne was famous enough for English dramatists to wax lyrical about it in 1676 (*The Man of Mode*, Sir George Etherege), 43 years before it is was first documented by the French. With this background it is little wonder that fizz is the fastest growing English wine. England and Wales are both so much on the cusp of what is and what is not possible in viticultural terms that there will be stark differences in vintages due to climatic conditions. Little sense can be made in this respect, however, because the learning curve is so steep and both elementary mistakes and accidental successes blur what should and will be an extremely clear picture. What we do know, however, is that Nyetimber is the clear leader and Ridgeview is increasing the pressure. This healthy competition can only be good for the quality of both wines and the fact that they are the only two vineyards planted and cultivated exclusively for sparkling wine should be a salutary lesson for all other aspiring fizzmakers.

88 ££ Nyetimber 1993 Première Cuvée, Chardonnay Blanc de Blancs

85 ££ Nyetimber 1993 Classic Cuvée

85 ££ Bloomsbury 1996 Cuvée Merret

84 ££ Nyetimber 1994 Classic Cuvée

82 ££ South Ridge 1996 Cuvée Merret, Brut (Bordeaux Direct)

77 £ Chapel Down 1995 Epoch Vintage Brut

76 £££ Chiltern Valley 1996 Brut Rosé

75 £ Carr Taylor NV Brut

75 ££ Chapel Down NV Millennium Magnum

75 ££ Chiltern Valley 1997 Millennium Cuvée 2000

75 £ Three Choirs NV Classic Cuvée Brut

75 ££ Warden Vineyard 1996 Brut

75 ££ Warden Vineyard 1996 Extra Brut

74 £ Beaulieu Bubbly 1997 Brut

74 £ Biddenden 1998 Brut

74 ££ Bookers 1995 Bart's Bubbly Rosé

74 £ Bothy 1996 Jessica Clare Fisher, Dry

74 £ Chapel Down NV Epoch

74 ££ Chilford Hundred 1996 Aluric de Norsehide

74 ££ Danebury 1994 Cossack

74 £ Heritage Brut NV

73 £ Davenport 1997

73 £ Hackwood NV Millennium Sparkling

73 £ Heritage Rosé NV

72 £ Leveret Sparkling Wine NV Dry

72 £ Biddenden 1997 Brut

72 ££ Cane End 1997 Dry

71 ££ Breaky Bottom 1996 Millennium Cuvée Maman Mercier Brut

70 ££ Bruisyard 1998 Millennium Brut

70 ££ Cane End 1996 Dry

70 £ Carr Taylor NV Rosé Réserve

70 ££ Lovejoy 1995 Brut

70 £ Windsor Forest 1996 Sparkling

GERMANY

Sekt has historically appealed to Germans and few others. Production is enormous, more than twice that of Champagne, but most of this is blended from the dregs of several countries and very little is exported. Until 1986 Deutscher Sekt was an oxymoron, but now it has to be the exclusive product of German wine. Smaller producers have always existed, but the quality of their wines was no better than that of the bigger bottlers until recently. It is only in the last few years that any of these individual estate wineries have tried to craft truly distinctive Sekt and the degree of finesse they achieve has leaped since only last year.

In the first edition I recommended 44 Sekte, but last year only 26. This decline was, I believe, due to two factors. Firstly, the number of wines submitted was smaller and the degree of pre-selection much less. Secondly, I researched the first edition of this guide at the same time as my Christie's Encyclopedia, for which I needed an historic perspective, thus I sought mature samples of any Sekt that in the opinion of its producer had aged well, and consequently received some excellent Sekt with beautifully mature Riesling aromas. For the second edition, I put the emphasis on current and future *cuvées*, thus denying myself a great tranche of special Sekt.

For this edition, however, I requested any mature vintages that were still commercially available, even if in limited quantities and no fewer than 83 Sekte qualified for recommendation. If Champagne is excluded, this is the best performance of any nation in terms of sheer numbers, although to qualify this, some countries have far more top-scoring sparkling wines than Germany. Just a few years ago I would have put Deutscher Sekt and Cava at level-pegging, but Germany has soared ahead, not only by the number of wines worth recommending, but also by their quality. Both countries may be lacking top-scoring wines, but Germany has no fewer than 55 Sekte that have scored 75 or above in this edition.

There are currently two styles of Sekte that stand out. The first is Riesling, while the second is Spätburgunder. While Riesling might be more traditional, its terpene-laden character overwhelms the subtle influence of autolysis, thus no sparkling wine made from this variety will ever achieve a classic bottle-fermented style. What it will achieve, however, is what any good still Riesling can accomplish and that is the development of those terpenes into a classic Riesling bottle-aroma, call it petrolly or what you like, but that usually takes a few years after disgorgement, hence the maturity factor. A Champagne-lover who is also a Riesling-lover will enjoy a mature Riesling Sekte, but only if all preconceived notions of what a sparkling wine should be are put to one side. More classic as far as most experienced sparkling wine will be concerned is Spätburgunder. Rosé is the best style. For some curious reason, few Spätburgunder made in the *blanc de noirs* style succeed, although some do. And I was rather taken by a sparkling red Spätburgunder this year (*see* Lergenmüller).

REMEMBER!

75 Points: "Any sparkling wine other than Champagne that receives this score is not just interesting, but good enough to grace the table of a self-confessed Champagne addict."
–TOM STEVENSON
Don't restrict your choice to 90-point wines – I don't!

DEUTSCHER SEKT: BRUT, VINTAGE & NON-VINTAGE

By far the most successful category.

85 Ⓔ Lergenmüller NV Spätburgunder Brut

79 Ⓔ Reichsrat von Buhl 1996 Spätburgunder Brut

79 ⒺⒺⒺ Dr. Thanisch, Erben Müller-Burggrae 1997 Bernkasteler Doktor

79 Ⓔ Wilhelmshof Riesling Brut 1998 Siebeldinger Königsgarten

78 Ⓔ Prinz Friedrich Riesling Brut 1998 Hattenheimer Deutesberg

78 Ⓔ August Kesseler 1998 Riesling Brut

78 Ⓔ Fürst Löwenstein Riesling Brut 1997 Hallgartener Hendelberg

78 Ⓔ Gehrig 1996 Spätburgunder Brut

78 ⒺⒺ Kloss & Foerster Riesling Brut 1997 Rüdesheimer Berg Rottland

78 Ⓔ Kloster Eberbach Riesling Brut 1998 Rauenthaler Baiken

78 Ⓔ Köwerich Riesling Brut 1994 MOUSEL

78 ⒺⒺ Markus Molitor Riesling Brut 1997 Bernkasteler Badstube

78 Ⓔ Reichsrat von Buhl 1998 Riesling Brut

78 Ⓔ SMW-Winzersekt Riesling Brut 1998 Dichtertraum

78 Ⓔ Weingut Rumpel Riesling Brut 1997 Trabener Gaispfad

78 Ⓔ Wilhelmshof Spätburgunder Blanc de Noirs 1998 Siebeldinger Königsgarten

77 Ⓔ Andres & Mugler Brut 1998 Chardonnay & Auxerrois

77 Ⓔ Carl Adelseck Riesling Brut 1998 Adelseck Juwel

77 Ⓔ Flein-Talheim Riesling Brut 1998 VEIT Fleiner Altenberg

77 Ⓔ H.-J. Fries Riesling Brut

1997 Noviander Klosterberg

77 Ⓔ St. Nikolaus Hospital Riesling Brut 1997 Bernkasteler Badstube

76 Ⓔ Friedhelm Rinklin 1995 Spätburgunder Weißherbst Brut

76 Ⓔ Fürstlich Castell'sches Domänenamt Brut 1998 Schloss Castell

76 Ⓔ Klaus Herres Riesling Brut 1998 St. Laurentius

75 Ⓔ Albert Kallfelz Riesling Brut 1998 Kallfelz Riesling

75 Ⓔ Andres & Mugler 1996 Spätburgunder Rosé Brut

75 Ⓔ Balthasar Ress Riesling Brut 1997 Von Unserm

75 Ⓔ Dr. Pauly-Bergweiler Spätburgunder Blanc de Noirs 1998 Wehlener Klosterberg

75 Ⓔ Josef Deppisch Silvaner Brut 1998 Franken Silvaner

75 ⒺⒺ Mäurer Spätburgunder 1996 Blanc de Noirs Brut

75 Ⓔ Ulrich Hahn 1997 Riesling Brut

75 Ⓔ Wv. Hagnau Grauer Burgunder Brut 1997 Rumore

75 Ⓔ Wolf 1997 Riesling Brut

74 Ⓕ Heim'sche Privat-Sektkellerei 1998 Riesling Brut

74 Ⓔ Ratzenberger Riesling Brut 1 996 Bacharacher Kloster Fürstental

74 Ⓔ Wg. Bischoffingen Spätburgunder B 1997 Bischoffinger Enselberg

74 Ⓔ Winzersekt 1998 Riesling Brut

73 Ⓔ Brogsitter Riesling Brut 1997 Brogsitters

73 ⒺⒺ Schloß Sommerhausen Riesling Brut 1995

	Sommerhäuser Stein	⑦②	ⓔ Schloss Saarstein Riesling Brut 1997 Schloss Saarstein
⑦②	ⓔ Badischer Winzerkeller Weißburgunder Brut 1996 Malterdinger Bienenberg	⑦①	ⓔ Anheuser Riesling Brut 1994 Niederhäuser Pfingstweide
⑦②	ⓔ Fürstlich Castell'sches Domänenamt Brut 1996 Schloss Castell	⑦①	ⓔ Walter Zimmer 1998 Riesling Brut
⑦②	ⓔ Joh. Geil I. Erben 1997 Weißburgunder Brut	⑦①	ⓔ Wg. Hambacher Schloß Riesling Bru 1996 Riesling Sekt
⑦②	ⓔ Longen-Schlöder 1996 Weißer Burgunder Brut		
⑦②	ⓔ Reichsgraf von Kesselstatt NV Riesling Brut		

DEUTSCHER SEKT: EXTRA BRUT

Although severely depleted from the number of wines submitted, I was nevertheless pleasantly surprised by the number of Extra Brut *cuvées* that survived the tasting with recommendations intact.

⑧⓪	ⓔ Freiherr zu Knyphausen Riesling Extra Brut 1993 Herrlichkeit Knyphausen		de Noirs Extra Brut
⑦⑥	ⓔ Freiherr von Gleichenstein Extra Brut 1996 Badischer Winzersekt	⑦⑤	ⓔ Fürst von Metternich Riesling Extra Brut 1998 Henkell & Söhnlein
⑦⑥	ⓔ Klaus Herres Riesling Extra Brut 1997 St. Laurentius	⑦⑤	ⓔ Hans Lang Riesling Extra Brut 1997 Johann Maximilian
⑦⑥	ⓔ Rainer Eymann Spätburgunder 1995 Blanc de Noirs Extra Brut	⑦④	ⓔ Schwahn-Fehlinger Riesling Extra Brut 1997 Westhofener Aulerde
⑦⑥	ⓔ Remstalkellerei Grauer Burgunder Extra Brut 1998 Grünbecher Klingle	⑦③	ⓔ Wg. Sasbach am Kaiserstuhl 1997 Weißer Burgunder Extra Brut
⑦⑥	ⓔ Wg. Sasbach am Kaiserstuhl 1997 Spätburgunder Blanc	⑦⓪	ⓔ Wv. Deidesheim Riesling Extra Brut 1998 Deidesheimer Paradiesgarten

REMEMBER!

75 Points: "Any sparkling wine other than Champagne that receives this score is not just interesting, but good enough to grace the table of a self-confessed Champagne addict."
–TOM STEVENSON
Don't restrict your choice to 90-point wines – I don't!

DEUTSCHER SEKT: EXTRA TROCKEN

Technically the same as Extra Sec, thus may have between 12 and 20 grams per litre of residual sugar.

⑦⑦	ⓔ Edith Stein Riesling Extra Trocken 1998 Nahe-Riesling		Baron zu Knyphausen
⑦⑦	ⓔⓔ Kloss & Foerster Spätburgunder Extra Trocken 1997 Assmannshäuser Höllenberg	⑦④	ⓔ Wachtenburg Winzer 1998 Spätburgunder Rosé Extra Trocken
⑦⑤	ⓔ Freiherr zu Knyphausen Riesling Extra Trocken 1997	⑦③	ⓔ Müller-Ruprecht Riesling NV Extra Trocken
		⑦③	ⓔⓔ Schales Rieslaner Auslese Extra Trocken 1991 Schales

73 £ Wg. Kallstadt Riesling Extra Trocken 1998 Kallstadter Kobnert — Rieslaner Sekt

72 £ Adam Müller Spätburgunder Rosé Extra Trocken 1998 Heidelberger Mannaberg

72 £ Friedel Russler Riesling Extra Trocken 1998

72 £ Josef Deppisch Riesling Extra Trocken 1998 Franken Riesling — Wallufer Oberberg

72 £ Winzersekt 1998 Spätburgunder Weißherbst

70 £ Schlosskellerei Affaltrach NV Baumann Rosé Extra Trocken

DEUTSCHER SEKT: TROCKEN & HALBTROCKEN
The equivalent of Sec and Demi-Sec, with 17-35 and 35-50 grams per litre of sugar respectively.

79 £ SMW-Winzersekt Riesling Trocken 1987 SMW Reserve

78 £ H.-J. Fries Riesling Halbtrocken 1997 Noviander Klosterberg

78 £ Studert-Prüm Riesling Trocken 1997 Maximiner Cabinet

77 £ Lebenshilfe Riesling Trocken 1998 Wachenheimer Schlossberg

77 £ Wg. Beckstein Riesling Trocken 1998 Becksteiner Kirchberg

76 £ Hex vom Dasenstein Spätburgunder Rosé Trocken 1998 Hex vom Dasenstein

76 £ Schales Riesling Halbtrocken

75 £ Schmitt Schenk Riesling Trocken 1998 Ockfener Scharzberg — 1996 Schales Riesling Sekt

75 £ Hauses Württemberg Riesling Trocken 1998 Maulbronner Eilfingerberg (*magnum*)

75 £ Weingut-Weinhandel Riesling Trocken 1998 Zeller Schwarze Katz

75 £ Wv. Deidesheim 1998 Spätburgunder Trocken

74 £ Wg. Cleebronn-Güglingen Riesling Trocken 1998 Cleebronner Michaelsberg

ITALY

The best response came from Franciacorta, the only Italian sparkling wine appellation that must be made by *méthode champenoise*. Franciacorta also happens to be the only compact wine area producing world-class sparkling wine in Italy. Why then hasn't a Champagne house set down some roots here? Franciacorta would be the ideal location for a Taittinger-style operation like Domaine Carneros. Satèn, by the way, is a *crémant* style and most of the best examples have also been barrel-fermented.

85 £££ Ca'del Bosco 1993 Brut Cuvée Annamaria Clementi

85 £££ Ca'del Bosco 1990 Brut Cuvée Annamaria Clementi

85 ££ Ricci Curbastro NV Satèn

82 ££ Bredasole NV Brut

82 ££££ Majolini 1996 Brut Millennio 2000

82 ££ La Montina 1995 Brut

82 ££ Lo Sparviere NV Extra Brut

82 ££ Villa 1996 Satèn

80 ££ Barone Pizzini 1995 Brut Bagnadore

80 £££ Ca'del Bosco 1988 Brut Cuvée Annamaria Clementi

80 £££ Ca'del Bosco 1996 Satèn

80 ££ Castelfaglia NV Extra Brut

80 ££ Castelveder 1995 Brut

80 £££ Cavalleri 1995 Brut Collezione
80 ££ Cola NV Brut
80 £££ Ricci Curbastro NV Extra Brut
80 ££ Faccoli NV Extra Brut
80 ££ Lantieri de Paratico 1995 Brut Arcadia
79 £££ Principe Banfi NV Extra Brut
78 ££ Barone Pizzini NV Satèn
78 ££ Boschi NV Brut
78 £££ Ca'del Bosco 1995 Satèn
78 ££ Cavalleri NV Satèn
78 ££ Cavalleri 1995 Pas Dosé Collection
78 ££ Cola 1996 Extra Brut
78 ££ Contadi Castaldi NV Zero
78 ££ Ferghettina NV Brut
78 ££ Tenuta Castellino NV Satèn
78 ££ Tenuta Castellino 1995 Brut
78 £££ Uberti 1995 Extra Brut Comari del Salem
78 ££ Villa 1996 Brut
77 £££ Bellavista 1993 Gran Cuvée Pas Opere
77 ££ Bersi Serlini NV Demisec Nuvola
77 £££ Ca'del Bosco 1996 Brut
77 ££ Faccoli NV Rosé
77 ££ Villa 1996 Cuvette Sec
76 ££ Barone Pizzini NV Extra Dry
76 £££ Bellavista NV Cuvée Brut
76 £££ Bellavista NV Gran Cuvée Satèn
76 £££ Bellavista 1996 Gran Cuvée Brut
76 £££ Berlucchi F.lli 1996 Satèn
76 ££ Bettinzana NV Brut
76 ££ Ca'del Bosco NV Brut
76 ££ Castelfaglia NV Brut Monogram
76 ££ Majolini NV Brut

76 ££ Monte Rossa NV Sec
76 ££ Monzio Compagnoni NV Satèn
76 ££ Il Mosnel NV Extra Brut
76 ££ Uberti NV Brut
76 ££ Villa 1994 Brut Selezione
75 £££ Bellavista 1995 Gran Cuvée Brut Rosé
75 ££ Berlucchi F.lli 1996 Brut
75 ££ Bersi Serlini NV Satèn
75 ££ Bredasole NV Extra Brut
75 ££ Castelveder NV Brut
75 ££ Contadi Castaldi NV Brut
75 ££ Cornaleto 1991 Brut
75 ££ Ricci Curbastro NV Brut
75 ££ Faccoli NV Brut
75 ££ Le Marchesine NV Brut
75 ££ La Montina NV Satèn
75 ££ Monzio Compagnoni NV Extra Brut
75 ££ San Cristoforo NV Brut
75 ££ Uberti NV Extra Brut
75 ££ Villa 1996 Rosé Demi Sec
74 £££ Principe Banfi NV Brut
74 £££ Ca'del Bosco 1996 Dosage Zero
74 £££ Ca'del Bosco 1996 Rosé
74 £££ Cavalleri 1995 Rosé Collezione
74 ££ Mirabella NV Rosé
74 ££ La Montina NV Rosé Demi Sec
74 £££ Il Mosnel 1996 Satèn
74 ££ Riccafana NV Brut
74 ££ Tenuta Castellino NV Brut
73 ££ Barone Pizzini NV Brut
72 ££ Mirabella NV Brut
72 ££ Monte Rossa NV Brut
72 ££ Monte Rossa NV Satèn
72 £££ Il Mosnel 1993 Brut
70 £ Majolini 1994 Brut

NEW ZEALAND

Because the centralized tasting was just as disappointing as the one for Australian fizz last year, my mind was made up: I just had to go downunder. I have long since realized that it is foolish to attempt to cover both New Zealand and Australia in one trip, so my trips now cover one of these countries intensively, merely stopping off in the other one for enough time to conduct a centralized tasting (albeit of far greater depth than I can accomplish in the UK). This trip I spent most of the time in New Zealand, next time it will be vice versa. In New Zealand I took the opportunity to drive through the hottest (but literally coolest) fizz area, Central Otago, in the south of South Island, although I spent most time in Marlborough, which is the proven provenance of the best New Zealand fizz.

Once again, both vintage and non-vintage are mixed for comparison, with Cloudy Bay leading the non-vintage pack with its relatively new release. In the vintage stakes, Hunter is threatening the 90-point barrier, when just a couple of years ago the same producer's Miru Miru was head and shoulders above Hunter's.

Most amazing of all, however, is that no fewer than 19 Kiwi sparkling wines have achieved scores five points above entry level Champagne and equivalent to the sort of quality I demand before a Champagne warrants a place in my own cellar.

(89) ££ Hunter's 1996 Brut

(88) ££ Pelorus 1987 Brut, Cloudy Bay

(87) ££ Pelorus 1988 Brut, Cloudy Bay

(87) ££ Miru Miru 1998 Hunters

(87) ££ Deutz Marlborough Blanc de Blancs 1996 Montana

(87) ££ Deutz Marlborough Blanc de Blancs 1994 Montana

(86) ££ Miru Miru 1997 Hunters

(85) ££ Arcadia 1996 Lake Hayes

(85) ££ Quartz Reef 1998 Brut Blanc de Blancs

(85) ££ Pelorus 1996 Brut, Cloudy Bay

(85) ££ Pelorus 1995 Brut, Cloudy Bay

(85) ££ Pelorus 1990 Brut, Cloudy Bay

(85) ££ Pelorus NV Brut, Cloudy Bay

(85) ££ Elstree 1996 Brut, Highfield Estate

(85) ££ Elstree 1995 Brut, Highfield Estate *(magnum)*

(85) ££ Miru Miru 1995 Hunters

(85) ££ Miru Miru 1996 Hunters

(85) ££ Deutz Marlborough Cuvée NV Montana

(84) ££ Voyage Special Cuvée Brut NV Giesen

(83) ££ Pelorus 1993 Brut, Cloudy Bay

(83) ££ Morton Black Label 1995 Bay of Plenty/Hawkes Bay

(82) ££ Daniel le Brun 1997 Brut

(82) ££ Hunter's 1995 Brut

(81) ££ Daniel le Brun 1997 Blanc de Blancs Brut

(80) ££ Quartz Reef NV Brut

(80) ££ Pelorus 1994 Brut, Cloudy Bay

(80) ££ Pelorus 1992 Brut, Cloudy Bay

(80) £ Amadeus 1996 Hawkes Bay

(80) ££ Elstree 1995 Brut, Highfield Estate

(80) £ Selaks Founders Reserve 1992 Marlborough

(76) ££ Kim Crawford Rory NV Marlborough

(76) £ Gillan 1995 Brut

(75) ££ Parker Firstlight NV Crackling Traminer

(75) ££ Parker Firstlight NV Merlot Brut

(73) £ Morton Estate NV Hawkes Bay/Marlborough

(72) ££ Lintz Estate 1997 Riesling Brut

(72) ££ Morton RD 1995 Marlborough

(70) £ Soljans Legacy 1997 Auckland/Marlborough

(70) £ Soljans Estate Pinotage NV Auckland

SOUTH AFRICA

The name reserved for sparkling wines fermented in the bottle in which it is sold is Cap Classique. The concept behind this wine is very similar to that determining Spain's Cava appellation, except that the area of production is at least as paramount as the designation Cap Classique. In Spain, however, it is not possible to specify the area of origin, even though we know where most of the best Cava is produced (in and around Sant Sadurní d'Anoia). There is good potential for Cap Classique and no one who has visited one of the leading producers, Graham Beck, can be anything but amazed by the elegance of its wines after seeing how flat and hot its Robertson vineyards are. What the industry needs now, however, is a much greater number of serious Cap Classique producers pushing each other to achieve higher standards.

80	ⓔ Graham Beck NV Cap Classique, Cuvée Two Thousand Brut	
80	ⓔ Boschendal 1993 Cap Classique	
80	ⓔⓔ Morgenhof 1997 Cap Classique, Reserve Centenaire	
78	ⓔ Graham Beck 1998 Cap Classique, Sparkling Pinotage	
75	ⓔ Graham Beck NV Chardonnay-Pinot Noir Brut	
75	ⓔ Pongracz NV Cap Classique	
72	ⓔ Buitenverwachting NV Cap Classique	

SPAIN

The number of Cavas recommended in this guide has increased for the second year in a row and although there is just one score in the 80s, there are more in the mid-to-upper 70s. There is still a long way to go, but there is a definite trend towards increasing quality despite the intrinsic limitation of Cava's traditional grape varieties (Parellada, Macabéo and Xarello) and that's straight from the mouth of a Cava-sceptic, so it must be true!

85 ⓔ Raimat NV Cava Gran Brut, Codorníu	76 ⓔ Marqués de Monistrol Selección Especiale 1996 Cava Brut Reserva
79 ⓔⓔ III Lustros Gramona 1993 Cava Brut Nature Gran Reserva	76 ⓔ Marqués de Monistrol Selección Especiale NV Cava Brut Rosé
78 ⓔⓔ Codorníu NV Cava Reserva Brut Rosé	75 ⓔⓔ Jaume de Codorníu NV Cava Brut, Codorníu
78 ⓔ Maria Casanovas NV Cava Brut Nature Gran Reserva	75 ⓔ Cuvée Raventós NV Cava Brut, Codorníu
78 ⓔⓔ Segura Viudas 1998 Cava Brut Nature	75 ⓔ Xenius 1998 Cava Brut, COVIDES
78 ⓔⓔ Segura Viudas, Reserva Heredad NV Cava Brut	75 ⓔ Ferret NV Cava Brut Reserva
76 ⓔⓔ Dioro Baco NV Cava Extra Brut, Bodegas Escudero	75 ⓔⓔ Celler Battle 1992 Cava Gran Reserva Brut, Gramona
76 ⓔⓔ Celler Battle 2001 1993 Cava, Gramona	75 ⓔ Castillo de Perelada NV Cava Brut Reserva

75 Ⓔ Reserva de Raventós i Blanc NV Cava Brut

75 Ⓔ Torre Oria NV Cava Brut Reserva

75 Ⓔ Castell de Vilarnau 1996 Cava Brut Gran Reserva

74 ⒺⒺ Colomer Bernat Siglo XXI 1996 Cava Brut Nature

74 Ⓔ Duc de Foix 1997 Cava Brut, COVIDES

74 Ⓔ Marqués de Monistrol, Gran Reserva de Familia NV Cava Rosé

74 Ⓔ Mont-Ferrant Medalla d'Or 1997 Cava Brut Reserva

74 ⒺⒺ Quercus 1997 Cava Brut Nature Reserva, Augustí Torelló

74 Ⓔ Torreblanca 1997 Cava Extra Brut Reserva, Viña Torreblanca

73 ⒺⒺ Parxet Aniversario 80 NV Cava Brut Nature

73 ⒺⒺ Gran Claustro 1998 Cava Brut Nature, Castillo de Perelada

73 Ⓔ Joan Raventós Rosell 1997 Cava Brut Nature

73 Ⓔ Cava NV Brut, Sevisa

73 Ⓔ Masblanc NV Cava Extra Brut, Viña Torreblanca

72 Ⓔ Anne Marie Comtesse NV Cava Brut Nature, Castell d'Age

72 Ⓔ Paul Cheneau Millennium 1997 Cava Brut, CIGRAVI

72 Ⓔ Rondell NV Cava Extreme Brut, Codorníu

72 Ⓔ Cavas Hill NV Cava Rosado Brut

72 ⒺⒺ Gran Juvé & Camps 1995 Cava Gran Reserva Brut

72 Ⓔ Llopart 1997 Cava Reserva Brut Nature

72 Ⓔ L'Hereu Brut de Raventós i Blanc NV Cava Brut

72 Ⓔ Vallformosa 1997 Cava Brut, Masía Vallformosa

71 Ⓔ Carolina de Masachs NV Cava Brut Reserva

71 ⒺⒺ Brut Reserva Heretat 1996 Cava Brut Natural, Joan Raventós Rosell

71 Ⓔ Aliger 1997 Cava Brut Vintage, Augustí Torelló

71 ⒺⒺ Gran Reserva Torelló 1995 Cava Brut Nature

71 Ⓔ Vallformosa 1997 Cava Brut Nature, Masía Vallformosa

70 Ⓔ Alsina & Sardà 1996 Cava Brut Reserva

70 Ⓔ Roger Goulart Gran Reserva 1996 Cava Brut Extra

70 Ⓔ Eudald Massana Noya Familia 1998 Cava Brut

70 Ⓔ Parxet Gran Reserva Millenium NV Cava Gran Reserva

70 Ⓔ Torelló 1997 Cava Brut

UNITED STATES OF AMERICA

California was the first New World area in which a Champagne house set up a serious *méthode champenoise* operation, when Moët established Domaine Chandon in 1973. This state still leads the way, but with Washington and Oregon in the wings. I also took time this year to visit New York and Michigan, where I tasted every sparkling wine in current production.

91 ⒺⒺⒺ Argyle 1995 Knudsen Vineyard Brut

91 ⒺⒺ Roederer Estate L'Ermitage 1993 Brut

90 ⒺⒺⒺ Argyle Knudsen Vineyard 1996 Julia Lee's Block

90 ⒺⒺ Argyle 1995 Brut

90 ⒺⒺⒺ Domaine Carneros by Taittinger 1994 Le Rêve

90 ⒺⒺⒺ Domaine Carneros by Taittinger 1993 Le Rêve

90 ⒺⒺ Roederer Estate NV Anderson Valley Brut Rosé

89 ⒺⒺⒺ Argyle 1988 Extended Tirage

89 ⒺⒺⒺ Domaine Carneros 1993 Le Rêve

REMEMBER!

75 Points: "Any sparkling wine other than Champagne that receives this score is not just interesting, but good enough to grace the table of a self-confessed Champagne addict."
–TOM STEVENSON

Don't restrict your choice to 90-point wines – I don't!

89	££	Mumm Cuvée Napa 1994 Winery Lake Brut
88	££	Argyle 1996 Brut
88	££	Mumm Cuvée Napa 1995 DVX Brut
87	£££	Argyle 1996 Knudsen Vineyard Brut
85	££	Mountain Dome NV Cuvée Forté, 2000 Brut
85	££	Roederer Estate NV Anderson Valley Brut
82	££	Domaine Carneros by Taittinger 1995 Brut
82	££	Iron Horse 1995 Russian Cuvée
82	££	Mountain Dome 1994 Brut
82	££	Schramsberg 1996 Blanc de Blancs Brut
80	££	Domaine Carneros by Taittinger 1996 Brut
80	££	Domaine Carneros by Taittinger 1997 Brut
80	££	Iron Horse 1995 Classic Vintage Brut
80	££	Iron Horse 1994 Brut Rosé
80	£	Lamoreaux Landing 1996 Brut
80	£	L. Mawby 1995 Mille, Blanc de Noirs, Leelanu Peninsula
78	££	Domaine Carneros 1994 Brut
78	£	Glenora 1998 Blanc de Blancs
77	£	Korbel NV Brut
77	£	Mountain Dome NV Brut
77	££	Mumm Cuvée Napa NV Blanc de Blancs Brut
76	££	Iron Horse 1997 Wedding Cuvée, Blanc de Noir
76	£	Domaine Ste. Michelle NV Cuvée Brut, Century Cuvée
75	£	Barefoot NV California
75	£	Bel Lago NV Brilliante
75	£	Bel Lago 1998 Brut, Leelanu Peninsula
75	£	Carpe Diem Semi-Dry Sparkling Wine NV Château Chantal
75	£	Carpe Diem NV Semi-Sweet Sparkling Wine
75	££	Chateau Frank 1995 Blanc de Blancs
75	££	Chateau Lafayette Reneau 1997 Blanc de Blancs
75	£	Glenora 1996 Brut
75	£	Glenora 1996 Extra Dry
75	£	Good Arbor NV Moonstruck Brut, Leelanu Peninsula
75	£	Lamoreaux Landing 1995 Brut
75	£	McGregor 1995 Blanc de Noirs
75	££	Mountain Dome NV Brut Rosé
75	££	Mumm Cuvée Napa NV Brut
75	££	Mumm Cuvée Napa NV Brut Rosé
75	£	Shady Lane 1997 Blanc de Blancs, Leelanu Peninsula
75	£	Domaine Ste. Michelle NV Blanc de Blanc, Century Cuvée
75	£	Hermann J. Wiemer 1997 Cuvée Brut 2000
74	££	Handley 1995 Brut
74	£	Pugliese 1997 Blanc de Blancs
74	££	Sakonnet Samson Brut 1995 Rhode Island
74	£	Shady Lane 1997 Riesling, Leelanu Peninsula
74	£	Thornton NV Cuvée Rouge, California
73	£	Glenora 1998 Blanc de Noirs
73	£	McGregor 1996 Sparkling Riesling
72	£	Bel Lago 1997 Brut
72	£	Glenora 1996 Blanc de Blancs
72	£	L. Mawby NV Crémant, Leelanu Peninsula (CV36)
72	£	Shady Lane 1997 Brut, Leelanu Peninsula
72	£	Swedish Hill 1996 Brut
72	£	Wagner 1997 Riesling Champagne
70	££	Chateau Frank 1995 Brut

70	ⓔ Chateau Frank 1997 Celebre
70	ⓔ Good Arbor NV Extra Dry, Leelanu Peninsula
70	ⓔ Korbel NV Blanc de Noirs
70	ⓔ Lamoreaux Landing 1992 Blanc de Blancs
70	ⓔ Lucas 1993 20th Anniversary
70	ⓔ L. Mawby NV Talisman Brut, Leelanu Peninsula

(CV28)

70	ⓔ L. Mawby 1994 Mille, Blanc de Noirs, Leelanu Peninsula
70	ⓔ Shady Lane 1995 Brut, Leelanu Peninsula
70	ⓔ Shady Lane 1994 Brut, Leelanu Peninsula
70	ⓔⓔ Westport Rivers 1993 Southeastern New England

WORLDWIDE GROUPING OF THE SWEETEST SPARKLING WINES

It has always been my contention that if you're going to make a sweet sparkling wine it really should be sweet, not semi or demi anything. This is also the one sparkling wine style that demands the most aromatic varieties and you don't get more aromatic than the Muscat or Moscato grape. Furthermore, to keep the freshness, vivacity and sheer exuberance of an aromatic grape variety the wine should have as little yeast contact as possible, thus *cuve close* is ideal for the purpose. If I'm right, then by having all the sweetest sparkling wines in the world compete, Asti, red Brachetto (a Moscato-like black grape) and the sparkling Muscat wines of Die should dominate. And as you can see below, they have.

90	ⓔⓔ La Selvatica Asti NV Caudrinia, Romano Dogliotti *(magnum)*
89	ⓔⓔ La Selvatica Asti NV Caudrina, Romano Dogliotti
88	ⓔ Beni di Batasiolo NV Asti Dolce
88	ⓔⓔ Tosti NV Asti 2000
87	ⓔⓔ De Miranda 1997 Asti
86	ⓔ Fontanafredda 1999 Brachetto d'Acqui
85	ⓔⓔ Alain Poulet Clairette de Die NV Méthode Dioise Ancestrale
85	ⓔ Arione NV Asti
85	ⓔⓔ Bava NV Malvasia di Castelnuovo don Bosco
85	ⓔⓔ Clairdie Tradition NV Méthode Dioise Ancestrale
85	ⓔ Conte di Cavour NV Asti
85	ⓔ Duchessa Lia NV Brachetto d'Acqui, Spumante Dolce
85	ⓔ Mondoro NV Asti
85	ⓔ Santero NV Brachetto d'Acqui
84	ⓔ Bersano NV Asti Dolce
83	ⓔ Bersano NV Brachetto d'Acqui Dolce

83	ⓔ Dezzani NV Brachetto d'Acqui Dolce
83	ⓔ Marenco NV Asti
83	ⓔ Toso NV Brachetto d'Acqui Dolce
82	ⓔⓔ Carod Frères Clairette de Die NV Méthode Dioise Ancestrale
82	ⓔ Fontanafredda 1999 Asti Millesimato
82	ⓔⓔ Marenco NV Brachetto d'Acqui
80	ⓔ Arione NV Piemonte Brachetto Dolce
80	ⓔⓔ Cave Didier Cornillon NV Méthode Dioise Ancestrale
80	ⓔⓔ Cerutti NV Asti Cesare
80	ⓔ Perlino NV Asti
80	ⓔ Valter Barbero NV Asti Acini Dolce
76	ⓔ Casa Martelletti NV Tradizione Asti
75	ⓔ Capetta NV Asti Dolce
75	ⓔⓔ Les Vignobles Vergnes de Martinolles NV Méthode Ancestrale
75	ⓔ Parxet Cuvée Dessert NV Cava Dulce Rosado

TASTING NOTES AND SCORES

ATTENTION CHAMPAGNE & SPARKLING WINE PRODUCERS!

If you are not already in contact with the author, but would like to submit wines for consideration in future editions, please contact Tom Stevenson at:

tom.stevenson@fizz.worldonline.co.uk

Warning: Any other unsolicited mail received at this address will be ignored.

Please note that recommendation in this guide involves no charge whatsoever beyond the cost of the samples and their delivery.

❖ **50 RED HILL ESTATE**, *see* Red Hill

ADAM
Alsace, France

JEAN-BAPTISTE ADAM NV CRÉMANT D'ALSACE BRUT

Some finesse and excellent acidity.
🍷 Now–2001 ⓔ

ADELSECK
Nahe, Germany

CARL ADELSECK RIESLING BRUT 1998 ADELSECK JUWEL

Very fresh, elevated fruit with fine acidity providing elegance on the finish. (*Méthode champenoise.*)
🍷 Now ⓔ DM11

AFFALTRACH
Schloßkellerei Affaltrach Württemberg, Germany

SCHLOSSKELLEREI AFFALTRACH NV BAUMANN ROSE EXTRA TROCKEN

Very fresh, easy-drinking fruit. (*Cuve close.*)
🍷 Now ⓔ 🍇 DM16

AGE
*Castell d'Age
Penedès, Spain*

ANNE MARIE COMTESSE NV CAVA BRUT NATURE, CASTELL D'AGE

The current 1998-based blend offers a good amount of flavour for Cava and possesses a mousse of some finesse.
🍷 Now ⓔ 🍇 750 Ptas

AIGLE
*Domaine de l'Aigle
Limoux, France*

DOMAINE DE L'AIGLE NV CRÉMANT DE LIMOUX BRUT

Elegant *barrique* aromas mingle with rich fruit on the palate, all of which is neatly underscored by excellent acidity to produce the best Limoux I have ever tasted.
🍷 Now–2002 ⓔ

DOMAINE DE L'AIGLE NV TRADITION

Fat, creamy-rich fruit, with excellent acidity.
🍷 Now–2001 ⓔ

ALL SAINTS
Victoria, Australia

ST LEONARDS CARYLYE 1997 SPARKLING SHIRAZ

This wine should carry a sanity warning, as it should only be approached by lovers of ultra-blackcurranty sparkling Shiraz made in the Seppelt Show Reserve style. This style is not for me, but it gets gongs and has a strong following.
❚ Now ⓔⓔ ⚑ A$20

ALSINA
Cellers Alsina
Penedès, Spain

ALSINA & SARDA 1996 CAVA BRUT RESERVA

Fuller style Cava with almondy fruit.
❚ Now ⓔ ⚑ 1,400 Ptas

ANDRES & MUGLER
Sektkellerei Andres & Mugler
Pfalz, Germany

ANDRES & MUGLER 1996 SPÄTBURGUNDER ROSÉ BRUT

Apricots and gamey Pinot fruit, underscored by true Brut dryness. (*Méthode champenoise.*)
❚ Now–2001 ⓔ ⚑ DM23

ANDRES & MUGLER BRUT 1998 CHARDONNAY & AUXERROIS

A really fresh and satisfying Sekt of some finesse and class. (*Méthode champenoise.*)
❚ Now–2001 ⓔ ⚑ DM28

❖ **ANGAS**, *see* Smith

ANHEUSER
Weingut Anheuser
Nahe, Germany

ANHEUSER RIESLING BRUT 1994 NIEDERHÄUSER PFINGSTWEIDE

Plenty of bottle-aged Riesling aromas and lots of fruit, but could do with more finesse to score higher.
❚ Now–2001 ⓔ

ARGYLE WINERY
Oregon, USA

ARGYLE 1996 BRUT

If not for the 1995, this light, ripe, elegant sparkling wine would be Argyle's best ever vintage. The fruit is elevated, making it very yummy, but detracting from the standard set by the 1995.
❚ Now–2002 ⓔⓔ

ARGYLE 1995 KNUDSEN VINEYARD BRUT

Absolutely classic!
❚ Now–2002 ⓔⓔⓔ

ARGYLE 1988 EXTENDED TIRAGE

The re-release of this old vintage is disgorged on demand (stated on front label), but the sample I tasted had a further 12 months' post-disgorgement ageing and I have to admit that I was amazed. I tasted this and the 1989 at the winery a year ago. It was nothing special, although not as bad as the 1989, which I could not get past my nose. I still cannot get the 1989 past my nose, but the 1988 has aged beautifully over the last year. The wine is now dominated by Chardonnay, which represents only 30% of the blend, but packs a peachy punch of fruit on both the nose and the palate.
❚ Now–2001 ⓔⓔⓔ

ARGYLE 1996 KNUDSEN VINEYARD BRUT

Although not quite so elevated as it is in Argyle's basic 1996 vintage, there is a noticeable touch of VA-lifted fruit, which detracts from the class of this otherwise fresh and delicious sparkling wine.
❚ Now–2002 ⓔⓔⓔ

ARGYLE 1995 BRUT

This exceptional sparkling wine is still extremely fresh with very slow development of post-disgorgement aromas since it was released 18 months ago.
❚ Now–2002 ⓔⓔ

ARGYLE, KNUDSEN VINEYARD 1996 JULIA LEE'S BLOCK, BLANC DE BLANCS

Barrique aromas add to this wine's complexity, giving it the edge over the classic Brut Knudsen Vineyard.

❗ Now–2003 ⓔⓔⓔ

ARIONE

Asti, Italy

ARIONE NV PIEMONTE BRACHETTO DOLCE

Light in colour and body, but with fresh, soapy Moscato fruit and a tangy, clean, very sweet finish. This soapiness is not unpleasant and usually develops into a distinctive fruit such as peach.

❗ Now ⓔ

ARIONE NV ASTI

Big, fresh, musky aromas followed by intensely sweet Moscato fruit with hints of orange in the fruit.

❗ Now ⓔ

ARNOULD

Champagne Michel Arnould & Fils
28 rue de Mailly 51360 Verzenay
☎(326) 49.40.06 ℻(326) 49.44.61

MICHEL ARNOULD & FILS NV BRUT GRAND CRU

The richness of Verzenay Pinot Noir comes through in both the current and forthcoming releases, but there is much more complexity waiting to build in both. The new release is a touch fatter and a tad less intense, but it is not fat and does not lack intensity. In fact, it is very Michel Arnould, very concentrated, very Pinot Noir and very Verzenay.

❗ Now–2003 ⓔⓔ

MICHEL ARNOULD & FILS NV BRUT, RÉSERVE GRAND CRU

The extraordinarily rich and satisfying Pinot Noir fruit in this wine is merely typical of Michel Arnould, but it really does repay keeping an extra year to let

the bouquet catch up with the palate.

▬ 2001–2004 ⓔⓔ

MICHEL ARNOULD & FILS NV BRUT ROSÉ, GRAND CRU

As Verzenay is super-expressive of Pinot Noir, Michel Arnould is super-expressive of Verzenay and the skin extraction for a rosé style allows the Pinot Noir to be even more expressive, this should be one of this producer's top *cuvées*. For some reason, however, it has not been, although it has usually been a Champagne I could wholeheartedly recommend, and this year's release is the best example I have tasted.

❗ Now–2004 ⓔⓔ

AUTREAU

Champagne Autreau-Lasnot
6 rue du Château 51480 Venteuil
℻(326) 58.65.44

AUTREAU-LASNOT 1992 BRUT PRESTIGE

Extraordinarily fresh for an eight-year-old Champagne, this wine is not only still in fruit-mode, it's in turbo-charged fruit-mode.

❗ Now–2005 ⓔⓔ

BADISCHER WINZERKELLER

Baden, Germany

BADISCHER WINZERKELLER WEIßBURGUNDER BRUT 1996 MALTERDINGER BIENENBERG

Some finesse on nose, with fresh, clean, frothy fruit on the palate. (*Méthode champenoise.*)

❗ Now ⓔ 🏅DM25

BAGBOROUGH

Pylle, Somerset, England, UK

LEVERET SPARKLING WINE
NV DRY

Fresh with crisp, aromatic fruit.
❙ Now–2001 ⓔ

❖ **BALTHASAR RESS**, *see* Ress

BANFI
Tuscany, Italy

PRINCIPE BANFI NV EXTRA BRUT

Lovely fruit-driven *cuvée*, nice
citrussy/apple-blossom fruit on finish.
❙ Now–2001 ⓔⓔⓔ ♚ 30,000 Lira

PRINCIPE BANFI NV BRUT

Finer autolysis on nose, apricot and
plums, an elegant try, but needs more
finesse to fully succeed.
❙ Now–2002 ⓔⓔⓔ ♚ 30,000 Lira

BARBERO
Asti, Italy

CONTE DI CAVOUR NV ASTI

Fresh, floral Moscato fruit with intensely
sweet, perfumed fruit.
❙ Now ⓔ

BARBERO, VALTER
Asti, Italy

VALTER BARBERO NV ASTI
ACINI DOLCE

Darker than all the other Asti tasted
(well over 50 in number), suggesting
additional bottle-age, which can be
unwelcome for Moscato because the
most important terpene in terms of its
distinctive aroma is geraniol and with
time this goes from wonderfully fresh to
a pungent geranium odour. However, this
wine is fresh and floral, with clean,
intensely sweet Moscato fruit, thus the
depth of colour might only be due to
concentrated fruit.
❙ Now ⓔ

BARDOUX

Champagne Bardoux
5–7 rue Saint-Vincent
51390 Villedommange
☎(326) 49.25.35 ℻(326) 49.23.15

BARDOUX PÈRE & FILS
NV BRUT PREMIER CRU

A bit rustic, but there's no denying the
strength of character in this *cuvée*. It
needs at least one year, however, for the
mousse to settle down and the bubbles to
be tinier and better integrated.
▬ 2001–2002 ⓔⓔ ♚ 88FF

BAREFOOT
California, USA

BAREFOOT NV CALIFORNIA

Estery-floral, muscatty aromas are at the
heart of this fresh, easy-drinking fizz,
making it perfect for its position in the
market place.
❙ Now ⓔ ♚ $6.99

BARNAUT

Champagne E. Barnaut
13 rue Pasteur
51150 Bouzy
☎(326) 57.01.54 ℻(326) 57.09.97

E. BARNAUT NV GRANDE
RÉSERVE, BRUT GRAND CRU

Good fruit and finesse. Should develop
slowly.
❙ Now–2003 ⓔⓔ ♚ 87FF

E. BARNAUT NV BLANC DE
NOIRS, BRUT GRAND CRU

Rich fruit with a touch of pineapple,
which is more elevated Chardonnay than
it is Pinot, but nice enough all the same.
❙ Now–2002 ⓔⓔ ♚ 87FF

BARON ALBERT

Champagne Baron Albert
1 rue des Chaillots Le Grand Porteron
02310 Charly-sur-Marne
C(23) 82.02.65 **FAX**(23) 82.02.44

BARON ALBERT NV BRUT ROSÉ **85**

An immediate impression of pure, concentrated Pinot fruit, even though I know that this *cuvée* contains 50% Chardonnay, or it always used to.
❘ Now–2003 €€ ❦ 78FF

BARON ALBERT NV BRUT CARTE D'OR **80**

The huge extract on this wine, which is so superior to Baron Albert's Cuvée An 2000, finishes so crisp that it is almost as sharp as a razor. The dosage, however, seems right, so it is merely a matter of time and I think two years should do it.
▬ 2002–2003 €€ ❦ 77FF

CUVÉE JEAN DE LA FONTAINE 1994 BRUT, BARON ALBERT **84**

Fresh, cool fruit with peachy-*barrique* aromas.
❘ Now–2002 €€

LA PRÉFÉRANCE DE BARON ALBERT 1994 BRUT MILLÉSIME **84**

Good, clean fun; this tasty Champagne is from the very western edge of the region, where the flavours do not always rack up quite so well, but this *cuvée* is nicely concentrated.
❘ Now–2002 €€

BARON-FUENTÉ

Champagne Baron-Fuenté
21 avenue Fernand Drouett
02310 Charly-sur-Marne
C(323) 82.01.97 **FAX**(323) 82.12.00

BARON-FUENTÉ NV BRUT TRADITION **84**

Tasty, aged fruit that is nicely crisp and satisfying on the finish. Much preferred to Baron Fuenté's Cuvée Prestige.
❘ Now–2003 €€

BARONE PIZZINI

Franciacorta, Italy

BARONE PIZZINI NV BRUT **73**

Estery, young, fresh, elegant fruit.
❘ Now–2002 €€

BARONE PIZZINI NV SATÈN **78**

Autolytic, but a touch of ferment aroma on the finish suggests this could have benefited from a little longer on yeast.
▬ 2001–2002 €€

BARONE PIZZINI NV EXTRA DRY **76**

Fresh, fine, excellent autolysis, lovely pin-cushion mousse, fresh and fruity finish.
❘ Now–2002 €€

BARONE PIZZINI 1995 BRUT BAGNADORE **80**

Fine *barrique* fruit, but needs cooler storage for second fermentation to achieve greater finesse.
❘ Now–2002 €€

BATASIOLO

Franciacorta, Italy

BENI DI BATASIOLO NV ASTI DOLCE **88**

Succulent, juicy-ripe, intensely sweet, rich-peachy fruit. Reminiscent of those huge peaches sold at the roadside in Greece and which are so ripe and fresh that you cannot bite into them without juice running all over the place.
❘ Now €

BAUGET-JOUETTE

Champagne Bauget-Jouette
6 rue Chaude-Ruelle
51200 Epernay
C(326) 54.44.05 **FAX**(326) 55.37.39

BAUGET-JOUETTE NV GRANDE RÉSERVE BRUT **84**

The dosage in this wine has been sulphured to allow for a slow

development, hence it will be at least one year before its elevated fruit adopts any toastiness.
 2001–2003 ⓔⓔ

BAUMARD

Loire, France

BAUMARD 1997 CRÉMANT DE LOIRE BRUT **72**

Rich and tasty.
❘ Now ⓔ

BAUMARD NV CARTE CORAIL, CRÉMANT DE LOIRE BRUT **75**

Fine, fresh aroma with a perfumed hint to the palate and a crisp, crunchy cranberry fruit finish.
❘ Now–2001 ⓔ

BAUR

Alsace, France

CHARLES BAUR 1996, CRÉMANT D'ALSACE BRUT **75**

Rich and creamy yeast-aged fruit with excellent acidity.
❘ Now–2001 ⓔ

BAVA

Asti, Italy

BAVA NV MALVASIA DI CASTELNUOVO DON BOSCO **85**

Relatively deep colour, with powerful Moscato aroma and great richness of sweet, musky fruit dominating the finish.
❘ Now ⓔⓔ

BEAULIEU

Brockenhurst, Hampshire, England, UK

BEAULIEU BUBBLY 1997 BRUT **74**

The best Beaulieu Bubbly I've tasted. I've

often wondered about the origin of "drunk as a lord", but I could well understand Lord Montagu over-imbibing on this particular vintage, with its fresh, crisp and utterly clean, aromatic fruit.
❘ Now–2001 ⓔ

BEAUMET

Champagne Beaumet
3 rue Malakoff
51207 Epernay
☎(326) 59.50.10 (326) 54.78.52

BEAUMET NV CUVÉE ROSÉ BRUT **83**

Although its chalk-dust aroma might not sound appealing, it is interesting and certainly not off-putting, and the fruit has nice spring-blossom aromas. Furthermore, it is streets ahead of Beaumet's rosé under Sainsbury's own-label at the same time.
❘ On sale–2001 ⓔⓔ 100FF

BEAUMONT DES CRAYÈRES

Champagne Beaumont des Crayères
64 rue de la Liberté
Mardeuil 51318 Epernay
☎(326) 55.29.40 (326) 54.26.30

BEAUMONT DES CRAYÈRES NV GRAND PRESTIGE BRUT **82**

Promising, but released too early and needs a couple of years for the carbonic gas to combine, the mousse to soften and the bubbles to get smaller.
 2002–2003 ⓔⓔ

BEAUMONT DES CRAYÈRES NV GRAND ROSÉ BRUT **82**

Fresh and tasty with bags of fruit.
❘ Now–2001 ⓔⓔ

BEAUMONT DES CRAYÈRES 1995 FLEUR DE ROSÉ, BRUT **85**

Tasty, perfumed-Pinot fruit with a juicy-sweet finish.
❘ Now–2001 ⓔⓔ

BEAUMONT DES CRAYÈRES 1995 FLEUR DE PRESTIGE, BRUT

A serious-styled, full-bodied, deeply flavoured Champagne with peach-stone fruit dominating.
❚ Now–2003 ⓔⓔ

BEAUMONT DES CRAYÈRES 1994 GRANDE PRESTIGE MILLÉSIME BRUT 85

I did not score this wine last year because the dominating biscuity-malo aromas were at odds with its lean fruit. One year later, however, and the wine has come together nicely. With maturity the fruit is plumper, the mousse softer, and the entire wine is now in harmony with its biscuity complexity, making a superior Champagne for such a lacklustre vintage as 1994.
❚ Now–2002 ⓔⓔⓔ

BEAUMONT DES CRAYÈRES, NUIT D'OR NV CUVÉE 2000 MILLÉNAIRE, BRUT PREMIÈRE CUVÉE

This Jeroboam is presented in a polished wooden box and the wine really has a profoundly deep and satisfying flavour, with a long, crisp finish. The aromas are rich in the flowery finesse of autolysis and there is great potential for this wine to improve throughout the entire first decade of the new millennium. My one gripe is the low quality wire used to secure the cork because it is only just acceptable now and will soon become nasty.
❚ Now–2009 ⓔⓔ

BEBLENHEIM

Producteurs Réunis Au Château de Beblenheim, Alsace, France

HEIMBERGER NV BLANC DE BLANCS, CRÉMANT D'ALSACE BRUT 78

Wonderfully fresh with succulent fruit, proving that cooperatives can produce the goods in Alsace. The mousse is somewhat firm, but will soften in bottle over the next year or two (if you cannot

wait, open the day before, drink one glass, reseal and store in fridge for 24 hours).
◣ 2001–2002 ⓔ

BARON DE HOEN BLANC DE NOIRS, CRÉMANT D'ALSACE BRUT

A good mouthful of fruit; this wine needs only a little more finesse to deserve a higher score.
❚ Now ⓔ

BECK

Robertson, South Africa

GRAHAM BECK NV CAP CLASSIQUE, CUVÉE TWO THOUSAND BRUT

Very pale salmon colour, and although fruit is elevated, this is countered by a delightful mousse of the tiniest bubbles.
❚ Now–2001 ⓔ ♗ R40

GRAHAM BECK NV CHARDONNAY-PINOT NOIR BRUT

The elegant, creamy fruit in this wine should go biscuity.
❚ Now–2001 ⓔ

GRAHAM BECK 1998 CAP CLASSIQUE, SPARKLING PINOTAGE

This pre-release sample is the Cape's answer to Australia's Sparkling Shiraz. Its Pinotage fruit is fresh, elegant and reminiscent of Maynards wine gums (the red ones).

🍷 Now–2002 ⓔ

BECKER
Alsace, France

BRUT DE BECKER 1998 BLANC DE BLANCS, CRÉMANT D'ALSACE BRUT

Fresher and lighter than the 1996, with plenty of elegant fruit and more finesse.

🍷 Now–2002 ⓔ

BRUT DE BECKER 1996 BLANC DE BLANCS, CRÉMANT D'ALSACE

Plenty of fruit and good acidity, but a touch too weighty.

🍷 Now ⓔ

BECKSTEIN
Winzergenossenschaft Beckstein Baden, Germany

WINZERGENOSSENSCHAFT BECKSTEIN RIESLING TROCKEN 1998 BECKSTEINER KIRCHBERG

Very fresh and classic in structure with excellent fruit. (*Méthode champenoise.*)

🍷 Now–2002 ⓔ 🍾 DM16

BEL LAGO
Michigan, USA

BEL LAGO NV BRILLIANTE

An easily accessible, off-dry sparkling wine made by the Cayuga, a hybrid that sucks at higher levels of ripeness, but which produces a fresh and fragrant wine when picked early, as it obviously was for this attractively light-styled fizz.

🍷 Now ⓔ

BEL LAGO 1997 BRUT

A well structured Chardonnay Pinot blend that has been spiced up with a smattering of Pinot Blanc, Pinot Gris and

Meunier. Good acidity, but needs some plumper fruit for a higher score.

🍷 Now–2002 ⓔ

BEL LAGO 1998 BRUT, LEELANU PENINSULA

Estery nose, but clean on the palate, with nice acid, focus and structure.

🍷 Now–2001 ⓔ

BELLAVISTA
Franciacorta, Italy

BELLAVISTA NV CUVÉE BRUT

Fresh, perfumed, light, Chardonnay aroma, crisp finish.

🍷 Now–2001 ⓔⓔⓔ 🍾 31,000 Lira

BELLAVISTA NV GRAN CUVÉE SATÈN

Very fresh, young and fruity. Not sure that I could classify this mousse as Satèn (i.e., lower pressure, akin to the original concept of *crémant*) under blind conditions, but good fruit nonetheless.

🍷 Now–2002 ⓔⓔⓔ 🍾 45,000 Lira

BELLAVISTA 1996 GRAN CUVÉE BRUT

Fat yet crisp.

🍷 Now–2002 ⓔⓔⓔ 🍾 43,000 Lira

BELLAVISTA 1995 GRAN CUVÉE BRUT ROSÉ

Fresh, crisp, toasty raspberry fruit with very crisp acidity.

🍷 Now–2002 ⓔⓔⓔ 🍾 45,000 Lira

BELLAVISTA 1993 GRAN CUVÉE PAS OPERE

White chocolate.

🍷 Now–2001 ⓔⓔⓔ

BERGKELDER
Stellenbosch, South Africa

PONGRACZ NV CAP CLASSIQUE

This wine is being released younger and younger, but it has a smooth presentation of fruit and pin-cushion

mousse in the mouth.
▮ Now–2002 ⓔ ☖ R45

BERLUCCHI, FRATELLI

Franciacorta, Italy

BERLUCCHI F.LLI 1996 BRUT

Almonds, fulsome, satisfying in its way, nice mousse, tiny bubbles.
▮ Now–2001 ⓔⓔ ☖ 26,000 Lira

BERLUCCHI F.LLI 1996 SATÈN

Full and satisfying with a touch of vanilla.
▮ Now–2002 ⓔⓔⓔ ☖ 32,000 Lira

BERSANO

Asti, Italy

BERSANO NV BRACHETTO D'ACQUI DOLCE 83

Intensely sweet, highly perfumed Moscato fruit.
▮ Now ⓔ

BERSANO NV ASTI DOLCE 84

Like a mouthful of concentrated Cox's Orange Pippin, only much sweeter.
▮ Now ⓔ

BERSI SERLINI

Franciacorta, Italy

BERSI SERLINI NV SATÈN 75

Fresh and easy, young and fruity.
▮ Now–2001 ⓔⓔ ☖ 25,000 Lira

BERSI SERLINI NV DEMISEC NUVOLA 77

Fresh and fine with excellent fruit on nose, very satisfying on nose.
▮ Now–2002 ⓔⓔ ☖ 23,000 Lira

BERTHET-BONDET

Jura, France

DOMAINE BERTHET-BONDET NV CRÉMANT DU JURA

This concoction of peppery fruit and excellent acidity makes for something different and interesting.
▮ Now–2001 ⓔ ☖ 44FF

BESSERAT DE BELLEFON

Champagne Besserat de Bellefon
19 Avenue de Champagne
51205 Epernay
☎(326) 59.51.00 🖷(326) 59.51.19

BESSERAT DE BELLEFON NV CUVÉE DES MOINES, BLANC DE BLANCS BRUT

Strong, expansive fruit that relies more on character than finesse.
▮ Now–2002 ⓔⓔⓔ ☖ 200FF

BESSERAT DE BELLEFON NV CUVÉE DES MOINES, BRUT

Rich, tasty and *vif*, with room for further development.
▮ Now–2002 ⓔⓔⓔ ☖ 160FF

BESTHEIM

Alsace, France

BESTHEIM NV CRÉMANT D'ALSACE BRUT 76

Fresh, frothy fruit and a darn sight more elegance than the label suggests!
▮ Now–2001 ⓔ

BESTHEIM NV AN 2000 PRESTIGE, CRÉMANT D'ALSACE BRUT 76

Just as much fresh fruit as the basic Bestheim Crémant d'Alsace, but in a more restrained style.
▮ Now–2001 ⓔ

CUVÉE MADAME SANS-GÈNE 1996 BLANC DE BLANCS, CRÉMANT D'ALSACE BRUT 72

Rich and fruity with a touch of creaminess, but the flavour could be more persistent on the finish, indicating that this wine was probably

at its peak last year.
❗ Now ⓔ

BETTINZANA
Franciacorta, Italy

**BETTINZANA NV
FRANCIACORTA BRUT**

Crisp, toasty fruit, fine acidity.
❗ Now–2001 ⓔⓔ

BIDDENDEN
Ashford, Kent, England, UK

BIDDENDEN 1997 BRUT

It might sound strange, but if someone
told me that this wine contains 10–20%
Pilsner, I would not disbelieve it.
Furthermore, I don't dislike the result!
❗ Now ⓔ

BIDDENDEN 1998 BRUT ⑦④

With just Reichensteiner and Pinot Noir
(the 1997 also included Ortega and
Muller-Thurgau), this is a much more
aromatic style with fresh muscatty aromas
and more focused fruit.
❗ Now–2001 ⓔ

BILLECART-SALMON
Champagne Billecart-Salmon
40 rue Carnot
51160 Mareuil-sur-Aÿ
☎(326) 52.60.22 📠(326) 52.64.88

**BILLECART-SALMON NV 2000
BRUT RÉSERVE** ⑧⑨

If this has been kept longer than the
normal Brut Réserve there is no
indication whatsoever of any ageing as
such. Perhaps there is an even greater
concentration of fruit, but Billecart-
Salmon's Brut Réserve is never short of
fruit. One thing is for sure and that is the
2000 is the best Brut Réserve in my
memory and I can remember some utterly
delicious releases of this *cuvée*.

❗ Now–2005 ⓔⓔⓔ 🍷 170FF

**BILLECART-SALMON NV
BRUT ROSÉ**

Few rosés can match Billecart-Salmon's
pale-peach coloured rosé for elegance.
This release has delicate raspberry-cherry
fruit aromas and a relatively fattish finish
brimming with sassy Pinot fruit.
❗ Now–2001 ⓔⓔⓔ 🍷 255FF

**BILLECART-SALMON NV
DEMI-SEC RÉSERVE**

I tasted well over 50 Demi-Sec
Champagnes this year and this was one
of just three that stood out because of its
real depth of flavour. While you can
certainly drink this Champagne now, only
a fool would. My advice is to keep it at
least 18 months.
❗ Now–2005 ⓔⓔ 🍷 170FF

**BILLECART-SALMON 1989
GRANDE CUVÉE**

I preferred the Cuvée Nicolas François,
but this Pinot-scented Champagne will
improve after 12 months further ageing.
▬ 2001–2002 ⓔⓔⓔⓔ 🍷 580FF

**BILLECART-SALMON 1990
GRANDE CUVÉE**

This is a later disgorged version of Cuvée
Nicolas François Billecart, Billecart-
Salmon's prestige *cuvée*, and the fruit-
laden 1990 is as stunning as anyone who
tasted the Cuvée Nicolas François could
possibly hope.
❗ Now–2015 ⓔⓔⓔⓔ 🍷 580FF

BISCHOFFINGEN
*Winzergenossenschaft Bischoffingen
Baden, Germany*

**WINZERGENOSSENSCHAFT
BISCHOFFINGEN
SPÄTBURGUNDER B 1997
BISCHOFFINGER ENSELBER**

Fresh, frothy fruit, so soft and creamy on
the finish.
❗ Now ⓔ

BLANCK

Domaine Paul Blanck
Alsace, France

BLANCK 1997 CRÉMANT D'ALSACE, EXTRA BRUT

This wine has some finesse for an Extra Brut, but it would have had a longer finish and thus more finesse if dosaged as a Brut.
❙ Now–2001 ⓔ

BLASS

Wolf Blass
South Australia, Australia

WOLF BLASS 1996 VINTAGE PINOT NOIR CHARDONNAY

Nice lightly balanced, satisfying, clean, sherbety fruit, but wouldn't this bottle look better with an understated label, possibly ticket-sized?
❙ Now–2001 ⓔ ❦ A$17

WOLF BLASS WINES NV BLASS BRUT

Fresh, frothy, easy drinking fruit.
❙ Now ⓔ ❦ A$13

BLIN

Champagne H. Blin
4 rue de Verdun
51700 Vincelles
☎(326) 58.20.04 ℻(326) 58.29.67

H. BLIN & CO NV BRUT TRADITION

The fruit might be a touch elevated, but it makes a nice, crisp aperitif style.
❙ Now–2001 ⓔⓔ

H. BLIN & CO 1995 BRUT

The pre-release sample I tasted was already starting to go biscuity, but there's at least three more years of prime-time drinking left in this rich, stylish Champagne.
❙ Now–2003 ⓔⓔ

BLONDEL

Champagne Th. Blondel
Domaine des Monts Fournois
51500 Ludes
☎(326) 03.43.92 ℻(326) 03.44.10

TH. BLONDEL NV CARTE OR BRUT, PREMIER CRU

Clean, focused fruit, capable of further development.
❙ Now–2002 ⓔⓔ ❦ 80FF

TH. BLONDEL 1995 BRUT MILLÉSIME, PREMIER CRU BLANC DE BLANCS

Classic biscuity-rich style with plenty of acidity.
❙ Now–2003 ⓔⓔ ❦ 100FF

BLUE PYRENEES ESTATE

Victoria, Australia

BLUE PYRENEES ESTATE NV MIDNIGHT CUVÉE

Perfumed, creamy fruit. Great for those who like a touch of the exotic.
❙ Now ⓔⓔ ❦ A$26

BLUE PYRENEES ESTATE RESERVE NV BRUT

Really quite sweet, but don't let that put Brut drinkers off because it's actually very good. Use this to accompany a savoury dish with a fruit sauce (cherries, orange, red fruits, etc).
❙ Now–2001 ⓔ ❦ A$19

BOIZEL

Champagne Boizel
14 rue de Bernon
51200 Epernay
☎(326) 55.21.51 ℻(326) 54.31.83

BOIZEL NV CHARDONNAY BRUT BLANC DE BLANCS

Nice mellow, creamy fruit on the palate, but the bouquet requires time to blossom.
➤ 2001–2003 ⓔⓔⓔ

BOIZEL 1990 CUVÉE SOUS BOIS, BRUT 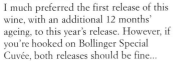 88

I much preferred the first release of this wine, with an additional 12 months' ageing, to this year's release. However, if you're hooked on Bollinger Special Cuvée, both releases should be fine...

➤ Wait and see ££££

BOIZEL 1991 JOYAU DE FRANCE, BRUT 89

This vintage of Boizel's prestige *cuvée* is drinking beautifully right now, yet there is so much more potential waiting to be released that true Champagne lovers will instantly recognize that it begs a further year or two in bottle.

❢ Now–2005 £££

BOIZEL 1989 JOYAU DE CHARDONNAY, BRUT 89

The *blanc de blancs* version of Boizel's prestige *cuvée* is new to me, but I have tasted pure Chardonnay Champagne dating back to 1928 from this house, so the idea of releasing a mature, top-quality *blanc de blancs* makes sense. This wine has exceptional finesse and complexity for a 1989 *blanc de blancs*, with a Pinot-like structure, particularly on the finish, although there are no black grapes in this *cuvée*, of course. A dazzling first release.

❢ Now–2009 £££

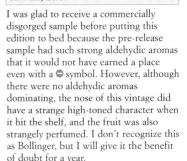

BOLLINGER

Champagne Jacques Bruère Blanc de Blancs
16 rue Jules Lobet
51160 Aÿ-Champagne
☎(326) 53.33.66 ☏(326) 54.85.59

BOLLINGER 1990 GRANDE ANNÉE, ROSÉ BRUT ⊖

Both samples of this year's release were marred by a murky mushroom aroma, but I've included it in the Guide to reassure readers who purchased this Champagne based on my last year's score of 89 points. After discovering that both samples of this wine were so dire, I dug out a sample cellared since last year and that was as clean as a whistle.

➤ Wait and see ££££

BOLLINGER 1992 GRANDE ANNÉE, BRUT ⊖

I was glad to receive a commercially disgorged sample before putting this edition to bed because the pre-release sample had such strong aldehydic aromas that it would not have earned a place even with a ⊖ symbol. However, although there were no aldehydic aromas dominating, the nose of this vintage did have a strange high-toned character when it hit the shelf, and the fruit was also strangely perfumed. I don't recognize this as Bollinger, but I will give it the benefit of doubt for a year.

➤ Wait and see ££££

BOLLINGER 1988 R.D. EXTRA BRUT 90

If you are worried about some disgorgements (such as 14 October 1999), my advice is to leave it in your cellar for a few years because the quality of the core-wine is beyond question. This will never age as gracefully as the Grande Année Brut (94 points) because of the lower dosage, but it will improve enormously.

➤ Wait and see ££££

BOLLINGER 1985 R.D. EXTRA BRUT 90

This year's release is even worse than last year's, yet I have had the original Grande Année disgorgement a number of times over the last 24 months and it has been every bit as sensational as when I first reviewed the wine (96 points). Proof positive that the choice of timing of a Champagne's disgorgement makes all the difference, and that extra time on yeast does not always improve a Champagne, even a great one.

➤ Wait and see ££££

BONIFACE

Savoie, France

LES ROCAILLES PIERRE BONIFACE NV BRUT 74

Fresh, floral, perfumed. Excellent après ski.

❢ Now £

BONNET

Champagne Alexandre Bonnet
138 rue du Général-de-Gaulle
10340 Les-Riceys
☎(325) 29.30.93 📠(325) 29.38.65

ALEXANDRE BONNET NV CUVÉE PRESTIGE BRUT — 84

A satisfying richness of fruit balanced by a crisp finish.
🍷 Now–2003 ⓔⓔ

ALEXANDRE BONNET NV BRUT ROSÉ — 83

Fresh strawberryish fruit with an aftertaste that builds in the mouth.
🍷 Now–2002 ⓔⓔ

ALEXANDRE BONNET 1993 BLANC DE BLANCS BRUT — 87

Old-fashioned, mature, toasty Chardonnay Champagne for aficionados only and even then to drink upon purchase.
🍷 Now ⓔⓔ

ALEXANDRE BONNET NV CUVÉE TRADITION, BRUT — 86

Rich fruit in a firm structure with truly splendid acidity.
🍷 Now–2004 ⓔⓔ

MADRIGAL 1993 BRUT, ALEXANDRE BONNET — 81

Some serious yeast-complexed fruit aromas, but lacks the degree of finesse necessary for a higher score.
🍷 Now–2002 ⓔⓔ

BOOKERS
Haywards Heath, Sussex, England, UK

BOOKERS 1995 BART'S BUBBLY ROSÉ — 74

A classic for those who love farmyard Pinot.
🍷 Now ⓔⓔ

BOSCHENDAL
Paarl, South Africa

BOSCHENDAL 1993 CAP CLASSIQUE, BRUT — 80

Biscuity aromas, excellent acidity, good mouth feel and a fruity finish.
🍷 Now–2001 ⓔ 🍇 R48

BOSCHI
Franciacorta, Italy

BOSCHI NV FRANCIACORTA BRUT — 78

1st corked. 2nd fine, clean fruit, crisp. Lovely structure.
🍷 Now–2003 ⓔⓔ

BOTHY
Frilford Heath, England, UK

BOTHY 1996 JESSICA CLARE FISHER, DRY — 74

This vintage is not due to be released until 2001, but it is ready now, with fresh, peachy aromas, soft fruit and a breezy finish. Another year on yeast could be a disadvantage for this style of sparkling wine.
🍷 Now–2001 ⓔ

BOULARD

Champagne Raymond Boulard
1 et 4 rue du Tambour
51480 La Neuville aux Larris
☎(326) 58.12.08 📠(326) 58.13.02

RAYMOND BOULARD NV BRUT GRAND CRU MAILLY-CHAMPAGNE — 82

Creamy fruit with a hint of biscuitiness that only comes out with warming in the glass, thus mature but very fresh for its age.
🍷 Now–2003 ⓔⓔ 🍇 119FF

RAYMOND BOULARD NV RÉSERVE BRUT

Good attack on palate, but needs more finesse on nose to achieve a higher score.
Now–2001 ©© ⚲ 110FF

RAYMOND BOULARD NV CUVÉE ROSE, BRUT

Plenty of strawberry-Pinot fruit, but closer to Extra-Sec or even Sec than Brut, although that makes it user-friendly for large gatherings and this impression of sweetness can be useful when partnering some savoury dishes with fruit ingredients.
Now–2001 ©© ⚲ 115FF

RAYMOND BOULARD NV BLANC DE BLANCS BRUT

Attractively fresh and crisp, pineapple fruit on the palate, but the estery aromas suggest that this should have been kept a further 6–12 months on yeast. However, cellaring the wine for a year after purchase should settle things down.
2001–2003 ©© ⚲ 112FF

❖ **BOURGEOIS**/J. Bourgeois, *see* Marne et Champagne

ATTENTION CHAMPAGNE & SPARKLING WINE PRODUCERS!

If you are not already in contact with the author, but would like to submit wines for consideration in future editions, please contact Tom Stevenson at:

tom.stevenson@fizz.worldonline.co.uk

Warning: Any other unsolicited mail received at this address will be ignored.

Please note that recommendation in this guide involves no charge whatsoever beyond the cost of the samples and their delivery.

BOURILLON-DORLÉANS

Loire, France

DOMAINE BOURILLON-DORLÉANS 1996 CUVÉE HÉLÈNE DORLÉANS BRUT MILLÉSIME, VOUVRAY

A generous Brut dosage makes this wine fresher than its years and extremely user-

---

friendly. A good reception aperitif.
Now–2002 ©

BOURSAULT

Champagne Château de Boursault
Boursault 51480 prés Epernay
☎(326) 58.42.21 ℻(326) 58.66.12

CHÂTEAU DE BOURSAULT NV BRUT TRADITION

Elegantly balanced, but the sulphur in the dosage demands at least 12 months' ageing before this will become evident. Should go toasty and has plenty of nice acidity to allow this to happen with some finesse.
 2001–2002 ©©

BOUVET

Loire, France

BOUVET NV CRÉMANT EXCELLENCE BRUT

An elegant wine with fresh, creamy, satisfying fruit, but let down by cheap wire cage securing the cork. Surely Bouvet can afford anodized wire for all its *cuvées*?
Now–2001 ©

BOUVET 1998 SAPHIR BRUT VINTAGE, SAUMUR

Very high acidity, but not at all unripe. This could have scored even higher with a larger, but balanced, dosage.
Now–2001 ©

BOUVET-LADUBAY 1997 TRESOR BRUT, SAUMU

The freshly disgorged, most recently shipped examples of this wine have fresh *barrique* aromas, with an attractively light body of fruit, whereas last year's release when aged tended to emphasize the structure and oakiness on the palate, with creamy richness of fruit on the finish. However, although the recent disgorgement showed some autolytic finesse on the nose, both lacked the degree of finesse required to break out of the scoring in the 70s, something last achieved by the 1995 (82 points).

❦ Now–2001 ⓔⓔ

BOUVET-LADUBAY 1998 SAPHIR, SAUMUR

A clean, fresh relief in a Saumur tasting. Smaller bubbles than most, good acidity.

❦ Now–2001 ⓔ

BOUVET-LADUBAY NV TRESOR ROSÉ, SAUMUR

Nice acidity, but let down by estery-oxidative aroma. Probably disgorged too early, wait and see.

➤ Wait and see ⓔⓔ

BREAKY BOTTOM

Lewes, England, UK

BREAKY BOTTOM, MILLENNIUM CUVÉE MAMAN MERCIER 1996 CUVÉE RÉSERVE BRUT

Very fresh, with initially attractive fruit that would have scored higher, but was let down by a touch of greenness on the finish.

❦ Now–2001 ⓔⓔ

BREDASOLE

Franciacorta, Italy

BREDASOLE NV FRANCIACORTA EXTRA BRUT

Fresh, crisp fruit, with a nicely prominent Chardonnay aroma.

❦ Now–2001 ⓔⓔ 🍇 28,000 Lira

BREDASOLE NV FRANCIACORTA BRUT

Distinctive Chardonnay aroma. Creamy, fruit-driven style, almost New World.

❦ Now–2002 ⓔⓔ 🍇 28,000 Lira

BREWERY HILL

South Australia, Australia
Formerly St Francis Winery

BREWERY HILL NV PREMIUM SPARKLING SHIRAZ

Mellow-toasty-creamy-oaky fruit with a snap of sweetness on the finish.

❦ Now–2001 ⓔ 🍇 A$14.40

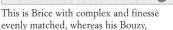

BRICE

Champagne Brice
3 rue Yvonnet
51150 Bouzy
☎(326) 52.06.60 ℻(326) 57.05.07

BRICE NV AŸ GRAND CRU BRUT 88

This is Brice with complex and finesse evenly matched, whereas his Bouzy, which vies with this wine to be his best, is weighted more on complexity than finesse. This *cuvée* has a lovely structure with beautifully fresh and elegant fruit.

❦ Now–2005 ⓔⓔ

BRICE NV BOUZY GRAND CRU BRUT

While serious Pinot aromas dominate this *cuvée* from the start, the palate can be deceptively easy with fresh, approachable fruit that can sometimes even seem simple and rather basic, but within a year everything comes together.

➤ 2001–2003 ⓔⓔ

BRICE NV CRAMANT GRAND CRU BRUT

Fresh, creamy Chardonnay fruit, with citrussy aromas mid-palate and a creamy-smooth finish.

❦ Now–2003 ⓔⓔ

BRICE NV VERZENAY GRAND CRU BRUT

Firm and fresh with creaminess just beginning to develop on the finish.

❦ Now–2004 ⓔⓔ

BRL HARDY

South Australia, Australia

LEASINGHAM CLASSIC CLARE SPARKLING SHIRAZ 1992

Extraordinarily fresh and at first

seemingly fruit-driven, but there's quite a bit of oak and tannin lurking in the background.

❚ Now–2002 ⓔ

SIR JAMES BRUT DE BRUT NV PINOT NOIR CHARDONNAY

This toasty sparkling wine has very good acidity and obviously comes from mature stock.

❚ Now ⓔ 🍇 A$12.95

SIR JAMES SHIRAZ NV

Sweet oaky-shiraz with bubbles and tannin! Nice creamy aftertaste.

❚ Now ⓔⓔ 🍇 A$21.95

YARRA BURN 1997 PINOT NOIR CHARDONNAY

Full and rich, with a soft vanilla aftertaste, but lacks the finesse necessary for higher score.

❚ Now ⓔ 🍇 A$19.95

BROGSITTER
Mosel-Saar-Ruwer, Germany

BROGSITTER RIESLING 1997 BRUT

Fresh and light, with peachy fruit. (*Cuve close*.)

❚ Now–2001 ⓔ 🍇 DM16

BROWN BROTHERS
Victoria, Australia

BROWN BROTHERS NV PINOT NOIR CHARDONNAY, KING VALLEY

This is the first really serious fizz I've tasted from Brown Brothers. A bit sweet on finish, but that makes it more user-friendly and allows some ageing potential for more experienced drinkers. I also tasted the next release of this *cuvée* and it scores just as highly and although it has slightly less Chardonnay in percentage terms, its varietal intensity is even greater in a lovely ripe, peachy way, and both releases are preferred to Brown Brothers 1995 vintage.

❚ Now–2002 ⓔ 🍇 A$15.70

BRUGNON
Champagne P. Brugnon
16 rue Carnot
51500 Rilly-la-Montagne
☏(326) 03.44.89 ℻(326) 03.46.02

PHILIPPE BRUGNON NV BRUT

Easy-drinking inexpensive Champagne with nice, mellow fruit.

❚ Now–2002 ⓔⓔ

PHILIPPE BRUGNON 1995 BRUT

Fine bead, fresh red-fruit aromas and crisp fruit finish.

❚ Now–2005 ⓔⓔ

BRUISYARD
Saxmundham, Suffolk, England, UK

BRUISYARD 1998 MILLENNIUM BRUT

Extremely fresh, nicely dry fruit.

❚ Now–2001 ⓔⓔ

BRUN, CELLIER LE
Marlborough, New Zealand

It is now evident that Daniel Le Brun's reputation at Cellier Le Brun was built on wines produced over just three years: 1989, 1990 and 1991. Forget the vintages from 1992 to 1996, when Daniel was enjoying the media spotlight so much that he took his eye off the *bulle* and allowed his grapes to be harvested far too green. That includes the 1996, which was sold as a non-vintage under the Terrace Road label and inexplicably won a number of awards. The quality and reputation of Cellier Le Brun is destined to return when the 1997s are released, albeit with another winemaker, Alan MacWilliams, and thus a different style.

DANIEL LE BRUN 1997 BRUT

I'm not sure when this will be released, but it is the first vintage Brut from this winery that can be recommended since the 1991. Although not in the classic, potentially biscuity style that made Daniel le Brun's reputation, the fresh, ripe citrus and tropical fruits in the 1997 has far more appeal than the green wines harvested 1992–1996 inclusive.

❦ Now–2001 ££

DANIEL LE BRUN 1997 BLANC DE BLANCS BRUT

Better balance, structure and ripeness than any *blanc de blancs* since 1991.

❦ Now–2001 ££

BRUN FAMILY ESTATE, LE

Marlborough, New Zealand

Daniel Le Brun's new family-owned specialist sparkling wine winery opened in 1999. His first release had a touch of greenness to the fruit, but the second release marks the maestro's return to form, while future *cuvées* include what promises to be a superb Daniel 1997 Virginie.

DANIEL NO.1 NV BRUT

The second release, due out soon, has a fuller style, with more Champagne-like fruit, and a touch of vanilla on the finish.

❦ Now–2001 ££

BUHL

Reichsrat v. Buhl
Pfalz, Germany

REICHSRAT VON BUHL 1998 RIESLING BRUT

Sherbety aroma, with deliciously fresh fruit and brimming with finesse.

❦ Now £

REICHSRAT VON BUHL 1996 SPÄTBURGUNDER BRUT

A classically structured Pinot of some class and finesse. Although delicious now, the structure and high, fine acidity suggest this should be interesting to age.

❦ Now–2003 £

BUITENVERWACHTING

Constantia, South Africa

BUITENVERWACHTING NV CAP CLASSIQUE, BRUT

Amylic aromas, but elegant fruit and fine acidity. Allow 12–18 months for amylic aromas to blow off. Tasteful presentation.

◀━ 2001–2002 £ ⚑ R35

CA'DEL BOSCO

Franciacorta, Italy

Hands-on owner Maurizio Zanella has always been a rebel, but one with a cause. Nothing expresses his cause at Ca'del Bosco more emphatically than a vertical of Cuvée Annamaria Clementi, although not all the vintages can be recommended, but as Arnold Bennett once wrote about a cause "like Champagne or highshoes, one must be prepared to suffer for it".

CA'DEL BOSCO NV BRUT

The first bottle was corked, but the second had fine autolytic aroma and a fresh, fruit-driven flavour supported by good structure and a crisp finish.

❦ Now–2001 ££ ⚑ 19,900 Lira

CA'DEL BOSCO 1996 DOSAGE ZERO

Clean, fruity, well-focused.

❦ Now–2001 £££ ⚑ 31,000 Lira

CA'DEL BOSCO 1996 BRUT

Too young when released, but very fruity.

❦ Now–2002 £££ ⚑ 30,000 Lira

CA'DEL BOSCO 1995 SATÈN

Sweet, ripe plums and other stone-fruit. Creamy aftertaste.

❦ Now–2002 £££ ⚑ 34,000 Lira

CA'DEL BOSCO 1996 ROSÉ

Fresh, clean, light, elegant, crisp fruit.

❦ Now–2002 £££ ⚑ 32,000 Lira

CA'DEL BOSCO 1993 BRUT CUVÉE ANNAMARIA CLEMENTI

Tasted both at the generic tasting and at Ca'del Bosco itself, this is a delicious,

rich and creamy *cuvée*, with very soft, biscuity fruit and a creamy-vanilla aftertaste. Not quite in the same class as last year's 1992 (85 points), but close.
❙ Now–2002 ⓔⓔⓔ ❧ 58,000 Lira

CA'DEL BOSCO 1990 BRUT CUVÉE ANNAMARIA CLEMENTI

A luxuriant mousse of minuscule bubbles merely serves to emphasise the intrinsic finesse of this wine's gorgeously soft and silky fruit.
❙ Now–2002 ⓔⓔⓔ

CA'DEL BOSCO 1988 BRUT CUVÉE ANNAMARIA CLEMENTI

Beautifully preserved on its first cork, with super-clean, fruity flavours that would be interesting to age for a year or two after disgorgement.
❙ Now–2002 ⓔⓔⓔ

CA'DEL BOSCO 1996 SATÈN

A sublime combination with *filetti di pesce persico dorato*.
❙ Now–2002 ⓔⓔⓔ ❧ 34,000 Lira

CABELIER
Jura, France

MARCEL CABELIER 1997 CRÉMANT DU JURA BRUT

Probably the best structure of all the Jura wines tasted this year.
❙ Now–2002 ⓔ

CAMEL VALLEY
Bodmin, Cornwall, England, UK

CAMEL VALLEY 1998 CORNWALL BRUT

Disgorged a month before the tasting, thus understandable that the dosage has not married, but the structure and fruit suggest this will be another Camel guzzler by the summertime and should go creamy-biscuity within 12–18 months.
➤ Wait and see ⓔⓔ

CANALS I MUNNE
Penedès, Spain

CANALS I MUNNE, GRAN DUC MILENIUM 1996 CAVA BRUT NATURE

De Venoge's Cuvée des Princes bottle! I ask you, who would bother to copy that? Some flavour and substance and the acidity is not bad, but it still has secondary ferment odours. Opinion reserved until I try this wine again in a year's time.
➤ Wait and see ⓔⓔ ❧ 2,995 Ptas

CANARD-DUCHÊNE
Champagne Canard-Duchêne
1 rue Edmond Canard
Ludes le Coquet
51500 Rilly-la-Montagne
☏(326) 61.10.96 ⅎ(326) 61.13.90

CANARD-DUCHÊNE NV BRUT

Creamy-rich, yeast-complexed fruit with excellent acidity and a nice mellowness developing on the finish. This particular release (L831 laser-printed on the bottle) is the best Canard-Duchêne non-vintage Brut I have ever tasted. Better than the current magnums, better even than *cuvée* used to relaunch this brand in its new livery a few years ago.
❙ Now–2003 ⓔⓔ

CANARD-DUCHÊNE NV BRUT (*magnum*)

Attractively fresh, floral fruit, but this release (L865) lacks the intensity, maturity and potential complexity of the same wine in normal 75cl bottles.
❙ Now–2003 ⓔⓔ

CANARD-DUCHÊNE NV BRUT ROSÉ

Perfumed Pinot fruit that is much fresher than its mature apricot colour suggests.
❙ Now–2001 ⓔⓔ

CANARD-DUCHÊNE 1990 BRUT

Naturally this vintage was much preferred to the 1991, which did not make the cut, but the pepperiness underneath this wine's rich fruit was something of a surprise. It's not something I remember when this vintage was recommended (88 points) in the first edition of this Guide.

❦ Now–2002 ⓔⓔⓔ

CANARD-DUCHÊNE NV CHARLES VII GRANDE CUVÉE, BRUT

The Charles VII has improved to the point where it can be recommended, but the malolactic remains dominant, it still lacks finesse and for a prestige *cuvée* has a long way to go.

❦ Now–2002 ⓔⓔⓔ

CANARD-DUCHÊNE NV CHARLES VII GRANDE CUVÉE, BLANC DE NOIRS BRUT

Where did this style of Charles VII pop-up from? This is the first time I have encountered a *blanc de noirs* version of this *cuvée*, which usually contains 40% Chardonnay. The mature, creamy-malo fruit is obvious, but interesting. However, Canard-Duchêne lose brownie points for sealing a prestige *cuvée* with the worst, mangy old wire cage seen on any Champagne this year.

❦ Now–2001 ⓔⓔⓔ

CANARD-DUCHÊNE NV CHARLES VII GRANDE CUVÉE, ROSÉ BRUT

Classic styled with delicately rich, biscuity fruit.

❦ Now–2002 ⓔⓔⓔ

CANE END
Oxfordshire, England, UK

CANE END 1997 DRY

Fresh, peachy aroma with rich, well-structured fruit, but needs a year or two to soften the mousse.

➤ 2001–2002 ⓔⓔ

CANE END 1996 DRY

Lovely peachy aromas, but the firm structure demands an even higher dosage!

➤ 2001–2002 ⓔⓔ

CAPETTA
Asti, Italy

CAPETTA NV ASTI DOLCE

Higher acidity gives this Asti a finer, longer flavour, lifting it above that of most of its peers.

❦ Now ⓔ

CARNEROS
Domaine Carneros
California, USA

DOMAINE CARNEROS 1993 LE RÊVE, BLANC DE BLANCS BRUT

This is last year's release with an additional 12 months' post-disgorgement ageing. The flavour has intensified and I imagine that there are further developments to come, but it is difficult to tell and it does not have quite as much finesse as it did a year ago, so it drops one point for the time being.

❦ Now–2002 ⓔⓔⓔ ⚱ $55

DOMAINE CARNEROS BY TAITTINGER 1996 BRUT

Very soft and satisfying.

❦ Now–2001 ⓔⓔ ⚱ $21.95

DOMAINE CARNEROS BY TAITTINGER 1995 BRUT

Really starting to peak now. This was the first year that the label of the basic vintage promoted Taittinger from small print to "by Taittinger" and why not?

❦ Now ⓔⓔ ⚱ $19.95

DOMAINE CARNEROS BY TAITTINGER 1997 BRUT

This vintage is due to be launched just before publication, but the pre-release sample already showed elegant, satisfying fruit.

❦ Now–2001 ⓔⓔ

DOMAINE CARNEROS BY TAITTINGER 1994 LE RÊVE, BLANC DE BLANCS BRUT

Not as complex as the 1993 was last year, but deliciously fresh and crisp, with at

least as much finesse.
❦ Now–2004 ⓔⓔⓔ

DOMAINE CARNEROS BY TAITTINGER 1993 LE RÊVE, BLANC DE BLANCS BRUT

The latest release of Le Rêve 1993 can be identified from the addition of "by Taittinger" on the label. After an extra year on yeast the *barrique* aromas have dropped away from the nose and have become immersed in the fruit on the palate, suggesting that the potential complexity and longevity is even greater than I had initially imagined.
❦ Now–2003 ⓔⓔⓔ 🍷 $55.00

DOMAINE CARNEROS 1994 BRUT

Not quite as crisp and invigorating as last year (five years seems the peak for Domaine Carneros basic vintage), but still retains freshness and beats a lot of younger California fizz.
❦ Now ⓔⓔ

CAROD
Rhône, France

CAROD 1995 CRÉMANT DE DIE BRUT

This fresh, fruity fizz is perhaps a touch sweet for a brut, but when no other Crémant de Die is worth recommending and 80% of the failures are rejected on the nose alone, who cares?
❦ Now–2001 ⓔ

CAROD FRÈRES CLAIRETTE DE DIE NV MÉTHODE DIOISE ANCESTRALE

Fresh, frothy, muscat fruit.
❦ Now ⓔⓔ

❖ **CARR TAYLOR**, *see* Chapel Down

CARTERS
Boxted, Essex, England, UK

LOVEJOY 1995 BRUT

This spiv's fizz would have benefited from higher first fermentation temperature and a year less on yeast, but its cool-fermented fruit is at least easy on the palate.
❦ Now–2001 ⓔⓔ

CASTELFAGLIA
Franciacorta, Italy

CASTELFAGLIA NV FRANCIACORTA EXTRA BRUT

Very fine aroma, fine lemony-aromatic fruit, excellent acidity and structure.
❦ Now–2002 ⓔⓔ

CASTELFAGLIA NV FRANCIACORTA BRUT MONOGRAM

Fine autolytic aroma, fine, crisply-structured fruit.
❦ Now–2001 ⓔⓔ

CASTELLINO
*Tenuta Castellino
Franciacorta, Italy*

Tenuta Castellino NV Franciacorta Brut

Very fresh, crisp aroma, focused lemony fruit.
❦ Now–2001 ⑥⑥ ⚜ 18,000 Lira

Tenuta Castellino NV Franciacorta Satèn

Rich and satisfying. Nice acidity, very soft and silky mousse, creamy.
❦ Now–2002 ⑥⑥ ⚜ 22,000 Lira

Tenuta Castellino 1995 Franciacorta Brut

A structurally impressive wine with oodles of fruit in support.
❦ Now–2002 ⑥⑥ ⚜ 22,000 Lira

CASTELL
Fürstlich Castell'sches Domänenamt
Franken, Germany

Fürstlich Castell'sches Domänenamt Brut 1996 Schloss Castell

The perfumed Riesling fruit might lack finesse, but I like the aftertaste. (*Méthode champenoise.*)
❦ Now–2001 ⑥ ⚜ DM24

Fürstlich Castell'sches Domänenamt Brut 1998 Schloss Castell

Fresh, frothy fruit. Ideal picnic wine for a picnic with a touch of class. (*Méthode champenoise.*)
❦ Now ⑥ ⚜ DM24

CASTELVEDER
Franciacorta, Italy

Castelveder NV Franciacorta Brut

Fresh, floral, creamy fruit, nice crisp finish, touch of malo creaminess on aftertaste.
❦ Now–2002 ⑥⑥ ⚜16,000 Lira

Castelveder 1995 Brut 80

Creamy rich fruit, satisfying.

❦ Now–2002 ⑥⑥ ⚜ 26,000 Lira

CATTIER
Champagne Cattier
6–11 rue Dom Pérignon
51500 Chigny-les-Roses
☎(326) 03.42.11 ℻(326) 03.43.13

Cattier NV Brut Rosé

Fresh and light with easy-going fruit.
❦ Now–2001 ⑥⑥

Cattier 1995 Brut Premier Cru 88

An ultra-fruity Champagne that will evolve slowly, eventually building up violety-vanilla finesse on the aftertaste.
❦ Now–2010 ⑥⑥⑥

Clos du Moulin NV Brut Premier Cru, Cattier

This blend of 1988, 1989 and 1990 (check the back label) is the best Clos du Moulin produced so far, with its wonderfully rich, mature, creamy-biscuity fruit. For aficionados only. Others won't believe it, but if you cellar this at a cool, even temperature for a few years, it will seem to get younger as it takes on more and more finesse.
❦ Now–2005 ⑥⑥⑥

CAVALLERI
Franciacorta, Italy

Cavalleri NV Franciacorta Satèn

Light and fresh, very fresh, Chardonnay driven fruit.
❦ Now–2002 ⑥⑥ ⚜ 28,700 Lira

Cavalleri 1995 Franciacorta Pas Dosé Collection 78

Crisp and creamy, with a touch of *barrique*.
❦ Now–2001 ⑥⑥ ⚜ 26,700 Lira

Cavalleri 1995 Franciacorta Brut Collezione

Rich and biscuity, fine acidity.
❦ Now–2002 ⑥⑥⑥ ⚜ 35,000 Lira

CAVALLERI 1995 FRANCIACORTA ROSÉ COLLEZIONE

Very firm, raspberry fruit.
Now–2002 ©©© ⚗ 35,000 Lira

CAZANOVE

Champagne Charles de Cazanove
1 rue des Cotelles
51204 Epernay
☎(326) 59.57.40 ℻(326) 54.16.38

CHARLES DE CAZANOVE NV BRUT CLASSIQUE

Better than last year, although not as good as it was two or three years ago, the current release just needs six months or so to bring the nose into line with the crisp, fresh, fruit-salad flavour on the palate.
2001–2003 ©© ⚗ 100FF

CHARLES DE CAZANOVE NV BRUT AZUR, PREMIER CRU

This is always fuller, firmer and more traditional in style than De Cazanove's Brut Classique, with higher acidity and plenty of biscuity richness on the finish, but this year's release is better than ever.
Now–2003 ©© ⚗ 130FF

CHARLES DE CAZANOVE NV GRANDE RÉSERVE AN 2000 BRUT

My goodness, De Cazanove is certainly on form this year! This *cuvée* reveals such lovely, rich, silky fruit and this is further enhanced by the creaminess of its mousse, which produces a wonderful finesse on the finish. Great potential complexity. And I just love the harlequin presentation. As soon as I saw the results, I purchased a case. Convinced?
Now–2003 ©© ⚗ 100FF

CHARLES DE CAZANOVE NV BRUT ROSÉ

A firm, fruity rosé that will go toasty.
Now–2003 ©© ⚗ 120FF

CHARLES DE CAZANOVE 1992 BRUT AZUR, PREMIER CRU

After a belly-full of oxidative Champagnes, it is getting to the point where I can only put up with those

aromas which also have a certain creaminess and are followed by a real amount of good fruit on the palate, as we have here.
Now–2002 ©© ⚗ 150FF

❖ **CELLER BATTLE,** *see* Gramona

❖ **CELLIER LE BRUN,** *see* Brun

CERUTTI

Asti, Italy

CERUTTI NV ASTI CESARE

The intensity of flavour in this bottle-fermented Asti is impressive, but the aroma is dulled by malo. No aromatic variety should ever go through malolactic and I cannot imagine that anyone in Asti would do this deliberately, but it can happen unintentionally in the bottle. Asti Cesare certainly has the makings of a very special wine indeed, thus I look forward to tasting non-malolactic *cuvées* in the future.
Now ©© ⚗ 25,000 Lira

CHANDON (AUSTRALIA)

*Domaine Chandon Australia
Victoria, Australia*

DOMAINE CHANDON NV BRUT PREMIUM CHARDONNAY PINOT NOIR

Fresh, easy-drinking, delicately perfumed fruit; ideal for drinking now, aperitif.
Now–2001 ©

DOMAINE CHANDON 1995 VICTORIA CUVÉE PINOT NOIR CHARDONNAY PINOT MEUNIER

Rich and tasty.
Now–2001 ©©

GREEN POINT BY CHANDON 1997 BRUT

Really very nice and soft, with a pin-cushion mousse and fresh, delicate, sherbety fruit.
Now ©© ⚗ A$26

GREEN POINT BY CHANDON 1997 BRUT ROSÉ

Fresh, easy-drinking, nice acidity.
Now–2002 ©© ❦ A$26

GREEN POINT BY CHANDON 1991 BRUT

I pulled a few different releases of the 1991 from my own cellar to see how this vintage has aged and was amazed by the beautiful integration of the mousse and fruit, although the fruit in EU Lot number L19 was starting to dry.
Now–2002 ©©

GREEN POINT BY CHANDON 1992 BRUT

More fruit but less finesse than the 1991.
Now ©©

GREEN POINT BY CHANDON 1993 BRUT

Succulent Pinot Noir dominated fruit.
Now ©©

CHANOINE
Champagne Chanoine
Avenue de Champagne
51100 Reims
☎ (326) 36.61.60 ⊠(326) 36.66.62

CHANOINE NV GRANDE RÉSERVE BRUT

This overtly fruity *cuvée* makes an ideal stepping stone from New World fizz to classic Champagne.
Now–2002 ©©

TSARINE NV TÊTE DE CUVÉE BRUT, CHANOINE

Fresh, easy-going fruit underscored by a fine filigree of pinprick size bubbles.
Now–2002 ©© ❦ 129FF

TSARINE 1995 BRUT MILLÉSIME, CHANOINE

A rich, creamy-biscuity Champagne made in a food-wine style.
Now–2002 ©©© ❦ 149FF

CHANTAL
Château Chantal
Michigan, USA

CARPE DIEM SEMI-DRY SPARKLING WINE NV CHÂTEAU CHANTAL

I hate to see "semi" on any wine, but this is a fun wine with lovely creamy fruit and immediate accessibility.
Now ©

CHAPEL DOWN
Tenterden, England, UK

In July 2000, Chapel Down merged with Lamberhurst, which had taken over Carr Taylor prior to its own acquisition by a business consortium in late 1999. The new owners of Lamberhurst had plans to focus on sparkling wine, which they saw as having the greatest potential of all English wines. Apparently their ideas were complementary with those of Chapel Down, thus instead of starting from scratch, they threw their investment into one merged pot. The combined company now owns 38 hectares of vineyards and access to a further 73 hectares under contract.

CARR TAYLOR NV BRUT

Carr Taylor is back on form with summertime quaffer. Its attractive peachy aroma would suggest ripe Chardonnay, but there isn't any in this 40% Pinot Noir *cuvée* as the rest of the blend is described as "other red varieties".
Now–2001 ©

CARR TAYLOR NV ROSÉ RÉSERVE

A perfumed nose leads into aromatic fruit with sweet fruit fatness on the finish.
Now–2001 ©

CHAPEL DOWN 1995 EPOCH VINTAGE BRUT

This vintage has always possessed less peachiness than previous years, but it makes a more serious accompaniment to food and does develop a lovely violetty-vanilla finesse on the finish if kept a year or more after purchase.
Now–2002 ©

CHAPEL DOWN NV EPOCH, BRUT

Much fresher than previous releases, the non-vintage Epoch is beginning to develop a serious, food-wine style.
❗ Now–2001 ⓔ

CHAPEL DOWN NV MILLENNIUM MAGNUM, BRUT

Initially there was an almost metallic edge to this blend of Pinot Noir, Rivaner and Reichensteiner from 1995, 1996 and 1997, but when I went back to it this had been replaced by a more focused crispness of nicely aromatic fruit, which suggests that it should be worth laying down for a year or two. A limited release of 2,000 magnums.
2001–2003 ⓔⓔ

CHAPEL DOWN 1995 CUVÉE PINOT, BRUT

Very Pinot (it's actually a blend of Pinot Noir and Pinot Blanc), but no autolysis and no post-disgorgement aromas.
❗ Now ⓔⓔ

CHARBAUT

Champagne Guy Charbaut
12 rue du Pont
51160 Mareuil-sur-Aÿ
☎(326) 52.80.59 ⅏(326) 51.91.49

GUY CHARBAUT NV CUVÉE DE RÉSERVE BRUT

Plenty of elevated fruit.
❗ Now–2002 ⓔⓔ

GUY CHARBAUT NV BRUT ROSÉ

I was unimpressed with the UK shipment in early 2000, but samples sent direct from France had bags of fresh, rich, cherry fruit. Obviously a Champagne that does not benefit from too much ageing.
❗ Now ⓔⓔ

GUY CHARBAUT 1995 MEMORY BLANC DE BLANC ⑧⑤

The first bottle stank like an overripe Brie de Meaux, but the second was as clean as a whistle, with fresh, lemony fruit that promised to go toasty. Rust marks around the lip of the bottle indicate the use of cheap crown-caps, when any vintage Champagne should really have stainless-steel caps, considering how long they are likely to be aged prior to disgorgement. This corrosion could explain the stinky bottle, due to an ingress of air and bacteria. The wire cage is also cheap and nasty. The good news is, however, that Charbaut is trying to replicate the classic, slow-maturing *blanc de blancs* that it was famous for under the Charbaut Certificate label, when this family owned the Epernay-based Champagne house bearing its name (since sold to Vranken). If Charbaut can match the quality of the cap and cage with the quality of the wine inside the bottle, it should be a winner.
❗ Now–2002 ⓔⓔⓔ

CHARD FARM

Central Otago, New Zealand

Failing miserably with local fruit, yet strangely successful with Arcadia from Marlborough.

ARCADIA 1996 LAKE HAYES

Very fine creamy-oxidative complexity on the nose, followed by excellent fruit with nicely understated malo-creaminess on the finish, and a superb mousse of slow-rising ultra-fine bubbles. Out of its class for Chard Farm. The use of Lake Hayes on the label is misleading because this wine is made from 100% Marlborough fruit.
❗ Now–2003 ⓔⓔ

CHARTOGNE-TAILLET

Champagne Chartogne-Taillet
37-39 Grande Rue
51220 Merfy
☎(326) 03.10.17 ⅏(326) 03.19.15

CHARTOGNE-TAILLET 1995 CUVÉE SAINTE-ANNE BRUT

A full, oxidatively complex aroma followed by biscuity-rich fruit.
❗ Now–2003 ⓔⓔⓔ

❖ **CHÂTEAU CHANTAL**, *see* Chantal

❖ **CHÂTEAU FRANK**, see Frank

❖ **CHÂTEAU DE BOURSAULT**, *see* Boursault

❖ **CHÂTEAU DE L'ETOILE**, *see* Etoile

❖ **CHÂTEAU DE MONTGUERET**, *see* Montgueret

❖ **CHAUVET**, *see* Quartz Reef

CHEURLIN-DANGIN

Champagne Cheurlin-Dangin
17 Grande-rue
10110 Celles-sur-Ource
☎(325) 38.50.26 ✉(325) 38.58.51

CHEURLIN-DANGIN NV CUVÉE SPÉCIALE, BRUT

Fresh, frothy fruit. More elegance than the basic non-vintage Brut, but picnic-style and less classic.
🍷 Now–2002 ⓔⓔ ▼ 88FF

CHEURLIN-DANGIN NV CUVÉE DU MILLÉNAIRE 2000 BRUT

The concentration and extract is testament to a high degree of selection, but the result is also strangely floral, thus although certainly interesting, opinion must be reserved.
🍷 Wait and see ⓔⓔ

CHEURLIN-DANGIN NV BRUT

Good basic non-vintage with classic fruit structure and an awful 1950s-type label.
🍷 Now–2002 ⓔⓔ ▼ 65FF

CHILFORD HUNDRED

Cambridge, England, UK

CHILFORD HUNDRED 1996 ALURIC DE NORSEHIDE, BRUT

An appealing rosé of some finesse, although nowhere near as good as the 1994 was two years ago.
🍷 Now ⓔⓔ

CHILFORD HUNDRED 1998 ALURIC DE NORSEHIDE, BRUT

Tasted some six months prior to commercial disgorgement and shows impressive structure and fruit, but it needs at least another year on yeast, thus judgement deferred.
🍷 Wait and see ⓔⓔ

CHILTERN VALLEY

Henley-on-Thames, Oxfordshire, England, UK

CHILTERN VALLEY 1996 BRUT ROSÉ

The beguiling muscatty aromas come from the Bacchus grape in this Bacchus-Dornfelder blend, making this an ideal summertime tipple.
🍷 Now–2001 ⓔⓔⓔ

CHILTERN VALLEY 1997 MILLENNIUM CUVÉE 2000, BRUT

This blend of Seyval Blanc, Pinot Noir and Huxelrebe has a lovely peachy aroma followed by very rich fruit on the palate. In fact the richness of fruit might have worried me but for the structure of the wine, which is more than adequate to cope with it.
🍷 Now–2001 ⓔⓔ

CHIQUET

Champagne Gaston Chiquet
912 avenue du Général-Leclerc
Dizy – 51318 Epernay
☎(326) 55.22.02 ✉(326) 51.83.81

GASTON CHIQUET NV BLANC DE BLANCS D'AŸ, BRUT GRAND CRU

Huge, ripe acidity and so much fruit that you could almost eat it. This *cuvée* is produced exclusively from Chardonnay grapes grown in Aÿ, a village famous for its Pinot Noir.
🍷 Now–2003 ⓔⓔ

GASTON CHIQUET NV TRADITION, BRUT PREMIER CRU

Excellent fruit, classic structure.

Now–2003 €€

GASTON CHIQUET 1995 BRUT, CLUB DE VITICULTEURS CHAMPENOIS

Full, serious, yeast-complexed fruit aromas followed by a mouthfilling richness on the palate. There is the barest hint of greenness on the finish, but this will drop out as the wine picks up its toasty post-disgorgement aromas.

2002–2004 €€€

CIGRAVI
Penedès, Spain

GIRO RIBOT 2000 NV CAVA BRUT NATURE, CIGRAVI

The nose of the 1997-based blend has finesse (which is more than I can say for the blue bottle or its optically-illusory label), but the acidity makes the fruit rather dour. This is one that I would like to follow for 12–18 months.

Now–2001 €€ 🍾 2,000 Ptas

PAUL CHENEAU MILLENNIUM 1997 CAVA BRUT, CIGRAVI

Plenty of fruit for a Cava, if you can put up with the gaudy gold plastic-film covered bottle.

Now € 🍾 795 Ptas

CLÉEBOURG
Cave Vinicole de Cléebourg, Alsace, France

CLÉROTSTEIN NV CRÉMANT D'ALSACE BRUT

A surprisingly serious, creamy fizz for the price.

Now–2002 € 🍾 26.30FF

CLEEBRONN-GÜGLINGEN
Weingärtner Cleebronn-Güglingen Württemberg, Germany

WEINGÄRTNER CLEEBRONN-GÜGLINGEN RIESLING TROCKEN 1998 CLEEBRONNER MICHAELSBERG

Fresh, gentle, soft and satisfying. Very clean. (*Cuve close.*)

Now € 🍾 DM14

CLEVELAND
Victoria, Australia

95ER CLEVELAND MACEDON BRUT

The high acidity in the 95er has kept its lime-like fruit nice and fresh, but I could not get the 92er past my nose and into my mouth!

Now–2001 €€ 🍾 A$28

❖ CLOS DE L'EPINAY (DOMAINE DU), *see* Epinay

CLOUDY BAY
Marlborough, New Zealand

The fuller, fatter style of Pelorus is not my preferred taste, but there is no denying the quality achieved and the remarkable finesse of some of the older vintages.

PELORUS NV BRUT, CLOUDY BAY

The first release was labelled as a pure Blanc de Blancs with lovely broad-brush Chardonnay aromas and tropical fruit on the finish. Since then, however, the term Blanc de Blancs has been removed, but the wine remains Chardonnay dominated. I was not impressed by the 1995-based *cuvée*, but the 1996-based *cuvée* shows fresh, toasty finesse.

Now–2001 €€

PELORUS 1996 BRUT, CLOUDY BAY

A pre-release sample was full and firmly structured with apricots and plums on the palate.

2001–2003 €€

PELORUS 1995 BRUT, CLOUDY BAY

Toasty-coffee aromas are already mellowing the fruit in this full and richly flavoured vintage.

◀■ 2001–2003 £€

PELORUS 1994 BRUT, CLOUDY BAY

A darker colour than any of the other recent vintages, due, apparently, to the skins of the Pinot Noir possessing particularly heavy pigmentation in 1994. Touch peppery on the finish.

❚ Now–2001 £€

PELORUS 1993 BRUT, CLOUDY BAY

Excellent balance between richness and acidity, but a touch of white pepper has started to develop on the finish and this detracts from the exceptional promise shown over the last two years.

❚ Now–2003 £€

PELORUS 1992 BRUT, CLOUDY BAY

Fresh for its age, but currently showing weak on the finish.

❚ Now–2001 £€

PELORUS 1990 BRUT, CLOUDY BAY

The darkest colour of the older vintages, but correspondingly richer and well preserved.

❚ Now–2001 £€

PELORUS 1988 BRUT, CLOUDY BAY

Beautifully preserved for a 12-year-old wine that is really quite fine and delicate.

❚ Now–2001 £€

PELORUS 1987 BRUT, CLOUDY BAY

Fresh and vigorous with beautifully pure fruit. Until now the 1988 has always stood out as the best of the two oldest vintages, but on this particular occasion the 1987 not only proved superior to the 1988, it was clearly the best of the lot.

❚ Now–2001 £€

ATTENTION CHAMPAGNE & SPARKLING WINE PRODUCERS!

If you are not already in contact with the author, but would like to submit wines for consideration in future editions, please contact Tom Stevenson at:

tom.stevenson@fizz.worldonline.co.uk

Warning: Any other unsolicited mail received at this address will be ignored.

Please note that recommendation in this guide involves no charge whatsoever beyond the cost of the samples and their delivery.

CLOUET

Champagne André Clouet
8 Rue Gambetta
Bouzy 51150 Tours-sur-Marne
☎(326) 57.00.82 📠(326) 51.65.13

ANDRÉ CLOUET NV UN JOUR DE 1911, BRUT GRAND CRU CLASSÉ

Last year this special blend of 50% 1990, 25% 1989 and 25% 1991 from 11 of Clouet's best Bouzy sites was in prime drinking condition. This year, however, it is beginning to firm up and although enjoyable to drink when tasted, I suspect that by the time the Guide is published, it will require at least one year additional post-disgorgement ageing. It is still fresh, but the fruit is really quite intense and the acidity nicely high. Such wines often go through a firming-up phase and it might be three or more years before it emerges as a much more complex Champagne. Keep watching this space!

◀■ 2001–2008 £££€ 🍾 350FF

CODORNÍU

Penedès, Spain

CODORNÍU NV CAVA RESERVA BRUT ROSÉ

Although this extremely elegant Cava states Monastrell and Parellada on the back label, it tastes like 100% strawberry Pinot Noir fruit to me. Still, they couldn't say that could they? Pinot Noir is not legal in Cava, is it?

Now–2001 ⓔⓔ

CUVÉE RAVENTÓS NV CAVA BRUT, CODORNÍU

Plenty of flavour, clean Chardonnay fruit dominating. Soft, creamy finish. Good acidity.

Now ⓔ ※ 1,715 Ptas

JAUME DE CODORNÍU NV CAVA BRUT, CODORNÍU

Good, but not as special as last year.

Now ⓔⓔ ※ 3,980 Ptas

RAIMAT NV CAVA GRAN BRUT, CODORNÍU

Definitely the best Cava this year, with good Chardonnay fruit, nice barrel aromas and a satisfying finish.

Now–2001 ⓔ ※ 1,975 Ptas

RONDELL NV CAVA EXTREME BRUT, CODORNÍU

Not that extreme. In fact a good balance between acidity and sweetness.

Now ⓔ

COFIELD
Victoria, Australia

COFIELD WINES 1997 SPARKLING SHIRAZ

Very fresh and fruity.

Now–2001 ⓔⓔ ※ A$24

COLA
Franciacorta, Italy

COLA NV FRANCIACORTA BRUT

Rich, crisp and satisfying. A rather full style and structure for Franciacorta but retains elegance.

Now–2003 ⓔⓔ ※ 13,000 Lira

COLA 1996 FRANCIACORTA EXTRA BRUT

Rich and tasty with classic biscuity richness. Fresh, crisp finish.

Now–2002 ⓔⓔ ※ 15,000 Lira

COLLET
Champagne Raoul Collet
14 Boulevard Pasteur
51160 Aÿ-Champagne
☎(326) 55.15.88 ☏(326) 54.02.40

RAOUL COLLET NV CARTE ROUGE, BRUT

A nice core of cool, frothy fruit, but let down in the finesse stakes by the barest hint of pepperiness on the finish. An extra year's ageing might be useful.

Now–2003 ⓔⓔ

RAOUL COLLET NV BRUT ROSÉ

More flavour than finesse, but the rich, creamy fruit is so easy to knock back.

Now–2001 ⓔⓔ

RAOUL COLLET 1991 CARTE D'OR, BRUT

A fine, firm-styled Champagne that needs some post-disgorgement mellowing.

➤ 2002–2004 ⓔⓔ

RAOUL COLLET 1993 CARTE D'OR BRUT

Excellent fruit, but needs a year or two to tame and smooth the mousse.

➤ 2001–2004 ⓔⓔ

COLOMER BERNAT
Penedès, Spain

COLOMER BERNAT SIGLO XXI 1996 CAVA BRUT NATURE

Bags of flavour, nice structure and a good mousse. With more finesse to the fruit this could have scored another 5 or 6 points.

Now ⓔⓔ ※ 2,500 Ptas

COMPAGNIE FRANÇAISE DES GRANDS VINS
France

COMPAGNIE FRANÇAISE DES GRANDS VINS NV L. PALAIS BLANC DE BLANC BRUT

Touch of floral fruit lifts it above most in its category.
Now ⓔ

COMPAGNIE FRANÇAISE DES GRANDS VINS NV VEUVE VALMANTE

Very clean, very fine, soft mousse, nice acidity.
Now ⓔ

CONTADI CASTALDI
Franciacorta, Italy

CONTADI CASTALDI NV FRANCIACORTA ZERO

Deeper colour, fat yet fresh, floral fruit, creamy apricot-fruit on finish.
Now–2002 ⓔⓔ ⚘ 18,800 Lira

CONTADI CASTALDI NV BRUT

Lime and lavender aromas, rich and satisfying fruit.
Now–2001 ⓔⓔ ⚘ 14,800 Lira

CONTRATTO
Asti, Italy

DE MIRANDA 1997 ASTI

This bottle-fermented Asti is immaculately labelled and presented in a wooden box, but let down by a cheap, crappy wire cage. Rich, peachy Moscato fruit stands out, but does not have the finesse that De Miranda 1995 showed two years ago (92 points!).
Now ⓔⓔ

CORBANS
Auckland, New Zealand

AMADEUS 1996 HAWKES BAY

Impressed by the combination of fruitiness and serious structure. Dosaged

to go toasty.
Now–2001 ⓔ ⚘ NZ$24.95

CORNALETO
Franciacorta, Italy

CORNALETO 1991 FRANCIACORTA BRUT

Really quite fresh for 9 years! Just lacks the finesse that Franciacorta has achieved in more recent times.
Now–2002 ⓔⓔ ⚘ 22,000 Lira

CORNILLON
Rhône, France

CAVE DIDIER CORNILLON NV MÉTHODE DIOISE ANCESTRALE, CLAIRETTE DE DIE

The best aromatics, as might be expected from the only Clairette de Die made from 100% Muscat, but obviously these wines benefit from the inclusion of the more acidic Clairette, which accounts for 5–25% of the blend in other Méthode Dioise Ancestrale.
Now ⓔⓔ

COVIDES
Penedès, Spain

DUC DE FOIX 1997 CAVA BRUT

Nice balance of fruit and acidity.
Now ⓔ ⚘ 850 Ptas

XENIUS 1998 CAVA BRUT

Good flavoursome fizz of some finesse.
Now ⓔ ⚘ 725 Ptas

CRAWFORD
Auckland, New Zealand

KIM CRAWFORD RORY NV MARLBOROUGH

What this lacks in complexity and finesse it makes up for in weight of fruit, fine structure and a freshness that brings a sense of elegance to the balance.
❦ Now–2001 ££ ❦ NZ$24.95

CRAY

Loire, France

When oh when are we going to see a more recent vintage? This is the third year that I've tasted Cray 1993s and I don't mind tasting them for another three years, but hopefully owner-winemaker Paul Boutinot will submit some of his more recent vintages next time.

CRAY 1993 CRÉMANT DE LOIRE BRUT

This wine did not even make the cut last year, but this release has lovely flowery autolytic finesse on the nose, suggesting a recent disgorgement, and satisfying, clean, fresh, elegant fruit on the palate. Quite a remarkable achievement for a seven-year-old Loire bubbly.
❦ Now £

CURBASTRO

*Ricci Curbastro
Franciacorta, Italy*

RICCI CURBASTRO NV FRANCIACORTA EXTRA BRUT

Fine autolytic aroma, soft-creamy fruit on mid-palate followed by crisp acidity on finish. Much better focus.
❦ Now–2002 £££ ❦ 30,000 Lira

RICCI CURBASTRO NV FRANCIACORTA BRUT

Fine autolysis on nose, malo-fruit on palate, nice structure.
❦ Now–2002 ££ ❦ 25,000 Lira

RICCI CURBASTRO NV FRANCIACORTA SATÈN

Oak *barrique* on nose! Very soft, silky mousse, very good fruit.
❦ Now–2003 ££ ❦ 25,000 Lira

DANEBURY

Stockbridge, Hampshire, England, UK

DANEBURY 1994 COSSACK, BRUT

Named after the infamous winner of the 1847 Derby, this is a serious, mature fizz that still has plenty of life.
❦ Now–2001 ££

DASENSTEIN

Baden, Germany

HEX VOM DASENSTEIN SPÄTBURGUNDER ROSÉ TROCKEN 1998 HEX VOM DASENSTEIN

Very fresh, lovely sweetish fruit, exquisitely clean and perfumed. (*Méthode champenoise.*)
❦ Now £ ❦ DM19

DAVENPORT

Rotherfield, East Sussex

DAVENPORT 1997

A very English fizz with fresh, herbaceous fruit and nice acidity on the finish.
❦ Now–2001 £

DEAKIN ESTATE

Victoria, Australia

DEAKIN ESTATE BRUT NV AUSTRALIAN SPARKLING WINE

Fresh fruity fizz for the price of a Cava.
❦ Now £

DEIDESHEIM

*Winzerverein Deidesheim
Pfalz, Germany*

WINZERVEREIN DEIDESHEIM 1998 SPÄTBURGUNDER TROCKEN

Very Pinot in character. Makes a great barbecue wine. (*Méthode champenoise.*)
❦ Now–2001 ⓔ ❧ DM10

WINZERVEREIN DEIDESHEIM RIESLING EXTRA BRUT 1998 DEIDESHEIMER PARADIESGARTEN

Nice ripe, honeyed Riesling aroma, but let down on palate, otherwise this Sekt would have scored higher. (*Méthode champenoise.*)
❦ Now–2001 ⓔ ❧ DM14

DELAMOTTE

Champagne Delamotte
5 & 7 rue de la Brèche d'Oger
51190 Le Mesnil-sur-Oger
France
☎(326) 57.51.65 ⒻⒶⓍ(326) 57.79.29

DELAMOTTE NV BLANC DE BLANCS BRUT

Ripe, sweet Chardonnay fruit dosaged to go toasty.
➤ 2001–2002 ⓔⓔ

DELAMOTTE 1990 BLANC DE BLANCS BRUT

A sensational 90-pointer in the first edition, this wine went through an awkward phase last year. I think it will improve from its current 86 points, but I'm not sure that it will ever be quite the corker it was when first released, so I recommend that anyone with a number of these bottles stashed away should drink up at least half now. Its lemony-oaky-toasty fruit is intriguing because no oak was used in the production of this Champagne. The exotic twist of fruit in the tail is reminiscent of this wine's early showing, thus it could still improve with age, hence my advice to keep at least some for the longer term.
❦ Now–2002 ⓔⓔⓔ

DELATITE

Victoria, Australia

DELATITE DEMELZA NV

An interesting fizz with good fruit and a dusting of vanilla on the finish.
❦ Now ⓔⓔ ❧ A$27.50

DELOUVIN NOWACK

Champagne Delouvin-Nowack
29 rue Principale
51700 Vandières
☎(326) 58.02.70 ⒻⒶⓍ(326) 57.10.11

DELOUVIN NOWACK NV BRUT

The clean, precise fruit is attractive to drink now, but the mousse is too assertive and would benefit from at least one year's further ageing.
➤ 2001–2004 ⓔⓔ ❧ 79FF

DEPPISCH

Franken, Germany

JOSEF DEPPISCH RIESLING EXTRA TROCKEN 1998 FRANKEN RIESLING

Fresh and gently fruity. (Transfer method.)
❦ Now ⓔ ❧ DM25

JOSEF DEPPISCH SILVANER BRUT 1998 FRANKEN SILVANER

Fresh, clean, tasty and quite solid, but not without some elegance. (Transfer method.)
❦ Now ⓔ ❧ DM20

DÉTHUNE

Champagne Paul Déthune
2 rue du Moulin
51150 Ambonnay
☎(326) 57.01.88 ⒻⒶⓍ(326) 57.09.31

PAUL DÉTHUNE NV BRUT GRAND CRU

Lovely freshness of fruit on both nose and palate, deliciously rich, well-focused fruit on palate.
❦ Now–2002 ⓔⓔ ❧ 88FF

PAUL DÉTHUNE NV BRUT ROSÉ, GRAND CRU

Lovely freshness of fruit, with finesse evident in the mouth.
❚ Now–2001 ⓕⓕ 🍷 95FF

PRINCESSE DES THUNES NV CUVÉE PRESTIGE BRUT, AMBONNAY GRAND CRU

Very clean and precise, with beautifully focused Pinot Noir fruit.
❚ Now–2004 ⓕⓕ 🍷 130FF

DEUTZ

Champagne Deutz
16 rue Jeanson
51160 Aÿ-Champagne
☎(326) 56.94.00 ℻(326) 56.94.10

DEUTZ NV BRUT CLASSIC

Fresh, crisp and, as the label says, classic. Will go biscuity and, indeed, some bottles I've tasted this year have been wonderfully rich and biscuity, indicating some mature stocks on the market despite the so-called millennium-effect.
❚ Now–2004 ⓕⓕ

DEUTZ 1995 BLANC DE BLANCS BRUT

It would be a shame to drink this now, when it is simply very fresh and crisp. Give it at least one year and it will open up and fill out, although it will remain crisp and elegant. The fruit should go creamy-toasty.
❚ 2001–2005 ⓕⓕⓕ

❖ **DEUTZ MARLBOROUGH**, *see* Montana

DEVAUX

Champagne Veuve A. Devaux
Domaine de Villeneuve
10110 Bar-sur-Seine
☎(25) 38.30.65 ℻(25) 29.73.21

VEUVE A. DEVAUX NV GRANDE RÉSERVE, BRUT

Soft and easy, giving lots of satisfaction.
❚ Now–2002 ⓕⓕ 🍷 110FF

VEUVE A. DEVAUX NV BLANC DE NOIRS, BRUT

Very fine indeed. Anyone who thinks the Aube cannot produce Champagnes of structure and class should taste the current release of this wine. Last year's *cuvée* scraped in with just 80 points.
❚ Now–2003 ⓕⓕ 🍷 110FF

VVE A. DEVAUX 2000 NV D DE DEVAUX, BRUT

There would seem to be some *barrique* ageing involved in the production of this *cuvée*, which is currently dominated by ripe, peachy, bottle-aromas, but there is no accompanying information, which is unusual for this normally *très* efficient cooperative.
🍾 2002–2004 ⓕⓕⓕ 🍷 250FF

VVE. A. DEVAUX 1995 BRUT

This tasty *cuvée* has good fruit, but needs a year to have a calming effect on the mousse and to bring a little more finesse.
🍾 2001–2003 ⓕⓕ

DEZZANI

Asti, Italy

DEZZANI NV BRACHETTO D'ACQUI DOLCE

A sweet, frothy red fizz with fresh Moscato fruit aromas.
❚ Now ⓕ

DOGLIOTTI

Asti, Italy

LA SELVATICA, ASTI NV CAUDRINA, ROMANO DOGLIOTTI

An equally beautiful presentation and although it is not quite in the same class as the magnum (90 points), it is close, with very similar orange-blossom style aromas mingling through its elegantly rich and sweet Moscato fruit. The freshness and finesse stand out.
❚ Now ⓕⓕ

LA SELVATICA, ASTI NV CAUDRINA, ROMANO DOGLIOTTI *(magnum)*

This magnum has a seductive floral, orange-water aroma, a wonderful peach-stone fruit, an impeccable mousse, and a lingering aftertaste, making it one of the few truly special wines of Asti. Beautifully presented.

❦ Now–2001 ££

❖ **DOMAINE BERTHET-BONDET,** *see* Berthet-Bondet

❖ **DOMAINE BOURILLON-DORLÉANS,** *see* Bourillon-Dorléans

❖ **DOMAINE CARNEROS,** *see* Carneros

❖ **DOMAINE CHANDON (AUSTRALIA),** *see* Chandon

❖ **DOMAINE DU CLOS DE L'EPINAY,** *see* Epinay

❖ **DOMAINE DUTERTRE,** *see* Dutertre

❖ **DOMAINE MARTIN FAUDOT,** *see* Faudot

❖ **DOMAINE PAUL BLANCK,** *see* Blanck

❖ **DOMAINE STE MICHELLE,** *see* Ste Michelle

DOPFF & IRION
Alsace, France

DOPFF & IRION NV CRÉMANT D'ALSACE BRUT

Much fruitier than its cousins (although this side of the Dopff family sold up in the 1990s), with lovely acids.
❦ Now £

DOPFF & IRION 1997 CRÉMANT D'ALSACE BRUT

A very fresh, fine and elegant *crémant* that is drinking well now, but could age gracefully for a year or two longer.
❦ Now–2002 £

DOQUET-JEANMAIRE
Champagne Doquet-Jeanmaire
44 Chemin Moulin Cense Bizet
51130 Vertus
☎(326) 52.16.50 ⊠(326) 59.36.71

DOQUET-JEANMAIRE NV BLANC DE BLANCS, CARTE OR BRUT PREMIER CRU

Finely aromatic Chardonnay fruit supported by Pinot-like structure, making this an interesting wine to age.
❦ Now–2003 ££ ✤ 79FF

DOQUET-JEANMAIRE 1990 BLANC DE BLANCS, BRUT PREMIER CRU

Amazingly fresh, ageless fruit. It could have benefited from more acidity, yet this itself illustrates how miraculous the eternal youth of this wine is because the higher the acidity the longer a Champagne remains fresh.
❦ Now–2005 ££ ✤ 102FF

DOYARD
Champagne Robert Doyard
63 avenue de Bammental
51130 Vertus
☎(326) 52.14.74 ⊠(326) 52.24.02

DOYARD 1995 COLLECTION DE L'AN I, BLANC DE BLANCS BRUT

Oxidative complexity followed by excellent fruit and acidity. Keep this 2–3 years and it could grow younger if and when the extract released overwhelms the aldehydes.
❦ Now–2003 £££ ✤ 155FF

DOYARD 1996 COLLECTION DE L'AN I, OEIL DE PERDRIX ROSÉ BRUT

A delicate pale-salmon colour, with lovely, fresh crisp fruit on the palate. Could be a white Champagne from taste alone.
❦ Now–2002 ££ ✤ 130FF

DRAPPIER

Champagne Drappier
Grande Rue
10200 Urville
☎(25) 27.40.15 ℻(25) 27.41.19

ANDRÉ ET MICHEL DRAPPIER NV BRUT NATURE, PINOT NOIR ZERO DOSAGE 80

The next release already tastes quite mature.
🍷 Now ⓕⓔ ❄ 125FF

DRAPPIER NV CARTE D'OR BRUT 85

This *cuvée* was fresh and elegantly fruity at the beginning of 2000, but had become ultra-fruity by the middle of the year, promising to go biscuity with another 12 months' ageing, during which time, of course, the next fruity release will be on the market.
🍷 Now–2002 ⓕⓔ ❄ 118FF

DRAPPIER NV VAL DES DEMOISELLES, ROSÉ BRUT 85

The next release has plenty of sweet-ripe fruit and promises to go creamy-biscuity.
🍷 Now–2001 ⓕⓔ ❄ 130FF

DRAPPIER 1995 CARTE D'OR BRUT 85

One of the firmer 1995s, this wine needs at least a year before approaching.
🍾 2001–2005 ⓕⓕⓔ ❄ 135FF

DRAPPIER 1995 GRANDE SENDREE, BRUT 00

The pre-release sample of Drappier's top

of the line *cuvée* was impressively rich, with pineapple fruit, but it won't be long before the biscuity-rich bottle-aromas set in, thanks to the low-sulphur regime used to produce this wine.
🍷 Now–2003 ⓕⓕⓔ ❄ 180FF

DRAPPIER 1990 GRANDE SENDRÉE, BRUT 89

This has greatly improved since last year (86 points), but dare I suggest the reason why might be the sulphur in the dosage? A low sulphur regime is one thing, but if a larger dose improves the wine, the producer should be big enough to go for it, as Drappier has done here. However, this will mean that it is more likely to go toasty than Drappier's normal biscuity style.
🍷 Now–2003 ⓕⓕⓔ ❄ 180FF

DRAPPIER 1989 GRANDE SENDRÉE, BRUT 88

Impressive acidity for a 1989, which probably explains why this is still in fruit-mode, but should quickly go biscuity.
🍷 Now–2002 ⓕⓕⓔ ❄ 195FF

DRAPPIER 1990 GRANDE SENDRÉE ROSÉ, BRUT 88

The fruit in this vintage is exceptionally fresh, soft and sassy, but it tastes really quite sweet for a Brut and I would not be able to drink more than one glass at its current stage of development. However, in a couple of years' time it should be biscuity, the impression of sweetness should convert to a rich creaminess, and I won't be able to get enough of the stuff!
🍾 2001–2003 ⓕⓕⓔ ❄ 230FF

DUCHESSA LIA

Asti, Italy

DUCHESSA LIA NV BRACHETTO D'ACQUI, SPUMANTE DOLCE 85

Good colour with elegant Moscato aromas and bags of sweet, tasty Moscato fruit on the palate and finish.
🍷 Now ⓕ

DUMANGIN

Champagne J. Dumangin Fils
3 rue de Rilly
51500 Chigny-les-Roses
☎(326) 03.46.34 📠(326) 03.45.61

J. DUMANGIN 1994 BRUT MILLÉSIMÉ, PREMIER CRU

Extremely fruity.
❚ Now–2003 €€

J. DUMANGIN NV GRANDE RÉSERVE, BRUT PREMIER CRU

A very traditional style Champagne with concentrated fruit, excellent acidity and a big finish.
❚ Now–2003 €€

DUMONT

Champagne Daniel Dumont
11 rue Gambetta
51500 Rilly-la-Montagne
☎(326) 03.40.67 📠(326) 03.44.82

DANIEL DUMONT NV GRANDE RÉSERVE BRUT

A relatively inexpensive grower Champagne of some finesse and complexity. A stylish wine that drinks well on release, whereas the non-vintage rosé is too oxidative.
❚ Now–2002 €€

DUMONT GRANDE RÉSERVE 1992 CUVÉE D'EXCELLENCE BRUT

MLF currently dominating fruit, which is rich and mellow, supported by a mousse of tiny bubbles. Food wine.
❚ Now–2002 €€

DUTERTRE

Loire, France

DOMAINE DUTERTRE NV CUVÉE SAINT GILLES, CRÉMANT DE LOIRE BRUT

Extremely fresh and *vif*. Ideal aperitif wine.

❚ Now–2001 €

DUVAL-LEROY

Champagne Fleur de Champagne
69 avenue de Bammental
F-51130 Vertus
☎(326) 52.10.75 📠(326) 57.54.01

FLEUR DE CHAMPAGNE NV BRUT, DUVAL-LEROY

This light, fresh, flowery Champagne has exceptional finesse and is typical of the elegant Duval-Leroy style and quality.
❚ Now–2003 €€

FLEUR DE CHAMPAGNE NV BRUT PREMIER CRU, DUVAL-LEROY

Unusual for Duval-Leroy, creamy-malo aromas are noticeable as soon as the wine hits the palate. The fruit is also creamier and less crisp. These are not, however, criticisms of the wine *per se*, which is of a good quality. I merely point out the differences so that regular Duval-Leroy drinkers do not expect anything different.
❚ Now–2002 €€

FLEUR DE CHAMPAGNE NV ROSÉ DE SAIGNÉE BRUT, DUVAL-LEROY

This delicious and delicately fruity Champagne has great class.
❚ Now–2003 €€€

FLEUR DE CHAMPAGNE 1992 BRUT, DUVAL-LEROY

Creamy-biscuity fruit, softer and fruitier than the same vintage of Duval-Leroy's LeRoy Neiman *cuvée*.
❚ Now–2004 €€€

FLEUR DE CHAMPAGNE 1995 BLANC DE CHARDONNAY BRUT, DUVAL-LEROY

Amazing complexity for such a fresh, tasty Champagne.
❚ Now–2003 €€€

FLEUR DE CHAMPAGNE 1992 EXTRA BRUT MILLÉSIMÉ, DUVAL-LEROY

This beautifully proportioned Champagne boasts exquisitely fine fruit supported by a perfect mousse of ultra-fine bubbles and interestingly is superior to the theoretically much greater 1990 vintage of the same *cuvée*.

Now–2001 ⓔⓔⓔ

FLEUR DE CHAMPAGNE 1990 EXTRA BRUT MILLÉSIMÉ, DUVAL-LEROY

Fine, firm and tasty with a crisp, almost sharp, finish.

Now–2001 ⓔⓔⓔ

FLEUR DE CHAMPAGNE, LEROY NEIMAN 1992 BRUT, DUVAL-LEROY

Compared to Duval-Leroy's basic 1992 vintage this is firmer, with greater extract, and has more in common with the 1992 Fin de Siècle Cuvée released last year.

Now–2004 ⓔⓔⓔ

FLEUR DE CHAMPAGNE, LEROY NEIMAN 1990 BRUT, DUVAL-LEROY

I preferred last year's sample (87 points) with 12 months' additional post-disgorgement ageing to this year's release.

2001–2003 ⓔⓔⓔ

CUVÉE DES ROYS 1990 BRUT, DUVAL-LEROY

Beautifully focused fruit in classic Duval-Leroy style.

Now–2002 ⓔⓔⓔ

CUVÉE DES ROYS 1990 BRUT, DUVAL-LEROY *(magnum)*

The magnum effect seems to have made the fruit a tad fatter, but it is so crisp and precise that it would be a mistake to think of this as being fat in any real sense. It's just a comparative term. The fruit also seems cooler; that's cool-fresh not cool-fermented.

Now–2004 ⓔⓔⓔ

CUVÉE DES ROYS 1986 BRUT, DUVAL-LEROY *(magnum)*

Duval-Leroy Cuvée des Roys 1986 is better than Cristal 1986, but it has to be admitted that Cristal 1986 has never been a good wine, although I fully expect that I shall be misquoted. More fool me for making such a deliberately provocative statement. To get back to the Cuvée des Roys 1986, this wine has exceptionally

fresh, nicely focused, fruit-salad flavours that slowly build to a certain smooth complexity in the mouth, but it is definitely in need of developing bottle-aromas to add interest to the nose and finish.

2001–2003 ⓔⓔⓔ

FEMME DE CHAMPAGNE 1990 BRUT, DUVAL-LEROY

This was so splendid last year (91 points), when it was in entirely fruit mode, and the same disgorgement tasted one year on still has exquisite fruit, but the current release is too oxidative. If you purchased the first release, you're very lucky, but the best I can offer those who have the current release is to hold on to them and watch this space.

Wait and see ⓔⓔⓔⓔ

EBERBACH

Kloster Eberbach
Rheingau, Germany

KLOSTER EBERBACH RIESLING BRUT 1998 RAUENTHALER BAIKEN

Very fresh, fine and elegant aromas followed by crisp fruit, with excellent extract on the finish. (Transfer method.)

Now–2002 ⓔ

ELLNER

Champagne Charles Ellner
1 & 6 rue Côte Legris
51207 Epernay Cedex
☎(326) 55.60.25 ☎(326) 51.54.00

CHARLES ELLNER 1989 BRUT

Traditional toasty style with piles of mature fruit.

Now–2002 ⓔⓔ ⚜ 115FF

❖ ELSTREE, *see* Highfield Estate

EPINAY

Domaine du Clos de l'Epinay
Loire, France

DOMAINE DU CLOS DE L'EPINAY 1997 TÊTE DE CUVÉE BRUT, VOUVRAY

Higher acidity than this domaine's basic 1997 and should therefore develop more slowly.
❚ Now–2002 ⓔ

ESCUDERO

Bodegas Escudero
Rioja, Spain

DIORO BACO NV CAVA EXTRA BRUT, BODEGAS ESCUDERO

One of the worst labels as far as both design and colour are concerned that I've ever seen, but although the wine itself is too oaky, its peachy Chardonnay fruit comes through, making it one of the better Cavas tasted this year.
❚ Now–2001 ⓔⓔ ⁂ 2,500 Ptas

ETOILE

Château de l'Etoile
Jura, France

CHÂTEAU DE L'ETOILE NV CRÉMANT DU JURA BRUT

If Bollinger sourced its grapes from the Jura, it would probably taste like this!
❚ Now ⓔ

EYMANN

Pfalz, Germany

RAINER EYMANN SPÄTBURGUNDER 1995 BLANC DE NOIRS EXTRA BRUT

Elevated strawberry-Pinot fruit. (*Méthode champenoise.*)
❚ Now–2001 ⓔ ⁂ DM22

FACCOLI

Franciacorta, Italy

FACCOLI NV FRANCIACORTA EXTRA BRUT

Very fresh, creamy floral apple blossom fruit. Not too dry, which is a mark of quality for extra brut.
❚ Now–2002 ⓔⓔ ⁂ 23,000 Lira

FACCOLI NV BRUT

Fresh, floral autolytic aroma, very fresh and crisp, keep a year to fill out.
➧ 2001–2002 ⓔⓔ ⁂ 21,000 Lira

FACCOLI NV ROSÉ

Very pale pink rosé. Fresh and fruity, crisp, fresh finish.
❚ Now–2002 ⓔⓔ ⁂ 23,000 Lira

FAUDOT

Domaine Martin Faudot
Jura, France

DOMAINE MARTIN FAUDOT NV CRÉMANT DU JURA BRUT

Excellent acidity, will go toasty.
➧ 2001 ⓔ

FERGHETTINA

Franciacorta, Italy

FERGHETTINA FRANCIACORTA NV BRUT

Very fresh, upfront, fruity aromas, attractive, focused Chardonnay fruit.
❚ Now–2002 ⓔⓔ ⁂ 19,000 Lira

FERRET

Penedès, Spain

FERRET NV CAVA BRUT RESERVA

The current 1996-based *cuvée* has gently rich fruit. Nice to taste a Cava of some substance.

▌ Now ⓔ 🍷 982 Ptas

FEUILLATTE

Champagne Nicolas Feuillatte
Chouilly
51206 Epernay
📞(326) 54.50.60 📠(326) 55.33.04

Do I detect an all round improvement, with
the wines showing more finesse?

ANDREW GARRETT & NICOLAS FEUILLATTE NV SIGNÉ, BRUT, CVC ⑧④

This traditionally structured wine is
similar to last year's *cuvée* (although
without the malo-biscuitiness) and
neither one is anything like the New
World styled first release, which prompts
me to ask the same question again: why
bother to have Aussie Garret's name on
the label if there is no evidence of any
New World influence on the wine?
▌ Now–2002 ⓔⓔ

NICOLAS FEUILLATTE 1995 BRUT ⊖

The aldehydic aromas would have been
worrying if it had not been a pre-release
sample I was tasting, but it is fairly
certain this character will not be present
in the final commercial product and the
rich, creamy fruit tells me this should be
one of this cooperative's better vintages.
It looks set to be a very fruity Champagne
when released and one that should in
time go biscuity rather than toasty.
▬▬ Wait and see ⓔⓔ

NICOLAS FEUILLATTE 1995 BLANC DE BLANCS MILLÉSIMÉ, BRUT PREMIER CRU ⑧⑥

Classic structure and fruit with
biscuitiness building.
▌ Now–2002 ⓔⓔⓔ

NICOLAS FEUILLATTE 1996 ROSÉ MILLÉSIME, BRUT PREMIER CRU ⑧③

A fresh, tasty melange of fruit on the
palate, but could do with more finesse
on the nose.
▌ Now–2001 ⓔⓔⓔ

NICOLAS FEUILLATTE 1995 CUVÉE SPÉCIALE, BRUT 1ER CRU ⑧⑤

Fresh, clean and well-structured.
▬▬ 2001–2005 ⓔⓔⓔ

NICOLAS FEUILLATTE 1992 BRUT ⑧④

Although evolving quickly, this wine has
excellent acidity, making it nicely
matured, with a while to go before it
peaks. It also has a degree of finesse not
noted in previous NF vintages.
▌ Now–2003 ⓔⓔ

❖ **FIRSTLIGHT**, *see* Parker MC

FLEIN-TALHEIM

Württemberg, Germany

FLEIN-TALHEIM RIESLING BRUT 1998 VEIT FLEINER ALTENBERG

The very pure Riesling aromatics in this
Sekt show great finesse and are followed
on the palate by delicious, early-drinking
Riesling fruit and a crisp finish. (*Méthode
champenoise.*)
▌ Now ⓔ 🍷 DM18

FLEURY

Champagne Fleury
43 Grande rue
10250 Courteron
📞(325) 38.20.28 📠(325) 38.24.65

FLEURY NV BRUT

This bio-dynamic *cuvée* is the first
Champagne to be certified by Demeter.
Very fresh and fruity with cool fruit on
the finish.
▌ Now–2001 ⓔⓔ

FLUTEAU 1996 BRUT BLANC DE BLANCS

Turbo-charged fruit!
▌ Now–2006 ⓔⓔ 🍷 88FF

FONTANAFREDDA
Asti, Italy

FONTANAFREDDA 1999 ASTI MILLESIMATO

The fresh, soapy Moscato fruit in this wine will go peachy within months.
❦ Now ⓔ ⚘ 14,000 Lira

FONTANAFREDDA 1999 BRACHETTO D'ACQUI

This fizzy red stood out on the nose amongst 20 other Brachetto d'Acqui and that's no mean feat when they are made from such an intensely aromatic grape variety. Not as sweet as some, but the most finesse of all.
❦ Now ⓔ ⚘ 17,000 Lira

FORGET-BRIMONT
Champagne Forget-Brimont
11 route de Louvois
51500 Craon de Ludes
☎(326) 61.10.45 ℻(326) 61.11.58

FORGET-BRIMONT NV BRUT ROSÉ, PREMIER CRU

Red fruits in creamy custard with a dusting of vanilla on the finish.
❦ Now–2001 ⓔⓔ

FORGET-BRIMONT NV CUVÉE AN 2000 BRUT

Rich, soft and smooth with a very satisfying, violety finesse on the finish. Can be consumed with pleasure now, but given a couple of years some understated vanilla should build into the violety finesse.
❦ Now–2003 ⓔⓔ

FORGET-BRIMONT 1991 CUVÉE PRESTIGE, BRUT PREMIER CRU

Although showing quite elegant and youthful now, the fruit in this wine is so gluggy that it could easily go over.
❦ Now ⓔⓔ

FORGET-CHEMIN
Champagne Forget-Chemin
15 Rue Victor Hugo
51500 Ludes Le Coquet
☎(326) 61.12.17 ℻(326) 61.14.51

FORGET-CHEMIN NV BRUT CARTE BLANCHE

Rich fruit and lovely acids, this Champagne has been dosaged to go toasty in a year or two.
❦ Now–2003 ⓔⓔ

FORGET-CHEMIN NV BRUT ROSÉ

Fresh and fruity with hints of peach on mid-to-end palate and aftertaste.
❦ Now–2001 ⓔⓔ

FORGET-CHEMIN 1995 BRUT

This Champagne, which is presented in the stylish, dumpy Club Viticulteurs Champenois bottle, is really rich and tasty, but needs more finesse to score higher, although perhaps with time it will achieve this.
❦ Now–2003 ⓔⓔ

FOX CREEK
South Australia, Australia

FOX CREEK VIXEN NV SPARKLING SHIRAZ CABERNET FRANC

Youthful, totally fruit-driven aroma, with some nice grippy tannins on the palate.
❦ Now–2001 ⓔⓔ ⚘ A$20

FRANK
*Chateau Frank
New York, USA*

CHATEAU FRANK 1995 BLANC DE BLANCS

Winey aromas, but with attractive creamy-fruit on palate and a touch of sweetness on the finish. Further ageing is required to bring the nose and palate more in tune with each other.

🥂 Now–2003 ⓒⓕ 🍾 $25

CHATEAU FRANK 1995 BRUT ⑦⓪

Simple, fresh and fruity style that will not repay keeping.
🥂 Now–2001 ⓒⓕ 🍾 $20

CHATEAU FRANK 1997 CÉLÈBRE ⑦⓪

Riesling style Sekt from New York state. The mousse is rather firm and the terpenes are not fully evolved, suggesting that a little ageing might be beneficial. If with time this wine does develop petrolly Riesling aromas, the score would jump.
▬▶ 2001–2002 ⓕ 🍾 $15

FRIEDRICH
Prinz Friedrich
Rheingau, Germany

PRINZ FRIEDRICH RIESLING BRUT 1998 HATTENHEIMER DEUTESBERG ⑦⑧

Young, fresh Riesling aroma gives way to great extract on palate. Deserves time. (*Méthode champenoise.*)
▬▶ 2001–2003 ⓕ

FRIES
Mosel-Saar-Ruwer, Germany

H.-J. FRIES RIESLING BRUT 1997 NOVIANDER KLOSTERBERG ⑦⑦

Bags of peachy fruit in an elegant style, yet with a firm backbone, and a very fine finish. (*Méthode champenoise.*)
🥂 Now–2001 ⓕ

H.-J. FRIES RIESLING HALBTROCKEN 1997 NOVIANDER KLOSTERBERG ⑦⑧

Classic matured peachy fruit. (*Méthode champenoise.*)
🥂 Now ⓕ

❖ FÜRST LÖWENSTEIN, *see* Löwenstein

GALLIMARD
Champagne Gallimard
18-20 rue du Magny
10340 Les Riceys
☎(25) 29.32.44 ℻(25) 38.55.20

GALLIMARD PÈRE & FILS NV CUVÉE AN 2000 BRUT ⑧⑤

This wine has shown a huge improvement after an extra year in bottle, with less volatile aromas and an evolution of the minerally extract. It would have been better with an extra 12 months on yeast (thus the more recent disgorgements released this year will be even better), but the excellent high acidity has kept the earlier disgorgement well focused and will continue to preserve the wine for a few more years to come.
▬▶ 2001–2004 ⓒⓕ

GARDEN GULLY
Victoria, Australia

GARDEN GULLY 1998 SPARKLING SHIRAZ ⑦⑤

Very fresh fruit that's not too sweet.
🥂 Now ⓒⓕ 🍾 A$27

GARDET

Champagne Gardet
13 rue Georges Legros
51500 Chigny-les-Roses
☎(326) 03.42.03 ℻(326) 03.43.95

GEORGES GARDET NV BRUT SPÉCIAL
82

Definitely a fruit-driven *cuvée* these days (used to be distinctly oxidative), but could do with more finesse.
▮ Now–2001 ©©

CUVÉE CHARLES GARDET 1995 BRUT
90

Extremely fine for such a rich, fruity Champagne, this wine is starting to develop an oxidative complexity of some finesse.
▮ Now–2004 ©©©

GARRETT

*Andrew Garrett
South Australia, Australia*

McLARENS ON THE LAKE SPARKLING NV BRUT CUVÉE
75

Fresh, light fruit salad nose, very soft, and aromatic, with an ultra-fine bead of minuscule bubbles. Off-dry to medium-dry. Very attractive for price and style and better in pure quality terms than Andrew Garrett's more expensive Pinot Noir Chardonnay.
Frontignan/Muscadelle/Sultana/Grenache.
▮ Now © A$10.75

McLARENS ON THE LAKE NV SPARKLING RED SHIRAZ
75

Sweetish, prune-like fruit that's very fresh, with good acidity.
▮ Now–2001 ©

ANDREW GARRETT NV SPARKLING BURGUNDY
77

This medium-bodied red fizz has a fresh, easy-drinking, fruit-driven style, with a drying finish.
▮ Now–2001 © A$15.95

ANDREW GARRETT 1996 CHARDONNAY PINOT NOIR
75

Definitely has the edge on the 1997, but needs another year.
▬ 2001–2002 © A$16

GATINOIS

Champagne Gatinois
7 rue Marcel Mailly
51160 Aÿ
☎(326) 55.14.26 ℻(326) 52.75.99

GATINOIS NV GRAND CRU BRUT
88

I have to be very specific because this is the sort of quality I have been expecting from Gatinois. The shipment offered on the British market in March-May 2000 had none of the unready estery aromas that has blighted other Gatinois wines I have tasted. It is a truly excellent example of fine quality, focused fruit that is just beginning to mellow and show true complexity of some finesse. Hopefully this is not a one-off, that owner-winemaker Pierre Cheval has everything licked and we can expect this level of refinement in all future releases. I have aged previous releases and the estery-oxidativeness does dissipate after a year or two, but they will never have the finesse that results from longer yeast-ageing.
▮ Now–2003 ©©

GATINOIS NV BRUT ROSÉ
85

Not quite as outstanding as the Grand Cru Brut, this Rosé is nevertheless very good, with excellent acidity underscoring fine fruit, but it will be even better in two or three years.
▮ Now–2003 ©©

GATINOIS NV DEMI-SEC
88

A retasting of last year's release reveals fabulously racy fruit, demonstrating yet again how much Gatinois Champagnes benefit from extended age.
▮ Now–2006 ©©

GEHRIG

Pfalz, Germany

GEHRIG 1996 SPÄTBURGUNDER BRUT

A fresh, classy rosé that is clean and softly crisp, which might sound like a contradiction in terms, but is nevertheless apt, as anyone who tastes this Sekt will discover. (*Méthode champenoise.*)

🥂 Now–2001 ⓔ 🍇 DM25

GEIL I. ERBEN

*Joh. Geil I. Erben
Rheinhessen, Germany*

JOH. GEIL I. ERBEN 1997 WEIßBURGUNDER BRUT

Interesting perfumed fruit with a touch of peach. (*Méthode champenoise.*)

🥂 Now ⓔ 🍇 DM17

GENELETTI

Jura, France

MICHEL GENELETTI ET FILS NV CRÉMANT DU JURA BRUT

Very creamy fruit.

🥂 Now ⓔ

GEOFFROY

Champagne René Geoffroy
150 rue du Bois-des-Jots
Cumières 51480 Damery
☎(326) 55.32.31 ℻(326) 54.66.50

RENÉ GEOFFROY NV CUVÉE PRESTIGE, BRUT PREMIER CRU

Smoother than Geoffroy's Cuvée de Réserve, a wine that has scored higher than the Cuvée Prestige in the previous two editions of this Guide, but failed to make the cut this year.

🥂 Now–2003 ⓔⓔ

RENÉ GEOFFROY NV BRUT ROSÉ

Young, easy-drinking style with fresh red-fruits on the palate and a touch of vanilla on the finish.

🥂 Now–2003 ⓔⓔ

RENÉ GEOFFROY 1996 CUVÉE SÉLECTIONNÉE, BRUT PREMIER CRU

The score is tentative; this is going to be special, but just how special we will have to wait and see because it needs at least another two years of post-disgorgement ageing.

▬ 2002–2010 ⓔⓔ

GIESEN

Canterbury, New Zealand

VOYAGE SPECIAL CUVÉE BRUT NV GIESEN

After the first release (1994-based), which was full of bright Pinot Noir fruit (85 points), I had great expectations, but the 1995-based second release was a big disappointment. The 1997-based third release (there being no 1996-based release) was an improvement, while 1998-based fourth release, which should still be available when the Guide is published, is better still (82 points). The 1999-based fifth release (84 points) almost comes up to the quality of the very first Voyage *cuvée*, although it does not have quite the same excitement and with 20% Chardonnay, it cannot be as vividly expressive of Pinot Noir fruit. Nevertheless it is an elegant wine with tropical fruits and a fine, light-bodied structure.

🥂 Now–2001 ⓔⓔ

GILLAN

Marlborough, New Zealand

Owned and run by Toni and Terry "Tellboy" Gillan. Tellboy is an ex-London builder turned sparkling winemaker who wears silk slacks, drips with gold and drives around in an E-Type complete with a personalized Tellboy number plate. According to Tellboy, he has had a few run-ins with the locals, but even those who count themselves as his friends love to tell stories about him. One I picked up from several sources concerned the rebuilding of Blenheim clocktower. This used to be a good-sized tower, something the locals really looked up to, but now it's on stilts and barely five feet off the ground. Tellboy is proud of his nice, cool winery, which of course he built himself, but there is a flaw because one of his thriving sidelines is to let it out for functions, when he puts tables between the stacks of wine and warms up the winery with heaters!

GILLAN 1995 BRUT　76

Light and easy-drinking style with plenty of elevated fruit.
❚ Now–2001 £

GIMONNET

Champagne Pierre Gimonnet & Fils
1 rue de la République
51530 Cuis
☎(326) 59.78.70 ℻(326) 59.79.84

PIERRE GIMONNET & FILS NV BLANC DE BLANCS BRUT, 1ER CRU　88

I tasted the 1997-based *cuvée* in the early part of 2000, when it was wonderfully fresh and focused with delicate fruit, making an ideal aperitif or an accompaniment to shellfish. A few months later I tasted the 1996-based *cuvée*, which was just as fresh and focused, but with much richer fruit and a firmer structure. Brilliant stuff!
❚ Now–2007 £££

PIERRE GIMONNET & FILS NV OENOPHILE, BLANC DE BLANCS, MAXI-BRUT　86

I cannot think of anyone who understands low and no dosage

Champagnes better than Didier Gimonnet. With no dosage a Champagne cannot age gracefully (although Gimonnet has occasionally produced one that breaks this rule), thus the lower the dosage the more ready a Champagne must be as soon as it is released. So what do we have here? Well, the Oenophile Maxi-Brut shipped throughout 2000 is in fact a pure 1993, although no vintage is mentioned. It is as fresh and crisp as any oyster-loving, Oenophile-drinking consumer could possibly ask for, yet there is a completeness to the wine that comes from the underlying soft, creamy and relatively fast-maturing 1993 fruit.
❚ Now–2002 £££

PIERRE GIMONNET & FILS 1995 PREMIER CRU-CHARDONNAY, BRUT　90

I admire anyone who was strong willed enough to resist drinking up every bottle of this seductive wine last year, but it will just get better and better. Presented in the special Club de Viticulteurs Champenois embossed bottle.
❚ Now–2009 £££

PIERRE GIMONNET & FILS 1995 FLEURON, BLANC DE BLANCS BRUT, 1ER CRU　90

If this is Gimonnet at its best, which it is, I cannot wait for the theoretically superior 1996 in magnums in a few years' time. Gimonnet excels in expressing purity of fruit with succulence and great finesse.
❚ Now–2009 £££

PIERRE GIMONNET & FILS 1995 BRUT GASTRONOME, BLANC DE BLANCS 1ER CRU　90

Anyone who has a few bottles of this stunning wine stashed away should still wait a year or two before drinking it on its own, although it has been drinking well at the table for more than a year now, the food bringing out the many different dimensions that will one day become apparent on their own.
❚ Now–2014 £££

PIERRE GIMONNET & FILS 1989 PREMIER CRU CHARDONNAY, BRUT　91

In the first edition this vintage scored 88

points and I noted that it needed either food or time. Well, just look what time did to the gorgeously concentrated toasty fruit in this release. I'm not sure if it is available commercially as there are only 500 bottles left, but I would try to prise a case or two out of Gimonnet if I were you.
🍷 Now–2005 ⓔⓔⓔ

PIERRE GIMONNET & FILS, MILLÉSIME DE COLLECTION 1990 LES CUVÉES DE L'AN 2000, BRUT *(magnum)* ⑨②

Quality tells and under blind conditions my notes were almost identical to last year's "deep and satisfying, with exquisitely rich fruit and an immaculate mousse". A beautifully matured Champagne that continues to develop gracefully. Presented in a wooden box.
🍷 Now–2009 ⓔⓔⓔ

GLEICHENSTEIN
Baden, Germany

FREIHERR VON GLEICHENSTEIN EXTRA BRUT 1996 BADISCHER WINZERSEKT ⑦⑥

Extremely pale peach in colour, with nicely crisp fruit that is fairly neutral, thus will benefit from some post-disgorgement ageing. (*Méthode champenoise.*)
🍷 Now–2001 ⓔ

GLENORA
New York, USA

GLENORA 1998 BLANC DE BLANCS ⑦⑧

Pre-release sample: has finesse, elegant apple-blossom fruit and an excellent mousse.
🍷 Now–2001 ⓔ

GLENORA 1998 BLANC DE NOIRS ⑦③

Pre-release sample: pale peach, touch amylic nose, light, elegant, easy-going style, fine mousse.
🍷 Now–2001 ⓔ

GLENORA 1996 BLANC DE BLANCS ⑦②

Sweet and sour fruit, tangy.
🍷 Now–2001 ⓔ 🥂 $14.99

GLENORA 1996 BRUT ⑦⑤

Rather a full colour, fuller, fatter than most, more of a classic style.
🍷 Now–2002 ⓔ 🥂 $14.99

GLENORA 1996 EXTRA DRY ⑦⑤

Crisp, zesty aromas, very fresh for its age.
🍷 Now–2002 ⓔ 🥂 $14.99

GOBILLARD

Champagne J.M. Gobillard
38 rue de l'Eglise
51160 Hautvillers
☎(326) 51.00.24 ℻(326) 51.00.18

A different family enterprise to Champagne Paul Gobillard of Pierry (who for some reason did not submit samples this year).

J.M. GOBILLARD NV ROSÉ BRUT ⑧②

This firm, fleshy rosé shows best at the table.
🍷 Now ⓔⓔ

J.M. GOBILLARD NV GRANDE RÉSERVE, BRUT PREMIER CRU ⑧⑤

Rich, well-focused fruit supported by excellent acidity.
🍷 Now–2003 ⓔⓔ

GONET

Champagne Michel Gonet
196 avenue Jean-Jaurès
51190 Avize
☎(326) 57.50.56 ℻(326) 57.91.98

MICHEL GONET NV BLANC DE BLANCS, BRUT GRAND CRU ⑧⑤

Firm structure and mousse, but should plump out within the next 12 months or so.
🍾 2001–2004 ⓔⓔ

MICHEL GONET NV BRUT RÉSERVE ⑧③

A very richly flavoured Champagne with fruit that is destined to go toasty.
❙ Now–2002 ©©

MICHEL GONET 1996 PRESTIGE 2000, BRUT GRAND CRU

Exquisitely rich and powerful fruit, but the wine has been dosaged for toastiness, and will benefit from laying down for at least one year.
▬▬ 2001–2004 ©©©

GONET

Champagne Philippe Gonet
1 rue de la Brèche d'Oger
51190 Le-Mesnil-sur-Oger
☎(326) 57.51.07 ⅺ(326) 57.51.03

PHILIPPE GONET NV BLANC DE BLANCS BRUT

For those who like mature, rustic-styled Champagne.
❙ Now–2001 ©© ⚘ 92FF

GOOD ARBOR

Michigan, USA

GOOD ARBOR NV MOONSTRUCK BRUT, LEELANU PENINSULA

A light airy fizz with a soft mousse of tiny bubbles supported by good fruit structure. I could be wrong, but it seems as if this wine could have a tendency to go oxidative and aldehydic when aged, so why bother keeping Moonstruck when it is perfectly nice to drink now?
❙ Now ©

GOOD ARBOR NV EXTRA DRY, LEELANU PENINSULA

Clean, fresh and tangy, with a firm mousse that could take some ageing.
❙ Now–2002 ©

GOSSET

Champagne Gosset
69 rue Jules Blondeau
51160 Aÿ-Champagne
☎(326) 55.14.18 ⅺ(326) 51.55.88

GOSSET NV GRANDE RÉSERVE BRUT

This year's sample tastes like the one released mid-1999 in which the fruit has merely gained intensity and is still three years away from picking up creamy-biscuity complexity.
▬▬ 2001–2010 ©©©

GOSSET NV GRAND ROSÉ BRUT

Full of promise, but so very young.
▬▬ 2002–2007 ©©©

GOSSET 1993 GRAND MILLÉSIME BRUT

This wine has edged up a point over last year, when it was peppery, sharp and all promise. Now the pepperiness has disappeared, the sharp edges softened and the first hints of complexity are just beginning to show through, which is pretty remarkable for a relatively fast-maturing vintage, thus it could well pick up a few more points in the future.
▬▬ 2001–2009 ©©©©

GOSSET 1989 GRAND MILLÉSIME BRUT

The good news is that this appears to have greater longevity than I had initially thought, but the bad news is that the pepperiness that underlies the fruit is still in evidence, so you must hang on to those bottles a while yet.
▬▬ 2002–2005 ©©©©

GOSSET CELEBRIS 1990 BRUT

The drop in score (it was 95 last year) probably reflects a developmental phase, although at 90 points this honeyed-biscuity Champagne can hardly be described as going through an awkward patch. If you have it in your cellar, just forget about it for a few years. Don't worry, you could lose a case of Celebris 1990 for a decade and it would be fine.
▬▬ 2002–2015 ©©©

GOULART

Penedès, Spain

ROGER GOULART GRAN RESERVA 1996 CAVA BRUT EXTRA ⑰

Not bad complexity for Cava. High acidity on finish. The Dom Pérignon shaped label looks odd on this type of bottle.
❦ Now ⓔ ♛ 1,100 Ptas

GOUTORBE

Champagne Henri Goutorbe
9 rue Jeanson
51160 Aÿ-Champagne
☎(326) 55.21.70 ℻(326) 54.85.11

GOUTORBE NV CUVÉE PRESTIGE, BRUT PREMIER CRU ⑧⑤

Creamy-biscuity aromas and huge extract.
❦ Now–2003 ⓔⓔ

HENRI GOUTORBE NV CUVÉE TRADITIONNELLE, BRUT ⑧⑤

Fresher and fruitier than the Cuvée Prestige, but in a more straightforward, less intense style, although it is merely a matter of comparison, as there is excellent concentration in this wine and it will achieve some biscuity complexity in a year or two.
❦ Now–2003 ⓔⓔ ♛ 77FF

HENRI GOUTORBE NV BRUT ROSÉ ⑧⑧

Electrifying acidity makes the fruit wonderfully fresh, racy and sherbety.
❦ Now–2002 ⓔⓔ ♛ 89FF

GRAMONA

Penedès, Spain

CELLER BATTLE 1992 CAVA GRAN RESERVA BRUT, GRAMONA ⑦⑤

Very rich with smooth, oaky-oxidative slant to the fruit.
❦ Now ⓔⓔ ♛ 4,500 Ptas

CELLER BATTLE 2001 1993 CAVA, GRAMONA ⑦⑥

Elegance and complexity.
❦ Now ⓔⓔ ♛ 2,800 Ptas

III LUSTROS GRAMONA 1993 CAVA BRUT NATURE GRAN RESERVA ⑦⑨

An excellent Cava with loads of flavour, a lovely fluffy mousse and fine acidity on the finish.
❦ Now–2001 ⓔⓔ ♛ 2,800 Ptas

GRAND FRÈRES

Jura, France

GRAND FRÈRES NV CRÉMANT DU JURA, BRUT PRESTIGE ⑦③

Elegant, creamy fruit with very good acidity. This wine would have scored higher had it been as immediately appealing on the nose as it was on the palate.
❦ Now–2001 ⓔ ♛ 42FF

GRANT BURGE

South Australia, Australia

GRANT BURGE NV BAROSSA PINOT NOIR CHARDONNAY ⑦⑤

Fresh, tangy fruit.
❦ Now ⓔⓔ ♛ A$20

GRATIEN

Champagne Alfred Gratien
30 rue Maurice Cerveaux
51201 Epernay
☎(326) 54.38.20 ℻(41) 51.03.55

ALFRED GRATIEN NV BRUT ⑧⑦

With such finesse on the nose and elegantly rich, classically structured fruit on the palate, what more could a Champagne drinker expect from a basic non-vintage?
❦ Now–2004 ⓔⓔ

ALFRED GRATIEN 1991 BRUT ⑧⑤

Not a top Gratien vintage, but promises to have greater longevity than most 1991s and better than Gratien's 1993.

➤ 2001–2005 ⓔⓔ

GRATIEN & MEYER
Loire, France

GRATIEN & MEYER NV CUVÉE ROYALE BRUT

A delicious wine that is so refreshing it might even be thirst-quenching.
❚ Now ⓔ

GRATIEN MEYER SEYDOUX NV CUVÉE FLAMME BRUT, SAUMUR

Embossed bottle, stylish presentation. Fine, direct, focused fruit with good acidity.
❚ 2001–2002 ⓔ

GRENELLE
Louis de Grenelle
Loire, France

LES CAVES LOUIS DE GRENELLE NV BRUT GRANDE CUVÉE 2000, SAUMUR

Sweet user-friendly style, but would have been better if the grapes had been riper and the dosage therefore smaller.
❚ Now–2002 ⓔ

GRUSS
Joseph Gruss
Alsace, France

GRUSS NV CRÉMANT D'ALSACE, BRUT PRESTIGE

Also VA lifted, but fresher and zippier.
❚ Now–2001 ⓔ

JOSEPH GRUSS & FILS NV CRÉMANT D'ALSACE BRUT

VA lifted fruit, but the VA is within acceptable levels.
❚ Now–2001 ⓔ

GUILLEMINOT
Champagne Michel Guilleminot
10340 Channes
☎(325) 29.17.31 ℻(325) 29.17.31

MICHEL GUILLEMINOT NV BRUT

The current *cuvée* has fine fruit, high acids and is dosaged to go toasty. The pre-release sample of the next *cuvée* is very similar, but with even more emphasis on fruit.
❚ Now–2003 ⓔⓔ 🍇 68FF

ATTENTION CHAMPAGNE & SPARKLING WINE PRODUCERS!
If you are not already in contact with the author, but would like to submit wines for consideration in future editions, please contact Tom Stevenson at:

tom.stevenson@fizz.worldonline.co.uk

Warning: Any other unsolicited mail received at this address will be ignored.

Please note that recommendation in this guide involves no charge whatsoever beyond the cost of the samples and their delivery.

GUINOT
Limoux, France

GUINOT NV IMPÉRIAL, CRÉMANT DE LIMOUX, BRUT-TENDRE

Malolactic aromas dominate, but very crisp, flavoursome fruit.
❚ Now–2001 ⓔ

HACKWOOD
Robertsbridge, East Sussex
England, UK

HACKWOOD NV MILLENNIUM SPARKLING

Easy-drinking style with plenty of fresh, breezy fruit. This may improve a year or two beyond 2002, but it is my first

---

experience of Hackwood, so it is best to be cautious.
❚ Now–2001 ⓔ

blanc de blancs that made Handley's early reputation?
 2001–2003 ⓔⓔ ☙ $28

HAGNAU

Winzerverein Hagnau
Baden, Germany

WINZERVEREIN HAGNAU GRAUER BURGUNDER BRUT 1997 RUMORE

Lovely fresh aroma, followed by very fresh, sweet, elegant fruit on the palate. (*Méthode rurale.*)
❚ Now–2001 ⓔ ☙ DM29

HAHN

Pfalz, Germany

ULRICH HAHN 1997 RIESLING BRUT

Beautiful Riesling nose, so fresh and *vif*, although not quite the promised finesse on the palate. (*Méthode champenoise.*)
❚ Now ⓔ ☙ DM15

HAMBACHER SCHLOSS

Baden, Germany

WINZERGENOSSENSCHAFT HAMBACHER SCHLOß RIESLING BRU 1996 RIESLING SEKT

Although rich and tasty, the Riesling fruit could have been better focused. (Transfer method.)
❚ Now–2001 ⓔ ☙ DM15

HANDLEY

California, USA

HANDLEY 1995 BRUT

The pre-release sample suggests that you will want to give this wine at least a year to soften, but it does promise to repay dividends. Where, I want to know, is the

---

HASELGROVE

South Australia, Australia

HASELGROVE NV-2 MT. GAMBIER CHARDONNAY PINOT NOIR

Tastes as if the wine has been matured with medium-toast American oak chips to impart coffee aromas. It's not my thing because I prefer the coffee aromas to take decades to evolve, but it is a style that has its following.
❚ Now ⓔ ☙ A$19.90

HASELGROVE NV McLAREN VALE GARNET SG-6 ⑧⓪

Much preferred to the aldehydic SG-5, which cannot be recommended, but not quite up to the SG-3 and SG-4 (81 points) tasted two years ago. The SG-6 has nicely balanced off-dry fruit-acidity and a surprising amount of autolytic finesse for a style that normally overwhelms the subtle effects of autolysis.
❚ Now ⓔ ☙ A$19.90

HEATHFIELD RIDGE

South Australia, Australia

HEATHFIELD RIDGE 1999 WONAMBI LIMESTONE COAST CHARDONNAY PINOT NOIR

This light rosé coloured fizz is very sweet. It is just like drinking sparkling pear juice. Not my sort of thing. Indeed, I've never tasted anything quite like it, but I'm sure somebody will love it.
❚ Now ⓔ ☙ A$9.50

HEIDSIECK

Champagne Charles Heidsieck
4 Blvd. Henry Vasnier
51100 Reims
☎(326) 84.43.50 📠(326) 84.43.99

CHARLES HEIDSIECK NV BRUT RÉSERVE, MIS EN CAVE EN 1996

Charles Heidsieck hits 90 points with the Mis en Cave en 1996 version of its basic non-vintage, which offers pure class in a glass. My only complaint is to wonder when this house will realize that each new Mis en Cave (MC) is released when this Guide is published, thus this wine should have been submitted last year because although it will still be available Charles Heidsieck will be onto the MC 1997 by the time this edition is published and the MC 1996 will be old news. Hopefully next year the penny will drop and they will submit the "old" MC 1997 (based on the amazing 1996 vintage), MC 1998 (which will be released when the next edition is published) and MC 1999 (due to be released at the end of the next edition's shelf-life).
❢ Now–2005 ⓔⓔⓔ 🥂 180FF

CHARLES HEIDSIECK NV BRUT RÉSERVE PRIVÉE, MIS EN CAVE EN 1990

This toasty-rich Champagne is definitely beginning to peak, but it is based on the fat 1989 vintage (plus 40% reserve wine), so perhaps this is understandable. Will Charles Heidsieck release Réserve Privée Mis en Cave en 1991 based on the 1990 vintage? Like this wine, such a wine was never released as a Mis en Cave, but merely slipped through as an undated Brut Réserve. However, when that wine was originally released it coincided with the widespread accolades Charles Heidsieck received for its recently relaunched non-vintage and at a vertical tasting a couple of years ago it stood out as the very best in the line up.
❢ Now–2002 ⓔⓔⓔ 🥂 300FF

CHARLES HEIDSIECK NV BRUT RÉSERVE, MIS EN CAVE EN 1993

Deliciously fat with strawberry Pinot fruit dominating the palate and oodles of delicate vanilla nuances from nose to finish.
❢ Now–2001 ⓔⓔⓔ

CHARLES HEIDSIECK NV BRUT RÉSERVE, MIS EN CAVE EN 1995

The last release of this *cuvée* was so fresh it even had a hint of green when held up to natural northern light, with beautifully crisp and biscuity fruit and a fresh, floral finish that will gradually take on an exquisitely smooth vanilla finesse.
❢ Now–2003 ⓔⓔⓔ

HEIDSIECK MONOPOLE

Champagne Heidsieck & Co Monopole
17 avenue de Champagne
51205 Epernay Cedex
☎(326) 59.50.00 FAX(326) 51.87.07

HEIDSIECK MONOPOLE 1995 BRUT

Some richness and class. This brand is part of the Vranken stable, which also includes Charbaut, Barancourt, Demoiselle, Charles Lafitte and, of course, Vranken. As a general comment on the group as a whole, the emphasis is definitely more on quantity than quality or individual expression, but there are often nuggets of pleasure waiting to be dug out. However, I seem to spend a disproportionate amount of time trying to coax samples from Vranken, so this year, as in future years, I will report on only those wines I happen to come across. Even when I'm successful in coaxing samples, Vranken openly declares that it is not worth submitting Charbaut or Barancourt, which speaks volumes about its regard for the customers of those brands.
❢ Now–2005 ⓔⓔⓔ

❖ HEIM, MARTIN HEIM, *see* Heim'sche

HEIM'SCHE

Pfalz, Germany

HEIM'SCHE PRIVAT-SEKTKELLEREI 1998 RIESLING BRUT

Nicely tart peachy fruit, not lacking in finesse. (*Méthode champenoise.*)
❢ Now–2001 ⓔ

HENKELL & SÖHNLEIN
Rheingau, Germany

FÜRST VON METTERNICH RIESLING EXTRA BRUT 1998 HENKELL & SÖHNLEIN

Quite elegant. This used to be one of the three best Sekte back in the bad old days and H&S are obviously trying hard to keep up. (*Méthode champenoise*.)
🍷 Now Ⓔ ⚱ DM22

HENRIET-BAZIN
Champagne D. Henriet-Bazin
9bis Rue Dom Pérignon
51380 Villers-Marmery
☎(326) 97.96.81 ℻(326) 97.97.30

D. HENRIET-BAZIN 1992 CARTE D'OR BRUT PREMIER CRU

Nutty-biscuity aromas followed by a mellow ripeness of fruit that tastes quite sweet for a Brut.
🍷 Now–2002 ⒺⒺ

HENRIOT
Champagne Henriot
3 Place des Droits de l'Homme
51100 Reims
☎(326) 89.53.00 ℻(326) 89.53.10

HENRIOT NV BRUT SOVEREIGN

Fresh and tasty with fruit as pure as driven snow, a fluffy mousse and a nicely crisp finish.
🍷 Now–2003 ⒺⒺ

HENRIOT NV BLANC DE BLANCS CHARDONNAY BRUT

Firm, fine and sharp. This wine deserves to be aged, when it will fatten and take on toasty aromas, but makes an excellent aperitif in the meantime.
🍷 Now–2003 ⒺⒺ

HENRIOT 1995 BRUT MILLÉSIMÉ

A touch too fat and more malo aromas than there should be, but

some will like that.
🍷 Now–2002 ⒺⒺⒺ

HENRIOT 1988 CUVÉE DES ENCHANTELEURS, BRUT

It looks as if Henriot has blown it by releasing this vintage now, when it's not ready, and in strict chronological order, when it needs at least another 12 months on yeast and, ironically, the 1989 (92 points) was begging to be disgorged last year.
🍾 2001–2006 ⒺⒺⒺⒺ

HERRES
*Klaus Herres
Mosel-Saar-Ruwer, Germany*

KLAUS HERRES RIESLING BRUT 1998 ST. LAURENTIUS

Fresh, sherbety aroma, with fine, soft, exquisitely clean fruit of good Brut dryness. (*Méthode champenoise*.)
🍷 Now Ⓔ ⚱ DM22

KLAUS HERRES RIESLING EXTRA BRUT 1997 ST. LAURENTIUS

Fresh, floral Riesling on the nose, already developing some bottle aromas on the palate. Soft finish. (*Méthode champenoise*.)
🍷 Now–2003 Ⓔ ⚱ DM22

HIGHFIELD ESTATE
Marlborough, New Zealand
Sparkling wine under the Elstree label has been produced at this Tuscan-style winery since 1993, but the quality did not come right until the 1995 vintage. The 1999 base wines seemed rather fat, but had good acidity.

ELSTREE 1996 BRUT, HIGHFIELD ESTATE

This was originally sold as a non-vintage millennium *cuvée,* and that was what I tasted when visiting Highfield. Thus its fine, crisp fruit I enjoyed can be considered an early-disgorged version of the 1996 vintage, which should have deeper, more yeast-complexed fruit

when released.
Now–2002 ⒺⒺ

ELSTREE 1995 BRUT, HIGHFIELD ESTATE (*magnum*)

This vintage is far more impressive in magnums than bottles.
Now–2003 ⒺⒺ

ELSTREE 1995 BRUT, HIGHFIELD ESTATE

Although this wine has jumped a full five points over last year's score and shows excellent autolysis on the nose, the fruit is less fine on the palate compared to the same vintage in magnums.
Now–2001 ⒺⒺ

HILL
Cavas Hill
Penedès, Spain

CAVAS HILL NV CAVA ROSADO BRUT

The creamy-peppery Garnacha fruit that dominates could so easily be from Roussillon in France.
Now Ⓔ 🍇 1,075 Ptas

HOSTOMME
Champagne M. Hostomme
5 rue de l'Allée
51530 Chouilly
☎(326) 55.40.79 ℻(326) 55.08.55

M. HOSTOMME NV CUVÉE TRADITION BRUT 83

The concentrated flavours in this *cuvée* require time to blossom.
▬ 2001–2002 ⒺⒺ

M. HOSTOMME NV BRUT GRAND CRU, BLANC DE BLANCS 82

Fresh, crisp aperitif style, with vaguely amylic hints and a surprisingly full finish for the weight of wine.
Now–2002 ⒺⒺ

M. HOSTOMME, GRANDE RÉSERVE NV BLANC DE BLANCS, BRUT GRAND CRU 80

Although richer than Hostomme's basic Grand Cru *blanc de blancs*, there is almost a muskiness that some will like and others will not.
Now–2001 ⒺⒺ

HUNTER'S
Marlborough, New Zealand

HUNTER'S 1995 BRUT

This malo-dominated wine is much fatter than I expected it might be when tasted last year. It has less acidity that the Miru Miru, with a leaner finish and an attractive biscuity complexity building on the finish.
Now–2002 ⒺⒺ

HUNTER'S 1996 BRUT

Hunter's Brut came of age with this vintage, setting itself apart from and above the Miru Miru, the first vintage of which (1995) had always trounced it, despite the simplicity of Miru Miru's unpretentious, fruit-driven style. Hunter's has always tried to be a bigger, more complex wine, but lacked finesse. The 1996, however, is a truly complex wine, with slow-building aromas and an undeniable finesse throughout. Perhaps now is the time for Hunter's to relaunch this wine internationally as Miru Miru Reserve.
Now–2002 ⒺⒺ

MIRU MIRU 1995 HUNTER'S

I'm constantly revising the drinking window of this wine, the first vintage of Miru Miru to be released, because it was initially so yummy and drinkable, yet has become progressively more serious as each year passes. It now has toasty bottle-aromas, yet the fruit is still very fresh and lively, with a fine structure and a gentle mousse of tiny bubbles.
Now–2002 ⒺⒺ

MIRU MIRU 1996 HUNTER'S

Just so moreish!
Now–2003 ⒺⒺ

MIRU MIRU 1997 HUNTER'S

Such soft and succulent fruit.
🍷 Now–2003 Ⓔ Ⓕ

MIRU MIRU 1998 HUNTER'S

The pre-release sample promised to be
the best Miru Miru yet. To produce a
fruit-driven wine that ages gracefully
must be every winemaker's dream. Due to
be released in 2001.
▬ 2001–2003 Ⓔ Ⓕ

❖ **III LUSTROS**, *see* Gramona

INGERSHEIM

Alsace, France

JEAN GEILER NV RIESLING BRUT, CRÉMANT D'ALSACE, PRESTIGE

A travesty as far as Riesling goes, but
better than a lot of Crémant d'Alsace,
whatever varieties they are produced
from.
🍷 Now–2002 Ⓔ

JEAN GEILER, CUVÉE AN 2000 NV CRÉMANT D'ALSACE, BLANC DE BLANCS BRUT PRESTIGE

Very fresh and a lot softer than most
Crémant d'Alsace, with fresh pear fruit,
although with finesse and not at all banal
amylic type.
🍷 Now–2001 Ⓔ

IRON HORSE

California, USA

IRON HORSE 1997 WEDDING CUVÉE, BLANC DE NOIR

Fresh, fruity and easy-drinking. The sort
of thing that won't offend anyone and yet
should also appeal to serious sparkling
wine drinkers.
🍷 Now–2001 Ⓔ Ⓕ 🍾 $28

IRON HORSE 1995 RUSSIAN CUVÉE

A deep, intensely flavoured fizz with
more than enough extract to balance
the sweetness, making Russian Cuvée
seem drier than many so-called Brut

sparkling wines.
🍷 Now–2004 Ⓔ Ⓕ 🍾 $26

IRON HORSE 1995 CLASSIC VINTAGE BRUT

Lots of malo, lots of extract and lots of
promise, but you will have to wait.
▬ 2002–2004 Ⓔ Ⓕ 🍾 $26

IRON HORSE 1994 BRUT ROSÉ

The creamy-butterscotchy aroma would
normally be a negative factor, but
although clearly defined, it is
unobtrusive, especially on the palate
where the fruit is so crisp and vital.
🍷 Now–2002 Ⓔ Ⓕ 🍾 $30

IRVINE

South Australia, Australia

IRVINE MERLOT NV BRUT

Creamy fruit on the nose, with very
smooth, creamy fruit on palate, tasting of
plums and raspberry ripple. A fruit-
driven style that is much drier than most.
🍷 Now–2001 Ⓔ Ⓕ

JACQUART

Champagne Jacquart
6 rue de Mars
51057 Reims
☎(326) 07.88.40 ℻(326) 07.12.07

JACQUART NV BRUT MOSAÏQUE

In the early part of 2000, this wine was
on top form (86 points), with crisp, floral,
stylish fruit showing more finesse than
many a *grande marque*, but the sample
received later in the year lacked finesse,
possessing rather simple lemony fruit.
🍷 Now–2002 Ⓔ Ⓕ 🍾 125FF

JACQUART NV DEMI-SEC

The flavours are more winey than
Champagne, with musky hints. This
Demi-Sec needs at least one year to settle
down and its score could increase as it
evolves.
▬ 2001–2005 Ⓔ Ⓕ 🍾 125FF

JACQUART 1992 CUVÉE MOSAÏQUE, BLANC DE BLANCS BRUT
88

The creamy fruit on the finish last year was an indication of skilful use of malolactic to add layers of texture rather than the heavier-handed approach, which merely lumbers a wine with buttery/caramel aromas that are so bloated they negate the elegance and finesse that should be intrinsic to the crisp style of a classic sparkling wine. This year I found some caramel, but because it has taken a year to emerge, the caramel is unobtrusive, integrating nicely with the biscuity complexity that is also developing. The result is a lovely, rich, mellow Champagne of true class. Consequently, while the straight vintage 1992 has maintained its score from last year, this Blanc de Blancs has edged ahead two points.
❚ Now–2003 ££££

JACQUART NV BRUT MOSAÏQUE
(magnum)
87

Lovely toasty aromas follow through onto the palate, where the high acidity keeps the mellow, matured fruit fresh, crisp and snappy. I would keep the wine at least another 12 months to smooth out the mousse.
❚ Now–2003 ££

JACQUART 1992 MOSAÏQUE MILLÉSIMÉ BRUT
86

This was ultra-fruity last year, but has quickly developed a toasty richness, with an excellent backbone of ripe acidity.
❚ Now–2003 £££ ⚘ 160FF

JACQUESSON

Champagne Jacquesson & Fils
68 rue du Colonel Fabien
51200 Dizy
☎(326) 55.68.11 ☏(326) 51.06.25

JACQUESSON & FILS NV PERFECTION BRUT
85

This *cuvée* seems to alternate between deep and rich, and light and elegant, although it is always crisp and classic. This year it's back to light and elegant.

❚ Now–2003 ££ ⚘ 160FF

JACQUESSON & FILS NV PERFECTION BRUT ROSÉ
84

The UK shipment tasted in early 2000 was definitely not up to the releases in the previous two years (88 points last year, 87 points the year before) and would have been lucky to scrape in at 80 points. However, the samples sent directly from France were a big improvement, with nice fluffy fruit for immediate drinking, but with the acidity and structure to improve awhile.
❚ Now–2001 £££ ⚘ 180FF

JACQUESSON & FILS 1995 BLANC DE BLANCS, BRUT GRAND CRU
86

Not quite as impressive as the 1993 was last year, but it is a year younger, and neither vintage can compare to exuberant 1990. The 1995 has a more restrained style and is thus more classic, but we will have to wait to see how much better it will get, although it is already developing a biscuitiness.
❚ Now–2005 £££ ⚘ 260FF

JACQUESSON & FILS 1985 BRUT, DÉGORGEMENT TARDIF
88

This year's release was disgorged in January 2000 and drops two points over last year's both as it was then, and, from cellaring the second sample, how it has aged since. This could well achieve a similar quality in years to come, but I am a great believer in windows of opportunity as far as disgorgements go and there was no time up to January 1999, when last year's release was disgorged, that it would have been possible and now it seems that the window has shut. At least for the time being.
 2002–2006 ££££ ⚘ 550FF

JACQUESSON & FILS 1990 GRAND VIN SIGNATURE, BRUT
91

The fruit in this year's release (disgorged July 1999) has intensified, the heavenly coffee-toasty after-aromas have yet to form and as far as serious Champagne drinkers will be concerned, this wine begs to be cellared for a couple of years.
 2002–2007 ££££ ⚘ 350FF

JACQUESSON & FILS 1990 GRAND VIN SIGNATURE, BRUT ROSÉ

The disgorgement tasted last year is starting to emerge from its tightening-up phase, but still needs a year or two, although it promises to mature very gracefully from then on. The more recent release of this vintage was disgorged in August 1999 and has already acquired a sumptuous, creamy-biscuity richness.

Now–2002 ⓔⓔⓔⓔ 🥂 390FF

JACQUESSON & FILS 1990 GRAND VIN SIGNATURE, BRUT *(magnum)*

The magnum effect on Jacquesson's 1990 has to be experienced to be believed. Just 850 magnums were produced and the sample I tasted was disgorged in November 1998. The fruit is slowly infusing with aromas of coffee-cream and toast, similar to the bottles of this wine last year, but with the finesse and ultimate complexity quadrupled.

Now–2009 ⓔⓔⓔⓔ

ATTENTION CHAMPAGNE & SPARKLING WINE PRODUCERS!

If you are not already in contact with the author, but would like to submit wines for consideration in future editions, please contact Tom Stevenson at:

tom.stevenson@fizz.worldonline.co.uk

Warning: Any other unsolicited mail received at this address will be ignored.

Please note that recommendation in this guide involves no charge whatsoever beyond the cost of the samples and their delivery.

JAMAIN

Champagne Pierre Jamain
1 rue des Tuileries
51260 La Celle-sous-Chantemerle
☎(326) 80.21.64 FAX(326) 80.29.32

PIERRE JAMAIN 1996 BRUT MILLÉSIME

I tasted a pre-release sample of this vintage, which is due to be launched two months after publication of this Guide

and from the nose alone, it obviously needed more time, but the fruit is excellent. Watch out for more comments on this wine.

Wait and see ⓔⓔ 🥂 78FF

❖ **JANSZ**, *see* Smith

JURA

*Les Grands Vins du Jura
Jura, France*

LES GRANDS VINS DU JURA 1996 BRUT DARGENT, MÉTHODE TRADITIONNELLE, CHARDONNAY

Age has given this wine an attractive oak-like dimension.

Now ⓔ

JUVÉ & CAMPS

Penedès, Spain

GRAN JUVÉ & CAMPS 1995 CAVA GRAN RESERVA BRUT

Some ripe fruit richness.

Now ⓔⓔ 🥂 3,500 Ptas

JUVÉ & CAMPS 1995 CAVA MILESIMÉ BRUT

This Cava stands out visually due to its Roederer lookalike presentation. Supposedly 100% Chardonnay, but needs better varietal quality. However, it does have sufficient potential to warrant keeping an eye on.

Wait and see ⓔⓔ 🥂 2,600 Ptas

KALLFELZ

Mosel-Saar-Ruwer, Germany

ALBERT KALLFELZ RIESLING BRUT 1998 KALLFELZ RIESLING

A very soft, yet very crisp Riesling (this grape usually infers a certain crispness) that is elegant and ready to drink. (*Méthode champenoise.*)

Now ⓔ 🥂 DM17

KALLSTADT

Pfalz, Germany

WINZERGENOSSENSCHAFT KALLSTADT RIESLING EXTRA TROCKEN 1998 KALLSTADTER KOBNERT

Fresh and frothy, closer to Brut than Extra Brut. (*Méthode champenoise.*)
🥂 Now ⓔ 🍾 DM10

KESSELER

Rheingau, Germany

AUGUST KESSELER 1998 RIESLING BRUT

Very crisp and fresh, with lime fruit and freshly-squeezed lemon acidity. This Brut is more Extra Brut than most Extra Brut are. (*Méthode champenoise.*)
🥂 Now–2001 ⓔ

KESSELSTATT

Mosel-Saar-Ruwer, Germany

REICHSGRAF VON KESSELSTATT NV RIESLING BRUT

More character than finesse, but clean, which characteristics alone would have been outstanding a few years ago. (*Méthode champenoise.*)
🥂 Now ⓔ 🍾 DM20

KLOSS & FOERSTER

Rheingau, Germany

KLOSS & FOERSTER RIESLING BRUT 1997 RÜDESHEIMER BERG ROTTLAND

Very fresh, fine floral aromas, followed by rich and tasty fruit. This Sekt does not lack finesse, but it does promise to get finer with age. (*Méthode champenoise.*)
🥂 Now–2003 ⓔⓔ 🍾 DM30

KLOSS & FOERSTER SPÄTBURGUNDER EXTRA TROCKEN 1997 ASSMANNSHÄUSER HÖLLENBERG

Classic Pinot aroma and fruit; the class of its origin shows through. (*Méthode champenoise.*)
🥂 Now–2001 ⓔⓔ 🍾 DM34

❖ **KLOSTER EBERBACH,** *see* Eberbach

KNYPHAUSEN

Rheingau, Germany

FREIHERR ZU KNYPHAUSEN RIESLING EXTRA BRUT 1993 HERRLICHKEIT KNYPHAUSEN

A very fresh, perfumed, soft-honeyed-petrol Riesling that works well with a low dosage. (*Méthode champenoise.*)
🥂 Now–2001 ⓔ 🍾 DM29

FREIHERR ZU KNYPHAUSEN RIESLING EXTRA TROCKEN 1997 BARON ZU KNYPHAUSEN

The fruit is very crisp, with a crunchy-grape sensation and plenty of extract. A Sekt that does not lack finesse. (*Cuve close.*)
🥂 Now–2003 ⓔ 🍾 DM19

KORBEL

California, USA

Don't run off to buy the basic non-vintage without reading my comments first.

KORBEL NV BRUT

If the Blanc de Noirs surprised me, this scared me to death by comparison. The sample I tasted was unlike any non-vintage Brut I've ever tasted from Korbel and as I encountered it in February 2000 I doubt that it will still be available when this edition is published, but this recommendation is for anyone who tucked away a bottle in the first quarter of 2000.
🥂 Now ⓔ 🍾 $10

KORBEL NV BLANC DE NOIRS

No one was more surprised than me when I discovered what this was, but its fruit is fresh, clean and easy to drink, so all credit to Korbel.

❦ Now ⓔ 🍾 $10

KÖWERICH

Mosel-Saar-Ruwer, Germany

KÖWERICH RIESLING BRUT 1994 MOUSEL

Rich Riesling fruit, very fresh and sherbety, with crisp finish. Amazingly fresh for 6-year-old Sekt. (*Méthode champenoise*.)

❦ Now–2001 ⓔ 🍾 DM11

❖ **KRAEMER**, *see* Landiras

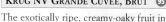

KRUG

Champagne Krug
5 rue Coquebert
51100 Reims
☎(326) 84.44.20 📠(326) 84.44.49

Krug can be classic Krug, but can never be classic Champagne. If it were there would be no other classic Champagnes because Krug is unique.

KRUG NV GRANDE CUVÉE, BRUT

The exotically ripe, creamy-oaky fruit in this Champagne is classic Krug.

❦ Now–2008 ⓔⓔⓔⓔ

KRUG ROSÉ NV BRUT 96

This *cuvée* is on sensational form. If you close your eyes and ignore the bubbles (which is not difficult, their being so microscopic and the mousse so soft), it's just like a gracefully matured red Burgundy from a great vineyard in a light year. Something like a perfectly preserved Charmes-Chambertin, with its ripe-fruit flavours and pure Pinot character set against a backdrop of beautifully integrated oak. Perhaps the most amazing thing is that Krug use 55% Pinot tops and the oak averages 40 years of age. Just where do those carefully crafted flavours come from?

❦ Now–2001 ⓔⓔⓔⓔ

KRUG 1988 BRUT

To die for!

❦ Now–2012 ⓔⓔⓔⓔ

KRUG COLLECTION 1979 BRUT

I've died and gone to heaven.

❦ Now–2005 ⓔⓔⓔⓔ

KUEHN

Alsace, France

BARON DE SCHIELE NV CRÉMANT D'ALSACE BRUT

VA lifted, but some finesse on finish. Let down by aftertaste.

❦ Now ⓔ

BARON DE SCHIELE NV RIESLING, CRÉMANT D'ALSACE BRUT

Also VA lifted, but less finesse, although finishes better.

❦ Now–2001 ⓔ

❖ **L'EPINAY**/Domaine du Clos de l'Epinay, *see* Epinay

❖ **L'ETOILE**/Château de l'Etoile, *see* Etoile

LABORIE

Paarl, South Africa

LABORIE 1994 CAP CLASSIQUE, BRUT

Cappuccino aroma followed by good acid on the palate, but where's the fruit? I must see how this strange brew develops before committing myself.

➤ Wait and see ⓔ 🍾 R35

CHATEAU LAFAYETTE RENEAU
New York, USA

CHATEAU LAFAYETTE RENEAU 1997 BLANC DE BLANCS

Soft, ripe, pears and apple fruit.
❦ Now–2001 ©© ❧ $24.95

LAGACHE
Champagne Lagache
12 rue de la Marquetterie
51530 Pierry
☎(326) 54.03.12 ℻(326) 55.47.60

LAGACHE 1995 PRESTIGE DE CONSORTS GRAND CRU

This rich, well-constructed Champagne is currently the best in the Lagache range, knocking spots off the Grande Réserve Premier Cru Brut, which was the best wine last year, but did not impress this time around.
❦ Now–2004 ©©©

❖ **L'AIGLE**, _see_ Aigle

LAISEMENT
Loire, France

LAISEMENT JEAN-PIERRE NV MÉTHODE TRADITIONNELLE BRUT, VOUVRAY

Can't deny the Chenin Blanc fruit, but it requires a touch more finesse and less angular structure to achieve a higher score.
❦ Now–2001 ©

LALLIER
Champagne René-James Lallier
4 place de la Libération
BP5 51160 Aÿ-Champagne
☎(326) 55.32.87 ℻(326) 55.79.93

RENÉ JAMES LALLIER NV BRUT ROSÉ

A serious rosé with firm strawberry-Pinot fruit.
❦ Now–2003 ©© ❧ 105FF

LAMIABLE
Champagne Lamiable
8 Rempart Est
51150 Tours-sur-Marne
☎(326) 58.92.69 ℻(326) 58.76.67

LAMIABLE NV EXTRA BRUT, GRAND CRU

Fine, firm, crisp fruit with plenty of extract. Ideal as an aperitif, providing the first wine served at the table is not overwhelmed. Equally at home with food, particularly with tomatoes baked in cream.
❦ Now–2002 ©© ❧ 85FF

LAMOREAUX LANDING
New York, USA

Although Glenora has the track record for making New York's best fizz, Lamoreaux Landing shows the greater promise. Even though its most successful _cuvées_ are really much too coconutty-oaky for a classic quality of sparkling wine, this cannot hide the finesse. Furthermore there is something about the winery, its design and the people who run it that tell me this is a class player.

LAMOREAUX LANDING 1996 BRUT

Although the _barrique_ aromas are too oaky for a classic sparkling wine, they are not quite as intrusive as those in the 1995 vintage and the softer, smoother mousse contributes considerably more finesse.
❦ Now–2002 © ❧ $16

LAMOREAUX LANDING 1995 BRUT

Fizzy coconut? For those who love coconut only.
❦ Now–2001 © ❧ $18

LAMOREAUX LANDING 1992 BLANC DE BLANCS

Tangy fruit with very much a _crémant_

mousse, creamy textured on the aftertaste.

❚ Now–2001 ⓔ 🥂 $16

LANDIRAS

France

LES CAVES DE LANDIRAS NV KRAEMER BLANC DE BLANCS

Very clean, with nice acidity, fine mousse of very tiny bubbles.

❚ Now ⓔ

SEPPI LANDMANN

Alsace, France

SEPPI LANDMANN NV CRÉMANT D'ALSACE, BRUT DE BRUT

Attractive Chardonnay aromas followed by stone fruits on the palate, particularly plums, underpinned by lime acidity, with a short creamy-biscuit finish. Would have scored higher, but for the short finish.

❚ Now–2001 ⓔ

SEPPI LANDMANN 1987 CRÉMANT D'ALSACE, BRUT DE BRUT *(magnum)*

What a pity! Although amazingly well preserved for a 13-year-old Crémant d'Alsace (6–8 years would normally be stretching it), a wine of this age in magnum cries out for a Brut dosage to ensure that any further ageing will be graceful.

❚ Now ⓔ

LANG

Rheingau, Germany

HANS LANG RIESLING EXTRA BRUT 1997 JOHANN MAXIMILIAN

Crisp, firm Riesling fruit front palate, although somewhat elevated mid-palate (*Méthode champenoise.*)

❚ Now–2001 ⓔ 🥂 DM24

LANGLOIS-CHÂTEAU

Loire, France

LANGLOIS NV CRÉMANT DE LOIRE BRUT

I prefer this simple fruity non-vintage brut to the upmarket Quadrille *cuvée*, which started out extremely disappointing, but deserved praise in the last edition only to slip back into the abyss this year.

❚ Now ⓔ

LANGLOIS NV CRÉMANT DE LOIRE, BRUT ROSÉ

A fresh easy-drinking fizz with light-bodied fruit sporting a hint of raspberry and rose-petal.

❚ Now ⓔ

LANGLOIS 1995 CRÉMANT DE LOIRE, BRUT RÉSERVE

Tasty and extremely youthful for a five-year-old Loire fizz.

❚ Now ⓔ

LANSON

Champagne Lanson
12 Boulevard Lundy
51100 Reims
☎(326) 78.50.50 📠(326) 78.50.99

Since this firm's acquisition in 1991 by the Marne et Champagne group, which purchased everything except its vast estate of highly rated vineyards, critics have been quick to pounce on this missing piece in the Lanson puzzle. They have suggested that its quality will suffer as a result, but they were too quick off the mark because the lost vineyards affect only Lanson's vintage *cuvées* (the bulk of Lanson's non-vintage Black Label having always been produced from bought-in grapes). There might be a drop in quality, but no one knows now, so they most certainly did not almost 10 years ago. This is because the best Lanson vintages have always needed time to show their true potential and 1995, the first true vintage under Lanson's new ownership, has yet to be released. And this is Champagne, not any old sparkling wine, so even when it is released we will still need to evaluate how the wine develops. Then what? You cannot

LANSON *(continued)*

build or destroy a *grande marque* reputation on a single vintage. However, other critics are less rational and I have to admit that Lanson does not do itself any favours by declaring 1994 a vintage.

LANSON NV BLACK LABEL, BRUT 87

Needs a touch more ageing than last year's *cuvée*, but excellent all the same, with a great depth of flavour and invigorating acidity.
▬ 2001–2005 ⓔⓔ ✿ 160FF

LANSON NV BLACK LABEL BRUT 84

Although there is an unusual smoothness to the fruit, this wine still needs ageing to show its true potential. Not in the same class as the previous two years.
▬ 2001–2003 ⓔⓔ ✿ 160FF

LANSON NV ROSE LABEL BRUT ROSÉ 86

An age-worthy rosé with excellent acidity and classic white Champagne flavours that build in the mouth.
❙ Now–2004 ⓔⓔⓔ ✿ 180FF

LANSON NV IVORY LABEL DEMI-SEC 88

Always one of the few top-quality demi-sec Champagnes, but please cellar it for a few years.
❙ Now–2006 ⓔⓔ

LANSON 1994 GOLD LABEL BRUT 80

This just scrapes in. I'm not sure why Lanson even bothered with this vintage. It was nowhere near as good a year as 1993 and, excellent though that was for Lanson, it was not exactly a top Lanson vintage. Hopefully, this wine has hidden depths that can push up the score at a later date.
❙ Now–2001 ⓔⓔⓔ ✿ 190FF

LANSON 1993 GOLD LABEL BRUT 88

An extra year on yeast has endowed the most recent disgorgements of this wine with greater potential longevity. The biscuity-rich fruit found in last year's release is now barely discernible as a lovely mellowness, but we know what's to come and the longer it takes the more

finesse the biscuity complexity will have.
❙ Now–2004 ⓔⓔⓔ

BLANC DE BLANCS DE LANSON 1994 BRUT 84

The expansive fruit here makes this one of the better 1994s, but watch out for oxidative aromas developing.
❙ Now–2001 ⓔⓔⓔⓔ

LANTIERI DE PARATICO
Franciacorta, Italy

LANTIERI DE PARATICO 1995 BRUT ARCADIA 80

Infused with vanilla custard.
❙ Now–2001 ⓔⓔ ✿ 25,000 Lira

LARMANDIER
Champagne Larmandier
46 rue du Mont Félix
51200 Cramant
☎(326) 57.52.19 ℻(326) 59.79.84

LARMANDIER NV BLANC DE BLANCS, BRUT 1ER CRU 80

Clean and fresh, but too cool-fermented for an artisanal Champagne. This could have been so much better had the first fermentation been a few degrees warmer. It does, however, make the cut, whereas Larmandier's Grand Cru Blanc de Blancs did not, due, ironically, to overly oxidative character, which is the opposite criticism of this *cuvée* (doubly ironic when the Grand Cru last year was amylic!).
❙ Now–2002 ⓔⓔ

LARMANDIER 1995 GRAND CRU CHARDONNAY, BRUT 90

Wonderfully pure fruit supported by a compact structure, suggesting considerable development to come, although already a joy to drink. Presented in the special, embossed Club de Viticulteurs Champenois bottle.
❙ Now–2005 ⓔⓔⓔ

LARMANDIER-BERNIER

Champagne Larmandier-Bernier
43 rue du 28 août
51130 Vertus
☎(326) 52.13.24 ᴀx(326) 52.21.00

LARMANDIER-BERNIER NV BRUT ROSÉ, PREMIER CRU 〈85〉

The sample I tasted was due to be released in August 2000 and would be labelled as a Champagne *rouge*, if such a thing existed. It doesn't exist because red Champagne is illegal; however, no regulations determine the colour of either rosé or red in Champagne so we will just have to regard this as a dark rosé. Needs ageing to convert the red wine aromas into Pinot fruit.

➤ 2001–2003 ⓒⓒ ⚭ 98FF

LARMANDIER-BERNIER NV NÉ D'UNE TERRE DE VERTUS, BRUT NATURE 〈83〉

Due to be released in August 2000, the name of this *cuvée* tells us that it is born of a specific *terroir* in Vertus at the tip of the Côte de Blancs. Although no vintage is indicated, it is also born of a specific year, 1996. Very fresh and tight-structured, this wine would have benefited from at least another year before disgorgement and a proper Brut dosage. Try keeping a year or two, but be careful as non-dosage wines seldom age gracefully.

❗ Now–2001 ⓒⓒ ⚭ 101FF

LARMANDIER-BERNIER NV BLANC DE BLANCS BRUT, PREMIER CRU 〈85〉

The pure, fresh, fluffy fruit in this *cuvée* makes delicious immediate drinking.

❗ Now–2002 ⓒⓒ ⚭ 98FF

LARMANDIER-BERNIER, VIEILLES VIGNES DE CRAMANT 1995 BLANC DE BLANCS, EXTRA BRUT GRAND CRU 〈88〉

This wine has scored a consistent 88 points on each and every tasting, but although last year's release would benefit from a few years' post-disgorgement ageing, it was also ready for immediate drinking, whereas this year's release positively needs at least 12 months'

ageing before it will be approachable.

➤ 2001–2005 ⓒⓒⓒ ⚭ 110FF

LASSALLE

Champagne J. Lassalle
21 rue Chataignier Fourchu
51500 Chigny-les-Roses
☎(326) 03.42.19 ᴀx(326) 03.45.70

J. LASSALLE NV CUVÉE IMPÉRIAL PRÉFÉRENCE, PREMIER CRU 〈85〉

As the score indicates, this is the sort of quality I would keep in my own cellar, but the amount of malolactic in the creamy-mellow is just at the cusp of being acceptable, whereas the toffee-malo character in the Brut Réserve Rosé is too much for a classic sparkling wine, and when fresh and silky the rosé used to be my favourite Lassalle *cuvée*.

❗ Now–2002 ⓒⓒ

J. LASSALLE 1989 BLANC DE BLANCS, PREMIER CRU 〈85〉

Still so young, presumably because of a fairly recent disgorgement.

➤ 2002–2005 ⓒⓒⓒ

LAUNOIS PÈRE & FILS

Champagne Launois Pere & Fils
3 avenue de la République
51190 Le Mesnil-sur-Oger
☎(326) 75.50.15 ᴀx(326) 57.97.82

LAUNOIS PÈRE & FILS NV BLANC DE BLANCS CUVÉE RÉSERVE GRAND CRU BRUT 〈86〉

Last year's disgorgement has benefited greatly from 12 months' additional bottle-age, its raw estery character having been replaced with succulent fruit of some complexity. A pity, then, that Launois did not submit any samples this year, and a good job that I methodically retaste one year later the second samples of any wines I include in the Guide under a "wait and see" proviso.

❗ Now–2004 ⓒⓒ

LAURENT-PERRIER

Champagne Laurent-Perrier
Domaine de Tours-sur-Marne
51150 Tours-sur-Marne
C(326) 58.91.22 **FAX**(326) 58.77.29

LAURENT-PERRIER NV BRUT L.P 🔵 **85**

A fine quality non-vintage Champagne with a firmer structure than normal, but still veering towards elegance rather than weight. No peppery fruit this time, thus ideal for immediate drinking.
❗ Now–2003 ⓔⓔ

LAURENT-PERRIER 1993 VINTAGE BRUT **88**

Not in the class of LP's 1990, but this rich flavoured wine is one of the potentially longer-lived 1993s and should go toasty after a couple of years' post-disgorgement ageing.
➤ 2001–2004 ⓔⓔⓔ

LAURENT-PERRIER 1990 VINTAGE BRUT **91**

Still stunning.
❗ Now–2010 ⓔⓔⓔ

LAURENT-PERRIER GRAND SIÈCLE NV LA CUVÉE **93**

After my report on last year's sumptuous *cuvée*, a peppery version was released onto the market. The sample received this year has no pepperiness, but is so pure and fruity that it needs two years to attain the depth and finesse that regular drinkers of Grand Siècle

"La Cuvée" expect.
➤ 2002–2007 ⓔⓔⓔⓔ

LAURENT-PERRIER GRAND SIÈCLE 1990 LUMIÈRE DU MILLÉNAIRE, BRUT MILLÉSIME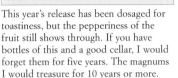

This year's release has been dosaged for toastiness, but the pepperiness of the fruit still shows through. If you have bottles of this and a good cellar, I would forget them for five years. The magnums I would treasure for 10 years or more.
➤ Wait and see ⓔⓔⓔⓔ

LAURENT-PERRIER GRAND SIÈCLE 1990 ALEXANDRA ROSÉ, BRUT **88**

Better dosage than the 1988, although nowhere near as special as the 1985 or 1982. There is some of the same pepperiness found in the 1990 Grand Siècle Brut, but it is partly covered by Pinot Noir fruit and thus not so prominent.
❗ Now–2003 ⓔⓔⓔⓔ

LAURENT-PERRIER GRAND SIÈCLE 1988 ALEXANDRA ROSÉ, BRUT **88**

Ripe, peachy Chardonnay fruit has come to the rescue of this wine, overwhelming the oxidativeness that had set in due to an unfavourably low dosage, but it could have much greater finesse had the dosage been higher.
❗ Now–2004 ⓔⓔⓔⓔ

LEBENSHILFE

Pfalz, Germany

LEBENSHILFE RIESLING TROCKEN 1998 WACHENHEIMER SCHLOSSBERG **77**

Very fresh, crispy fruit. Makes a great food wine.
❗ Now–2001 ⓔ

LEMAIRE-RASSELET

Champagne Lemaire-Rasselet
5 rue de la Croix St Jean
51480 Boursault-Villesaint
C(326) 58.44.85 **FAX**(326) 59.46.08

LEMAIRE-RASSELET 1995 AN 2000, BRUT

Plenty of flavour, but keep to develop finesse and complexity.
➤ 2001–2003 £££

LENOBLE

Champagne A.R. Lenoble
35-37 rue Paul Douce
51480 Damery
☎(326) 58.42.60 ⅎ(326) 58.65.57

A.R. LENOBLE NV BRUT RÉSERVE 85

Fresh, tasty fruit underscored by plenty of mouthwateringly ripe acidity.
❢ Now–2002 ££

A.R. LENOBLE 1992 BLANC DE NOIRS PREMIER CRU, BRUT MILLÉSIME 85

Surprisingly estery for an eight-year-old Champagne, but that augurs well for the finesse of this potentially rich yet elegant *cuvée* when everything comes together in a couple of years' time.
➤ 2002–2005 ££

A.R. LENOBLE 1990 GENTILHOMME, BRUT GRAND CRU 85

Soft, smooth and mature with almondy fruit.
❢ Now–2002 ££

LERGENMÜLLER

W. Lergenmüller Söhne
Pfalz, Germany

LERGENMÜLLER NV SPÄTBURGUNDER BRUT 85

This is a serious red Spätburgunder Sekt in a true Brut style, with cranberries and redcurrants on the aftertaste. (*Méthode champenoise.*)
❢ Now–2001 £

❖ **LINDAUER**, *see* Montana

LINTZ

Martinborough, New Zealand

LINTZ ESTATE 1997 RIESLING BRUT 72

Autolysis fighting Riesling's aromatic varietal aromas on the nose, but with crisp, clean citrus fruit on the finish. Would have benefited from one year less on yeast, but one year more after disgorgement, as this would have avoided conflict with the autolysis.
❢ Now–2001 ££ ⅋ NZ$30

LLOPART

Penedès, Spain

LLOPART 1997 CAVA RESERVA BRUT NATURE 72

Smooth and fresh with nice acidity.
❢ Now £ ⅋ 1,300 Ptas

LONGEN-SCHLÖDER

Mosel-Saar-Ruwer, Germany

LONGEN-SCHLÖDER 1996 WEIßER BURGUNDER BRUT 72

Attractive, if elevated, perfumed fruit on the nose, followed by somewhat fat fruit on the palate. (*Méthode champenoise.*)
❢ Now £ ⅋ DM17

LÖWENSTEIN

Fürst Löwenstein
Franken, USA

FÜRST LÖWENSTEIN RIESLING BRUT 1997 HALLGARTENER HENDELBERG 78

Plenty of extract in this already elegant wine. (*Méthode champenoise.*)
❢ Now–2003 £ ⅋ DM24

LUBIANA

Stefano Lubiana
Tasmania, Australia

STEFANO LUBIANA 1995   ㉘

Has considerable finesse for a fruit-driven style.
❦ Now–2001 ⓔ ⚘ A$45

LUCAS

New York, USA

LUCAS 1993 20TH ANNIVERSARY   ㉚

Nicely balanced, fresh and crisp.
❦ Now–2001 ⓔ ⚘ $11.99

MAILLY

Champagne Mailly
28 rue de la Libération
51500 Mailly-Champagne
℡(326) 49.41.10 ☎(326) 49.42.27

MAILLY NV BLANC DE NOIRS, BRUT GRAND CRU   ㉜

Peppery-oxidative aromas over smooth fruit and a soft mousse.
❦ Now–2002 ⓔⓔ ⚘ 144FF

MAILLY NV CASSIOPEE, BRUT NATURE, GRAND CRU   ㉟

I thought Cassiopee was a palmtop computer. I found the next release of this *cuvée* to be deeply flavoured and very expressive of Northern Montagne Pinot Noir, but it deserves to be aged and that would be better achieved with a proper Brut dosage.
❦ Now ⓔⓔⓔ ⚘ 215FF

MAILLY 1995 BRUT GRAND CRU MILLÉSIME   ㉝

A big mouthful of complex fruit, a touch of vanilla and a smooth, creamy-vanilla finish.
❦ Now–2002 ⓔⓔⓔ ⚘ 153FF

MAILLY 1988 CUVÉE LES ECHANSONS, BRUT GRAND CRU   ㉧

This *cuvée* has a real intensity of fruit and having looked back, the word intensity has featured in the tasting note of every single Cuvée Les Echansons tasted. Has finesse and although this comes out in the glass, it needs more to match the size of this wine and attract the sort of score it should have.
❦ Now–2003 ⓔⓔⓔ ⚘ 305FF

MAJOLINI

Franciacorta, Italy

MAJOLINI NV FRANCIACORTA BRUT   ㉖

Creamy-buttery aroma, going for a fuller, more Champagne style.
❦ Now–2002 ⓔⓔ ⚘ 23,000 Lira

MAJOLINI 1996 FRANCIACORTA BRUT MILLENNIO 2000   ㉜

Oaky-creamy aroma, a bit obvious, but very moreish all the same.
❦ Now–2002 ⓔⓔⓔⓔ ⚘ 120,000 Lira

MAJOLINI 1994 FRANCIACORTA BRUT   ㉚

Apricot and plums.
❦ Now–2002 ⓔ

MALARD

Champagne Jean-Louis Malard
21 avenue de Champagne
51203 Epernay
℡(326) 57.77.24 ☎(326) 52.75.54

CUVÉE COMPAGNIE DES WAGONS-LITS NV PULLMAN ORIENT-EXPRESS, BRUT GRAND CRU   ㉟

More substance and more potential than Malard's Grand Cru Pinot Noir-Chardonnay.
❦ Now–2004 ⓔⓔ ⚘ 129FF

JEAN LOUIS MALARD NV BRUT GRAND CRU PINOT NOIR-CHARDONNAY   ㉜

A fresh, elegant Champagne that is capable of some complexity.
❦ Now–2003 ⓔⓔ ⚘ 109FF

JEAN-LOUIS MALARD NV GRAND CRU CHARDONNAY

This wine has lovely fruit and a soft, seductive mousse, but often requires a year or two for the bouquet to be running at the same speed as the rest of the wine.

▼ Now–2003 ⓔⓔ 🍇 109FF

MANDOIS

Champagne Henri Mandois
66 rue du Général de Gaulle
51530 Pierry
☎(326) 54.03.18 ᴬˣ(326) 51.53.66

The more I taste Mandois, the more impressed I become.

HENRI MANDOIS NV CUVÉE DE RÉSERVE BRUT

Very fruity in a clean and elegantly focused style. The style and its enjoyability have not changed, although the quality edges up every year.

▼ Now–2002 ⓔⓔ 🍇 68FF

HENRI MANDOIS NV BRUT ROSÉ, PREMIER CRU

Sweet and ripe on the nose, with high acids on the palate. Can be enjoyed now, but cellaring it for a modest six months might not be such a bad idea.

▼ Now–2003 ⓔⓔ 🍇 73FF

HENRI MANDOIS 1995 BRUT MILLÉSIMÉ, BRUT PREMIER CRU

Serious, rich, silky fruit capable of considerable complexity.

▼ Now–2005 ⓔⓔ 🍇 75.50FF

HENRI MANDOIS 1995 CHARDONNAY, BRUT PREMIER CRU

If you enjoyed the 1993, which was "ridiculously easy to drink", then you will love the 1995, with its extremely racy, mouthwatering, sherbety fruit.

▼ Now–2005 ⓔⓔⓔ 🍇 77FF

HENRI MANDOIS 1995 CUVÉE VICTOR MANDOIS, BRUT

Mandois excelled itself with the 1993 vintage of this *cuvée* and the 1995 shows even greater class.

▼ Now–2005 ⓔⓔⓔ 🍇 100.50FF

HENRI MANDOIS 1993 CUVÉE DES TROIS GÉNÉRATIONS, BRUT

Amazingly young, fresh and vital for a 1993, with extremely rich, clean, pure fruit, refreshing acidity and a classic structure.

▼ Now–2005 ⓔⓔⓔ 🍇 90.50FF

MANN

Albert Mann
Alsace, France

BARON DE CASTEX NV CRÉMANT D'ALSACE BRUT

Very fresh, but needs 6–12 months to soften mousse.

▬ 2001–2002 ⓔ

MARCHESINE

Le Marchesine
Franciacorta, Italy

LE MARCHESINE NV FRANCIACORTA BRUT

The buttered-toast aromas are for toast lovers only (and if you are one, you can add 5 points!).

▼ Now–2001 ⓔⓔ 🍇 18,000 Lira

MARENCO

Asti, Italy

MARENCO NV ASTI

The peachy-styled Moscato fruit is attractive and puts this wine way ahead of most Asti, but it does not have the richness, sweetness or finesse of the very best Asti.

▼ Now ⓔ

MARENCO NV BRACHETTO D'ACQUI

This fizzy red has an attractive raspberry colour, more winey aromas than most Brachetto and comparatively less sweetness, although certainly on the sweet side.

🍷 Now ⓔⓕ

MARGUET-BONNERAVE

Champagne Marguet-Bonnerave
14 rue de Bouzy
51150 Ambonnay
☎(326) 57.01.08 📠(326) 57.09.98

MARGUET-BONNERAVE NV BRUT ROSÉ GRAND CRU

Full yet soft, perfumed fruit.

🍷 Now–2001 ⓔⓕ

MARGUET-BONNERAVE NV BRUT TRADITION GRAND CRU ⑧⑤

Pin-cushion mousse gives finesse to the fruit, but promises to go oxidatively complex so drink up unless you like that style.

🍷 Now–2001 ⓔⓕ

MARNE ET CHAMPAGNE

22 rue Maurice-Cerveaux
51205 Epernay
☎(326) 78.50.50 📠(326) 54.55.77
Makers of over 250 brands!

J. BOURGEOIS NV CUVÉE AN 2000, CARTE OR BRUT ⑧⓪

Plenty of flavour, but needs to be kept a year to develop toastiness, and has the acidity to do this without going flabby.

◄━ 2001–2003 ⓔⓕ

GAUTHIER 1993 BRUT MILLÉSIME ⑧⑦

Rich, creamy fruit with a refreshing crispness on the palate and a touch of vanilla and plums on the finish.

🍷 Now–2003 ⓔⓕ 🍇 150FF

MARNIQUET

Champagne Marniquet
8 rue des Crayères
51480 Venteuil
☎(326) 58.48.99

JEAN-PIERRE MARNIQUET NV BRUT TRADITION ⑧⓪

A couple of years ago this *cuvée* had a Muscat-like twist to the fruit, but there is nothing so exotic in the fruit of this light, firm fizz. Some releases shipped shortly after disgorgement can have an amylic character, but this fades after six months.

🍷 Now–2002 ⓔⓕ

MARQUÉS DE MONISTROL

Penedès, Spain

MARQUÉS DE MONISTROL SELECCIÓN ESPECIAL NV CAVA BRUT ROSÉ ⑦⑥

Delicate and soft with elegant red fruits, nice acidity and fine mousse.

🍷 Now ⓕ

MARQUÉS DE MONISTROL, GRAN RESERVA DE FAMILIA NV CAVA ROSÉ ⑦⑤

Perfumed red fruits that are delicate and charming for this quality level.

🍷 Now ⓕ

MARQUÉS DE MONISTROL SELECCIÓN ESPECIAL 1996 CAVA BRUT RESERVA ⑦⑥

A serious sparkling wine that offers more fruitiness and substance than most Cava.

🍷 Now ⓕ

MARTEL

Champagne GH Martel
69 avenue de Champagne
51318 Epernay Cedex
☎(326) 51.06.33 📠(326) 54.41.52

PAUL-LOUIS MARTIN NV GRAND CRU BOUZY ⑧⑥

This mono-cru is produced by GH Martel and shows true Pinot complexity.

🍷 Now–2003 ⓔⓕ

GH MARTEL 1995 CUVÉE VICTOIRE ⑧⑧

This rich, satisfying, toasty Champagne is typical of the surprising quality that often lurks behind the gaudy label of Martel's prestige *cuvée*.

Now–2003 £££

MARTELLETTI
Asti, Italy

CASA MARTELLETTI NV TRADIZIONE ASTI

Rich, intensely sweet, peachy-Moscato fruit.

Now £

MARTINOLLES
Limoux, France

LES VIGNOBLES VERGNES DE MARTINOLLES NV MÉTHODE ANCESTRALE VERGNES

Ferment odours, boiled sweet richness lifted by VA fruitiness. A motley description perhaps, but not an unpleasant experience.

Now–2002 ££

MASACHS
Penedès, Spain

CAROLINA DE MASACHS NV CAVA BRUT RESERVA

Although the fruit is a touch elevated, this is certainly above average for a Cava.

Now £ ♦ 1,800 Ptas

MASSANA NOYA
Eudald Massana Noya
Penedès, Spain

EUDALD MASSANA NOYA FAMILIA 1998 CAVA BRUT

My preferred *cuvée* from Massana is its cheapest, simple, unpretentious fruity fizz.

Now £ ♦ 535 Ptas

MATHIEU
Champagne Serge Mathieu
6 rue des Vignes
10340 Avirey-Lingey
☎(25) 29.32.58 ℻(25) 29.11.57

SERGE MATHIEU NV CUVÉE PRESTIGE BRUT

A supremely elegant Champagne brimming with beautifully smooth, mouthwateringly fresh, succulent fruit.

Now–2003 ££

SERGE MATHIEU NV TÊTE DE CUVÉE SELECT, BRUT

Deeper and fuller than the Cuvée Prestige, with far more yeast-complexed flavours and white peach fruit on the finish.

Now–2004 £££

SERGE MATHIEU NV CUVÉE TRADITION, BLANC DE NOIRS, BRUT

Very fresh, tasty, frothy fruit.

Now–2002 ££

SERGE MATHIEU NV ROSÉ BRUT

The sight of a rosé tends to conjure up red fruits, but this *cuvée* has a distinctively peachy aftertaste.

Now–2001 ££

SERGE MATHIEU 1995 BRUT MILLÉSIME

Concentrated and tasty, but as often happens with Mathieu, not up to its non-vintage *cuvées*, which are exceptional. Perhaps more strangely the 1995 is not as good as the 1993.

Now–2003 £££

MATHIEU-GOSZTYLA
Champagne Mathieu-Gosztyla
26 cour des Dames
51700 Baslieux sous Chatillon
☎(326) 58.11.78 ℻(326) 58.11.78

MATHIEU-GOSZTYLA NV BRUT TRADITION

A sweetish Brut with a fleeting glimpse of

coconut when the wine hits the palate.
▌ Now–2001 ⓔⓔ ⚑ 71FF

MÄURER

Mäurer's Sekt-u.Weingut
Pfalz, Germany

MÄURER SPÄTBURGUNDER 1996 BLANC DE NOIRS BRUT

Very fresh aromas followed by crisp, tasty fruit with a touch of greengage on finish. (*Méthode champenoise.*)
▌ Now ⓔⓔ ⚑ DM40

ATTENTION CHAMPAGNE & SPARKLING WINE PRODUCERS!
If you are not already in contact with the author, but would like to submit wines for consideration in future editions, please contact Tom Stevenson at:

tom.stevenson@fizz.worldonline.co.uk

Warning: Any other unsolicited mail received at this address will be ignored.

Please note that recommendation in this guide involves no charge whatsoever beyond the cost of the samples and their delivery.

MAWBY

L. Mawby
Michigan, USA

Michigan's most enthusiastic follower of the bubble has at least as many failures as credits to his name, but that's what happens when you pursue a goal, rather than play safe.

L. MAWBY NV CRÉMANT, LEELANU PENINSULA (CV36)

Made from the Vignoles (a Seibel × Pinot Noir hybrid otherwise known as Ravat), this is a well-made sparkler with a vanilla aroma and creamy-tangy fruit. It has a certain distinctive character, but lacks the finesse for a higher score.
▌ Now ⓔ

L. MAWBY NV TALISMAN BRUT, LEELANU PENINSULA (CV28)

The previous release was easy-going, soft and fruity, with nicely balanced acidity, while the next release has a fragrant vanilla aroma and elegant, creamy fruit that make this Vignoles *cuvée* a similar, but softer version of the Crémant (CV36).
▌ Now ⓔ

L. MAWBY 1995 MILLE, BLANC DE NOIRS, LEELANU PENINSULA

This carefully crafted pure-Pinot *cuvée* was easily the best sparkling wine I tasted from Michigan so far. The tiny bubbles in its softly effervescent mousse are the hallmark of a quality sparkling wine and the lovely, creamy-rich fruit gently supported by ripe acidity is an indication that world-class sparkling wine may one day be produced from Pinot Noir grown in this state.
▌ Now–2003 ⓔ

L. MAWBY 1994 MILLE, BLANC DE NOIRS, LEELANU PENINSULA

The vanilla aroma and creamy fruit are more Vignoles than Pinot Noir and it is too soft, lacking the acidity and finesse of the 1995.
▌ Now ⓔ

McGREGOR

New York, USA

McGREGOR 1996 SPARKLING RIESLING

Some petrolly Riesling aromas, fresh and zesty fruit.
▌ Now–2001 ⓔ

McGREGOR 1995 BLANC DE NOIRS ⊖

An off-aroma, but not bad on palate. A phase perhaps?
▌ Now–2001 ⓔ

❖ **McLARENS ON THE LAKE**, *see* Garrett

MELTON
South Australia, Australia

CHARLES MELTON NV BAROSSA VALLEY SPARKLING RED

Tremendously elegant, impeccably oak-driven style, with heaps of fruit and a sweetness that is not overpowering. Skilful blending.

Now–2002 ⓒⓔ ❦ A$39.90

MERCIER
Champagne Mercier
68/70 avenue de Champagne
51200 Epernay
☎(326) 51.22.00 ℻(326) 54.84.23

MERCIER NV BRUT

Fuller than Moët, but fresh, clean and correctly crisp without any Chablis-greenness. For those who like the Mercier mellowness, age for a further year or two.

Now–2003 ⓒⓔ

EUGÈNE MERCIER NV CUVÉE DU FONDATEUR, BRUT

Not as fat or as rich as a couple of years ago, when this *cuvée* achieved 87 points, but it does have a creamy-richness of fruit that will go toasty and is a darn sight better than last year's release, which did not even deserve recommendation.

Now–2003 ⓒⓔ

MERCIER NV BRUT ROSÉ

A characterful *cuvée* that is fuller than Moët's non-vintage Rosé, but without the finesse of that wine (when it is on form).

Now–2002 ⓒⓔ

MERCIER 1995 VENDANGE BRUT

Quite fat for the vintage, but that is Mercier's house style showing through. Will go toasty.

Now–2004 ⓒⓔ

MESNIL
Champagne Le Mesnil
Union des Propriétaires Récoltants
51390 Le Mesnil-sur-Oger
☎(326) 57.53.23

LE MESNIL 1995 RÉSERVE SÉLECTION, BLANC DE BLANCS BRUT

The creamy-brazilnut-biscuity fruit in this *cuvée* always makes it worth the premium over this cooperative's other more ubiquitous Champagnes.

Now–2003 ⓒⓔⓔ

MESTRES
Penedès, Spain

MESTRES ROSADO 1998 CAVA BRUT NATURAL

This deliberately oxidized Cava is a must for anyone who longs for Spanish wines as they used to be!

Now ⓒⓔ ❦ 2,200 Ptas

MIGNON & PIERREL
Champagne Mignon & Pierrel
24 Rue Henri Dunant
51200 Epernay
☎(326) 51.93.39 ℻(326) 51.69.40

PIERREL CUVÉE 1995 BRUT

I can thoroughly recommend Pierrel's Cuvée 1995, but not the more expensive Grand Cuvée 1992, so save some money and buy this fine quality Champagne, with excellent acidity and concentration of fruit.

Now–2003 ⓒⓔ

MILAN
Champagne Milan
6 route d'Avize
51190 Oger
☎(326) 57.50.09 ℻(326) 57.78.47

JEAN CHARLES MILAN, CUVÉE DE RÉSERVE NV BLANC DE BLANCS, BRUT GRAND CRU

80

Rich and tasty, with better acidity than Milan's An 2000, but less aromatic potential.

Now–2002 ££

JEAN MILAN, AN 2000 NV BLANCS DE BLANCS, BRUT SPÉCIAL, GRAND CRU

82

Estery aromas suggest this should not have been disgorged until the end of 2000, but that would have missed the point, wouldn't it? Still quite young, but promises to evolve elegantly if kept well-cellared for at least a year.

2001–2003 ££ ☙ 86FF

TERRES DE NOËL, AN 2000 BRUT SÉLECTION 1995 GRAND CRU BLANC DE BLANCS

There is something high-tone about the front palate that prevents me from making a judgement at this moment, but the lovely citrussy fruit from mid-palate through to finish and the tangy-lemony fruit acidity on the finish offer much hope.

Wait ££

MIRABELLA
Franciacorta, Italy

MIRABELLA NV FRANCIACORTA BRUT

72

Attractive initially and even seems to have complexity and finesse, then leaves a hollow finish.

Now–2002 ££ ☙ 13,500 Lira

MIRABELLA NV ROSÉ

74

Pale peachy rosé. Fresh, nicely structured.

Now–2002 ££ ☙ 13,500 Lira

MIRANDA
South Australia, Australia

MIRANDA BRUT NV BLANC DE BLANC

70

The cheapest Australian fizz tasted this year and its Trebbiano/Colombard fruit is clean and quaffing.

Now £ ☙ A$4.95

MIRANDA 1994 SPARKLING SHIRAZ BAROSSA OLD VINE

77

Jammy Shiraz with a coffee-toffee twist on the finish.

Now ££ ☙ A$23.95

❖ **MIRU MIRU**, *see* Hunter's

MITCHELL
South Australia, Australia

MITCHELL NV CLARE VALLEY SPARKLING PEPPERTREE

75

A nice well-rounded sparkling Shiraz, but overpriced in Australia, although it would be worth importing elsewhere if the price was right.

Now ££ ☙ A$30

MOËT & CHANDON

Champagne Moët & Chandon
20 avenue de Champagne
51200 Epernay
☎(326) 51.20.00 FAX(326) 51.20.37

The Esprit du Siècle is the only wine in the Guide that was not tasted during the year of publication. I got the chance to taste it at a special presentation in London towards the end of 1999. It's not exactly a snip at 20,000 Euros (£13,000 or $20,000), but I knew that I would seldom if ever get the opportunity to taste it again, so I made sure I got my fair share on the day. In fact I had three good glassfuls. That's $5,000-worth to you and me! We were sat at the table carefully preserving our glasses of this precious liquid and all of us too polite to ask for more, when I thought this is ridiculous – any leftovers are going to go to waste. I therefore excused myself from the table and took a circuitous route to the loo, noticing on the way that there was nearly half a magnum left in the ice-bucket. After spending the world's most expensive penny,

MOËT & CHANDON NV ESPRIT DU SIÈCLE — 98

Just 320 magnums of this, the world's most expensive wine, were produced and of this pitifully small quantity, only 30 will ever be sold, the rest having been allocated for charity auctions and various special events at Moët up to and including its 300th birthday celebration in 2043. This *cuvée* consists of 11 exceptional 20th century vintages (1900, 1914, 1921, 1934, 1943, 1952, 1962, 1976, 1983, 1985 and 1995). Generally the older the year the less wine used, but if Moët is to be believed the two youngest years comprise no more than one-third of the total blend, so the older vintages are not a meaningless gesture, but form the backbone of this wine. The blending is masterful, the vintages seamless and, most extraordinary of all, the wine has a paradoxical quality of being unquestionably mature, yet fascinatingly fresh. The maturity comes across as merely a creamy feel on the palate.

❚ Now–2050 ⓕⓕⓕⓕ ♚ 130,000FF

MOËT & CHANDON NV BRUT IMPÉRIAL — 80

Not the floweriness of some shipments, but typical light-bodied structure and like all Moët NV Brut Impérial this wine will go toasty within 12 months.

❚ Now–2002 ⓕⓕ

MOËT & CHANDON NV CUVÉE CLAUDE MOËT — 85

According to the back label this Champagne is served to Moët's guests at Château Saran. Maybe things have changed since I last had that privilege, but it always used to be the previous vintage in magnum for the aperitif, followed by older vintages and Dom Pérignon, of course. The Saran Coteaux Champenoise usually cropped up at some

point in the menu, but I honestly cannot remember ever seeing this *cuvée*. In fact, the first time I encountered this wine in its purple livery was in the Duty Free at Singapore airport. This is a fuller style than the Premier Cru, which itself is fuller than the Brut Impérial, but it is not at all heavy. The fruit is smooth and Pinot dominated, with lots of extract on the finish.

❚ Now–2003 ⓕⓕ

MOËT & CHANDON NV BRUT PREMIER CRU — 84

Rich, but tart with youth and really should have had another year on yeast. Still, as all serious fizz-drinkers know, you should always keep Moët Brut Impérial one year. Now it looks as if you might have to keep the Brut Premier Cru a year as well.

◀ 2001–2004 ⓕⓕⓕ

MOËT & CHANDON NV BRUT ROSÉ — 80

I tasted this *cuvée* several times in 2000 and not once did it remind me of the wonderfully fresh, soft, delicate rosé encountered last year. They all lacked the finesse and all showed a certain greenness, but this will turn toasty and thus scrapes in on potential alone.

◀ 2001–2002 ⓕⓕⓕ

MOËT & CHANDON NV NECTAR IMPÉRIAL — 88

Of all the Demi-Sec tasted this year (and there were over 50), this was the only one to stand out on the nose alone. It was also the most elegant on the palate. Deliciously fresh and fruity.

❚ Now–2005 ⓕⓕⓕ

MOËT & CHANDON 1993 BRUT IMPÉRIAL — 88

The fruit has become plumper since last year, but the acidity seems much fresher and keener on the palate, suggesting that the more recent disgorgements should be kept a year or so before broaching.

◀ 2001–2007 ⓕⓕⓕ

MOËT & CHANDON 1993 BRUT IMPÉRIAL ROSÉ — 87

This rich, food-wine rosé is fresher than last year's release (good though that was), but it still remains fairly mature and this seems at odds with the house style. In the last edition I thought that Moët should release its vintage rosé at a younger age. Ideally this house would be on 1995 or 1996 by now, not 1993 for the second year running.

▌ Now–2001 ⒼⒼⒼ

MOËT & CHANDON 1992 BRUT IMPÉRIAL

Just as toasty as last year, the structure of this 1992 vintage has however softened, while the finish is much smoother, with a lovely floral-Meunier aftertaste, making it much more accessible on its own.

▌ Now–2003 ⒼⒼⒼ

MOËT ET CHANDON 1992 CUVÉE DOM PÉRIGNON BRUT

This vintage has come a long way in the last 12 months, dropping some of its greenness and gradually picking up nuances of toast and prunes, but there is still another year or two to go before it will possess the refinement and finesse expected in any vintage of Dom Pérignon.

➤ 2002–2011 ⒼⒼⒼⒼ

MOËT ET CHANDON 1990 CUVÉE DOM PÉRIGNON ROSÉ BRUT

The nose is quite pungent and reminiscent of the smell of raspberries reducing prior to becoming a jam or preserve. This could be off-putting to some, although the delightful red-fruits on the palate should do nothing but delight. I need to taste this in a year's time to decide whether ageing the wine will accentuate or minimize the pungency.

➤ Wait and see ⒼⒼⒼⒼ

MOLITOR

Weingut Markus Molitor
Mosel-Saar-Ruwer, Germany

MARKUS MOLITOR RIESLING BRUT 1997 MOLITOR PRESTIGE, BERNKASTELER BADSTUBE

Lovely concentration of peachy fruit. It's a pity that money has been spent on a premium quality bottle only to have the

presentation end up looking like Piat d'Or! (*Méthode champenoise.*)

▌ Now–2001 ⒼⒼ 🍇 DM32

MONCUIT

Champagne Pierre Moncuit
11 rue Persault-Maheu
51190 Le Mesnil-sur-Oger
☎(326) 57.52.65 📠(326) 57.97.89

PIERRE MONCUIT, CUVÉE NICOLE MONCUIT 1991 VIEILLE VIGNE, BLANC DE BLANCS, BRUT GRAND CRU

What this needs now is to build some post-disgorgement aromas, but the fruit is ready to drink and the wine is not at all heavy despite the concentration of flavour on the palate. Far more impressive than the 1992 vintage of this *cuvée*.

▌ Now–2003 ⒼⒼⒼ

MONT-FERRANT

Gerona, Spain

MONT-FERRANT MEDALLA D'OR 1997 CAVA BRUT RESERVA

Some biscuity complexity on finish.

▌ Now Ⓔ 🍇 850 Ptas

MONTANA

Marlborough, New Zealand

Large wineries have let down the efforts of quality-minded smaller producers in many regions throughout the world, but the fact that Montana has never done that and is in fact one of the top three best sparkling wine producers in New Zealand is proof that big does not necessarily mean bad.

LINDAUER NV BRUT

Lemon meringue pie fruit.

▌ Now Ⓔ

LINDAUER NV ROSÉ

Soft, creamy red fruits.
❦ Now ⓔ

LINDAUER NV SPECIAL RESERVE, MARLBOROUGH/HAWKES BAY

The current *cuvée* of this soft, easy-drinking fruity fizz is the best release yet.
❦ Now–2001 ⓔ

LINDAUER NV SPECIAL RESERVE, MARLBOROUGH/HAWKES BAY *(magnum)*

If you enjoy the Special Reserve, try it in magnum and you'll be blown away. Its crisper, even fresher fruit is not simply part of the magnum effect, but the whole blend seems to me to be different. A selection of a selection perhaps?
❦ Now–2003 ⓔⓔ

DEUTZ MARLBOROUGH CUVÉE NV MONTANA

The current release is the 1997-based *cuvée* and what a very fresh, vibrantly fruity wine it is, with its fluffy-creamy mousse and crisp, ripe acidity.
❦ Now–2001 ⓔⓔ

DEUTZ MARLBOROUGH BLANC DE BLANCS 1996 MONTANA

Beautifully rich, lusciously creamy fruit underscored by fine, ripe acidity to give long, lingering finish.
❦ Now–2002 ⓔⓔ

DEUTZ MARLBOROUGH BLANC DE BLANCS 1994 MONTANA

This has shaken off its maltiness and emerged from last year's "wait and see" category to score a point higher than the 1991, which was an exciting wine for its time. This should improve for a year or two, as its vanilla-laced fruity aromas will need that time to develop the toastiness required to balance the same on the palate.
❦ Now–2002 ⓔⓔ

DEUTZ MARLBOROUGH BLANC DE NOIRS 1994 MONTANA

This new *cuvée* with its toasty, vanilla and cherry fruit is a tinted New World *blanc de noirs* rather than a classic, white champenois influenced rendition.
❦ Now–2002 ⓔⓔ

MONTE ROSSA
Franciacorta, Italy

MONTE ROSSA NV BRUT

Fresh, fine, nicely fragrant, but could have done with more finesse and this would bring a greater sense of satisfaction.
❦ Now–2001 ⓔⓔ

MONTE ROSSA NV SATÈN

Fruit-driven aromas, creamy fruit, just let down by a touch of VA (which lifted the aroma) on the finish.
❦ Now–2001 ⓔⓔ

MONTE ROSSA NV SEC

Fresh and fine with almondy fruit and excellent acidity (almondy without crisp acidity is a bad sign, this good).
❦ Now–2002 ⓔⓔ

MONTGUERET
Château de Montgueret
Loire, France

CHÂTEAU DE MONTGUERET 1997 TÊTE DE CUVÉE, SAUMUR

Fuller, food-wine style. Fresh.
❦ Now–2002 ⓔ

MONTINA
La Montina
Franciacorta, Italy

LA MONTINA NV FRANCIACORTA SATÈN

Creamy, almondy, vanilla fruit, quite distinctive, lovely soft mousse and very small bubbles.
❦ Now–2001 ⓔⓔ 🍾 15,400 Lira

LA MONTINA NV ROSÉ DEMI SEC

Sweetish fresh fruit.
❦ Now–2001 ⓔⓔ 🍾 15,000 Lira

LA MONTINA 1995 BRUT

Vanilla fruit, satisfying. Serious stuff.

Now–2003 ⓔⓔ

MONTLOUIS
*Caves des Producteurs de Montlouis
Loire, France*

CAVES DES PRODUCTEURS DE MONTLOUIS NV CUVÉE RÉSERVÉE SEC
 ⓑ

Not too sweet, the dosage merely emphasizes the fruitiness. Excellent acidity.

Now–2002 ⓔ

MONZIO
Franciacorta, Italy

MONZIO COMPAGNONI NV FRANCIACORTA EXTRA BRUT
ⓑ

Although estery aromas suggest this could have benefited from slightly longer on yeast, it is coming together nicely on palate and should be an elegant wine by the time of publication.

Now–2002 ⓔⓔ ♥ 21,900 Lira

MONZIO COMPAGNONI NV FRANCIACORTA SATÈN
ⓑ

Fresh, mature, vanilla aromas, *barrique* fruit on palate, but not as creamy-silky as other Satèn.

Now–2001 ⓔⓔ ♥ 24,000 Lira

MORGENHOF
Stellenbosch, South Africa

MORGENHOF 1997 CAP CLASSIQUE, RESERVE CENTENAIRE
ⓑ

Oak-ferment aromas followed by nice fruit on palate, with a good structure. Certainly warrants following.

 2001–2003 ⓔⓔ ♥ R95

MORTON
Bay of Plenty, New Zealand

MORTON ESTATE NV HAWKES BAY/MARLBOROUGH
ⓑ

Not a complex wine when released, but the current *cuvée* has nice clean fruit, excellent acidity, and should go biscuity in 6–9 months.

Now–2001 ⓔ ♥ NZ$18

MORTON RD 1995 MARLBOROUGH
ⓑ

There was none of the autolytic floral aromas that a recently disgorged sparkling wine usually has. In fact the toasty bottle-aromas building on the palate would suggest that the sample I tasted had not been recently disgorged.

Now–2001 ⓔⓔ ♥ NZ$24.95

MORTON BLACK LABEL 1995 BAY OF PLENTY/HAWKES BAY
ⓑ

Gosset-like bottle and label. Oaky aromas are too dominant for purists, but others will love this and it is supported by excellent fruit and acidity.

 2001–2002 ⓔⓔ ♥ NZ$32.95

MOSNEL
*Il Mosnel
Franciacorta, Italy*

IL MOSNEL NV FRANCIACORTA EXTRA BRUT
ⓑ

Mellow aroma, biscuity-malo fruit palate and finish.

Now–2001 ⓔⓔ ♥ 25,000 Lira

IL MOSNEL 1996 FRANCIACORTA SATÈN
ⓑ

Sweet, ripe plum, with a touch of underripeness in the background, but overall this is an enjoyable sparkling wine that will turn toasty in a year or two.

Now–2002 ⓔⓔⓔ ♥ 32,000 Lira

IL MOSNEL 1993 FRANCIACORTA BRUT
ⓑ

Fresh and biscuity.

Now–2002 ⓔⓔⓔ ♥ 36,000 Lira

MOUNTADAM
South Australia, Australia

MOUNTADAM 1994 PINOT NOIR CHARDONNAY

Malo aromas continue to dominate the Mountadam style, but this vintage is pure *crème brûlée* compared to the caramel found in the 1992.
Now Ⓔ ❧ A$36

MOUNTAIN DOME
Washington, USA

MOUNTAIN DOME NV BRUT

This *cuvée* needs at least one year for the aromas on the nose to settle down, but the fruit underneath is wonderfully rich and creamy with excellent acidity.
2001–2003 Ⓔ

MOUNTAIN DOME NV CUVÉE FORTÉ, 2000 BRUT

My crazy friend who really does live in a dome on a mountain has made something special here. To be super-critical, however, the acidity could be higher, as this would not only give the fruit a finer structure, it would also leave no doubt as to how the wine would age. This is a serious quality wine and if it can maintain its finesse while developing mellow bottle-aromas, it could achieve an interesting level of complexity.
Now–2003 ⒺⒺ

MOUNTAIN DOME NV BRUT ROSÉ

A creamy-fruity aroma is followed by strawberry fruit on the palate and a touch too much dosage on the finish. Unless you want the sweetness to dominate, you should give this wine at least two years for the dosage to work its creamy-biscuity way on the strawberry fruit.
2002–2004 ⒺⒺ

MOUNTAIN DOME 1994 BRUT

Although I'm surprised just how much this vintage has improved, please do not broach the bottle for at least one year after purchase.

 2001–2002 ⒺⒺ

MOUNT WILLIAM
Victoria, Australia

MOUNT WILLIAM WINES NV

This wine should carry a warning! I think that even regular Seppelt Show Reserve drinkers would be shocked by what can only be described as a triple concentration of Seppelt Show Reserve (however, there is no commercial or winemaking connection with Seppelt), but maybe devotees of Show Reserve will actually love it.
Now Ⓔ

MOUTARD
Champagne Moutard
6 rue des Ponts
Buxeuil
10110 Buxeuil
☎(25) 38.50.73 ℻(25) 38.57.72

MOUTARD NV BRUT RÉSERVE

A simple sweet fruitiness saves the day for this *cuvée*. If you've purchased this and like it, then let me suggest trying the Brut Grande Réserve, which is well worth the small premium in price.
Now–2001 ⒺⒺ ❧ 72FF

MOUTARD NV BRUT GRANDE RÉSERVE

Fine, lemony fruit of some elegance and more finesse than the toffee-edged fruit in Moutard's 1989 vintage.
Now–2005 ⒺⒺ ❧ 80FF

MOUTARD NV CUVÉE PRESTIGE, BRUT

The silkiness of the mousse emphasizes the natural softness of fruit in this wine, but there is good acidity underneath as evidenced by its long finish.
Now–2004 ⒺⒺ ❧ 95FF

MOUTARD NV BRUT ROSÉ

Just as dark as Larmandier-Bernier's so-called rosé, although this red Champagne in all but name has a more mature, brick-red tone. If you tasted the exquisite, delicately perfumed Pinot fruit in this *cuvée* literally blind, you would never imagine anything quite so dark in colour.

❚ Now–2003 ⓔⓔ ✻ 74FF

MÜLLER

Adam Muller
Baden, Germany

ADAM MÜLLER SPÄTBURGUNDER ROSÉ EXTRA TROCKEN 1998 HEIDELBERGER MANNABERG

Fresh, rich and tasty. (*Méthode champenoise*.)

❚ Now ⓔ ✻ DM16

MULLER-KOEBERLE

Alsace, France

MULLER-KOEBERLE NV CUVÉE MARIANNE, CRÉMANT D'ALSACE BRUT ROSÉ

Sweet, ripe perfumed Pinot fruit aromas, followed by attractive strawberry/redcurrant Pinot fruit on the palate.

❚ Now–2001 ⓔ

MÜLLER-RUPRECHT

Pfalz, Germany

MÜLLER-RUPRECHT RIESLING NV EXTRA TROCKEN

Strangely tart, yet surprisingly appealing. Very dry; not Extra Trocken, more like Extra Brut!

❚ Now ⓔ

MUMM

Champagne G.H. Mumm & Cie
29 rue du Champ-de-Mars
51053 Reims
☎(326) 49.59.69 🖷(326) 77.40.69

With this house under new ownership, its reputation turning around and the future quality of its Champagne assured by young Dominique Demarville, now is the time to revamp the kitsch labelling. A good graphics designer should be able to come up with something tasteful, yet still maintain the *cordon rouge* banner that helped Mumm walk off the shelf even in its grimmest quality days.

MUMM CORDON ROSÉ NV BRUT

A firm, serious-styled rosé that will repay keeping.

▬ 2001–2003 ⓔⓔⓔ

MUMM CORDON ROUGE NV BRUT

Not as exciting as last year's *cuvée*, but that was 1996-based and this is, I suppose, 1997-based. However, it is as clean as a whistle and a few years ago that alone would have been sufficient to hold a street party.

❚ Now–2002 ⓔⓔ

MUMM DE CRAMANT NV CHARDONNAY, BRUT GRAND CRU

Much softer than normal, but very fresh and that is how this *cuvée* is best enjoyed.

❚ Now ⓔⓔⓔ

MUMM CORDON ROUGE 1996 BRUT 88

Classic Mumm lightness of body, with young, fresh, elegant fruit. In theory this should rate higher than 89 points because that was the score the 1995 vintage achieved last year and I'm certain that Mumm 1996 will be significantly superior over the long haul. However, under blind conditions 88 was the score and so 88 it will remain. As this was a pre-release sample, I could have given the wine a ⊖ symbol and reserved opinion, but 88 is an excellent score and thus gives a better impression than "Wait and see". The odds are that this score will go up rather than down in future issues.

▬ 2001–2005 ⓔⓔⓔ

MUMM CORDON ROUGE 1995 BRUT MILLÉSIMÉ

Fresh, zesty fruit aromas follow through onto the palate, making this one of the finest and most elegant of Mumm vintages in many years.

Now–2005 £££

MUMM CORDON ROUGE 1990 CUVÉE LIMITÉE, BRUT MILLÉSIMÉ

Reprehensibly for Mumm, the real 1990 Cordon Rouge is dead and buried. This, however, is the 1990 Grand Cordon prestige, so you're getting more than you bargained for and, miraculously, this wonderfully fruity Champagne was made during Mumm's darkest years. Furthermore, the (clean) malolactic aromas that dominated this wine last year have disappeared. I don't know what Dominique Demarville put in this year's dosage, but it's worked wonders.

Now–2005 £££

ATTENTION CHAMPAGNE & SPARKLING WINE PRODUCERS!

If you are not already in contact with the author, but would like to submit wines for consideration in future editions, please contact Tom Stevenson at:

tom.stevenson@fizz.worldonline.co.uk

Warning: Any other unsolicited mail received at this address will be ignored.

Please note that recommendation in this guide involves no charge whatsoever beyond the cost of the samples and their delivery.

MUMM NAPA
California, USA

MUMM CUVÉE NAPA NV BRUT

The Granny Smith fruit in the current release will develop a toastiness in 12–18 months.

Now–2002 ££

MUMM CUVÉE NAPA NV BLANC DE BLANCS BRUT

Not as fresh or as vivacious as last year's *cuvée*, this release is already toasty and will go even toastier, but it has the acidity to withstand the mellowing effect without going too fat.

Now–2001 ££

MUMM CUVÉE NAPA NV BRUT ROSÉ

Tart apple-pie juice.

Now–2002 ££

MUMM CUVÉE NAPA 1995 DVX BRUT

A serious quaffer, if that's not a contradiction in terms. It's a pity that Mumm Napa did not submit both this and the 1994, as it would be interesting to hold a taste-off between the two vintages.

Now–2002 ££

MUMM CUVÉE NAPA 1994 WINERY LAKE BRUT

I cannot put in print the exclamation I made when typing up this note only to discover the identity. Winery Lake shows well in the States, but has not travelled well in the past or, at least, it has not travelled well to the UK in commercial shipments. This sample was, however, brilliant. The fruit was both delicate and intense, which is characteristic of the Winery Lake vineyard. Also zesty. Lovely. Will mature beautifully.

Now–2003 ££

MURÉ
Alsace, France

RENÉ MURÉ NV CRÉMANT D'ALSACE, BRUT CUVÉE PRESTIGE

This would achieve more finesse if the malolactic was throttled back.

Now–2001 £

NYETIMBER

West Chiltington, England, UK

England's leading sparkling wine specialist can hack it out in the real world against all comers.

NYETIMBER 1994 CLASSIC CUVÉE, BRUT 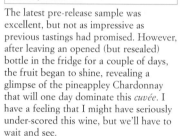 84

The latest pre-release sample was excellent, but not as impressive as previous tastings had promised. However, after leaving an opened (but resealed) bottle in the fridge for a couple of days, the fruit began to shine, revealing a glimpse of the pineappley Chardonnay that will one day dominate this *cuvée*. I have a feeling that I might have seriously under-scored this wine, but we'll have to wait and see.

2002–2004 ⓔⓔ

NYETIMBER 1993 CLASSIC CUVÉE, BRUT 89

The richness of the fruit is now beginning to dig in, yet it remains elegant with a silky finesse and the exquisite *cordon* is evidence of excellent mousse retention. It is quite extraordinary that an English sparkling wine actually needs seven years before it starts coming right!

Now–2002 ⓔⓔ

NYETIMBER 1993 PREMIÈRE CUVÉE, CHARDONNAY BLANC DE BLANCS, BRUT 88

Without doubt the Classic Cuvée is the best of Nyetimber's two 1993s and it's getting better each year, but the Chardonnay has at long last shed itself of most of its herbaceousness and is really starting to shine. Herbaceousness can be one of the most attractive aspects of other English sparkling wines, but it simply detracts from the class and quality of Nyetimber. So, if you've kept a case of last year's disgorgement, you will have a wonderfully creamy-biscuity wine and now is the time to start drinking it.

Now–2003 ⓔⓔ

ORLANDO WYNDHAM GROUP

South Australia, Australia

ORLANDO TRILOGY CUVÉE NV BRUT 75

Nicely balanced fruit for the price.
Now ⓔ 🍾 A$12.45

MORRIS NV SPARKLING SHIRAZ DURIF 80

The sweet oaky-cedary-plummy fruit in this red fizz is surprisingly fresh and elegant for such a sizeable wine.
Now–2001 ⓔ 🍾 A$16

ORSCHWIHR

Château d'Orschwihr
Alsace, France

CHÂTEAU D'ORSCHWIHR NV CUVÉE 2000, CRÉMANT D'ALSACE BRUT 74

Leaning more towards classic, but with plenty of fruit, albeit with a buttery-malo character with a smooth creamy finish.
Now–2001 ⓔ

OUDINOT

Champagne Oudinot
12 rue Godart-Roger
51207 Epernay
☎(326) 54.60.31 📠(326) 54.78.52

OUDINOT NV CUVÉE BRUT 80

Good intensity of peachy fruit on the palate, but could do with more finesse on the nose.
Now–2002 ⓔⓔ 🍾 90FF

PAILLARD

Champagne Bruno Paillard
avenue du Champagne
51100 Reims
☎(326) 36.20.22 📠(326) 36.57.72

BRUNO PAILLARD NV BRUT PREMIÈRE CUVÉE

Fresh, floral aromas, crisp fruit and an accent on finesse. (Disgorged October 1999.)

Now–2003 ££

BRUNO PAILLARD NV CHARDONNAY RÉSERVE PRIVÉE, BRUT

After two years of post-disgorgement ageing (the sample was disgorged in October 1998), a richness to the fruit has built up on the palate, but the bouquet still needs to blossom. The Chardonnay in this wine typically goes soft and creamy.

2001–2004 £££

BRUNO PAILLARD NV BRUT ROSÉ PREMIÈRE CUVÉE

A light, fresh, perfumed rosé of some elegance.

Now–2001 £££

BRUNO PAILLARD 1995 BRUT

Serious, classically structured Champagne with rich, yeast-complexed fruit.

Now–2004 £££

BRUNO PAILLARD 1990 N.P.U. NEO PLUS ULTRA, BRUT

This new wine should have been disgorged three years ago, not one, but the fruit has enough concentration, albeit somewhat elevated, and the *barrique* aromas are so nicely understated, that it will improve greatly over the next two years or so.

2002–2005 ££££

❖ **PALAIS, L.,** *see* Compagnie Française des Grands Vins

PALMER

Champagne Palmer
67 rue Jacquart
51100 Reims
☎(326) 07.35.07 ☎(326) 07.45.24

PALMER NV BRUT

A soft, fine and flavoursome *cuvée* that is satisfying to drink on its own, but also makes a good, general-purpose food wine.

Now–2003 ££ 98FF

AMAZONE DE PALMER NV BRUT

Fine, complex nose followed by fine, rich fruit with delicate toasty aromas demonstrate that this is a mature Champagne of class and quality. Should continue to age gracefully for several more years.

Now–2007 £££

PALMER 1995 BLANC DE BLANCS BRUT

If you like unoaked Chablis, you'll love this!

Now–2002 ££ 133FF

PALMER 1992 BRUT

Eight years old and this Champagne still needs time. A full-bodied, true Brut style that should go toasty.

2002–2005 ££ 140FF

PALMER 1991 BRUT

Should start going toasty by the time this Guide is published, but has the acidity to achieve this with some degree of finesse.

Now–2003 ££

PANNIER

Champagne Pannier
23 rue Roger Catillon
02406 Château-Thierry
☎(323) 69.51.30 ☎(323) 69.51.31

PANNIER NV BRUT SÉLECTION

This truly enjoyable, scrumptious, fruity Champagne is the best-ever release of Pannier Brut Sélection and much preferred to the premium-priced Cuvée Louis Eugène, which failed to make the cut this year.

Now–2003 ££ 86FF

PANNIER NV BRUT ROSÉ

Light, fresh, thirst-quenching fruit with a touch of vanilla dusting the finish.

Now–2001 ££ 91FF

PANNIER NV CUVÉE LOUIS EUGÈNE, ROSÉ BRUT

A curious but not unlikeable rosé with an almost musky style of fruit that strangely went well with food.

▍ Now–2002 ⓔⓔ ☙ 120FF

EGÉRIE DE PANNIER 1995 BRUT

A bit too fat and over-the-top in richness, this vintage needs a spark of finesse and elegance to lift it above its current score, and this could possibly be achieved with additional ageing, but I would not want to keep it very long.

▍ Now–2001 ⓔⓔⓔ ☙ 142FF

PARKER MC

Gisborne, New Zealand

Phil Parker's old winery has a DC3 aircraft perched on top and a yellow Morris Minor tumbling out of one of the windows. That, however, is Parker past. Phil is moving on to run Acton Estate, where he plans to build a new winery and live a respectable life. The thought of respectability may make Parker's friends smile with disbelief; after all, this is the man who named his son Robert so that 18 years later he might be able to sell wines under a Robert Parker label.

PARKER FIRSTLIGHT NV CRACKLING TRAMINER

Fresh rose-petal nose followed easy-drinking fruit on the palate. There is a touch of spice to the fruit and this promises to develop with some bottle-age, but the wine has no dosage and thus further ageing cannot be recommended. The no-dosage style is not a matter of choice, it is simply a necessity because Phil Parker has not been able to cadge a dosage machine!

▍ Now ⓔⓔ

PARKER FIRSTLIGHT NV MERLOT BRUT

A dry tannic red fizz showing a good depth of colour, but in need of a good Brut dosage.

▍ Now ⓔⓔ

PARXET

Penedès, Spain

PARXET CUVÉE DESSERT NV CAVA DULCE ROSADO

The palate has a candied fruit sweetness followed by vanilla. Only let down by sulphur, but this is clean and not bound, so it should dissipate.

▍ Now ⓔ ☙ 1,225 Ptas

PARXET GRAN RESERVA MILLENIUM NV CAVA GRAN RESERVA

A touch of perfume to the fruit. Very soft.

▍ Now ⓔ ☙ 1,570 Ptas

PARXET ANIVERSARIO 80 NV CAVA BRUT NATURE

This Pinot Noir-Chardonnay blend offers more fruit than the basic Parxet Brut Nature.

▍ Now ⓔⓔ ☙ 5,000 Ptas

PAULY-BERGWEILER

Dr. Pauly-Bergweiler
Mosel-Saar-Ruwer, Germany

DR. PAULY-BERGWEILER SPÄTBURGUNDER BLANC DE NOIRS 1998 WEHLENER KLOSTERBERG

This Sekt is nothing if not interesting, starting off in a conventional manner with very fresh, delightful aromas, then followed by really quite sweet fruit for a Brut and an intriguing aroma of Ceylon tea on finish. (*Méthode champenoise.*)

▍ Now ⓔ ☙ DM23

PELLETIER

Champagne Jean-Michel Pelletier
22 rue Bruslard
51700 Passy-Grigny
☎(326) 52.65.86 ☏(326) 52.65.86

JEAN-MICHEL PELLETIER NV BRUT SELECTION

I much prefer this rich, fruity Champagne to Pelletier's extremely aldehydic Grande Réserve, but the dosage is a bit blatant on the finish and needs time to marry.
➤ 2001–2002 ££ ♚ 71FF

PELLIN
France

TÊTE DE CUVÉE ROSÉ DEMI-SEC NV PRESTIGE, VIN PÉTILLANT, PELLIN

Elevated strawberry fruit aromas.
❦ Now £

❖ **PELORUS**, *see* Cloudy Bay

PERELADA
Ampurdán-Costa Brava, Spain

CASTILLO DE PERELADA NV CAVA BRUT RESERVA

Light, elegant and fruity style. Very soft with perhaps a touch too much sweetness on the finish, but that is preferable to a much drier Cava without any fruit or charm.
❦ Now £ ♚ 775 Ptas

GRAN CLAUSTRO 1998 CAVA BRUT NATURE, CASTILLO DE PERELADA

I tasted a pre-release sample of the *cuvée* due to be released the month before this edition is published and found it nicely fresh, elegant and fruity, with no secondary-ferment odours, even though some fully commercial Cavas have.
❦ Now–2001 ££ ♚ 2,600 Ptas

PERLINO
Asti, Italy

PERLINO NV ASTI

The extremely rich, concentrated Moscato fruit in this wine and true

sweetness lift the Perlino above most other Asti.
❦ Now £

PERRIER
Champagne Joseph Perrier
69 avenue de Paris
51016 Châlons-en-Champagne
☎(326) 68.29.51 ℻(326) 70.57.16

JOSEPH PERRIER NV CUVÉE ROYALE BLANC DE BLANCS

Those who know this ultimately biscuity *cuvée* will give it at least four years, although it starts to become approachable after three.
➤ 2003–2007 £££

JOSEPH PERRIER 1995 BRUT CUVÉE ROYALE

Excellent combination of richness and finesse, lifted by a pin-cushion mousse of tiny bubbles.
❦ Now–2010 £££

JOSEPH PERRIER 1996 BRUT CUVÉE ROYALE

Really needs another two years on yeast, but the quality is clear, with an interesting minerally complexity leading to great finesse. My score might well be on the conservative side.
➤ 2001–2010 £££

PERRIER-JOUËT
Champagne Perrier-Jouët
28 avenue de Champagne
51201 Epernay
☎(326) 53.38.00 ℻(326) 54.54.55

PERRIER-JOUËT NV GRAND BRUT

Fresh and floral, with elegant fruit and a clean, crisp finish.
❦ Now–2003 ££

PERRIER-JOUËT NV BLASON DE FRANCE, BRUT

Creamy-biscuity malo aromas dominate, with crisp, clean fruit on palate and finish.

▌ Now–2001 ⓕⓕⓕ

PERRIER-JOUËT NV BLASON DE FRANCE ROSÉ BRUT ⑧⑨

A welcome back into the land of high-scoring recommendation for this *cuvée*, which was spoilt last year by atypical butterscotch malo aromas. Those who loved the beautiful strawberry Pinot fruit in Blason Rosé can buy it with confidence once again. The fruit is really quite substantial, with a touch of vanilla underlying the strawberry flavour on the finish.

▌ Now–2002 ⓕⓕⓕ

PERRIER-JOUËT 1992 GRAND BRUT ⑧⑧

I was surprised to see this vintage still on the market in 2000, when Perrier-Jouët's Belle Epoque, which is traditionally released one year behind, was already onto 1995, but it is and therefore makes its third successive appearance in this annual Guide. Paradoxically the more recent the disgorgement, the more it resembles the earliest releases, with its fruit showing beautifully young and crisp, with a touch of floral-almond aroma mid-palate.

▌ Now–2004 ⓕⓕⓕ

PERRIER-JOUËT 1995 BELLE EPOQUE BRUT ⑨⓪

Nose extremely closed, but that is probably due to the wine tasted coming from a pre-release sample, and the quality is clear from the beautiful Cramant-influenced fruit on the palate.

◂▬ 2001–2006 ⓕⓕⓕⓕ

PERRIER-JOUËT 1989 BELLE EPOQUE ROSÉ BRUT ⑨⓪

Last year's reserved opinion is singing a good 90 points this year. In the last edition of the Guide I noted caramel-malo aromas that were far too dominant and Pinot fruit that could go farmyardy, but the current release could not be cleaner. No malo, no farmyardy hints, only freshness and fruit, this wine is going between red-fruit-driven mode and Cramant-influenced fruit.

▌ Now–2009 ⓕⓕⓕⓕ

PERRIER-JOUËT 1993 BELLE EPOQUE BLANC DE BLANCS ⑧⑨

This mono-cru Belle Epoque is made exclusively from Chardonnay grapes grown in Perrier-Jouët's finest vineyards of Cramant. If you do not chill this wine as much as a normal Champagne you should notice the first hints of biscuitiness mingling with exquisite citrussy-floral fruit. I cannot wait to see what this *cuvée* is like in a truly great year such as 1995 or 1996.

▌ Now–2004 ⓕⓕⓕⓕ

PETALUMA

South Australia, Australia

A complete vertical with Brian Croser downunder was a most instructive experience, especially the huge difference in quality and staying power of those wines aged after disgorgement compared to the same wines kept on yeast. Now if only he could get this point over to his chums at Bollinger!

CROSER 1998 PETALUMA ⑧⑧

Softer than and superior to the 1997, the fruit in this vintage shows a lovely elegance. Although two years away from being released, there is no hiding the finesse of this beautifully balanced, potentially great vintage, which should age gracefully and increase its score in the process.

▌ Now–2003 ⓕⓕ 🍇 A$29

CROSER 1997 PETALUMA ⑧④

In the company of other Australian fizz, this tastes like a serious sparkling wine indeed, but everything is relative and compared to some other Croser vintages this is just a middling effort with good fruit.

▌ Now–2003 ⓕⓕ

CROSER 1996 PETALUMA ⑧⑤

If this firmly structured, newly released Croser follows in the same vein as previous vintages, we can expect a softening of the fruit, including a tasteful degree of fatness, a touch of vanilla and finesse building over the next few years, along with an increase in score of 3–5 points.

▌ Now–2003 ⓕⓕ

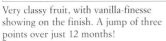

CROSER 1995 PETALUMA (88)

Very classy fruit, with vanilla-finesse showing on the finish. A jump of three points over just 12 months!
❚ Now–2003 ©©

CROSER 1994 PETALUMA (90)

Classy stuff! It was instructive to find this vintage so impressive two years after writing "strangely foursquare if served too cold, but has a soft, gentle fatness with nice vanilla fruit finesse on the finish when not over-chilled" (85 points).
❚ Now–2003 ©©

CROSER 1993 PETALUMA (87)

Both the recent and the original disgorgement were fresh and clean, with vanilla and apricots in the fruit. Excellent.
❚ Now–2003 ©©

CROSER 1992 PETALUMA (87)

The recently disgorged version was fresher than the 1992, but the normally disgorged bottle was once again as clean as a whistle and as fresh a daisy.
❚ Now–2003 ©©

CROSER 1991 PETALUMA (86)

The excellent freshness here should be an object lesson to those who believe that yeast-ageing preserves sparkling wine better than cellaring the same wine after disgorgement because the recently disgorged version of this vintage has smelly, cabbage odours, whereas this is fresh and fine, with no hint of any off-odours. Furthermore it has a fine structure and acidity, suggesting that further ageing is indeed possible.
❚ Now–2003 ©©

PETIT

Désiré Petit
Jura, France

DÉSIRÉ PETIT NV CUVÉE DE L'AN 2000, CRÉMANT DU JURA BRUT (71)

This wine stood out from most other Crémant du Jura on the nose, being elegant and immediately appealing, but it did not compare to the others

on the palate.
❚ Now ©

ATTENTION CHAMPAGNE & SPARKLING WINE PRODUCERS!
If you are not already in contact with the author, but would like to submit wines for consideration in future editions, please contact Tom Stevenson at:

tom.stevenson@fizz.worldonline.co.uk

Warning: Any other unsolicited mail received at this address will be ignored.

Please note that recommendation in this guide involves no charge whatsoever beyond the cost of the samples and their delivery.

PHILIPPONNAT

Champagne Philipponnat
13 rue du Pont
51160 Mareuil-sur-Aÿ
☎(326) 56.93.00 ℻(326) 56.93.18

PHILIPPONNAT NV RÉSERVE ROSÉ, BRUT (84)

A serious rosé that showed fine, attractive fruit and delicious acidity at the beginning of the year, gaining mature, mellow fruitiness in the following months. Good food wine.
❚ Now–2002 ©© 🍷 167FF

PHILIPPONNAT NV LE REFLET DU MILLÉNAIRE AN 2000, BRUT (86)

The first release of Le Reflet that will not only benefit from ageing, but positively requires it. I'm not certain if this is a permanent change of style or a one-off for a millennium *cuvée*, but there does appear to be more emphasis on Pinot Noir and high extract, whereas Le Reflet has always made easy immediate drinking and attempts to age it have not been successful. However, with 50% of the wine coming from Clos des Goisses, there should be the potential for development.
➤ 2002–2004 ©©© 🍷 170FF

PHILIPPONNAT 1991 GRAND BLANC, BRUT (85)

Lovely perfumed Chardonnay aroma with
crisp fruit on the palate, lemony acidity
lengthening the finish and peach-stone
fruit on the aftertaste.

❦ Now–2003 ££££ 🍾 236FF

❖ **PIERREL**, *see* Mignon & Pierrel

PIPER-HEIDSIECK

Champagne Piper-Heidsieck
51 Boulevard Henri Vasnier
51100 Reims
☎ (326) 84.41.94 FAX (326) 84.43.49

For some reason Rémy-Cointreau
submitted only Charles Heidsieck this year,
which was a pity. I was rather hoping that I
might receive the Jean-Paul Gaultier
cuvée, which has the bottle strapped into a
bright red corset! The wines below were
both tasted at the annual Champagne
tasting in London.

PIPER-HEIDSIECK NV BRUT (80)

The step-up in quality noticed with the
1992-based *cuvée* of this wine some three
years ago seems to have been forgotten.
Although this wine dropped a point last
year, that was hardly worth worrying
about, but this year the amylic aroma and
raw pepperiness have an oppressive effect
on the sunny Aube fruit at the heart of
Piper NV Brut. Consequently it has
barely scraped through with the sort of
score that I expect from any decent BOB
Champagne. It is time, I think, that
Daniel Thibault took a firm grip of the
team responsible for this wine.

➤ 2001–2002 ££

PIPER-HEIDSIECK 1995 BRUT (85)

While this might not be up to Piper's
1990, that was an exceptional vintage.
There is nothing wrong with the 1995
that a couple of years' additional ageing
will not rectify. A truly fine wine with
excellent acidity.

➤ 2002–2006 ££

PIPER'S BROOK

Tasmania, Australia

PIPERS BROOK 1996 DELAMERE CUVÉE (79)

The hint of something good, but too
much oak for the weight of wine merely
leaches out the finesse.

❦ Now–2002 £

PIRIE 1996 PIPERS BROOK (91)

I sent Andrew Pirie a copy of my notes
on his first vintage (91 points) prior to
publication last year and told him that I
had considered prefacing these with a
warning that it could just be a flash in the
pan. The only reason I did not was
because I did not want anything to spoil
the sense of excitement I was trying to
convey, but I must confess that more than
once I wondered whether I would come
to regret such unqualified praise.
Naturally enough Andrew was confident
about the quality of his forthcoming Pirie
1996, but when he poured me a glass
earlier this year, did I detect just the
slightest hint of anxiety when he asked
"Well?". I thought I did, so I kept him
dangling a while, then announced, "Well
Andrew, that's another flash in the pan
then." If anything the 1996 is better, but
it will take a few years to be certain.

❦ Now–2006 ££ 🍾 A$39.80

PIRIE 1995 PIPERS BROOK (91)

I came across an oxidized bottle in the
Barossa earlier this year, which made me
anxious to get home and taste a bottle
that had been in my cellar since the year
before. That, I can happily say, was in
perfect condition, still in full-throttle
fruit-driven mode and evolving slowly
and gracefully.

❦ Now–2004 ££ 🍾 A$39.80

PLUNKETT

Victoria, Australia

PLUNKETT WINES 1997 STRATHBOGIE RANGES CHARDONNAY PINOT NOIR (80)

Fresh, fruity, but with some elegance.
Very clean and refreshing.

❦ Now ££ 🍾 A$27

POL ROGER

Champagne White Foil
1 rue Henri Lelarge
51206 Epernay
☎(326) 59.58.00 ☏(326) 55.25.70

POL ROGER NV BRUT WHITE FOIL, EXTRA CUVÉE DE RÉSERVE — 84

I could not believe how good this wine was at the Annual Champagne tasting in London at the beginning of the year. Following the exhaustion of stock due to the millennium, the UK shipment had no landing-age whatsoever, yet was really quite biscuity (87 points). I wish I had taken a note of the EU Lot Number because the *cuvée* submitted to my tastings needed ageing, thus had no biscuitiness, and although it was showing some intensity of flavour, there was none of the fresh, floral Meunier fruit that the White Foil is so famous for. Furthermore there was little of Pol Roger's finesse on the nose.
▮ Now–2003 ⓔⓔ

POL ROGER NV RICH SPECIAL DEMI-SEC — 88

I somehow doubt that Pol Roger wants its Demi-Sec to become a high-profile product, but every now and then it comes out with an absolute cracker and it always ages well, so it will just have to put up with something of a reputation for this style. The current *cuvée* has greatest richness, as opposed to simply bags of sweetness. In fact it was the richest of all the Demi-Sec tasted this year, and I tasted some pretty good ones. The fruit brought back childhood memories of a perfectly ripe Beauty of Bath apple.
▮ Now–2005 ⓔⓔⓔ

POL ROGER 1993 BRUT — 89

Neither a great year nor a top Pol Roger, yet such is the quality of Pol Roger's vintage Champagnes that even its "second raters" can score 89 points and almost 20 years' potential longevity (it will in fact be much more, but the when-to-drink range in this guide is both conservative and restricted to prime drinking). The purity of fruit in this wine is so delightful.

▮ Now–2012 ⓔⓔⓔ

POL ROGER 1993 BRUT ROSÉ — 87

Not the immediate drinkability or sensual experience of the 1990 rosé, but the firmer fruit will plump out with a little cellaring.
▬▬ 2001–2003 ⓔⓔⓔⓔ

POL ROGER 1990 BRUT — 96

I see this has edged up one point in my tasting, which I put down to the more recent disgorgement. The earliest disgorgement was tremendous, but some of the releases in between have not matured cleanly. This, however, is extraordinary quality even by Pol Roger's exalted standards.
▮ Now–2020 ⓔⓔⓔ

POL ROGER 1993 BRUT CHARDONNAY — 88

Another minor classic, this *blanc de blancs* really needs to be kept a few years.
▬▬ 2003–2007 ⓔⓔⓔⓔ

POL ROGER 1990 CUVÉE SIR WINSTON CHURCHILL BRUT — 98

Simply stunning!
▬▬ 2001–2020 ⓔⓔⓔⓔ

POL ROGER 1988 CUVÉE SIR WINSTON CHURCHILL BRUT — 95

Last year's prediction that it will take three years before this starts drinking well seems on target, but even then it will only show a fraction of its potential. Anyone lucky enough to have cases of both this and CSWC 1990 should start drinking the latter first.
▬▬ 2002–2030 ⓔⓔⓔⓔ

POMMERY

Champagne Pommery
5 Place du Général Gouraud
51053 Reims
☎(326) 61.62.63 ☏(326) 61.62.99
This house is on terrific form.

POMMERY NV BRUT ROYAL — 85

Beautifully fresh, crisp and elegant. If Pommery keeps this quality up much longer, I'll stop calling for its Brut Royal to be delisted!

🍾 Now–2003 ⓕⓕ ✿ 160FF

POMMERY NV BRUT ROYAL (*magnum*) 89

A more mature *cuvée* than in the 75cl, current magnums have slightly more mellowness to the fruit, but it is relative and probably not noticeable to most consumers drinking, who should find this wine equally fresh and crisp. Lovely finesse.

🍾 2002–2008 ⓕⓕⓕ ✿ 900FF

POMMERY NV BRUT ROYAL APANAGE 88

After dipping one percentile point last year, Apanage is back on form as a substantially flavoured non-vintage Brut that somehow retains the elegance expected of Pommery at its best.

🍾 Now–2004 ⓕⓕⓕ ✿ 185FF

POMMERY NV SUMMERTIME, BLANC DE BLANCS BRUT 86

Great richness of fruit, fresh and sherbety.

🍾 Now–2002 ⓕⓕⓕ ✿ 180FF

POMMERY NV ROSÉ BRUT 86

This applies to the *cuvée* available in the UK at the beginning of 2000, which was exceptionally fresh and invigorating, not the sample submitted, which I expect to be in general distribution by the time this edition of the Guide is published.

🍾 Now–2002 ⓕⓕⓕ ✿ 180FF

POMMERY 1995 BRUT, GRAND CRU 86

This powerful tasting Champagne is not too full-bodied, but certainly is one of Pommery's bigger vintages, such as the stunning 1989, but this is another Grande Marque using grotty uncoated wire cages: why?

🍾 2001–2005 ⓕⓕⓕ ✿ 220FF

POMMERY 1992 BRUT, GRAND CRU 88

Extraordinary richness and grace. All Champagne lovers who have shunned Pommery in the past really should take a look at its vintage wines and ask themselves how many other houses can claim their vintage Champagnes are 100% Grand Cru?

🍾 Now–2005 ⓕⓕⓕ ✿ 220FF

POMMERY 1992 BRUT, GRAND CRU (*magnum*) 89

Nuances of toast and coffee mingle with the fruit in this magnum version of Pommery's excellent 1992 vintage, yet it still needs time.

🍾 2002–2008 ⓕⓕⓕ ✿ 450FF

POMMERY 1989 LOUISE, BRUT 86

Quite fat, still needs time.

🍾 2002–2008 ⓕⓕⓕⓕ ✿ 550FF

POMMERY 1990 LOUISE ROSÉ BRUT 92

Luscious, creamy fruit. Irresistible!

🍾 Now–2002 ⓕⓕⓕⓕ ✿ 700FF

VEUVE POMMERY 1979 FLACON D'EXCELLENCE NATURE (*magnum*) 95

This magnificent magnum of one of Pommery's very best vintages is presented in a wicker picnic basket and although available only from its own cellars where the price is officially "subject to negotiation", readers of last year's edition of the Guide will know that was then a mere FF900, which made it the best-value wine out of no fewer than 40 vintages dating back to 1904 that this firm offered in celebration of the new millennium. This magnum of 1979 is so young and fresh with exquisitely pure fruit. However, there is no dosage, hence it should be drunk sooner rather than later. Hopefully Pommery might release some of these magnums with a small dosage so that aficionados can age this great Champagne for a few more years.

🍾 Now–2002 ⓕⓕⓕ

POUILLON

Champagne Roger Pouillon
3 Rue de la Couple
51160 Mareuil-sur-Aÿ
(326) 52.60.08 (326) 59.49.83

ROGER POUILLON NV LE BRUT VIGNERON, PREMIER CRU 80

Rich and tasty, but rather straightforward

and needs both finesse and complexity to achieve a higher score.

❚ Now–2001 ⓔⓔ ❄ 90FF

ROGER POUILLON, 50 ÈME ANNIVERSAIRE NV FLEUR DE MAREUIL, BRUT PREMIER CRU 89

Succulent fruit with *barrique* aromas on the nose and front palate, and peachy fruit on the mid-palate through to the finish.

❚ Now–2003 ⓔⓔ ❄ 120FF

POULET
Rhône, France

ALAIN POULET CLAIRETTE DE DIE NV MÉTHODE DIOISE ANCESTRALE, TRADITION 85

Delicious, muscatty fruit. Like a restrained Asti or a turbo-charged demi-sec!

❚ Now ⓔⓔ

PRIMO ESTATE
South Australia, Australia

JOSEPH NV SPARKLING RED 88

Extremely rich and creamy fruit, but perhaps too much on the creamy side to match the Charles Melton this year (last year both wines scored 90 points).

❚ Now–2001 ⓔⓔ ❄ A$50

PUGLIESE
New York, USA

PUGLIESE 1997 BLANC DE BLANCS 74

Bright, crisp colour. Tangy, citrussy fruit with sherbety fruit on finish.

❚ Now–2001 ⓔ ❄ $17.99

QUARTZ REEF
Central Otago, New Zealand

Rudi Bauer and Clotilde Chauvet are the first sparkling winemakers in Central Otago to move successfully from Marlborough to local fruit.

QUARTZ REEF NV BRUT 80

The second release of this wine is a darn sight better than the first release. A fresh and fluffy wine that is full of fruit and ridiculously easy to quaff. Both releases were, however, made from Marlborough and Canterbury fruit. The third release, which will not leave the cellar doors until February 2001, is the first to contain any Central Otago fruit, albeit just 13%, and the advance sample has an even greater intensity of fruit, although with another year *sur lie* this wine should develop a more layered, yeast-complexed style.

❚ Now–2001 ⓔⓔ

CHAUVET 1998 BRUT BLANC DE BLANCS, QUARTZ REEF 85

The first pure Central Otago sparkling wine from Quartz Reef, 100% from the Rafters Road vineyard in Gibston Valley, 100% malolactic and almost 100% Chardonnay (in fact 7% Pinot Noir was added for balance). This is also the very first pure Central Otago sparkling wine I can be enthusiastic about (forget Rippon, which no longer makes fizz thank goodness, and Chard Farm, which has more teething troubles than a dentist's surgery), although it will not be released until February 2002 or thereabouts. The advance sample was very promising, with exquisitely rich pineapple fruit and brilliantly vivid acidity. Book your case now!

➤ Wait and see ⓔⓔ

RATZENBERGER
Mittelrhein, Germany

RATZENBERGER RIESLING BRUT 1996 BACHARACHER KLOSTER FÜRSTENTAL 74

A fuller-bodied Riesling style that deserves to develop bottle aromas. (*Méthode champenoise.*)

 2001 Ⓔ 🥂 DM18

RAVENTÓS

Raventós i Blanc
Penedès, Spain

L'HEREU BRUT DE RAVENTÓS I BLANC NV CAVA BRUT

This 1998-based Cava has really good acidity, making it interesting to age for 6–12 months after purchase.

🥂 Now–2001 Ⓔ 🥂 850 Ptas

RESERVA DE RAVENTÓS I BLANC NV CAVA BRUT

In Cava terms this 1997-based *cuvée* is ultra-fruity.

🥂 Now Ⓔ 🥂 1,100 Ptas

RAVENTÓS ROSELL

Joan Raventós Rosell
Penedès, Spain

BRUT RESERVA HERETAT 1996 CAVA BRUT NATURAL, JOAN RAVENTÓS ROSELL

Chic presentation, with good, lightly fruity fizz inside.

🥂 Now ⒺⒺ 🥂 2,340 Ptas

JOAN RAVENTÓS ROSELL 1997 CAVA BRUT NATURE

Would be better with a dosage.

🥂 Now Ⓔ 🥂 1,510 Ptas

RED HILL

50 Red Hill Estate
Victoria, Australia

50 RED HILL ESTATE MORNINGTON PENINSULA 1997 PINOT NOIR CHARDONNAY

A serious attempt at a serious style, with creamy yeast-complexed fruit and

potential to improve.

🥂 Now–2003 ⒺⒺ 🥂 A$28

REMSTALKELLEREI

Württemberg, Germany

REMSTALKELLEREI GRAUER BURGUNDER EXTRA BRUT 1998 GRÜNBECHER KLINGLE

Fat, creamy fruit that promises to develop some spice. (Transfer method.)

🥂 Now–2001 Ⓔ 🥂 DM17

RENAUDIN

Champagne R. Renaudin
Domaine des Conardins
Moussy
51200 Epernay
📞(326) 54.03.41 📠(326) 54.31.12

R. RENAUDIN NV BRUT ROSÉ

High acids supporting plenty of flavour, this wine deserves to be kept at least one year, after which the yeast-complexed fruit aromas will blossom.

 2001–2003 ⒺⒺ

RESS

Balthasar Ress
Rheingau, Germany

BALTHASAR RESS RIESLING BRUT 1997 VON UNSERM

Great intensity of flavour, but not particularly fruity, which is not necessarily a bad thing. Needs time to gain finesse. (*Méthode champenoise.*)

🥂 Now–2003 Ⓔ 🥂 DM22

RICCAFANA

Franciacorta, Italy

RICCAFANA NV FRANCIACORTA BRUT

Very fresh and fine, but with a touch of

toast, although finish is again very fresh, light fruit.
❚ Now–2001 €€

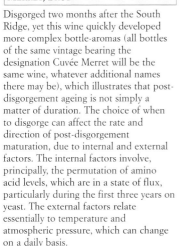

RIDGEVIEW

Ditchling Common, Sussex England, UK

The second commercial winery in the UK to develop an estate entirely designated to sparkling wine production, Ridgeview is beginning to push Nyetimber and competing for quality can only be good for the consumer.

BLOOMSBURY 1996 CUVÉE MERRET, BRUT ⑧⑤

Disgorged two months after the South Ridge, yet this wine quickly developed more complex bottle-aromas (all bottles of the same vintage bearing the designation Cuvée Merret will be the same wine, whatever additional names there may be), which illustrates that post-disgorgement ageing is not simply a matter of duration. The choice of when to disgorge can affect the rate and direction of post-disgorgement maturation, due to internal and external factors. The internal factors involve, principally, the permutation of amino acid levels, which are in a state of flux, particularly during the first three years on yeast. The external factors relate essentially to temperature and atmospheric pressure, which can change on a daily basis.
❚ Now–2001 €€

SOUTH RIDGE 1996 CUVÉE MERRET, BRUT (BORDEAUX DIRECT) ⑧②

Disgorged in August 1999, this release is exquisitely fruity, whereas the earlier disgorged Bloomsbury achieved a creamy-biscuity complexity of excellent finesse at a much faster rate. This wine therefore has a wider drinking window and should in theory not only have a greater potential longevity, but should also achieve its complexity with more finesse, yet I have scored it lower: why? My 100-point system is universal, thus a 90-point Australian fizz or whatever is

equal in pure quality to a 90-point Champagne. In assessing these scores I take into account the potential quality of a wine, but give priority to current drinkability and despite South Ridge's faster development it does have finesse and will not fall over too quickly.
❚ Now–2002 €€

RIEFLÉ

Alsace, France

RIEFLÉ NV CRÉMANT D'ALSACE BRUT ⑦⑧

This is serious stuff, with an attractive melange of varietal flavours. Fresh and crisp with a suggestion of VA lift. If this wine had more acid it would achieve a score in the 80s.
❚ Now–2003 €

RINKLIN

Weingut Friedhelm Rinklin Baden, Germany

FRIEDHELM RINKLIN 1995 SPÄTBURGUNDER WEIßHERBST BRUT ⑦⑥

Rich and tangy fruit of good brut dryness. (*Méthode champenoise.*)
❚ Now € DM22

ROEDERER ESTATE

California, USA

Sold as Quartet on some export markets.

ROEDERER ESTATE NV ANDERSON VALLEY BRUT ⑧⑤

Now that Roederer Estate has embraced malolactic, there is an incongruity when first released between the wine's mellow aromas and crispness of fruit that only time can redress. So for an entirely different reason, aficionados of Roederer Estate will still want to cellar the wine, although for 1–2 years instead of the previous minimum of 2–3.

2001–2004 ⓔⓔ

ROEDERER ESTATE NV ANDERSON VALLEY BRUT ROSÉ 〈90〉

The best release so far of this wine, with its magnificent creamy-biscuity complexity lording itself over the crisp, creamy fruit from nose to finish. Great finesse.

❚ Now–2003 ⓔⓔ

ROEDERER ESTATE L'ERMITAGE 1993 BRUT 〈91〉

This complex, biscuity classic remains one of the best three non-Champagne sparkling wines ever produced.

❚ Now–2007 ⓔⓔ ☙ $38

ATTENTION CHAMPAGNE & SPARKLING WINE PRODUCERS!

If you are not already in contact with the author, but would like to submit wines for consideration in future editions, please contact Tom Stevenson at:

tom.stevenson@fizz.worldonline.co.uk

Warning: Any other unsolicited mail received at this address will be ignored.

Please note that recommendation in this guide involves no charge whatsoever beyond the cost of the samples and their delivery.

ROEDERER

Champagne Louis Roederer
21 Boulevard Lundy
51053 Reims
☎(326) 40.42.11 ☎(326) 47.66.51

LOUIS ROEDERER NV BRUT PREMIER 〈88〉

Roederer's basic non-vintage Brut slips two percentile points from its usual, if quite extraordinary, score of 90 because, contrary to claims that the age of this *cuvée* would gradually increase despite the pressure of Millennium demand, this wine has less post-disgorgement ageing than normal. The potential is just as high, but the current shipment begs to be aged

---

at least two years, by which time its fruit should have developed its famous creamy-biscuity mellowness.

 2002–2005 ⓔⓔ ☙ 180FF

LOUIS ROEDERER NV RICH 〈88〉

The sweet biscuity aroma that pervades every aspect of this wine is reminiscent of a tin of custard creams.

❚ Now–2005 ⓔⓔⓔ

LOUIS ROEDERER 1994 BRUT 〈82〉

Since the very minimum score I expect from any Roederer *cuvée*, vintage or otherwise, is 85, this can only be described as a disaster. As Roederer has demonstrated on many occasions that it can by strict selection produce Champagne well above the class of the year in question, I can only assume that the reason for its failure in the 1994 vintage is insufficient selection. Based on Roederer's track-record I'm willing to consider the possibility that this Champagne might improve beyond my wildest dreams, and if it had been a pre-release sample I would have slapped on a ⊖ symbol and immediately reserved judgement, but it isn't, Roederer has made mistakes (i.e., Cristal 1986) and I must call the shots as I see them. I hope I'm wrong!

❚ Now–2002 ⓔⓔⓔⓔ ☙ 275FF

LOUIS ROEDERER 1994 VINTAGE ROSÉ, BRUT 〈87〉

The colour in Roederer's rosé is famous for its absence and the 1994 is a classic in this respect. The tasty fruit supported by a pin-cushion mousse hardly shows the potential of this wine. Keep one year for the fruit to deepen and two to three to start going creamy-biscuity.

 2001–2003 ⓔⓔⓔⓔ ☙ 275FF

LOUIS ROEDERER 1990 BRUT VINTAGE 〈90〉

Apart from one batch I tasted at a wine competition that had obviously been improperly stored, this vintage remains remarkably youthful for a 10-year-old Champagne. It certainly has one of the firmest structures amongst the top 1990s, suggesting that it will take a few years yet to achieve its creamy-biscuity potential.

❚ Now–2005 ⓔⓔⓔⓔ

LOUIS ROEDERER CRISTAL 1994 BRUT

Extraordinary finesse for the year, but Cristal is the ultimate expression of Roederer's vineyard philosophy of severe pruning, bunch thinning and strict selection of only the healthiest grapes. This illustrates how thin the line is between a successful and a mediocre vintage in Champagne, and how those with a quality first mentality can always cross it for a price.
➤ 2002–2006 ⓔⓔⓔⓔ ❦ 650FF

ROIG
Penedès, Spain

MARIA CASANOVAS NV CAVA BRUT NATURE GRAN RESERVA

The pre-release sample I tasted had finesse on nose, complexity on palate and very good acidity. It was not vintaged, although I imagine it must be 1997-based, and I much preferred it to the current 1996 vintage.
❦ Now–2001 ⓔ

ROLET
Arbois, France

ROLET 1996 CRÉMANT DU JURA BRUT

Good acidity supporting creamy fruit makes for ready drinking.
❦ Now ⓔ ❦ 60FF

ROSEMOUNT
New South Wales, Australia

ROSEMOUNT KIRRI BILLI 1997 VINTAGE BRUT

This sparkling wine has a New World *blanc de noirs* colour and some finesse.
➤ 2001–2003 ⓔⓔ ❦ A$25

ROTHBURY
Victoria, Australia

THE ROTHBURY WINE SOCIETY 1996 CHARDONNAY PINOT NOIR

Full, rich fizz of Krug-like dimensions, but although exceptionally good, not quite of Krug-like quality.
❦ Now–2002 ⓔ ❦ A$17.95

ROYER
Champagne Royer Père
120 Grande Rue
10110 Landreville
☏(325) 38.52.16 ℻(325) 29.92.26

ROYER PÈRE ET FILS NV CUVÉE PRESTIGE, BLANC DE BLANCS BRUT

The most stunning aspect of this wine is its balance of acidity, fruit and dosage on the mid-palate, but for those who can wait, there is much more to come, particularly when the bouquet has blossomed.
❦ Now–2004 ⓔⓔ

RUINART
Champagne Ruinart
4 rue des Crayères
51053 Reims
☏(326) 77.51.51 ℻(326) 82.88.43

R DE RUINART NV BRUT

Very young and so very fresh that there is almost a Chablis dimension to the fruit, although there is no greenness and indeed even a certain roundness. Keep at least one year, three if you want the toastiness to build.
➤ 2001–2003 ⓔⓔ

R DE RUINART NV BRUT ROSÉ

A delightful and delicious melange of strawberry and raspberry fruit.
❦ Now–2001 ⓔⓔⓔ

R DE RUINART 1995 BRUT

For some reason Ruinart vintages are often forward, yet that does not affect their longevity. This one even has coffee notes on the bouquet. The rich fruit and excellent acidity assure its long life.
🍸 Now–2005 ⓔⓔⓔ

R DE RUINART 1993 BRUT　　⑧⑦

Although this will shortly be replaced by the 1995 and there is a nice, smooth hint of vanilla beginning to build on the finish, the 1993 still tastes recently disgorged and needs at least another year to show its true potential.
➤ 2001–2005 ⓔⓔⓔ

RUMBALL

Peter Rumball
South Australia

RUMBALL NV SPARKLING SHIRAZ　⑦⑥

Peppery-Shiraz, with heaps of rich, plummy-cherry fruit and a dusting of ground white pepper.
🍸 Now–2001 ⓔ

RUMPEL

Rheingau, Germany

WEINGUT RUMPEL RIESLING BRUT 1997 TRABENER GAISPFAD　⑦⑧

Deliciously fresh, sherbety Riesling fruit. A lovely, elegant, refreshing wine for summer drinking. (*Méthode champenoise.*)
🍸 Now ⓔ

RUSSLER

Rheingau, Germany

FRIEDEL RUSSLER RIESLING EXTRA TROCKEN 1998 WALLUFER OBERBERG　⑦②

Fresh, crisp and quite firm. (*Méthode champenoise.*)
🍸 Now ⓔ 🥂 DM13

SAARSTEIN

Schloss Saarstein
Mosel-Saar-Ruwer, Germany

SCHLOSS SAARSTEIN RIESLING BRUT 1997 SCHLOSS SAARSTEIN　⑦②

Although this Sekt lacks a touch of finesse on the nose, its peachy fruit on palate pushes it above the breadline score. (*Méthode champenoise.*)
🍸 Now ⓔ 🥂 DM20

SACY

Champagne Louis de Sacy
6 rue de Verzenay
51380 Verzy
☎(326) 97.91.13 🖷(326) 97.94.25

LOUIS DE SACY NV BRUT GRAND CRU　⑧⑤

A very fruity Champagne with a classic structure, this will represent the best of both worlds to some consumers.
🍸 Now–2003 ⓔⓔ 🥂 98FF

SAINT-ROCH

Loire, France

BLANC FOUSSY NV BRUT TOURAINE, GRANDES CAVES SAINT-ROCH　⑦②

Unsweetened apple-pie juice.
🍸 Now ⓔ

SAKONNET

New York, USA

SAKONNET SAMSON BRUT 1995 RHODE ISLAND　⑦④

Clean and well structured with ripe fruit.
🍸 Now ⓔⓔ 🥂 $35

SAN CRISTOFORO
Franciacorta, Italy

SAN CRISTOFORO NV FRANCIACORTA BRUT

Fine and fresh, satisfying, but could have done with more acidity.
🍾 Now–2001 ©© ❧ 18,000 Lira

SANTERO
Asti, Italy

SANTERO NV BRACHETTO D'ACQUI

A pale Burgundy colour with fresh, highly perfumed Moscato aromas and very sweet, intense Moscato fruit on the finish.
🍾 Now ©

SASBACH
Winzergenossenschaft Sasbach am Kaiserstuhl, Baden, Germany

WINZERGENOSSENSCHAFT SASBACH AM KAISERSTUHL 1997 WEIßER BURGUNDER EXTRA BRUT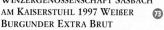

Good attempt at crossing over to a Champagne style, but needs an extra year's bottle-age. (*Méthode champenoise.*)
▬ 2001 © ❧ DM20

WINZERGENOSSENSCHAFT SASBACH AM KAISERSTUHL 1997 SPÄTBURGUNDER BLANC DE NOIRS EXTRA BRUT

Malo provides a creaminess for palate. Could tone the MLF down a bit, but a satisfying wine nonetheless. (*Méthode champenoise.*)
🍾 Now–2001 © ❧ DM20

SAUMUR
Cave des Vignerons de Saumur Loire, France

CAVE DES VIGNERONS DE SAUMUR 1997 CUVÉE DE LA CHEVALERIE

Clean, fresh and soft.
🍾 Now–2001 ©

SCARPANTONI
South Australia

SCARPANTONI BLACK TEMPEST NV

Drier than most, with firm, minty-Shiraz fruit.
🍾 Now–2001 ©© ❧ A$26

SCHALES
Rheinhessen, Germany

SCHALES RIESLANER AUSLESE EXTRA TROCKEN 1991 SCHALES RIESLANER SEKT

Very rich and peachy fruit of huge extract, but could do with more finesse. (*Méthode champenoise.*)
▬ 2001–2002 ©© ❧ DM30

SCHALES RIESLING HALBTROCKEN 1996 SCHALES RIESLING SEKT 76

Far better focused than this producer's previous vintage. Rich, almost sugary (barley sugar), but that makes it attractive for many to drink now. (*Méthode champenoise.*)
🍾 Now–2001 © ❧ DM20

❖ **SCHLOSS SAARSTEIN**, *see* Saarstein

SCHMITT SCHENK
Mosel-Saar-Ruwer, Italy

SCHMITT SCHENK RIESLING TROCKEN 1998 OCKFENER SCHARZBERG

Very fresh, crisp and peachy. (*Méthode champenoise.*)
▌ Now Ⓔ ❧ DM16

SCHRAMSBERG
California, USA

SCHRAMSBERG 1996 BLANC DE BLANCS BRUT 82

A lovely mouthful of fresh, breezy, succulent fruit.
▌ Now–2001 ⒺⒺ ❧ $26.50

SCHWAHN-FEHLINGER
Rheinhessen, Germany

SCHWAHN-FEHLINGER RIESLING EXTRA BRUT 1997 WESTHOFENER AULERDE 74

Fuller style, should develop well. (*Méthode champenoise.*)
➤ 2001–2003 Ⓔ ❧ DM18

SEAVIEW
South Australia, Australia

SEAVIEW 1997 CHARDONNAY BLANC DE BLANCS 83

Very fresh with lovely acid-fruit balance. This is a serious sparkling wine that can take some ageing.
▌ Now–2002 Ⓔ

SEAVIEW 1995 CHARDONNAY BLANC DE BLANCS 76

Juicy-fat Chardonnay fruit with toasty aromas dominating.
▌ Now Ⓔ

SEGURA VIUDAS
Penedès, Spain

SEGURA VIUDAS, RESERVA HEREDAD NV CAVA BRUT 78

An excellent Cava with clean, elegant fruit showing sweetness and ripeness.
▌ Now ⒺⒺ

SEGURA VIUDAS 1998 CAVA BRUT NATURE 78

Two different samples of apparently the same wine were submitted to my tasting this year, the only difference being that one claimed 5% more Xarello, the other 5% more Macabéo. On both samples I detected *barrique*-fermented aromas, but the one with 5% more Xarello had more *barrique* aromas, and a tad less finesse.
▌ Now ⒺⒺ

SELAKS
Auckland, New Zealand

SELAKS FOUNDERS RESERVE 1992 MARLBOROUGH 80

Refined biscuity aromas over barley-sugar fruit.
▌ Now–2002 Ⓔ ❧ NZ$18.50

SEPPELT
South Australia, Australia

CONNISTON AUSTRALIAN SPARKLING WINE NV BRUT RESERVE, B. SEPPELT & SON 72

Sherbet-dip fruit!
▌ Now Ⓔ

SEPPELT 1987 SHOW RESERVE SHIRAZ SPARKLING 85

Just so Seppelt Show! The pungently blackcurrant nose is absolutely typical of Seppelt Show Reserve, whatever the vintage, but it can be a shock to the system of the uninitiated.
▌ Now ⒺⒺ ❧ A$52.90

SEPPELT ORIGINAL SPARKLING SHIRAZ 1995 80

Beautifully balanced with a hint of spicy-spearmint. Not as sweet as most.
▌ Now–2002 Ⓔ ❧ A$15.90

SEPPELT SALINGER 1993 MÉTHODE CHAMPENOISE

This wine would be better with 2 years less on lees and one year more before shipping after disgorgement.
▌ Now ©© ❧ A$21.90

SERAFINO
Asti, Italy

MONDORO NV ASTI

Concentrated, sweet Moscato fruit of some elegance.
▌ Now © ❧ 11,000 L

SEVISA
Penedès, Spain

CAVA NV BRUT, SEVISA

Creamy-malo nose followed by nicely crisp fruit.
▌ Now ©

SHADY LANE
Michigan, USA

SHADY LANE 1997 RIESLING, LEELANU PENINSULA

Fresh, crisp and clean with a clear varietal character that only requires a year or so of post-disgorgement ageing to build up the Riesling bottle-aromas.
▌ Now–2002 ©

SHADY LANE 1997 BLANC DE BLANCS, LEELANU PENINSULA

Fresh and clean with some autolytic finesse on the nose and a lovely, creamy pin-cushion mousse of tiny bubbles supporting lively fruit well balanced by acidity on the palate. The second-best Michigan fizz tasted this year.
▌ Now–2003 ©

SHADY LANE 1997 BRUT, LEELANU PENINSULA

A touch of sulphur that should clear by

publication to reveal an elegant, stylish fizz with a soft mousse of small bubbles and nicely balanced fruit and acidity.
▌ Now–2001 ©

SHADY LANE 1995 BRUT, LEELANU PENINSULA

A fresh and tangy fizz with a talcum powder perfumed finish.
▌ Now ©

SHADY LANE 1994 BRUT, LEELANU PENINSULA

The fruit on both the nose and palate is a compote of strawberry and raspberry preserve, which is not classic, but not too jammy and therefore not unattractive either. Firm mousse with small bubbles.
▌ Now ©

SIEUR D'ARQUES
Limoux, France

AIMERY SIEUR D'ARQUES NV ST-HILAIRE

Fresh and clean, with good structure. Food wine.
▌ Now–2002 ©

GRANDE CUVÉE 1531 DE AIMERY NV CRÉMANT DE LIMOUX, TÊTE DE CUVÉE BRUT

Very fresh and fine aromas followed by tangy fruit.
▌ Now–2001 ©

SIEUR D'ARQUES 1997 CRÉMANT DE LIMOUX BRUT

Soft and charming fruit of some finesse.
▌ Now 2001 ©

SIPP MACK
Alsace, France

SIPP MACK NV CRÉMANT D'ALSACE BRUT

Tastes like a *blanc de noirs*, although there is no indication of what grape varieties have been used and no accompanying literature to refer to after

the tasting. Good finesse on the palate and if it had the same on the nose this wine would have scored higher.
❢ Now–2001 ⓔ

ATTENTION CHAMPAGNE & SPARKLING WINE PRODUCERS!

If you are not already in contact with the author, but would like to submit wines for consideration in future editions, please contact Tom Stevenson at:

tom.stevenson@fizz.worldonline.co.uk

Warning: Any other unsolicited mail received at this address will be ignored.

Please note that recommendation in this guide involves no charge whatsoever beyond the cost of the samples and their delivery.

SMITH

Samuel Smith & Son
South Australia, Australia

JANSZ NV AUSTRALIA PREMIUM NON VINTAGE CUVÉE

Sweet, easy drinking, user-friendly fizz.
❢ Now ⓔⓔ ✠ A$18

JANSZ 1996 TASMANIA BRUT CUVÉE

One of the best vintages so far. Elegant fruit with firm structure and the potential to age.
❢ Now–2002 ⓔⓔ ✠ A$30

YALUMBA D 1997 CUVÉE 97-1 85

Although a touch soapy when tasted, this will disperse after 12 months and the fruit is very fresh on the palate. A million miles away from the leesy style that used to be so hit-and-miss for Yalumba D.
➤ 2001–2002 ⓔⓔ ✠ A$25

YALUMBA D 1996 BLACK 96-1

A fruit-driven style that is drier and more serious than most, with attractive menthol aromas mingling through its very elegant fruit.
❢ Now–2002 ⓔⓔ ✠ A$25

SMW-WINZERSEKT

Mosel-Saar-Ruwer, Germany

SMW-WINZERSEKT RIESLING BRUT 1998 DICHTERTRAUM

The *cordon rouge* on the label no doubt attracts sales. This wine has a lovely construction and finesse, with aromatics penetrating palate and intensity of extract on the finish. (*Méthode champenoise*.)
❢ Now–2003 ⓔ ✠ DM20

SMW-WINZERSEKT RIESLING TROCKEN 1987 SMW RESERVE

The peachiness of this Sekt begins on the nose and follows right through the palate to a long finish. (*Méthode champenoise*.)
❢ Now–2002 ⓔ ✠ DM20

SOLJANS

Henderson, New Zealand

SOLJANS ESTATE PINOTAGE NV AUCKLAND

Not dissimilar to a sweetish Yugoslav red of the style produced in the 1970s, only with bubbles. Should remind New Zealand's many Dalmatians of home.
❢ Now ⓔ

SOLJANS LEGACY 1997 AUCKLAND/MARLBOROUGH

The fruit is good on the nose and palate, but a touch elevated on the finish, although nowhere near as elevated as on the 1996. If you like your oak rather blatant and coconutty, then add 5 points or so to the score.
❢ Now–2001 ⓔ

SOMMERHAUSEN

Franken, Germany

SCHLOß SOMMERHAUSEN RIESLING BRUT 1995 SOMMERHÄUSER STEIN

Although lacking finesse on nose and front palate, this wine has good attack

mid-palate, nice length and a clean, crisp finish. (*Méthode champenoise.*)
🍷 Now–2001 ⓔ️ⓔ️ 🏆 DM36

SOUTHCORP
New South Wales, Australia

KILLAWARRA K SERIES NV SPARKLING SHIRAZ CABERNET   85

This fruit-driven styled fizz is not as dry as the driest Australian sparkling reds, but definitely on the drier side, with blackcurrant and blackberry fruits, pepper and menthol aromas.
🍷 Now–2001 ⓔ️

SOUTIRAN-PELLETIER
Champagne Soutiran-Pelletier
3 rue de Crilly
51150 Ambonnay
☎(326) 57.07.87 ℻(326) 57.81.74

A. SOUTIRAN-PELLETIER NV GRAND CRU BRUT   83

Fresh and fruity.
🍷 Now–2001 ⓔ️ⓔ️

SPARR
Alsace, France

PIERRE SPARR NV CRÉMANT D'ALSACE, BRUT RÉSERVE 75

Fine aroma and fruit, excellent acidity. Definitely a food wine.
🍷 Now–2001 ⓔ️

PIERRE SPARR 1995 DYNASTIE, CRÉMANT D'ALSACE, BRUT MILLÉSIMÉ 72

A firm-styled *crémant* that should go biscuity, but needs a larger brut dosage to do that gracefully, thus it drops a few points and should be consumed sooner rather than later.
🍷 Now ⓔ️

PIERRE SPARR 1995 GLORIUS 2000, CRÉMANT D'ALSACE, BRUT R.D.   72

More tangy-fruity than Sparr's Dynastie, but also would be improved by a larger brut dosage. If you think the purple-labelled Dynastie was vulgar, take a look at the rocket-propelled Crunchie bar on the front of this wine.
🍷 Now ⓔ️

SPARVIERE
*Lo Sparviere
Franciacorta, Italy*

LO SPARVIERE NV FRANCIACORTA EXTRA BRUT   82

Lovely flowery autolytic nose, top quality low-dosage Franciacorta, excellent structure. Can age. After a while, biscuity.
🍷 Now–2004 ⓔ️ⓔ️

SPIROPOULOS
Greece

ODE PANOS NV BRUT, DOMAINE SPIROPOULOS   71

The current release of this family-owned, organically grown *cuve close* sparkling wine is somewhat sweeter and more amylic than in previous years, but still deserves recommendation and had it not been for the arrival of Villa Amalia, would still be the best Greek sparkling wine.
🍷 Now ⓔ️

STEIN
Nahe, Germany

EDITH STEIN RIESLING EXTRA TROCKEN 1998 NAHE-RIESLING   77

A very fresh, elegant wine of some finesse, this Riesling can function as either an aperitif or a food-wine. Not as sweet as its Extra Trocken designation might suggest: could be labelled as a Brut

and few would query it. (*Cuve close.*)
🥂 Now–2001 €

ST. NIKOLAUS HOSPITAL
Mosel-Saar-Ruwer, Germany

ST. NIKOLAUS HOSPITAL RIESLING BRUT 1997 BERNKASTELER BADSTUBE

Lovely Riesling aromatics on the nose and palate, followed by ripe, peachy finish.
🥂 Now–2001 €

STE MICHELLE
*Domaine Ste Michelle
Washington, USA*

DOMAINE STE. MICHELLE NV CUVÉE BRUT, CENTURY CUVÉE

The top *cuvées* from this winery are nudging up in quality, as the fresh, fluffy fruit in this wine demonstrates. Crisp and refreshing.
🥂 Now–2001 € 🍸 $12

DOMAINE STE. MICHELLE NV BLANC DE BLANC, CENTURY CUVÉE

Fresh, chewy-creamy-yeasty fruit.
🥂 Now–2001 € 🍸 $12

STUDERT-PRÜM
Mosel-Saar-Ruwer, Germany

STUDERT-PRÜM RIESLING TROCKEN 1997 MAXIMINER CABINET

Deliciously rich, clean and smooth, with tasty fruit and a sherbety finish. Very tangy. (*Méthode champenoise.*)
🥂 Now–2001 € 🍸 DM18

SUD-EST APPELLATIONS
Rhône, France

SUD-EST APPELLATIONS, CLAIRDIE TRADITION NV MÉTHODE DIOISE ANCESTRALE

Wonderfully floral Muscat aroma followed by fresh, frothy fruit and a lovely soft, sensuous finish.
🥂 Now €€

SUSS
Champagne Jean-Paul Suss
10110 Buxeuil
☎(325) 38.56.22 ⒻⒶⓍ(325) 38.58.58

JEAN-PAUL SUSS NV BRUT RÉSERVE

Plenty of fruit, although somewhat elevated, but this makes for immediate drinking. Much preferred to Cuvée 2000.
🥂 Now–2001 €€

SWEDISH HILL
New York, USA

SWEDISH HILL 1996 BRUT

Young for its year with an intriguing tangerine nuance to its soft fruit.
🥂 Now–2001 € 🍸 $16.99

TAITTINGER
Champagne Taittinger
9 Place Saint-Niçaise
51061 Reims
☎(326) 85.45.35 ⒻⒶⓍ(326) 85.84.65

TAITTINGER NV BRUT RÉSERVE

Light, fresh and easy, but not so easy that it does not possess finesse.
🥂 Now–2003 €€

TAITTINGER NV BRUT PRESTIGE ROSÉ

Until recently this used to be all black

grapes (70% Pinot Noir, 30% Meunier), but now includes 20% or more Chardonnay and the result is impressive for the current 1995-based *cuvée*, with its softer, more accessible structure and very fresh, elegant fruit.

Now–2003 ©©

TAITTINGER 1996 BRUT MILLÉSIMÉ

The best 1996 released so far. As soon as you put this wine to your nose, its finesse hits you between the eyes (literally: that's where your olfactory bulb is!) and this carries right through the wine to the finish.

Now–2008 ©©© ⚘ 180FF

TAITTINGER 1995 BRUT MILLÉSIMÉ

Malo aromas and surprisingly fat fruit for Taittinger ensure that this vintage will never have the finesse of the 1996, but for those who are patient it will certainly have its moment of glory.

➤ 2001–2004 ©©© ⚘ 180FF

TAITTINGER 1992 BRUT MILLÉSIMÉ

An elegant and stylish wine that already has some complexity and this should develop more along biscuity than toasty lines.

Now–2004 ©©©

TAITTINGER COMTES DE CHAMPAGNE 1994 BLANC DE BLANCS BRUT 89

Taittinger's UK shipper promised samples of this vintage, although there was so little produced that the Irish market snapped up the lot. Funny that, because I came across it in Singapore and Spain, and a good job too because the promised samples never turned up. In many respects this is a typically lush Comtes de Champagne with its attractive broad-brush Chardonnay imprint, but although fresh and youthful, its creamy fruit is almost five years in advance of its age. Lovely though, and I'm glad the Irish didn't nab the lot.

Now–2005 ©©©© ⚘ 620FF

TAITTINGER COMTES DE CHAMPAGNE 1995 BLANC DE BLANCS BRUT

Although this wine can be drunk with much pleasure now, I would not recommend it because this will turn out to be one of the very best vintages of Comtes de Champagne and it would be a shame to miss out on all it has to offer. What stands out at the moment is the impeccable balance between its lush Chardonnay fruit and lovely ripe acidity, which will ensure its freshness and finesse for at least a decade.

➤ 2002–2010 ©©©© ⚘ 620FF

TALTARNI
Victoria, Australia

TALTARNI CLOVER HILL 1996

VA-elevated, but not as high as some and resulting in a deeply fruit-driven style.

Now ©© ⚘ A$30

TARLANT
Champagne Tarlant
51480 Oeuilly
☎(326) 58.30.60 FAX(326) 58.37.31

TARLANT NV BRUT ZERO

Tastier and better balanced than most non-dosage Champagnes.

Now ©©

TATACHILLA
South Australia, Australia

TATACHILLA NV BRUT MCLAREN VALE

A light, refreshing fruit-driven style with fresh, sherbety, Pinot fruit.

Now–2001 ©

TATACHILLA NV SPARKLING MALBEC PADTHAWAY 85

The very floral, violet aromas on this wine are typical of Malbec, but time on

yeast has added a creamy element. A fruit-driven style that is drier than most. Wonderful with roast pork and crackling.
▼ Now–2002 ⓔⓔ

❖ **TENUTA CASTELLINO**, *see* Castellino

TESTULAT

Champagne V. Testulat
23 rue Léger Bertin
51201 Epernay
☎(326) 54.10.65 ⚆(326) 54.61.18

CLAUDE RENOUX NV BRUT   85

The fresh, clean, pineappley fruit in this Champagne was a relief after a run of over-oxidative *cuvées* from producers who have obviously attempted to achieve complexity, but have merely ended up with something too aldehydic.
▼ Now–2002 ⓔⓔ

THANISCH

Weingut Witwe Dr. Thanisch
Mosel-Saar-Ruwer, Germany

WEINGUT WITWE DR. THANISCH, ERBEN MÜLLER-BERGGRAEF 1997   79 BERNKASTELER DOKTOR

Exquisitely perfumed, elegant fruit. (*Méthode champenoise.*)
▼ Now ⓔⓔⓔ 🍶 DM80

THIENOT

Champagne Alain Thienot
14 rue des Moissons
51100 Reims
☎(326) 77.50.10 ⚆(326) 77.50.19

ALAIN THIENOT NV BRUT   84

Hint of aniseed on the nose, clean fruit and zippy acidity.
▼ Now–2001 ⓔⓔ

ALAIN THIENOT NV BRUT ROSÉ   85

Very fresh and *vif* with excellent, racy acidity.

▼ Now–2001 ⓔⓔ

ALAIN THIENOT 1993 BRUT   85

Although a typically forward 1993, the creamy-biscuity malo-mellowness already present will provide satisfaction for at least another two years.
▼ Now–2002 ⓔⓔ

THORNTON

California, USA

THORNTON NV CUVÉE ROUGE,   74 CALIFORNIA

The cherries and strawberries on the nose, strawberries on the palate might sound pretty outgoing, but compared to many sparkling red wines this *cuvée* is understated. Needs a bit more flamboyance to stand out in this category.
▼ Now ⓔ $10.99

THREE CHOIRS

Newent, Gloucestershire

THREE CHOIRS NV CLASSIC   75 CUVÉE BRUT

This *cuvée* demonstrates a good balance between structure and elegance, with fine acidity and freshness.
▼ Now–2001 ⓔ

TISSOT

André & Mireille Tissot
Jura, France

ANDRÉ & MIREILLE TISSOT NV   74 CRÉMANT DU JURA BRUT

The freshest and technically best Crémant du Jura on the nose out of those tasted this year, with a good follow through of light-bodied fruit on the palate.
▼ Now–2001 ⓔ

TISSOT

Jacques Tissot
Jura, France

JACQUES TISSOT NV 2000, CRÉMANT DU JURA BRUT

The most elegant and interesting Crémant du Jura I've ever tasted.
❚ Now–2001 ⓔ

TORELLÓ

Penedès, Spain

ALIGUER 1997 CAVA BRUT VINTAGE, AUGUSTÍ TORELLÓ

Amylic aromas, but with more fruit than any of Augustí Torelló's other *cuvées*.
❚ Now ⓔ

QUERCUS 1997 CAVA BRUT NATURE RESERVA, AUGUSTÍ TORELLÓ

Fermented in new oak, although very little is noticeable. This has the best acidity of all Augustí Torelló's *cuvées*, making it the most interesting to age a year or two.
❚ Now–2002 ⓔⓔ ⚐ 2,400 Ptas

TORELLÓ LLOPART

Penedès, Spain

GRAN RESERVA TORELLÓ 1995 CAVA BRUT NATURE

Some interesting, mellow aromas followed by sound fruit and acidity on the palate, and complex bottle-aromas on the aftertaste.
❚ Now ⓔⓔ ⚐ 2,900 Ptas

TORELLÓ 1997 CAVA BRUT

Another mellow, relatively complex Cava.
❚ Now ⓔ ⚐ 1,260 Ptas

TORNAY

Champagne Bernard Tornay
2 rue Colbert
51150 Bouzy
☎ (326) 57.08.58

BERNARD TORNAY NV BRUT CARTE D'OR

Ultra-fruity style with a pineapple finish.
❚ Now–2001 ⓔⓔ

TORREBLANCA

Penedès, Spain

MASBLANC NV CAVA EXTRA BRUT, TORREBLANCA

Very similar to the 1997.
❚ Now ⓔ ⚐ 1,055 Ptas

TORREBLANCA 1997 CAVA EXTRA BRUT RESERVA

Very smooth fruit on nose and palate, with a touch of smooth sweetness on the finish.
❚ Now ⓔ ⚐ 1,200 Ptas

TORRE ORIA

Utiel-Requena, Spain

TORRE ORIA NV CAVA BRUT RESERVA

The 1997-based blend of this *cuvée* is so much better and fresher than any of Torre Oria's other Cavas.
❚ Now ⓔ ⚐ 610 Ptas

TOSO

Asti, Italy

TOSO NV BRACHETTO D'ACQUI DOLCE

This sweet, fizzy red has a deepish colour, with quite intense Moscato aromas and fruit.
❚ Now ⓔ

TOSTI
Asti, Italy

TOSTI NV ASTI 2000 88

Powerful Moscato aromatics and intense sweetness force this wine almost to the very top of all the Asti tasted this year.
🍷 Now ⓕⓕ

TRENTHAM
New South Wales, Australia

TRENTHAM ESTATE RUBY SPARKLING RED 1998 85

Essentially a fruit-driven style, but with a touch of oak, this full coloured fizzy red has smooth Cabernet-like aromas, with rich, soft, medium-sweet fruit.
🍷 Now–2001 ⓕ 🍸 A$15

TSELEPOS
Domaine Tselepos
Greece

VILLA AMALIA NV BRUT 80

I was stunned by the extraordinarily high quality of this new arrival on the Greek sparkling wine scene, with its extremely rich, pineapple fruit, excellent structure and beautifully balanced acidity.
🍷 Now–2001 ⓕ

TWEE JONGE GEZELLEN
Tulbagh, South Africa

KRONE BOREALIS NV CAP CLASSIQUE, BRUT ⊖

After a hiccup in production (hardly any grapes were harvested in 1999 after Nicky Krone was too zealous in his eco-friendly farming!), this *cuvée* is now non-vintage. The structure seems fine, but I want to see how this "new" Krone Borealis develops.
▸ Wait and see ⓕ 🍸 R42

UBERTI
Franciacorta, Italy

UBERTI NV FRANCIACORTA EXTRA BRUT 75

Some aged characteristics mingling with fresh, citrus fruit.
🍷 Now–2001 ⓕⓕ 🍸 27,000 Lira

UBERTI NV FRANCIACORTA BRUT 76

Lemon-lavender autolysis nose. Full, fresh and interesting.
🍷 Now–2002 ⓕⓕ 🍸 27,000 Lira

UBERTI NV FRANCIACORTA SATÈN MAGNIFICENTIA ⊖

A richly flavoured wine with lovely elevated fruit aroma, very fine, attractive and elegant fruit on the palate.
🍷 Now–2002 ⓕⓕⓕ 🍸 38,000 Lira

UBERTI 1995 FRANCIACORTA EXTRA BRUT COMARI DEL SALEM 78

Lovely fruit aroma. Fine, crisp finish.
🍷 Now–2002 ⓕⓕⓕ 🍸 48,000 Lira

ATTENTION CHAMPAGNE & SPARKLING WINE PRODUCERS!
If you are not already in contact with the author, but would like to submit wines for consideration in future editions, please contact Tom Stevenson at:

tom.stevenson@fizz.worldonline.co.uk

Warning: Any other unsolicited mail received at this address will be ignored.

Please note that recommendation in this guide involves no charge whatsoever beyond the cost of the samples and their delivery.

UNION CHAMPAGNE

7 rue Pasteur
51190 Avize
☎(326) 57.94.22 ⟨FAX⟩(326) 57.57.98

DE SAINT GALL NV BRUT PREMIER CRU 82

Fresh, cool-fermented fruit with good

acidity, but keep it a year to knock back some of those amylic aromas.

▬ 2001–2002 ⓔⓔ ⚑ 99.50FF

PIERRE VAUDON NV PREMIER CRU BRUT ⑧⓪

The shipment available in the UK in the first quarter of 2000 was not up to the standard of releases made in the previous 12 months. Furthermore, it promised to go malty, so drink it up unless you are partial to that particular style. The sample submitted to my blind tastings and which should be in full distribution when this edition is published is much better (83 points). A rich, traditionally-styled Champagne of good age, but will need more bottle maturation before its mellow, biscuity aromas kick in.

❚ Now–2003 ⓔⓔ

PIERRE VAUDON NV PREMIER CRU BRUT ROSÉ ⑧⑤

This is recommended for immediate consumption because its rich, fresh, crisp berry-flavoured fruit makes such easy drinking that there is little point ageing it any further.

❚ Now ⓔⓔ

DE SAINT GALL 1995 BLANC DE BLANCS, BRUT PREMIER CRU ⑧⑦

The rich, creamy fruit in this *cuvée* has a lovely fresh finish, making it taste much younger than a number of far more famous 1995s.

❚ Now–2005 ⓔⓔⓔ ⚑ 121.50FF

PIERRE VAUDON 1985 PREMIER CRU BRUT ⑧⑥

The fruit in this Champagne is beautifully balanced between richness and elegance.

❚ Now–2003 ⓔⓔⓔ

VALLEY VINEYARDS
Twyford, Berkshire, England, UK

HERITAGE BRUT NV ⑦④

Fresh, herbaceous fruit tempered by a little MLF creaminess on the finish.

▬ 2001–2002 ⓔ

HERITAGE ROSÉ NV ⑦③

Those who like gamey Pinot Noir will find the varietal aroma very attractive, while others might think it too mature or too quickly matured, but there is a good weight of fruit to back it up.

❚ Now ⓔ

VALLFORMOSA
Penedès, Spain

VALLFORMOSA 1997 CAVA BRUT NATURE, MASÍA VALLFORMOSA ⑦①

Fresh, fruity and uncomplicated. Ideal summertime-drinking Cava.

❚ Now ⓔ ⚑ 1,125 Ptas

VALLFORMOSA 1997 CAVA BRUT, MASÍA VALLFORMOSA ⑦②

Just a tad fuller and more satisfying than the Brut Nature.

❚ Now ⓔ ⚑ 954 Ptas

❖ **VALMANTE**, *see* Compagnie Française des Grands Vins

❖ **VAUDON**, Pierre Vaudon, *see* Union Champagne

VAUVERSIN
Champagne F. Vauversin
9bis rue de Flavigny
51190 Oger
☎(326) 57.51.01 ℻(326) 51.64.44

AUBELINE DE VAUVERSIN NV BLANC DE BLANCS, GRAND CRU, SEC ⑧②

Estery aromas indicate that this should have been kept on yeast another 6–9 months. Not as sweet as expected. In fact, not as sweet as some of the Extra-Sec Champagnes tasted this year.

▬ 2001–2002 ⓔⓔ ⚑ 82FF

F. VAUVERSIN NV BLANC DE BLANCS, BRUT GRAND CRU ⑧⓪

Rustic Chardonnay richness.

❚ Now–2001 ⓔⓔ ⚑ 80FF

F. VAUVERSIN 1993 BLANC DE BLANCS, BRUT GRAND CRU (84)

Big, biscuity Chardonnay Champagne for aficionados only.

🍷 Now–2001 £E 🍇 107FF

VENOGE

Champagne de Venoge
30 avenue de Champagne
51204 Epernay
☎(326) 55.01.01 📠(326) 54.73.60

DE VENOGE NV BRUT SÉLECT, CORDON BLEU (88)

The current 1996-based *cuvée* is one of those rare non-vintage Champagnes that you should really snap up and lay down. Although the substantial yeast-aged flavour in this wine is already bursting with fruit and finesse, a few more years in bottle will turn this into a minor masterpiece.

🍷 Now–2006 £E

DE VENOGE NV BRUT BLANC DE NOIRS (90)

The score and notes apply exclusively to those bottles carrying the EU Lot number L6169. The fine coffee-toasty aromas that form the bouquet of this beautifully preserved mature Champagne and mingle throughout its elegantly ripe fruit are curiously reminiscent of those found on the De Venoge Blanc de Blancs 1976 and 1979 with five years' landed-age, which just goes to show how little the post-disgorgement aromas reflect the grape varieties used in the *cuvée* in question. They are more to do with an interaction between the autolysis and dosage.

🍷 Now–2002 £E£

DE VENOGE NV PRINCESSE ROSÉ BRUT (85)

Rosé? Ha! Who do they think they're kidding? Did they label the wrong batch? I had better qualify this with EU Lot number L5029 because there is not the slightest hint of colour in the wine, not even enough to describe it as apricot. Not that De Venoge is trying to trick anyone. How could they with a clear bottle that reveals exactly what colour the wine is?

From sight alone I expected a mature Champagne and that's exactly what I got, with heaps of mature, rich, mellow, toasty fruit.

🍷 Now–2001 £E£

DE VENOGE 1990 BRUT BLANC DE NOIRS (89)

A fabulously mellow Champagne showing a real depth of biscuity richness.

🍷 Now–2003 £E£

DE VENOGE 1992 GRAND VIN DE PRINCES BRUT ⊖

I nearly rejected this wine because of its rapid ageing, but although I hate the hideous bottle and kitsch stopper, I have had a number of stunning vintages of this Champagne and more than a few have appeared to age fast at some point in their development. Most memorable in this respect is the 1976, which I once gave up on, but still have a couple of bottles in prime condition to remind me how wrong I was. This review, then, is not the result of a blind tasting, but its very antithesis. The sight of a label is, as they say, worth a lifetime's experience. Well, at the moment this vintage is dominated by biscuity-caramel malo aroma and a bitter finish, but the bitterness could be undeveloped extract and might just be its saviour. Do not expect any miracle transformations, but rather a slow unfolding over at least four or five years.

▶ Wait £E££

VESSELLE

Champagne Georges Vesselle
16 rue des Postes
51150 Bouzy
☎(326) 57.00.15 📠(326) 57.09.20

GEORGES VESSELLE NV BRUT GRAND CRU (85)

Lovely, clean, cool fruit that is well-defined and should go biscuity.

🍷 Now–2003 £E 🍇 108FF

GEORGES VESSELLE NV BRUT ROSÉ GRAND CRU (85)

Lovely sherbety, perfumed fruit.

❚ Now–2001 ⓔⓔ

GEORGES VESSELLE NV CUVÉE JULINE GRAND CRU BRUT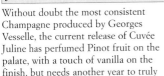

Without doubt the most consistent Champagne produced by Georges Vesselle, the current release of Cuvée Juline has perfumed Pinot fruit on the palate, with a touch of vanilla on the finish, but needs another year to truly blossom.

▬► 2001–2005 ⓔⓔ ☕ 162FF

GEORGES VESSELLE 1995 BRUT MILLÉSIMÉ GRAND CRU ⑧⑤

This Champagne is already showing lovely strawberry fruit, which is so classic for Bouzy Pinot Noir, but it needs time to develop complex aromas and a more focused finish.

▬► 2001–2005 ⓔⓔⓔ ☕ 128FF

GEORGES VESSELLE 1990 BRUT MILLÉSIME GRAND CRU ⑧⑦

This very fresh and young 1990 could have done with a gram or two more sugar in the dosage, but it is already developing nice creamy-biscuit complexity and has the structure and fruit to improve further in bottle.

❚ Now–2005 ⓔⓔⓔ

VESSELLE
Champagne Jean Vesselle
4 rue Victor-Hugo
51150 Bouzy
☎(326) 57.01.55 ℻(326) 57.06.95

JEAN VESSELLE NV BRUT PRESTIGE EXTRA BRUT ⑧②

A food wine style that needs two years to go toasty.

▬► 2002–2003 ⓔⓔ

VEUVE AMBAL
France
Nothing rip-roaring here, but some of the better non-appellation French fizz.

VEUVE AMBAL NV MÉTHODE TRADITIONNELLE TRADITION ⑦⓪

Very clean, frothy fruit.
❚ Now ⓔ

VEUVE AMBAL 1997 MÉTHODE TRADITIONNELLE MILLÉSIMÉE ⑦⓪

Surprisingly rich for such a light, delicate balance of fruit. Would have scored higher if the wine had higher acidity, but much preferred to Veuve Ambal's 1997 Crémant de Bourgogne, with its strange white-pepper fruit.

❚ Now ⓔ

VEUVE AMIOT
Loire, France

VEUVE AMIOT NV CLUB DEMI-SEC, VOUVRAY ⑦②

Fresh, richly flavoured Chenin with a liquorice finish. Not too sweet.
❚ Now–2001 ⓔ

VEUVE AMIOT NV CUVÉE RÉSERVÉE BRUT, SAUMUR ⑦⓪

Excellent flowery autolysis on nose, but MLF notes on finish lower the score.
❚ Now–2001 ⓔ

VEUVE AMIOT NV CLUB BRUT, VOUVRAY ⑦⓪

A Chenin that will go toasty if kept 12 months.
❚ Now–2002 ⓔ

VEUVE CLICQUOT

Champagne Veuve Clicquot-Ponsardin
12 rue du Temple
51054 Reims
📞(326) 89.54.40 📠(326) 40.60.17

VEUVE CLICQUOT PONSARDIN NV BRUT — 88

Although the shipment at the beginning of 2000 required ageing, it was nevertheless very light-bodied for Veuve Clicquot (85 points). However, the release submitted to my tasting (L894) had a vastly more mature, creamy-malo turning biscuity bouquet. The latter, upon which the rating below is based, will retain crispness and freshness for several years to come, thus the optimum drinking period applies to both. The wine submitted had a cheap wire cage, which was not anodized, lacquered, painted or coated in any way. Come on guys, do you really think this is how a Grande Marque Champagne should be presented?
🍷 Now–2005 ⓕⓕ 🍾 160FF

VEUVE CLICQUOT PONSARDIN NV DEMI-SEC — 80

A good Demi-Sec that will get richer, but not as impressive as last year's *cuvée*.
🍷 Now–2002 ⓕⓕⓕ 🍾 160FF

VEUVE CLICQUOT PONSARDIN 1991 BRUT VINTAGE RESERVE — 88

This precocious Veuve Clicquot vintage is getting more classy by the day, as it evolves from relatively simple biscuity mellowness to a much richer, creamier, more complex biscuitiness. The fruit is plumper and more focused, and the potential longevity is beginning to stretch away from initial predictions.
🍷 Now–2006 ⓕⓕⓕ

VEUVE CLICQUOT PONSARDIN 1993 BRUT VINTAGE RESERVE — 86

As last year, this vintage is too malo-dominated with peppery fruit underneath, but slips a percentile point because the malolactic character has become buttery. It should still go biscuity, but whereas other vintages of Veuve Clicquot have been enjoyable in their own fresh, fruity right when first released, the 1993 will, as predicted last year, take much longer to become approachable.
 2002–2005 ⓕⓕⓕ

VEUVE CLICQUOT PONSARDIN 1995 ROSÉ RESERVE, BRUT — 90

A great rosé in the making, although its crisp, racy red-fruits and refreshing acidity make a mouthwateringly delicious youthful drink.
🍷 Now–2005 ⓕⓕⓕ 🍾 250FF

VEUVE CLICQUOT PONSARDIN 1995 RICH RESERVE — 85

Not as good as the 1993 (87 points), which itself was not in the same class as the 1989 (90 points), yet still rates as the third best Demi-Sec tasted this year (out of over 50). The malo aromas suggest this will go biscuity with a touch of caramel.
 2002–2005 ⓕⓕⓕ 🍾 250FF

VEUVE CLICQUOT PONSARDIN 1990 LA GRANDE DAME BRUT — 95

Stunning richness, length and finesse. Still in fruit mode, with a few years to go before its complex toasty aromas set in.
🍷 Now–2020 ⓕⓕⓕⓕ

VEUVE CLICQUOT PONSARDIN 1990 LA GRANDE DAME ROSÉ, BRUT — 94

The creaminess is currently overwhelming the biscuity aromas and there is a sweet pimento slant to the fruit that needs to be smoothed out. From the score, however, readers should realize that these comments are not negatives, but merely an explanation for why this wine should be cellared for at least one year.
 2001–2004 ⓕⓕⓕⓕ 🍾 800FF

❖ **VEUVE VALMANTE,** *see* Compagnie Française des Grands Vins

VILARNAU

*Castell de Vilarnau
Penedès, Spain*

CASTELL DE VILARNAU 1996 CAVA BRUT GRAN RESERVA — 75

The fruit could have more finesse, but there's heaps of flavour, very good acidity and a satisfying finish. Definitely a step up from Vilarnau's Brut Nature Reserve.

❦ Now ⓔ ❦ 1,500 Ptas

VILLA

Franciacorta, Italy

It was not until after an intensive tasting in which all these wines were strung out amongst all the other Franciacorta that I realized how highly and consistently I rated Villa.

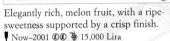

VILLA 1996 FRANCIACORTA BRUT 78

Elegantly rich, melon fruit, with a ripe-sweetness supported by a crisp finish.

❦ Now–2001 ⓒⓔ ❦ 15,000 Lira

VILLA 1996 FRANCIACORTA SATÈN 82

Very fresh, fruit-driven, modern Franciacorta.

❦ Now–2002 ⓒⓔ ❦ 18,000 Lira

VILLA 1996 FRANCIACORTA CUVETTE SEC 77

Very fresh and breezy, clean racy fruit.

❦ Now–2002 ⓒⓔ ❦ 19,000 Lira

VILLA 1996 FRANCIACORTA ROSÉ DEMI SEC 75

Fresh, clean strawberry fruit.

❦ Now–2002 ⓒⓔ ❦ 18,000 Lira

VILLA 1994 FRANCIACORTA BRUT SELEZIONE 76

Estery when released, but the potential is obvious and will be achieved if kept 12 months.

❦ Now–2002 ⓒⓔ ❦ 25,000 Lira

VILMART

Champagne Vilmart & Cie
4 rue de la République
51500 Rilly La Montagne
☎(326) 03.40.01   🖷(326) 03.46.57

VILMART NV GRAND CELLIER, BRUT PREMIERS CRUS 85

Plenty of flavour, lovely high acids

and no oak.

 2001–2004 ⓒⓔ ❦ 113FF

VILMART NV CUVÉE CELLIER, BRUT 90

The full, satisfying, smooth flavours in this *cuvée* build slowly in the mouth and despite fearing that I might sound like an overly pretentious French wine journalist, I really did detect vanilla, cocoa-butter, white chocolate and mandarins, although I felt as if I was stretching my imagination as much as my palate! In any case this is an extraordinary quality Champagne that harks back to the best of Vilmart's pre-new-oak days and represents brilliant value for money.

❦ Now–2006 ⓒⓔ ❦ 140FF

VILMART NV CUVÉE RUBIS, BRUT 85

Mature apricot colour, with attractive peachy fruit on palate and finish. The best rosé from Vilmart I can remember.

❦ Now–2001 ⓒⓔ ❦ 93FF

VILMART 1993 COEUR DE CUVÉE, BRUT PREMIERS CRUS 93

A beautiful wine by any standards, the *barrique* aromas create *crème anglaise* taste and texture in the fruit.

❦ Now–2007 ⓒⓒⓒⓒ ❦ 205FF

VILMART 1995 CUVÉE CRÉATION IIIe MILLÉNAIRE, BRUT ⊖

Although the less overtly oaky character is welcome, there is something high-toned about the aromas that I found somewhat disturbing, so I opened the back-up sample. However, that was the same, so I tried inserting the wine at various places in the tasting to see if its positioning was a factor (the same wine coming after different wines can alter our perception of that wine), but the high-tone character remained. I should remind readers that the tastings are blind, thus I had no idea what the Champagne was, but I felt there was sufficient to be curious about to give it a ⊖ symbol and now that I know what it is, I certainly think I should at least reserve judgement for two or three years.

 Wait and see ⓒⓒⓒ ❦ 195FF

VOLLEREAUX

Champagne Vollereaux
48 rue Léon-Bourgeois
51530 Pierry
☎(326) 54.03.05 ℻(326) 54.88.36

DOMAINE DE CORRIGOT NV EXTRA-DRY, VOLLEREAUX
82

This is in fact a *blanc de noirs* and currently it is the 40% of Meunier that dominates the wine, with its fresh, flowery aromas and sherbety fruit on the aftertaste.
🍷 Now–2001 €€ 🥂 74FF

VOLLEREAUX 1993 CUVÉE MARGUERITE BRUT
80

Fresh and tasty now, but soon due to go quite full and toasty.
🍷 Now–2002 €€ 🥂 115FF

❖ **VON BUHL**, *see* Buhl

❖ **VON UNSERM**, *see* Ress

❖ **VOYAGE**, *see* Giesen

VOUVRAY
Caves des Producteurs de Vouvray

CAVES DES PRODUCTEURS DE VOUVRAY 1997 TÊTE DE CUVÉE
74

Classic Chenin, soft, frothy mousse and extremely clean fruit.
🍷 Now–2001 €

WACHTENBURG
Pfalz, Germany

WACHTENBURG WINZER 1998 SPÄTBURGUNDER ROSÉ EXTRA TROCKEN
74

A dark rosé rather than light red, but the fresh, strawberry Pinot fruit will win more admiration than the colour. (Transfer method.)
🍷 Now € 🥂 DM19

WAGNER
New York, USA

WAGNER 1997 RIESLING CHAMPAGNE
72

The second-best Riesling fizz I tasted from New York state this year, this is a sweetish Sekt-style with nicely developed Riesling aromas that increase in the glass. Although Champagne is legal for bottle-fermented sparkling wines produced and sold in the USA, Riesling Champagne is a contradiction in terms as far as I'm concerned.
🍷 Now–2001 €

WANTZ
Alsace, France

CH. WANTZ NV CARTE NOIRE BRUT TRADITION, CRÉMANT D'ALSACE
72

Fresh, clean and tasty fruit, with some finesse on the palate, but lacking this on the nose.
🍷 Now–2001 €

WARDEN VINEYARD
Biggleswade, Bedfordshire England, UK

WARDEN VINEYARD 1996 BRUT
75

Still full of wonderfully muscatty fruit, but where are the more recent vintages. This style is best consumed as youthful as possible.
🍷 Now–2001 €€

WARDEN VINEYARD 1996 EXTRA BRUT
75

An irresistible summertime quaffer packed with mouthwatering muscat-like fruit.
🍾 2001–2002 €€

WEINHANDEL

Weingut-Weinhandel
Mosel-Saar-Ruwer, Germany

WEINGUT-WEINHANDEL RIESLING TROCKEN 1998 ZELLER SCHWARZE KATZ

Very fresh and fruity, easy to drink.
(*Méthode champenoise.*)
🍷 Now Ⓔ 🥂 DM20

WESTPORT RIVERS

Massachusetts, USA

WESTPORT RIVERS 1993 SOUTHEASTERN NEW ENGLAND

Rich, tangy fruit with a citric slant and a good long finish.
🍷 Now ⒺⒺ 🥂 $39.95

WIEMER

Hermann J. Wiemer
New York, USA

HERMANN J. WIEMER 1997 CUVÉE BRUT 2000

Winey aromas but has some finesse and is an attempt at a serious style.
🍷 Now–2001 Ⓔ

ATTENTION CHAMPAGNE & SPARKLING WINE PRODUCERS!

If you are not already in contact with the author, but would like to submit wines for consideration in future editions, please contact Tom Stevenson at:

tom.stevenson@fizz.worldonline.co.uk

Warning: Any other unsolicited mail received at this address will be ignored.

Please note that recommendation in this guide involves no charge whatsoever beyond the cost of the samples and their delivery.

WILHELMSHOF

Pfalz, Germany

WILHELMSHOF SPÄTBURGUNDER BLANC DE NOIRS BRUT 1998 SIEBELDINGER KÖNIGSGARTEN

This very fresh Sekt has finesse on nose and palate, with surprising length on the finish. (*Méthode champenoise.*)
🍷 Now–2001 Ⓔ 🥂 DM26

WILHELMSHOF RIESLING BRUT 1998 SIEBELDINGER KÖNIGSGARTEN

A deliciously fresh and elegantly fruity Sekt of some class. (*Méthode champenoise.*)
🍷 Now–2001 Ⓔ

WILLM

Alsace, France

WILLM NV CRÉMANT D'ALSACE BRUT

Rich pineapple fruit underscored by crisp acidity.
🍷 Now Ⓔ

WILSON

South Australia

THE WILSON VINEYARD HIPPOCRENE NV SPARKLING RED

Elegant, off-dry, fruit-driven style with a youthful melange of fruit and bubbles.
🍷 Now–2001 ⒺⒺ 🥂 A$23

WINDSOR FOREST

Ascot, Berkshire, England, UK

WINDSOR FOREST 1996 SPARKLING

A touch too much dosage, but interesting wet-pebble fruit.
🍷 Now Ⓔ

WINZERSEKT
Rheinhessen, Germany

WINZERSEKT 1998 RIESLING BRUT 74

Gently perfumed Riesling has some finesse (certainly more finesse than this Winzersekt *cuvée* used to have). (*Méthode champenoise.*)
🍷 Now Ⓔ 🥂 DM14 .

WINZERSEKT 1998 SPÄTBURGUNDER WEIßHERBST 72

Very fresh, elevated fruit with clean, crisp finish. (*Méthode champenoise.*)
🍷 Now Ⓔ 🥂 DM15

WIRRA WIRRA
South Australia, Australia

WIRRA WIRRA 1996 THE COUSINS, PINOT NOIR CHARDONNAY 85

Smooth, integrated toasty fruit. Good acidity.
🍷 Now–2001 ⒺⒺ 🥂 A$25

WIRRA WIRRA 1991 LIMITED EDITION THE COUSINS 80

Very smooth and sophisticated.
🍷 Now–2002 ⒺⒺ 🥂 A$69

WOLF
Pfalz, Germany

WOLF 1997 RIESLING BRUT 75

First sample unfortunately corked, but the second sample was totally clean of any off-odours and although quite austere, it has exceptional extract and will develop. (*Méthode champenoise.*)
🥢 2001–2002 Ⓔ

WOLFBERGER
Alsace, France

WOLFBERGER NV CRÉMANT D'ALSACE BRUT 75

Fresh, rich, breezy fruit of some elegance and finesse.
🍷 Now–2001 Ⓔ

WOLFBERGER NV RIESLING, CRÉMANT D'ALSACE BRUT 72

Plenty of lemony Riesling character, but this wine would have scored higher if it had less weight and more finesse.
🍷 Now–2001 Ⓔ

WOLFBERGER NV BLANC DE NOIRS, CRÉMANT D'ALSACE BRUT 77

Excellent Pinot Noir fruit, rich and full, but not too weighty.
🍷 Now–2002 Ⓔ

WOLFBERGER NV CRÉMANT D'ALSACE ROSÉ, BRUT 75

A soft and elegant wine brimming with pure strawberry flavoured Alsace Pinot Noir fruit.
🍷 Now Ⓔ

WOLFBERGER NV CRÉMANT D'ALSACE DEMI-SEC 78

Extremely fresh and really quite luscious, yet this will improve if aged a year or so.
🍷 Now–2003 Ⓔ

WOLFBERGER NV TOKAY PINOT GRIS, CRÉMANT D'ALSACE BRUT 70

Fat and soft, when Pinot Gris should have more acidity, but enough freshness to the fruit to deserve recommendation.
🍷 Now Ⓔ

WOLFBERGER NV CHARDONNAY, CRÉMANT D'ALSACE EXTRA BRUT 70

Fizzy Granny Smiths!
🍷 Now–2001 Ⓔ

WOLFBERGER, CUVÉE DE L'AN 2000 NV CRÉMANT D'ALSACE, PRESTIGE BRUT 80

More excellent Pinot Noir fruit, but this time with a hint of floral Riesling and even better acidity.
🍷 Now–2002 Ⓔ

WOLFBERGER 1995 CRÉMANT D'ALSACE 70

Sweet, peachy fruit.
🍷 Now Ⓔ

WÜRTTEMBERG

Weingut des Hauses Württemberg
Württemberg, Germany

WEINGUT DES HAUSES WÜRTTEMBERG RIESLING TROCKEN 1998 MAULBRONNER EILFINGERBERG *(magnum)*

Rich and satisfying with plenty of extract, but developing nicely and should age well in magnum. (*Méthode champenoise.*)
▌ Now–2003 ⓔ ☙ DM20

❖ **XENIUS**, *see* Covides

YALDARA

South Australia, Australia

YALDARA NV CUVÉE RESERVE, BRUT ROSÉ

Apricot and strawberry jam.
▌ Now ⓔ

YALDARA NV CUVÉE RESERVE BRUT

Fresh, clean, simple, easy-drinking picnic fizz.
▌ Now ⓔ

❖ **YALUMBA**, *see* Samuel Smith & Son

❖ **YARRABANK**, *see* Yering Station

YELLOWGLEN

Victoria, Australia

YELLOWGLEN NV PINOT NOIR CHARDONNAY

Excellent aroma showing finesse, but not quite the elegant balance of fruit on the palate as previous releases.
▌ Now–2001 ⓔ ☙ A$15

YELLOWGLEN "YELLOW" NV BRUT

Sweetish-autolytic aromas mingle with sweet, juicy-fruity aromas in this fresh, ready-drinking, excellent value fizz.
▌ Now ⓔ ☙ A$10

YELLOWGLEN "RED" NV

A light sparkling Burgundy colour; very soft, frothy fruit tasting of winegums, only sweeter. Fruit-driven style.
▌ Now ⓔ ☙ A$10

YELLOWGLEN VINTAGE 1997

Lovely soft, plump fruitiness encased in classic structure. Really shows well and should age better than previous vintages.
▌ Now–2003 ⓔ

YELLOWGLEN "Y" NV SPARKLING BURGUNDY

Deeper, richer colour than Yellowglen Red, with a touch of tannin to give added grip to this medium-sweet, fruit-driven fizz.
▌ Now–2002 ⓔ ☙ A$18.50

YERING STATION

Victoria, Australia

YARRABANK 1995 TIBAULT AND GILLET CUVÉE

Ageing fast on nose, but very interesting Champagne-like fruit followed by vanilla-complexity on finish.
▌ Now–2001 ⓔⓔ ☙ A$42

YARRABANK 1994 TIBAULT AND GILLET CUVÉE

The 1994 has the greatest finesse on the nose of the four different vintages I tasted this year (1993 to 1996 inclusive), with lovely mellow lemony-biscuity fruit, huge extract and high acidity combining to produce intense flavours of surprising finesse. The five-year drinking window errs on the side of caution as this vintage could possibly improve for 10 years or more.
▌ Now–2005 ⓔⓔ ☙ A$42

YARRABANK 1993 TIBAULT AND GILLET CUVÉE

Probably a year past its best, but still holds interest.
▌ Now ⓔⓔ ☙ A$42

ZANETTI

Martino Zanetti
Veneto, Italy

CASE BIANCHE, VIGNA DEL CUC 1999 PROSECCO DI CONEGLIANO VALDOBBIADENE, BRUT 73

If you're into Prosecco, this one offers more depth and acidity than most.
❚ Now ⓔ

ZIMMER

Weigut Hirschhof
Rheinhessen, Germany

WALTER ZIMMER 1998 RIESLING BRUT 71

Fresh, sherbety aroma followed by clean Riesling fruit. (*Méthode champenoise.*)
❚ Now ⓔ 🍇 DM22

UK Stockists

A listing of major stockists of Champagnes and sparkling wines in the UK, including a key to where to find over 650 major brands.

BRAND FINDER

Brands are in **bold** type for easy indexing. Only regularly stocked products are included, and not all are recommended in *This Year's Tastings*. Note that not all stockists carry the full range of every brand they sell, and are bound to de-list brands from time to time.

Abell & Cie Edward Sheldon
Ackerman Ubiquitous Chip
Acquese Christopher Piper, Noel Young
Aigle Lea & Sandeman, Nicolas, Christopher Piper
Ailerons et Baie Pavilion Wine Company
Aimery The Haslemere Cellar, Waverley Vintners
Albecourt The Haslemere Cellar, Lay & Wheeler
Albert Etienne Safeway
Alderic John Arkell Vintners
Aldridge Estate Connolly's, George Hill, Christopher Piper, Shaws of Beaumaris, The Wine Bureau, The Wright Wine Company
Aliança Booths
Aliguer Selfridges
Amour de Paris Waverley Vintners
Amyot The Winery
Angas Fuller's, James Nicholson, Sommelier Wine Co, Tesco, Unwins
Antech The Wine Society
Antoine Champagne Exchange, Quellyn Roberts
Araldica Somerfield, Valvona & Crolla, Villeneuve Wines, Noel Young
Ardinat Vinceremos
Arenberg Bibendum
Argyle Booths, Rodney Densem Wines, Harrods, Harvey Nichols, House of Townend
Archard Vincent Vinceremos
Arione Averys, Oddbins
Arnaud Jeroboams
Arnould (Michel) T&W Wines, Tanners
Arques *See* Sieur d'Arques
Aubac Brian Coad Fine Wines
Aubry Wine Raks
Augustí Torelló Mata The Wine Society
Aurigny Morrisons
Autreau Bouteille d'Or
Avril ChateauOnline
Ayala Majestic Wine, Nicolas, Planet Wine, Quellyn Roberts

Backsberg Terry Platt
Bailli The Vintry
Bailly (Caves de) La Réserve
Bailly (Charles) Hedley Wright,

Quellyn Roberts, Smedley Vintners
Bailly (Coopérative de) Somerfield, Stevens Garnier
Balachat Charles Hennings
Baldovino Addison, Terry Platt, Waters Wine Merchants
Banfi The Butlers Wine Cellar
Barancourt Planet Wine
Barnaut Philglas & Swiggot, Rogers Wine Co, Satchells
Barnier Charterhouse Wine Emporium
Baron Addison, Charles Hennings, Unwins, Waters Wine Merchants
Baron Albert Howard Ripley
Baron de Beaumont Waitrose
Baron de Marck Lay & Wheeler
Baron de Monceny Pallant Wines, Safeway
Barramundi Asda, Booths, Co-op, Co-operative, Morrisons
Bass Tuba-Bava The Nobody Inn
Bauchet Majestic Wine
Bauchet Frères Châteaux Wines
Baudry Villeneuve Wines
Bauget-Jouette Andrew Chapman, High Breck Vintners, Trout Wines, Noel Young
Baumard Eldridge Pope, La Reserve, Sommelier Wine Co
Bava The Butlers Wine Cellar
Beaumet Le Pont de la Tour
Beaumont des Crayeres John Armit Wines, Oddbins, La Reserve
Beauvolage Wine Raks
Beck (Graham) Bibendum, Fortnum & Mason, Unwins, Waverley Vintners
Beerens Bibendum
Bellavista Valvona & Crolla, Noel Young
Belle Fleur Waters Wine Merchants
Bellevue James Nicholson
Benedick Lea & Sandeman
Berger Justerini & Brooks, Yapp Brothers
Berlucchi Mitchells Wine Merchants, Roberson
Bernard-Massard Eldridge Pope Fine Wines
Besserat de Bellefon Nicolas, Planet Wine, Wine Direct
Billecart-Salmon Adnams, Amathus Wines, Berry Bros & Rudd, The Champagne House, Corney & Barrow, Ben Ellis, Fortnum & Mason, Goedhuis & Company, Harrods, Harvey Nichols, High Breck Vintners, Michael Jobling, Justerini & Brooks, Lea & Sandeman, James Nicholson, Oddbins, Pallant Wines, Philglas & Swiggot, Planet Wine, Le Pont de la Tour, Roberson, Sandiway Wine

Company, Savage Selection, Selfridges, Shaws of Beaumaris, Frank Stainton, Ubiquitous Chip, Valvona & Crolla
Billiot Bibendum, madaboutwine.com, Raeburn Fine Wines
Binet Berry Bros & Rudd
Blanc Foussy Heyman Barwell Jones
Blin Charles Hennings, Pallant Wines, Oddbins, Villeneuve Wines
Blue Lake Ridge Asda
Blossom Hill Budgens
Bluff Hill Marks & Spencer
Bochingen Amathus Wines
Boeckel Allez Vins!
Boheme Frank Stainton
Bohemia Regal Waitrose
Boizel Four Walls Wine Co
Bolla Noel Young
Bollinger Addison, Amathus Wines, John Arkell Vintners, John Armit Wines, Asda, Averys, Balls Brothers, Berry Bros & Rudd, Bibendum, Booths, Bordeaux Direct, Budgens, The Butlers Wine Cellar, Champagne Exchange, The Champagne House, Charterhouse Wine Emporium, ChateauOnline, Connolly's, Co-op, Co-operative, Corkscrew Wines, Corney & Barrow, Rodney Densem Wines, Direct Wine Shipments, Drinks Direct, Eldridge Pope, Ben Ellis, First Quench, Forth Wines, Fortnum & Mason, Four Walls Wine Co, Friarwood, Fuller's, Goedhuis & Company, Great Western Wine Company, Hall Batson & Co, Handford-Holland Park, Harrods, Harvey Nichols, The Haslemere Cellar, Haynes Hanson & Clark, Hedley Wright, Pierre Henck Wines, Charles Hennings, Heyman Barwell Jones, Hicks & Don, George Hill, House of Townend, Jeroboams, Michael Jobling, S.H. Jones, Justerini & Brooks, Lay & Wheeler, Laytons, Lea & Sandeman, Lloyd Taylor Wines, madaboutwine.com, Majestic Wine, Mitchells Wine Merchants, Morris & Verdin, Morrisons, Nickolls & Perks, Nicolas, The Nobody Inn, Oddbins, The Oxford Wine Company, Pallant Wines, Pavilion Wine Company, Penistone Court Wine Cellars, Philglas & Swiggot, Christopher Piper, Planet Wine, Terry Platt, Le Pont de la Tour, Portland Wine Company, Quellyn Roberts, Raeburn Fine Wines, Reid Wines, La Reserve, Roberson, Rogers Wine Co, Safeway, Sainsbury's,

Sandiway Wine Company, Satchells, Scatchard, Sebastopol Wines, Selfridges, Shaws of Beaumaris, Edward Sheldon, Somerfield, Frank Stainton, John Stephenson, Stevens Garnier, Stratford's Wine Shippers, T&W Wines, Tanners Wines, Tesco, Ubiquitous Chip, Unwins, Valvona & Crolla, La Vigneronne, Villeneuve Wines, Waitrose, Waterloo Wine Co, Waters Wine Merchants, Waverley Vintners, Wine Raks, The Winery, The Wine Society, Woodhouse Wines, The Wright Wine Company, Peter Wylie, Yapp Brothers, Noel Young
Bonaval Adnams, Andrew Chapman, Le Fleming Wines, Philglas & Swiggot, Shaws of Beaumaris, Wine Raks, Noel Young
Bonnamy Nicolas
Bonnet (A.) Le Pont de la Tour
Bonnet (F.) Addison, Kwik-Save, Oddbins
Bonval Ramsbottom Victuallers
Borelli Mitchells Wine Merchants, Stevens Garnier
Bortoli Le Fleming Wines, The Wright Wine Company
Bortolotti Harrods
Boschendal Terry Platt
Bosio Majestic Wine
Botter Forth Wines
Boucheron The Wine Treasury
Bourgeois Père et Fils Safeway
Bourillon Dorléans Morris & Verdin
Bourisset Noel Young
Boursault Fuller's, Unwins
Bouvet *See* Bouvet-Ladubay
Bouvet-Ladubay Brian Coad Fine Wines, Co-operative, Fortnum & Mason, Harrods, Harvey Nichols, Justerini & Brooks, Majestic Wine, James Nicholson, Nicolas, Terry Platt, Roberson, Selfridges, Edward Sheldon, The Wright Wine Company
Bracieux Co-op
Brassart ChateauOnline
Brédif S.H. Jones, Frank Stainton, The Wine Bureau
Bredon Waitrose
Brémont ChateauOnline, The Fine Champagne Company
Breuer Direct Wine Shipments
Brézé York Wines
Bricout Lea & Sandeman, madaboutwine.com, Planet Wine
Brigand Raeburn Fine Wines
Brizé Great Western Wine Company
Brochet-Hervieux Handford-Holland Park
Brossault Booths, Budgens, Fuller's
Brouette Nicolas
Brown Brothers Co-op, Rodney Densem Wines, Direct Wine Shipments, Hall Batson & Co,

Penistone Court Wine Cellars, Christopher Piper, Terry Platt, John Stephenson, Stevens Garnier, The Wright Wine Company, Noel Young
Brugnon The Oxford Wine Company
Brummel The Wright Wine Company
Brun (Albert le) The Champagne House, Satchells
Brun (Cellier le) Andrew Chapman, Fortnum & Mason, Great Western Wine Company, Hedley Wright, The Nobody Inn, Roberson, Shaws of Beaumaris, Smedley Vintners, Noel Young
Brun de Neuville Trout Wines, Waterloo Wine Co
Bründlmayer Raeburn Fine Wines
Bruyne (de) King Wines
Bry Edward Sheldon, Frank Stainton
Busin ChateauOnline

Ca'del Bosco Valvona & Crolla
Cadre Noir Addison, Waters Wine Merchants
Cairolle Oddbins
Calissano Balls Brothers, House of Townend, S.H. Jones, Portland Wine Company
Callot Budgens, Growers & Châteaux
Camuset Bibendum, Sainsbury's
Canard-Duchêne Barrels & Bottles. Booths, Champagne Exchange, Corkscrew Wines, Edencroft Fine Wines, Four Walls Wine Co, Fuller's, Great Grog, Charles Hennings, George Hill, Jeroboams, S.H. Jones, Majestic Wine, Morris & Verdin, Morrisons, New London Wine, Oddbins, The Oxford Wine Company, Pallant Wines, Planet Wine, Roberson, Rogers Wine Co, Sandiway Wine Company, Unwins, Waitrose, The Winery
Carneros Terry Platt
Carpene Malvolti Lea & Sandeman, Roberson
Carrington *See* Orlando
Carr Taylor Budgens, Ramsbottom Victuallers
Ca'Rugate Valvona & Crolla
Casa del Valle Oddbins
Casarito The Butlers Wine Cellar, Corkscrew Wines, Sommelier Wine Co
Cascina Castelet Sandiway Wine Company, Noel Young
Ca'Solare Bordeaux Direct
Castell d'Olerdola The Haslemere Cellar, Haynes Hanson & Clark, S.H. Jones, Lay & Wheeler, Portland Wine Company
Castell de Vilarnau Brian Coad Fine Wines, Somerfield
Castellane Budgens, Growers & Châteaux, Wine Raks

Castellblanch Bibendum, Corkscrew Wines, First Quench, S.H. Jones, Waitrose, Waters Wine Merchants, The Winery
Castelnau Justerini & Brooks
Cattier The Butlers Wine Cellar, Four Walls Wine Co, Wine Raks
Cavalier Amathus Wines, Booths, Co-operative, Oddbins
Cavalino The Butlers Wine Cellar
Cavas Hill Budgens
Cavicchioli The Butlers Wine Cellar, Valvona & Crolla
Cavini Mitchells Wine Merchants
Cazanove Hall Batson & Co, The Wright Wine Company
Cesari The Butlers Wine Cellar
Champalou Sommelier Wine Co
Chandon (Domaine, Australia) *See* Green Point
Chandon (Domaine, Cava) Addison
Chandon (Domaine, USA) *See* Shadow Creek
Channay Morrisons
Chanoine Sainsbury's
Chanson Averys, S.H. Jones,
Chantelore Majestic Wine
Chapel Down Bat & Bottle, Booths, Fortnum & Mason, Hicks & Don, S.H. Jones, The Oxford Wine Company, Roberson, Safeway, Selfridges, Tesco, Waitrose, Woodhouse Wines
Charbaut Penistone Court Wine Cellars, Stratford's Wine Shippers, The Vintry
Charlemagne Bouteille d'Or
Charnay Bibendum
Chartogne-Taillet Safeway
Chassenay First Quench
Chassey Corney & Barrow
Chaudron Nicolas
Chevalier de France Rodney Densem Wines, Nicolas, The Wright Wine Company
Chevaliers de Malte The Butlers Wine Cellar, Pierre Henck Wines, Lloyd Taylor Wines, The Oxford Wine Company, York Wines
Chidaine Pavilion Wine Company
Chilford Hundred Noel Young
Chimere Forth Wines
Cinzano Brian Coad Fine Wines
Clairveaux Co-operative
Clos Naudin-Philippe Foreau Direct Wine Shipments
Cloudy Bay *See* Pelorus
Clouet T&W Wines, Tanners
Clover Hill Penistone Court Wine Cellars, Frank Stainton
Cocchi Penistone Court Wine Cellars
Cockatoo Ridge Oddbins, Sainsbury's, Tesco, Vin du Van
Codorníu Asda, Co-op, Co-operative, Great Grog, Safeway, Somerfield, Tesco, Woodhouse Wines
Codorníu Napa Asda
Collin et Bourisset Brian Coad

Fine Wines, Selfridges
Comte de France Woodhouse Wines
Comte Royer de Bravard Hicks & Don
Conde de Caralt The Butlers Wine Cellar, Great Western Wine Company
Conte Collalto Heyman Barwell Jones
Cornillon Eckington Wines
Cotte The Butlers Wine Cellar
Courbet First Quench
Cranswick Asda
Cray Booths, The Butlers Wine Cellar, Connolly's, Corkscrew Wines, Sandiway Wine Company, Shaws of Beaumaris, Wine Raks, Noel Young
Cristalino Woodhouse Wines

Darwin's Path Waters Wine Merchants, York Wines
Deakin Estate Bibendum, Great Grog, Oddbins, Ramsbottom Victuallers
Debesson Rodney Densem Wines
Deinhard John Arkell Vintners, Budgens, John Stephenson
Delahaie ChateauOnline
Delamotte Corney & Barrow, King Wines
Delbeck Bordeaux Direct, ChateauOnline
Delmas Pallant Wines, Vinceremos
Delorme Selfridges, Waterloo Wine Co
Delot Hedley Wright
Demets Raeburn Fine Wines
Demoiselle Nicolas
Denizot Great Western Wine Company
Denois *See* Aigle
Derose Oddbins
Desroches Marks & Spencer
Deutz John Armit Wines, Berkmann Wine Cellars, Forth Wines, Harvey Nichols, Laytons, Mitchells Wine Merchants, Nicolas, John Stephenson, Turville Valley Wines
Deutz Marlborough *See* Montana
Devaux Majestic Wine, Frank Stainton, The Wine Bureau
Deva Azulle Somerfield
Devilliers Justerini & Brooks, Noel Young
Diane de Poitiers House of Townend
Diebolt-Vallois Eckington Wines
Dinet-Peuvrel Handford-Holland Park, The Wine Treasury
Divinoude Nicolas
Dom Pérignon *See* Moët & Chandon
Dopff au Moulin Harrods, House of Townend, Terry Platt, Roberson
Drappier Amathus Wines, Barrels & Bottles, Anthony Byrne Fine Wines, Corkscrew Wines, First Quench, Le Fleming Wines,

ItsWine.com, Nickolls & Perks, Satchells, Scatchard
Dubois-Martin Smedley Vintners
Duc de Breux Ben Ellis, Le Fleming Wine, New London Wine, Stevens Garnier
Duc de Foix Scatchard, Trout Wines, Young's
Duc de Lavigny Heyman Barwell Jones
Duc de Raybaud Barrels & Bottles
Duc de Roucher Waverley Vintners
Duchatel Unwins
Dumangin (J.) Yapp Brothers
Dumont Fuller's
Dumont, Daniel Ramsbottom Victuallers, Sandiway Wine Company
Duret Tesco
Duval-Leroy Addison, Adnams, Bordeaux Direct, ChateauOnline, Rodney Densem Wines, Lay & Wheeler, Penistone Court Wine Cellars, Terry Platt, Portland Wine Company, John Stephenson, Tanners Wines

Egly-Ouriet La Vigneronne
Ellner Balls Brothers, Bouteille d'Or, S.H. Jones, Lay & Wheeler
Elysée Heyman Barwell Jones
Epoch *See* Chapel Down
Eschenauer Somerfield
Espinosa de los Monteros Somerfield
Estrand House of Townend, Portland Wine Company

Fairview Sandiway Wine Company
Faubert Selfridges
Faustino Martinez Amathus Wines, Mitchells Wine Merchants
Férat Bibendum
Féraud Charles Hennings, John Stephenson
Ferrari Handford-Holland Park
Feuillatte Asda, First Quench, Pierre Henck Wines, Planet Wine, Roberson, Safeway, Scatchard, Tesco, Unwins
Fiddler's Creek Budgens
Fita Azul Morrisons
Flavy La Vigneronne
Fleuret Berkmann Wine Cellars
Fleury Raeburn Fine Wines, The Wine Society
Florancy ChateauOnline
Fontanafredda Fortnum & Mason, Harrods, Roberson, Ubiquitous Chip, Valvona & Crolla
Fox Creek Sommelier Wine Co, Noel Young
Freixenet Addison, Amathus Wines, John Arkell Vintners, Averys, Balls Brothers, Booths, Co-op, Co-operative, Rodney Densem Wines, First Quench, Fuller's, Hall Batson & Co,

Harrods, Charles Hennings, George Hill, House of Townend, Majestic Wine, Mitchells Wine Merchants, Morrisons, The Oxford Wine Company, Christopher Piper, Terry Platt, Portland Wine Company, Quellyn Roberts, Roberson, Safeway, Sainsbury's, Satchells, Selfridges, Edward Sheldon, Edward Sheldon, Somerfield, John Stephenson, Stevens Garnier, Tesco, Ubiquitous Chip, Unwins, Waitrose, Waters Wine Merchants

Gailen Nicolas
Gallimard Ben Ellis, Shaws of Beaumaris, The Wine Bureau
Gallo Asda, Budgens, Co-op, Co-operative, Forth Wines, Mitchells Wine Merchants, Safeway, Sainsbury's, First Quench
Gancia Amathus Wines, Co-op, Hall Batson & Co, Hedley Wright, Nicolas, Quellyn Roberts, Waverley Vintners
Ganioud The Wine Society
Gardet Ballantynes of Cowbridge, Bat & Bottle, Charterhouse Wine Emporium, Connolly's, Goedhuis & Company, The Haslemere Cellar, Hicks & Don, House of Townend, S.H. Jones, New London Wine, The Nobody Inn, Sommelier Wine Co, Young's
Gardin Hicks & Don
Gareoult High Breck Vintners
Garnotel The Butlers Wine Cellar
Gatinois Haynes Hanson & Clark
Gaucher John Arkell Vintners, Stevens Garnier
Gaudrelle James Nicholson
Gemma Connolly's
Geoffroy Tanners Wines, The Winery
Germain Budgens
Gianni Morrisons
Gilbert Corney & Barrow
Gimonnet Oddbins
Gioiosa Valvona & Crolla
Giordano The Butlers Wine Cellar
Gloria Ferrer George Hill, Majestic Wine, Terry Platt, John Stephenson
Gobillard ChateauOnline, Lay & Wheeler
Goerg The Champagne House
Golan Heights Averys
Gonet Somerfield
Gosset Amathus Wines, Ballantynes of Cowbridge, Balls Brothers, The Butlers Wine Cellar, ChateauOnline, Rodney Densem Wines, Fortnum & Mason, Four Walls Wine Co, Handford-Holland Park, Harrods, The Haslemere Cellar, Hedley Wright, Charles

Hennings, Hicks & Don, Lea & Sandeman, The Nobody Inn, The Oxford Wine Company, Pallant Wines, Philglas & Swiggot, Le Pont de la Tour, Portland Wine Company, La Reserve, Roberson, C.A. Rookes, Scatchard, Selfridges, Sommelier Wine Co, Stratford's Wine Shippers, La Vigneronne, The Wine Bureau, The Wright Wine Company, Noel Young

Goulet Harrods, Nicolas

Gramey Mitchells Wine Merchants

Grand Marque (Saumur) Balls Brothers, House of Townend

Grandin Co-operative, Stevens Garnier

Grands Crus (Caves de) The Butlers Wine Cellar

Grant Burge Connolly's, The Oxford Wine Company

Gratien (Alfred) Connolly's, Fortnum & Mason, Sainsbury's, Wine Raks, The Wine Society

Gratien & Meyer Connolly's, George Hill, Morrisons, Oddbins, Quellyn Roberts, The Wine Society, The Wright Wine Company

Great Western Andrew Chapman, Connolly's, First Quench, Pierre Henck Wines, Christopher Piper, Woodhouse Wines

Green (Douglas) Tesco

Green Point Addison, Amathus Wines, Averys, Berry Bros & Rudd, Bibendum, Rodney Densem Wines, Direct Wine Shipments, First Quench, Forth Wines, Fortnum & Mason, Four Walls Wine Co, Fuller's, Harrods, Haynes Hanson & Clark, S.H. Jones, Lay & Wheeler, Majestic Wine, Mitchells Wine Merchants, Philglas & Swiggot, Terry Platt, Portland Wine Company, Raeburn Fine Wines, Roberson, Sainsbury's, Sebastopol Wines, Selfridges, Edward Sheldon, Sommelier Wine Co, John Stephenson, Tesco, Unwins, Villeneuve Wines, Waitrose, Waters Wine Merchants, Waverley Vintners, The Wine Society, Noel Young

Gregoletto Harvey Nichols

Gregoria Noel Young

Gremillet Christopher Piper, Sandiway Wine Company, The Burgundy Shuttle, Noel Young

Grenelle (Louis de) Sommelier Wine Co,

Guidon Selfridges

Guilleminot Lay & Wheeler

Hamilton Noel Young

Hardy (Dominique) C.A. Rookes

Hardys Mitchells Wine Merchants, Nicolas, Safeway, John Stephenson, Tesco,

Villeneuve Wines

Harlin Oddbins

Haselgrove Andrew Chapman, Sommelier Wine Co, Vin du Van, Wine Raks

Heidsieck (Charles) Amathus Wines, John Arkell Vintners, Averys, Booths, Champagne Exchange, First Quench, Forth Wines, Fortnum & Mason, Goedhuis & Company, Charles Hennings, S.H. Jones, Justerini & Brooks, Majestic Wine, Mitchells Wine Merchants, Nicolas, The Nobody Inn, Christopher Piper, Planet Wine, Selfridges, Unwins, Villeneuve Wines, Waters Wine Merchants, Noel Young

Heidsieck Monopole John Arkell Vintners, Budgens, Champagne Exchange, Charterhouse Wine Emporium, Rodney Densem Wines, House of Townend, S.H. Jones, New London Wine, Oddbins, Tesco, Waverley Vintners

Heidsieck (Piper) *See* Piper Heidsieck

Heidt Bordeaux Direct

Henkell Amathus Wines, Booths, Mitchells Wine Merchants, Morrisons, Satchells

Henriet La Bouteille d'Or

Henriet-Bazin La Bouteille d'Or

Henriot Bordeaux Direct, Anthony Byrne Fine Wines, Michael Jobling, Justerini & Brooks, Nicolas, Penistone Court Wine Cellars, Planet Wine

Herard (Paul) Lloyd Taylor Wines, Morrisons, James Nicholson, Scatchard, Ubiquitous Chip

Herard (Philippe) High Breck Vintners, Lloyd Taylor Wines, Edward Sheldon

Hollick Le Fleming Wines, Lay & Wheeler, James Nicholson, Vin du Van, Noel Young

Hostomme The Nobody Inn, Selfridges

Huet Bibendum, Justerini & Brooks, Raeburn Fine Wines, The Wine Society

Huguenot Hills Somerfield

Huia Bibendum

Hunter's Harrods, Michael Jobling, Justerini & Brooks, Majestic Wine, Philglas & Swiggot, Christopher Piper, Noel Young

Hurlingham Justerini & Brooks

Husson Budgens, Growers & Châteaux

Inviosa The Nobody Inn

Jackson Hedley Wright, Portland Wine Company, Sandiway Wine Company

Jacobs Creek Fuller's, Tesco, Unwins

Jacquart Booths, Majestic Wine,

Planet Wine, Selfridges, John Stephenson, Trout Wines

Jacquart (André) The Butlers Wine Cellar, Morris & Verdin, Sandiway Wine Company, Noel Young

Jacquesson & Fils Mayfair Cellars, Pallant Wines, Selfridges

Jarry Yapp Brothers

Jeanson Oddbins

Jeeper Barrels & Bottles

Jordan Harvey Nichols

Juvé y Camps Bat & Bottle, Berry Bros & Rudd, Fortnum & Mason, Harrods, Pierre Henck Wines, Laymont & Shaw, Philglas & Swiggot, Roberson, Satchells, Selfridges, Shaws of Beaumaris, Frank Stainton, Ubiquitous Chip, Villeneuve Wines, The Wright Wine Company

Killawarra Addison, Fuller's, Great Western Wine Company, Charles Hennings, S.H. Jones, Lay & Wheeler, Lloyd Taylor Wines, The Oxford Wine Company, Pallant Wines, Sommelier Wine Co, Vin du Van, Waverley Vintners, Young's

Kindler Budgens

Kripta Selfridges

Kriter Selfridges, John Stephenson

Kröne Borealis Waitrose

Krug Addison, Adnams, Amathus Wines, John Arkell Vintners, John Armit Wines, Averys, Balls Brothers, Barrels & Bottles, Berry Bros & Rudd, Bibendum, The Butlers Wine Cellar, Champagne Exchange, ChateauOnline, Charterhouse Wine Emporium, Connolly's, Corney & Barrow, Rodney Densem Wines, Edencroft Fine Wines, Eldridge Pope, Ben Ellis, First Quench, Forth Wines, Fortnum & Mason, Four Walls Wine Co, Goedhuis & Company, Hall Batson & Co, Harrods, Harvey Nichols, The Haslemere Cellar, Haynes Hanson & Clark, Pierre Henck Wines, Charles Hennings, Heyman Barwell Jones, House of Townend, Michael Jobling, S.H. Jones, Justerini & Brooks, Lay & Wheeler, Laytons, Lea & Sandeman, madaboutwine.com, Majestic Wine, Mitchells Wine Merchants, Nickolls & Perks, Nicolas, The Nobody Inn, The Oxford Wine Company, Pavilion Wine Company, Penistone Court Wine Cellars, Philglas & Swiggot, Christopher Piper, Planet Wine, Le Pont de la Tour, Portland Wine Company, Quellyn Roberts, La Reserve, Roberson, Scatchard, Sebastopol Wines, Selfridges, Edward Sheldon, Sommelier Wine Co, Frank Stainton, John Stephenson, T&W Wines,

Tanners Wines, Tesco, Turville Valley Wines, Ubiquitous Chip, Unwins, Valvona & Crolla, Villeneuve Wines, Waterloo Wine Co, Waters Wine Merchants, Waverley Vintners, Wine Raks, The Winery, The Wright Wine Company, Peter Wylie, Noel Young
Kuentz-Bas The Wine Bureau

Laborie Charles Hennings, The Wright Wine Company
Lafitte Nicolas, Planet Wine
Laithwaite Bordeaux Direct
Lamiable High Breck Vintners
Lamoure Stevens Garnier
Lamoureux ChateauOnline
Lancelot Noel Young
Landiras Somerfield
Langlois Addison, Rodney Densem Wines, Majestic Wine, Villeneuve Wines
Lanson Addison, Amathus Wines, John Arkell Vintners, Asda, Averys, Budgens, Champagne Exchange, Connolly's, Co-op, Co-operative, Rodney Densem Wines, Drinks Direct, Eldridge Pope, First Quench, Fuller's, Charles Hennings, Heyman Barwell Jones, S.H. Jones, Justerini & Brooks, Majestic Wine, Mitchells Wine Merchants, Morrisons, Nickolls & Perks, Nicolas, Oddbins, Pallant Wines, Planet Wine, Terry Platt, Rogers Wine Co, Safeway, Sainsbury's, Selfridges, Somerfield, Frank Stainton, John Stephenson, Tesco, Unwins, Waitrose, Waters Wine Merchants, Waverley Vintners, Wine Direct, Woodhouse Wines, The Wright Wine Company
Lantage 3D Wines
H. Lanvin Hall Batson & Co
Larmandier Tanners
Lassalle ChateauOnline
La Tour Grise C.A. Rookes
Launois Addison
Laurent-Perrier Addison, Adnams, Amathus Wines, John Armit Wines, John Arkell Vintners, Averys, Balls Brothers, Bibendum, Bordeaux Direct, Budgens, The Butlers Wine Cellar, Châteaux Wines, Champagne Exchange, Connolly's, Corney & Barrow, Drinks Direct, Eldridge Pope, First Quench, Fortnum & Mason, Friarwood, Fuller's, Goedhuis & Company, Great Western Wine Company, Hall Batson & Co, Harrods, Harvey Nichols, Haynes Hanson & Clark, Hedley Wright, Pierre Henck Wines, Charles Hennings, Heyman Barwell Jones, High Breck Vintners, George Hill, House of Townend, Jeroboams, S.H. Jones, Justerini

& Brooks, Lay & Wheeler, Laytons, Lea & Sandeman, madaboutwine.com, Majestic Wine, Mitchells Wine Merchants, Morris & Verdin, New London Wine, Nickolls & Perks, Nicolas, Oddbins, The Oxford Wine Company, Penistone Court Wine Cellars, Christopher Piper, Planet Wine, Terry Platt, Le Pont de la Tour, Quellyn Roberts, Reid Wines, Roberson, Rogers Wine Co, Sainsbury's, Sebastopol Wines, Selfridges, Smedley Vintners, Frank Stainton, John Stephenson, Stratford's Wine Shippers, Tesco, Unwins, Valvona & Crolla, Villeneuve Wines, Waters Wine Merchants, Waverley Vintners, Wine Raks, The Winery, The Wine Society, The Wright Wine Company, Noel Young, Young's
J.B. Lechere Ballantynes of Cowbridge
Legendre New London Wine
Leger Wine Direct
Legras Lea & Sandeman
Lemoine Addison, Hedley Wright, Quellyn Roberts, Rogers Wine Co, Smedley Vintners, John Stephenson
Lenoble Brian Coad Fine Wines, ChateauOnline, Nickolls & Perks
Lenz Moser Forth Wines
Lepitre Harvey Nichols
Leprince La Reserve
Letourneau The Burgundy Shuttle
Liards See Berger
Lilbert The Champagne House, T&W Wines
Lindauer See Montana
Listel Booths, Edward Sheldon, C.A. Rookes, Satchells
Longridge Brian Coad Fine Wines, Hedley Wright, Ramsbottom Victuallers, Roberson
Lonsdale Ridge Bibendum
Loredan Gasparini Averys, Penistone Court Wine Cellars
Lorent Averys
Lorentz Forth Wines
Loriot York Wines
Louis St Croix Averys
Lourmel Asda
Lugny Haynes Hanson & Clark, Oddbins, Christopher Piper, Sommelier Wine Co, Waitrose

Madeba Cellars Lay & Wheeler, Oddbins, Safeway, Sainsbury's, First Quench
Magenta The Wright Wine Company
Mailly Grand Cru Friarwood
Maire Averys
Malard First Quench
Mancey The Haslemere Cellar
Mandois Andrew Sheepshanks, Somerfield
Mann Lay & Wheeler

Mansard Forth Wines, Champagne Exchange
Marca First Quench, Waitrose
Marcarini Raeburn Fine Wines
Margaine La Vigneronne
Marguerite Christel Hall Batson & Co
Marguet-Bonnerave Addison, Barrels & Bottles, The Burgundy Shuttle
Marimont Budgens
Marino Co-op
Marlin Bay Marks & Spencer
Marniquet The Oxford Wine Company
Marques de Alella Harvey Nichols
Marques de Monistrol Amathus Wines, Berkmann Wine Cellars, Budgens, Corkscrew Wines, Ben Ellis, Raeburn Fine Wines, Scatchard, Stevens Garnier
Marquis d'Auvigne New London Wine
Marquis de la Tour First Quench
Marquis d'Estrand See Estrand
Martel Barrels & Bottles, The Fine Champagne Company, Springfield Wines
Martial-Couvreur The Butlers Wine Cellar
Martini Addison, Amathus Wines, Asda, Booths, Budgens, Co-op, Co-operative, Rodney Densem Wines, Eldridge Pope, Forth Wines, Fuller's, Charles Hennings, George Hill, Heyman Barwell Jones, S.H. Jones, Mitchells Wine Merchants, Morrisons, Oddbins, Pallant Wines, Terry Platt, Safeway, Sainsbury's, Satchells, Scatchard, Selfridges, Shaws of Beaumaris, Edward Sheldon, Somerfield, Frank Stainton, John Stephenson, Tesco, First Quench, Unwins, Waitrose, Waters Wine Merchants, Woodhouse Wines, The Wright Wine Company
Martinolles Stevens Garnier
Mascaro The Butlers Wine Cellar
Mascaro Monarch Terry Platt
Masse Champagne Exchange, Somerfield
Mathieu Great Grog
Mauler Selfridges
Maxim's Budgens, Growers & Châteaux
Mazegrand Stratford's Wine Shippers, The Vintry
Medot Harvey Nichols, Adam Bancroft Associates, James Nicholson
Melton Adnams, Le Fleming Wines, Harrods, Harvey Nichols, Hedley Wright, Sandiway Wine Company, Vin du Van, Wine Raks, Noel Young
Mercier Addison, Amathus Wines, John Arkell Vintners, Asda, Budgens, Champagne Exchange, Co-op, Drinks Direct, First Quench, Forth Wines,

Fuller's, Heyman Barwell Jones, S.H. Jones, Lay & Wheeler, Laytons, Mitchells Wine Merchants, Morrisons, Planet Wine, Roberson, Safeway, Sainsbury's, John Stephenson, Tesco, Unwins, Villeneuve Wines, Waters Wine Merchants, Waverley Vintners, Woodhouse Wines

Mesnil Adnams, Balls Brothers, Justerini & Brooks, Raeburn Fine Wines, Ramsbottom Victuallers, Richards Walford, Noel Young

Meyer-Fonné Lay & Wheeler

Mignon The Fine Champagne Company

Mills Reef Forth Wines

Mionetto Reid Wines

Miranda Averys, Connolly's

Miraucourt George Hill

Miru Miru *See* Hunters

Mitchell Lay & Wheeler

Moët & Chandon Addison, Amathus Wines, John Arkell Vintners, Asda, Averys, Balls Brothers, Barrels & Bottles, Berry Bros & Rudd, Bibendum, Booths, Budgens, The Butlers Wine Cellar, Champagne Exchange, The Champagne House, Charterhouse Wine Emporium, Connolly's, Co-op, Co-operative, Corkscrew Wines, Corney & Barrow, Rodney Densem Wines, Drinks Direct, Eckington Wines, Eldridge Pope, Ben Ellis, First Quench, Forth Wines, Fortnum & Mason, Four Walls Wine Co, Friarwood, Fuller's, Goedhuis & Company, Hall Batson & Co, Harrods, Harvey Nichols, The Haslemere Cellar, Haynes Hanson & Clark, Charles Hennings, Heyman Barwell Jones, George Hill, House of Townend, Jeroboams, S.H. Jones, Justerini & Brooks, Lay & Wheeler, Laytons, Lea & Sandeman, madaboutwine.com, Majestic Wine, Mitchells Wine Merchants, Morrisons, Nickolls & Perks, Nicolas, Oddbins, The Oxford Wine Company, Pallant Wines, Christopher Piper, Philglas & Swiggot, Planet Wine, Terry Platt, Le Pont de la Tour, Portland Wine Company, Quellyn Roberts, Raeburn Fine Wines, Roberson, Safeway, Sainsbury's, Scatchard, Sebastopol Wines, Selfridges, Shaws of Beaumaris, Edward Sheldon, Somerfield, Frank Stainton, John Stephenson, Stevens Garnier, Stratford's Wine Shippers, T&W Wines, Tanners Wines, Tesco, Turville Valley Wines, Ubiquitous Chip, Unwins, Valvona & Crolla, La Vigneronne, Villeneuve Wines, Waitrose, Waterloo Wine Co, Waters Wine Merchants, Waverley Vintners, Wine Direct,

Wine Raks, The Winery, Woodhouse Wines, The Wright Wine Company, The Wright Wine Company, Peter Wylie, Noel Young

Moingeon Heyman Barwell Jones

Moncontour James Nicholson, Stevens Garnier

Moncuit Amathus Wines, ChateauOnline, Winefinds, Noel Young

Monluc Satchells

Monmousseau Nicolas, C.A. Rookes

Montana Addison, Amathus Wines, John Arkell Vintners, Asda, Averys, Booths, Budgens, Co-op, Co-operative, Corkscrew Wines, First Quench, Fuller's, Harvey Nichols, Hedley Wright, Charles Hennings, S.H. Jones, Mitchells Wine Merchants, Morrisons, Oddbins, Pallant Wines, Christopher Piper, Portland Wine Company, Quellyn Roberts, Roberson, Safeway, Sainsbury's, Satchells, Edward Sheldon, Edward Sheldon, Smedley Vintners, Somerfield, John Stephenson, Tesco, Unwins, Villeneuve Wines, Waitrose, Waverley Vintners, Woodhouse Wines, Young's

Montarlau Woodhouse Wines

Montaudon Mitchells Wine Merchants, Satchells

Monteau First Quench

Mont Marçal Booths

Montoy First Quench

Moondarra Waverley Vintners

Morette The Fine Champagne Company

Morin ChateauOnline

Morton Estate Berkmann Wine Cellars, Noel Young

Motte Asda

Mottura Penistone Court Wine Cellars

Moulin (Domaine du) C.A. Rookes

Mountadam Adnams, Connolly's, Le Fleming Wines, The Wright Wine Company, Noel Young

Moutardier Addison, Edencroft Fine Wines, Great Western Wine Company, C.A. Rookes, Winefinds

Muller Forth Wines, Somerfield

Mumm Amathus Wines, Champagne Exchange, Charles Hennings, Charterhouse Wine Emporium, Corney & Barrow, First Quench, Harvey Nichols, Michael Jobling, Mitchells Wine Merchants, Oddbins, Planet Wine, Roberson, Sainsbury's, Selfridges, Tesco, Unwins, The Wright Wine Company

Mumm Cuvée Napa Amathus Wines, John Arkell Vintners, Booths, Budgens, Co-op, Co-operative, Corkscrew Wines, Rodney Densem Wines, Drinks

Direct, First Quench, Fuller's, Harvey Nichols, House of Townend, Majestic Wine, Mitchells Wine Merchants, Morrisons, Oddbins, Portland Wine Company, Safeway, Sainsbury's, Satchells, Selfridges, Edward Sheldon, Somerfield, John Stephenson, Tesco, Unwins, Villeneuve Wines, Waitrose, Waverley Vintners, Woodhouse Wines

Muré Nicolas

Nautilus Amathus Wines, Le Fleming Wines, Majestic Wine, Christopher Piper, Sommelier Wine Co, Vin du Van, The Winery

Nederburg Eldridge Pope, The Oxford Wine Company

Neufchatel John Arkell Vintners, Hall Batson & Co, The Wright Wine Company

Noirot York Wines

Northbrook Springs Charles Hennings

Nutbourne Manor Charles Hennings

Nyetimber Corkscrew Wines, Fortnum & Mason, Four Walls Wine Co, Charles Hennings, S.H. Jones, Pallant Wines, Reid Wines, La Reserve, The Wine Bureau

Ode Panos The Greek Wine Centre

Omar Khayyam Adnams, Amathus Wines, Budgens, Co-op, Mitchells Wine Merchants, The Nobody Inn, Christopher Piper, John Stephenson, Wine Raks

Ondarre Averys

Orlando Rodney Densem Wines, Forth Wines, S.H. Jones, New London Wine, Pallant Wines, Quellyn Roberts, Selfridges, Ubiquitous Chip, Unwins, Vin du Van, The Winery

Orpale *See* St Gall

Oudinot Marks & Spencer

Padthaway The Wine Bureau

Paillard Berkmann Wine Cellars, Bibendum, Bordeaux Direct, Champagne Exchange, Nicolas, Philglas & Swiggot, The Winery, Noel Young

Palau Connolly's

Paleine Handford-Holland Park

Palmer The Champagne Company, Justerini & Brooks, Somerfield

Pannier Amathus Wines, Direct Wine Shipments, Heyman Barwell Jones, Oddbins

Pannier (Remy) Forth Wines, Majestic Wine, New London Wine

Parxet Direct Wine Shipments, Fortnum & Mason, Nicolas

Pavy 3D Wines

Pelcino Somerfield

Pelorus Addison, Amathus Wines, Balls Brothers, Corkscrew Wines, Corney & Barrow, First Quench, Le Fleming Wines, Fortnum & Mason, Four Walls Wine Co, Fuller's, Great Grog, Haynes Hanson & Clark, Charles Hennings, House of Townend, S.H. Jones, Justerini & Brooks, Lea & Sandeman, Majestic Wine, Mitchells Wine Merchants, Morris & Verdin, James Nicholson, The Nobody Inn, The Oxford Wine Company, Pallant Wines, Penistone Court Wine Cellars, Philglas & Swiggot, Terry Platt, Raeburn Fine Wines, Sandiway Wine Company, Scatchard, Sebastopol Wines, Selfridges, Frank Stainton, John Stephenson, Tesco, Ubiquitous Chip, Unwins, Villeneuve Wines, Vin du Van, Wine Raks, The Wright Wine Company, Noel Young

Penley Lay & Wheeler, Villeneuve Wines, The Wine Treasury

Pere Ventura Waverley Vintners

Pérignon (Dom) *See* Moët & Chandon

Perlage Vinceremos

Perlino First Quench

Perrier (Joseph) Balls Brothers, The Butlers Wine Cellar, Charterhouse Wine Emporium, Eckington Wines, Fuller's, Great Western Wine Company, Hall Batson & Co, Hicks & Don, Michael Jobling, madaboutwine.com, New London Wine, The Oxford Wine Company, Roberson, Edward Sheldon, Stevens Garnier, Jeroboams, Stratford's Wine Shippers, Tanners Wines, Ubiquitous Chip, Woodhouse Wines

Perrier-Jouët Addison, Amathus Wines, Averys, Bordeaux Direct, Champagne Exchange, Corkscrew Wines, Corney & Barrow, Rodney Densem Wines, Drinks Direct, First Quench, Forth Wines, Fortnum & Mason, Friarwood, Fuller's, Harrods, Harvey Nichols, Heyman Barwell Jones, Laytons, Majestic Wine, Mitchells Wine Merchants, Nicolas, Oddbins, Pallant Wines, Christopher Piper, Planet Wine, Le Pont de la Tour, Roberson, Edward Sheldon, Ubiquitous Chip, Villeneuve Wines, Waverley Vintners, Wine Raks, The Wright Wine Company

Perrin ChateauNet

Perrone Harvey Nichols, Reid Wines

Petaluma Fortnum & Mason, Harrods, Harvey Nichols, Sebastopol Wines, Vin du Van, Noel Young

Peters Bouteille d'Or

Philipponnat Sommelier Wine Co, Stevens Garnier

Pierrel The Fine Champagne Company

Pignoletto The Butlers Wine Cellar

Pilton Manor Harrods

Piper-Heidsieck Amathus Wines, John Arkell Vintners, Averys, Booths, Bordeaux Direct, Champagne Exchange, Co-op, Rodney Densem Wines, Drinks Direct, First Quench, Forth Wines, Charles Hennings, Heyman Barwell Jones, Mitchells Wine Merchants, Morrisons, Nicolas, Oddbins, Christopher Piper, Planet Wine, Safeway, Sainsbury's, Selfridges, Somerfield, John Stephenson, Tesco, Ubiquitous Chip, Unwins, Villeneuve Wines, Waitrose, Waverley Vintners, Woodhouse Wines, The Wright Wine Company

Pirie Sommelier Wine Co, Tesco, Wine Raks

Plageoles Raeburn Fine Wines

Plantagenet Stevens Garnier

Pol Acker Budgens, Co-operative, Safeway

Pol Aime Tesco

Pol d'Ambert Bordeaux Direct

Pol Pasquier Fuller's

Pol Remy Majestic Wine

Pol Roger Adnams, Amathus Wines, Averys, Balls Brothers, Barrels & Bottles, Berry Bros & Rudd, Bibendum, Bordeaux Direct, Andrew Bruce, The Butlers Wine Cellar, Champagne Exchange, The Champagne House, ChateauOnline, Connolly's, First Quench, Forth Wines, Fortnum & Mason, Fuller's, Goedhuis & Company, Harrods, Harvey Nichols, Haynes Hanson & Clark, Pierre Henck Wines, Charles Hennings, House of Townend, Michael Jobling, S.H. Jones, Justerini & Brooks, Lay & Wheeler, Laytons, Lea & Sandeman, Lloyd Taylor Wines, Majestic Wine, Mitchells Wine Merchants, Morris & Verdin, Nickolls & Perks, Nicolas, Oddbins, The Oxford Wine Company, Penistone Court Wine Cellars, Planet Wine, Portland Wine Company, Quellyn Roberts, Reid Wines, La Reserve, Roberson, Sandiway Wine Company, Selfridges, Sommelier Wine Co, Frank Stainton, Tanners Wines, Ubiquitous Chip, Unwins, Valvona & Crolla, Villeneuve Wines, The Wine Bureau, The Wine Society, The Wright Wine Company, Noel Young

Pommery Amathus Wines, Bibendum, Champagne

Exchange, Rodney Densem Wines, Fuller's, Fortnum & Mason, House of Townend, Lay & Wheeler, Majestic Wine, Oddbins, Planet Wine, Le Pont de la Tour, Roberson, Selfridges, Edward Sheldon, Stratford's Wine Shippers, Tesco, Villeneuve Wines

Pongracz Amathus Wines, Charles Hennings, S.H. Jones, Majestic Wine, Mitchells Wine Merchants, Quellyn Roberts, Sandiway Wine Company, Selfridges, John Stephenson, Stevens Garnier

Poniatowski Four Walls Wine Co, Frank Stainton

Praisac Drinks Direct, First Quench

Prieure Waterloo Wine Co

Primo Australian Wine Club

Quartet Adnams, Amathus Wines, Balls Brothers, Corkscrew Wines, Fortnum & Mason, Four Walls Wine Co, Handford-Holland Park, Harrods, Harvey Nichols, S.H. Jones, Majestic Wine, The Nobody Inn, Terry Platt, Portland Wine Company, Reid Wines, La Reserve, Sandiway Wine Company, Selfridges, Frank Stainton, Waitrose, Waters Wine Merchants, Wine Raks, The Winery, The Wine Society

Rare Print Australian Wine Club

Raymond Kwik-Save

Raventós Waterloo Wine Co

Raventós L'Hereu Waterloo Wine Co

Raventós Rosell Hedley Wright, Smedley Vintners

Redbank Hicks & Don, Roberson

Reminger Morrisons

Renaudin Bordeaux Direct

Rennesson The Vintry

Renoux Amathus Wines

Reynier Eldridge Pope Fine Wines

Rheinach Fuller's

Rialto Co-operative

Richard The Champagne House

Richmond Terry Platt

Richmond Royal Addison, Waters Wine Merchants

Rion Morris & Verdin

Rivetti Adnams

Robe d'Or Balls Brothers, House of Townend, S.H. Jones

Robert (Alain) Sommelier Wine Co,

Robert (J.P.) The Winery

Roche Lacour Bordeaux Direct, The Butlers Wine Cellar

Roederer (Louis) Addison, Adnams, Amathus Wines, John Armit Wines, Balls Brothers, Barrels & Bottles, Berry Bros &

Rudd, Bibendum, Booths, Champagne Exchange, ChateauOnline, Connolly's, Corkscrew Wines, Corney & Barrow, Rodney Densem Wines, Eldridge Pope, Ben Ellis, First Quench, Forth Wines, Fortnum & Mason, Four Walls Wine Co, Friarwood, Fuller's, Goedhuis & Company, Great Western Wine Company, Handford-Holland Park, Harrods, Harvey Nichols, Haynes Hanson & Clark, Hedley Wright, Pierre Henck Wines, Charles Hennings, George Hill, House of Townend, Jeroboams, S.H. Jones, Justerini & Brooks, Lay & Wheeler, Laytons, Lea & Sandeman, madaboutwine.com, Majestic Wine, Mitchells Wine Merchants, Morris & Verdin, James Nicholson, Nickolls & Perks, Nicolas, The Nobody Inn, Oddbins, Pallant Wines, Pavilion Wine Company, Penistone Court Wine Cellars, Philglas & Swiggot, Planet Wine, Terry Platt, Le Pont de la Tour, Portland Wine Company, Quellyn Roberts, Raeburn Fine Wines, Reid Wines, La Reserve, Roberson, Sandiway Wine Company, Scatchard, Selfridges, Frank Stainton, Stevens Garnier, Stratford's Wine Shippers, T&W Wines, Tanners Wines, Tesco, Turville Valley Wines, Unwins, Valvona & Crolla, La Vigneronne, Waitrose, Waters Wine Merchants, Waverley Vintners, The Wine Bureau, Wine Raks, The Winery, The Wine Society, The Wright Wine Company

Roederer (Théophile) Berry Bros & Rudd, Brian Coad Fine Wines, Villeneuve Wines

Roederer Estate *See* Quartet

Rolet La Bouteille d'Or

Rolleston Vale Connolly's, Corkscrew Wines, George Hill, Michael Jobling, Portland Wine Company, Villeneuve Wines

Rosemount Forth Wines, Majestic Wine

Rothschild Planet Wine,

Roura Heyman Barwell Jones

Rowlands Brook Averys, Haynes Hanson & Clark, House of Townend, S.H. Jones, Lay & Wheeler, Portland Wine Company

Royal Marquissac Nicolas

Royal St Charles Pallant Wines

Royer La Bouteille d'Or

Ruelle Pertois Roger Harris Wines

Ruggeri The Butlers Wine Cellar, Selfridges, Sommelier Wine Co, Valvona & Crolla

Ruinart Amathus Wines, John Arkell Vintners, Berry Bros & Rudd, Andrew Bruce, The

Champagne House, First Quench, Fortnum & Mason, Harrods, Heyman Barwell Jones, S.H. Jones, Justerini & Brooks, Lay & Wheeler, Lea & Sandeman, Mitchells Wine Merchants, Nicolas, Planet Wine, Scatchard, Selfridges, John Stephenson, La Vigneronne, Villeneuve Wines, Wine Direct, The Winery

Rumigny T&W Wines

RV Growers & Châteaux

Rymill Estate Raeburn Fine Wines

Sacred Hill Stevens Garnier, Frank Stainton

Saint-Ceran Lay & Wheeler

Saint Flavy Hicks & Don

St Gall Bordeaux Direct, Marks & Spencer

St Honore First Quench

Ste Michelle Hedley Wright, Michael Jobling

Salon Corney & Barrow, Fortnum & Mason, Harvey Nichols, Nickolls & Perks, Planet Wine, Le Pont de la Tour, Selfridges, The Winery

San Carlo Corkscrew Wines, Forth Wines

Sandro Waterloo Wine Co

Santa Carolina Morrisons

Sarcey Justerini & Brooks

Saumur (Caves de) S.H. Jones, Nicolas

Saumur (Vignerons de) Yapp Brothers

Savs ChateauOnline

Scharffenberger Asda

Schloss Trier Budgens

Schlumberger Mitchells Wine Merchants, Penistone Court Wine Cellars,

Schramsberg Adnams, Four Walls Wine Co, Lay & Wheeler, Roberson

Seaview Addison, Amathus Wines, John Arkell Vintners, Asda, Booths, Budgens, Co-op, Co-operative, Corkscrew Wines, First Quench, Fuller's, Charles Hennings, S.H. Jones, Lay & Wheeler, Majestic Wine, Mitchells Wine Merchants, Morrisons, Oddbins, The Oxford Wine Company, Pallant Wines, Portland Wine Company, Safeway, Sainsbury's, Sandiway Wine Company, Sebastopol Wines, Edward Sheldon, Somerfield, Sommelier Wine Co, John Stephenson, Tesco, Unwins, Villeneuve Wines, Vin du Van, Waitrose, The Wine Society, Woodhouse Wines, Noel Young

Sécade Nicolas, The Wright Wine Company

Segura Viudas Direct Wine Shipments, Oddbins, Noel Young

Selaks Stevens Garnier

Selosse The Champagne House,

Lea & Sandeman, Ramsbottom Victuallers, Sandiway Wine Company

Seltz Waterloo Wine Co

Seppelt John Arkell Vintners, Booths, Co-operative, Corkscrew Wines, Eldridge Pope, First Quench, Fuller's, Hall Batson & Co, George Hill, Majestic Wine, Mitchells Wine Merchants, Morrisons, The Nobody Inn, Oddbins, The Oxford Wine Company, Pallant Wines, Philglas & Swiggot, Christopher Piper, Portland Wine Company, Roberson, Sainsbury's, Sandiway Wine Company, Satchells, Selfridges, Somerfield, John Stephenson, Unwins, Waitrose, Waterloo Wine Co, Noel Young

Serafina & Vidotto Hicks & Don, Winefinds

Serres John Arkell Vintners

Servin Rodney Densem Wines

Shadow Creek Addison, Adnams, Budgens, First Quench, Fuller's, Harrods, Harvey Nichols, House of Townend, S.H. Jones, Majestic Wine, Mitchells Wine Merchants, Oddbins, Christopher Piper, Terry Platt, Raeburn Fine Wines, Sommelier Wine Co, John Stephenson, Trout Wines, Unwins, Waverley Vintners, Noel Young

Sieur d'Arques ChateauOnline

Signat Eldridge Pope

Silver Ridge Co-op

Silver Swan Waitrose

Simon (André, Champagne) Corkscrew Wines, Mitchells Wine Merchants, Portland Wine Company, Satchells, Scatchard

Simon (André, Mousseux) Budgens, Corkscrew Wines, John Stephenson

Simonnet-Febvre The Burgundy Shuttle

Simonsig Kaapse Vonkel Corney & Barrow, The Nobody Inn

Soljan's Estate The Haslemere Cellar, Wine Raks, Noel Young

Sonoma Pacific Berry Bros & Rudd

Soutiran Eckington Wines, Springfield Wines

Soutiran-Pelletier Allez Vins!, Handford-Holland Park

Souza ChateauOnline

Sorevi Stevens Garnier

Stary Pizenec Rodney Densem Wines

Sumarroca The Wine Society

Sunnycliff Balls Brothers, Haynes Hanson & Clark, Lay & Wheeler, Portland Wine Company

Taittinger Addison, Amathus Wines, John Armit Wines, Averys, Bordeaux Direct, Budgens, Champagne Exchange, Drinks Direct, Ben Ellis, Forth Wines, Fortnum & Mason, Four

Walls Wine Co, Fuller's, Great Western Wine Company, Harrods, Harvey Nichols, House of Townend, Justerini & Brooks, Lay & Wheeler, Lea & Sandeman, madaboutwine.com, Majestic Wine, Mitchells Wine Merchants, Nicolas, Oddbins, The Oxford Wine Company, Penistone Court Wine Cellars, Planet Wine, Terry Platt, Le Pont de la Tour, Portland Wine Company, Roberson, Sainsbury's, Sommelier Wine Co, T&W Wines, Tesco, Ubiquitous Chip, Valvona & Crolla, Waters Wine Merchants, Waverley Vintners, The Winery

Taltarni Adnams, Averys, Connolly's, First Quench, Handford-Holland Park, Penistone Court Wine Cellars, Reid Wines, C.A. Rookes, Sandiway Wine Company, Selfridges, Edward Sheldon, Sommelier Wine Co, Frank Stainton, John Stephenson, Stevens Garnier, Unwins, Waters Wine Merchants, The Wine Bureau, Wine Raks, The Wright Wine Company

Tarlant Laytons

Tatachilla Adam Bancroft Associates, Philglas & Swiggot, Vin du Van

Teixidor Corkscrew Wines, George Hill

Telmont Majestic Wine

Tenuta San Vito Vinceremos

Terrace Road York Wines

Thévenin ChateauOnline

Thienot madaboutwine.com, Le Pont de la Tour, Unwins

Thiers Yapp Brothers

Tollana Averys

Törley Wines of Westhorpe

Tornay La Bouteille d'Or

Torre del Gall Amathus Wines, Averys, Budgens, First Quench, Fuller's, Hall Batson & Co, Harvey Nichols, House of Townend, Lay & Wheeler, Mitchells Wine Merchants, Terry Platt, Quellyn Roberts, Raeburn Fine Wines, Sommelier Wine Co, John Stephenson, Unwins, Villeneuve Wines

Torrerossa Majestic Wine

Torres Amathus Wines, Direct Wine Shipments, Ramsbottom Victuallers

Tribaut ChateauOnline

Trudel Waitrose

Turckheim Wine Raks, Noel Young

Tyrrell's The Wright Wine Company

Vaillant Booths

Val Brun Hedley Wright, Smedley Vintners

Valdivieso Bibendum, Sainsbury's

Valentin Friarwood

Vallformosa Forth Wines, Mitchells Wine Merchants

Van Loveren Villeneuve Wines

Varichon et Clerc Balls Brothers, Corney & Barrow, Ben Ellis, Lay & Wheeler, Reid Wines

Vaudon Haynes Hanson & Clark

Venoge Addison, Corkscrew Wines, Fuller's, Nicolas

Venus Tesco

Verdier Co-operative

Vergere The Butlers Wine Cellar

Vesselle (Georges) Nicolas, Jeroboams

Vesselle (Jean) Bouteille d'Or

Veuve Ambal King Wines

Veuve de Bomonde Connolly's, Corkscrew Wines, Great Western Wine Company, Hedley Wright, Shaws of Beaumaris, John Stephenson

Veuve Borodin Roberson

Veuve Chapelle Averys

Veuve Clicquot Ponsardin Addison, Adnams, Amathus Wines, John Arkell Vintners, John Armit Wines, Asda, Averys, Balls Brothers, Barrels & Bottles, Berry Bros & Rudd, Bibendum, Booths, Bordeaux Direct, Champagne Exchange, Connolly's, Co-op, Corkscrew Wines, Corney & Barrow, Rodney Densem Wines, Drinks Direct, Edencroft Fine Wines, Eldridge Pope, Ben Ellis, First Quench, Le Fleming Wines, Forth Wines, Fortnum & Mason, Four Walls Wine Co, Fuller's, Goedhuis & Company, Great Grog, Hall Batson & Co, Handford-Holland Park, Harrods, Harvey Nichols, Haynes Hanson & Clark, Charles Hennings, Heyman Barwell Jones, George Hill, House of Townend, Jeroboams, S.H. Jones, Justerini & Brooks, Lay & Wheeler, Laytons, Lea & Sandeman, Lloyd Taylor Wines, Majestic Wine, Mitchells Wine Merchants, Morris & Verdin, Morrisons, New London Wine, Nickolls & Perks, Nicolas, Oddbins, The Oxford Wine Company, Pallant Wines, Penistone Court Wine Cellars, Philglas & Swiggot, Christopher Piper, Planet Wine, Terry Platt, Le Pont de la Tour, Portland Wine Company, Quellyn Roberts, Raeburn Fine Wines, Reid Wines, La Reserve, Roberson, Rogers Wine Co, Safeway, Sainsbury's, Sandiway Wine Company, Satchells, Scatchard, Selfridges, Edward Sheldon, Sommelier Wine Co, Frank Stainton, John Stephenson, Stevens Garnier, Stratford's Wine Shippers, Tanners Wines, Tesco, Unwins, Valvona & Crolla, La Vigneronne,

Villeneuve Wines, Waitrose, Waters Wine Merchants, Waverley Vintners, The Wine Bureau, Wine Raks, The Winery, The Wine Society, Woodhouse Wines, The Wright Wine Company, Peter Wylie, Noel Young, Young's

Veuve Corbin Waterloo Wine Co

Veuve Delaroy Bibendum

Veuve Fourny Christopher Piper, Shaws of Beaumaris, The Wine Bureau

Veuve Honorain Co-op

Veuve Lorin Berry Bros & Rudd

Veuve Noiziers Co-operative

Veuve Oudinot Mitchells Wine Merchants, Penistone Court Wine Cellars

Veuve Pelletier Eckington Wines

Veuve Truffeau Marks & Spencer

Veuve Valmante Addison, Terry Platt, Waters Wine Merchants

Veuve du Vernay Booths, Budgens, Co-op, Co-operative, First Quench, Forth Wines, Mitchells Wine Merchants, Waters Wine Merchants, Waverley Vintners, The Wright Wine Company

Viardot La Bouteille d'Or

Vicomte d'Almon Balls Brothers

Villa Pigna Tesco

Villelonge S.H. Jones

Vilmart Direct Wine Shipments, Selfridges, Shaws of Beaumaris, Noel Young

Windy Peak Brian Coad Fine Wines

Wissembourg George Hill

Wolfberger The Butlers Wine Cellar, C.A. Rookes

Wolf Blass Mitchells Wine Merchants

Wunsch et Mann Penistone Court Wine Cellars

Yaldara Booths, The Butlers Wine Cellar, Brian Coad Fine Wines, Hedley Wright, Majestic Wine, Oddbins, Terry Platt, Satchells, Scatchard, Stratfords's Wine Shippers

Yalumba Adnams, Booths, Co-op, First Quench, Fuller's, Majestic Wine, Mitchells Wine Merchants, James Nicholson, Oddbins, Quellyn Roberts, Safeway, Sainsbury's, Somerfield, Sommelier Wine Co, Stevens Garnier, Unwins, Vin du Van, Waitrose

Yarden Averys

Yellowglen Majestic Wine, Mitchells Wine Merchants, Oddbins, John Stephenson

Young & Saunders Ubiquitous Chip

Zonin Booths, House of Townend

STOCKIST PROFILES

OWN LABELS
All the stockists were asked to submit their own-label Champagnes and other sparkling wines to the author for tasting, and those recommended are listed below. Since the NM (*négociant-manipulant*) number is the code to who produced the own-label in question and stockists occasionally change their suppliers, I have included this important detail as part of the name of the wine in question.

PRICES
The prices given in this section are inclusive of VAT, and correct at the time of tasting, but like the price of most products can be expected to increase rather than decrease. Readers are advised not to compare prices between retail and mail-order outlets, since one sells wine by the single bottle, while the other is effectively a wholesaler with a minimum quantity of 12 bottles. Furthermore, a retailer may offer various special discounts for multiple purchases, which cannot be taken into account here, whereas mail-order operations have many variables that affect the per bottle price (mixed or unbroken cases, delivery charges, free delivery, quantity discount). Comparing prices between different mail-order firms is thus impossible, let alone comparing mail-order with retail prices.

✉ Mail order available

3D Wines
Holly Lodge, High Street, Swineshead, Lincs PE20 3LH
☎ 01205 820745
🖷 01205 821042 ✉
info@3dwines.com
www.3dwines.com
3D Wines is an "innovative wine club for Francophiles", supplying wines from over 30 vineyards in France, including two in Champagne and one that produces sparkling wine in Touraine. They host regular tastings and events in the UK and France, including banquets in Champagne cellars.
🔟 CHAMPAGNE MICHEL LENIQUE NV BRUT SÉLECTION, 3D WINES
More character than finesse, but there's an honesty about this rustic, lemony Champagne I like.
❗ Now–2001 £12.18

Addison Wines
Village Farm, Lilleshall, Newport, Shropshire TF10 9HB
☎ 0800 197 3555
🖷 01952 677309 ✉
sales@addisonwines.com
www.addisonwines.com
Addison has recently dropped its BOB offerings in exchange for exclusive and semi-

exclusive agreements with growers. With the Vallée de la Marne, Montagne de Reims and Cotes des Blancs all represented, Addison hopes to provide a greater sense of terroir and varietal character in its Champagne offerings.

Adnams
The Crown, High Street, Southwold, Suffolk IP18 6DP
☎ 01502 727222
🖷 01502 727273 ✉
wines@adnams.co.uk
Visiting sleepy Southwold is like entering a time-warp, with Victorian bathing huts by the beach and beer delivered by horse and cart. Adnams has one of the best wine lists in the country, including a select range of Champagnes and sparkling wines, including own-label Champagne, which is back in the recommended category, and Adnams Fizz, a sparkling French Chardonnay.
🔟 ADNAMS SPÉCIAL CUVÉE CHAMPAGNE NV BRUT
Made by SEDI Champagne Chouilly, this cuvée is fresh, light and sweetish in an amylic style, although the peardrop aroma should gradually dissipate.
❗ Now–2002 £15.25

Allez Vins!
PO Box 1019, Long Itchington, Rugby, Warwickshire CV23 8ZU
☎ 01926 811969
🖷 01926 811969 ✉
avsales@bigfoot.com
www.allezvins.co.uk
Owner John Bouttal specializes in French regional wines from quality-minded growers such as Soutiran-Pelletier in Champagne (*see Tasting Notes and Scores*).

Amathus Wines
Unit 20, Mowlem Industrial Estate, Leeside Road, London N17 OQJ
☎ 020 8808 4181
🖷 020 8808 8538 ✉
amathus.wines@dial.pipex.com
Unlike most retail or wholesale operations, Amathus tends to list the whole range of *cuvées*, including different bottle-sizes and various vintages for each of the producers it deals with. House Champagne Claude Renoux is produced by Vincent Testulat.

Arkell's Vintners
Arkell's Brewery Ltd, Stratton St Margaret,

Swindon SN2 6RU
☎ 01793 823026
📠 01793 828864 ✉
arkells@compuserve.com
www.swindonweb.com
Nick Arkell runs the wine division of his family's brewery, which owns 95 licensed outlets and supplies 400 free houses, pubs, hotels and restaurants. Bernard Gaucher is the house Champagne.

John Armit Wines
5 Royalty Studios,
105 Lancaster Road,
London W11 1QF

ATTENTION UNLISTED STOCKISTS

It is hoped to build this section into the most comprehensive fizz buyer's reference available in the UK, so if you would like to be included in a future edition, please contact Tom Stevenson at:

tom.stevenson@
fizz.worldonline.co.uk

Warning: Any other unsolicited mail received at this address will be ignored

Please note that inclusion in this guide involves no charge whatsoever, although stockists are expected to update or correct any factual information given in their profiles below, and those with own-label products are requested to submit tasting samples at their own cost. Stockists in previous editions who have not updated their information have been deleted for the sake of accuracy, but are most welcome to appear in future editions.

☎ 020 7727 6846
📠 020 7727 7133 ✉
info@armit.co.uk
www.armit.co.uk
An upmarket, beautifully produced list, with a small selection of Champagne, John Armit considers the highly reputable Beaumont des Crayères cooperative

as its house Champagne. No other sparkling wines listed.

Asda
Asda House, Southbank, Great Wilson Street, Leeds LS1 5AD
☎ 0113 243 5435
📠 0113 241 8666
www.asda.co.uk
One of the country's leading supermarket groups, Asda has more than 230 superstores, and a range of own-label fizz that usually does well in blind tastings.

Australian Wine Club
Kershaw House, Great West Road, Hounslow, Middlesex TW5 0BU
☎ 020 8538 0718
📠 020 8572 5200 ✉
orders@austwine.demon.
  co.uk
www.australian-wine.co.uk
This by-the-case mail-order club ships just two sparkling wines, but one of them is the fabulous Joseph from the Primo Estate (*see Tasting Notes and Scores*).

Averys
Orchard House, Southfield Road, Nailsea Bristol BS48 1JN
☎ 01275 811100
📠 01275 811101 ✉
averywines@aol.com
A large range of alternative sparkling wines, including sparkling red Burgundy, and such obscurities as Israeli fizz and Vin Fou ("Mad Wine") from the Arbois, plus a complete range of Averys own-label Champagne.

Ballantynes of Cowbridge
3 Westgate, Cowbridge, Vale of Glamorgan CF71 7AQ
☎ 01446 774840
📠 01446 775253 ✉
enq@ballantynes.co.uk
www.ballantynes.co.uk
A small range of Champagnes from Gosset, Gardet and Lechere.

Balls Brothers
313 Cambridge Heath, Road London E2 9LQ
☎ 020 7739 1642
📠 020 7729 0258 ✉
sales@ballsbrothers.co.uk
www.ballsbrothers.co.uk
In addition to Vicomte d'Almon, Balls Brothers' house Champagne, there is a selection of mostly quality *grandes marques*, plus a few New World goodies such as Pelorus and Quartet.

Adam Bancroft Associates
Eastbridge Office North, New Covent Garden Market, London SW8 5JB
☎ 020 7627 8700
📠 020 7627 8766 ✉
This mail-order only business remains the best source for Champagne Médot and Tatachilla Sparkling Malbec.

Barrels & Bottles
3 Oak Street, Sheffield S8 9UB
☎ 0114 255 6611
📠 0114 255 1010 ✉
sales@barrelsandbottles.
  co.uk
www.barrelsandbottles.co.uk
The retail arm of The Wine Schoppen offers a small but good selection of Champagne.

Bat & Bottle
Knightley Grange Office, Grange Road Knightley Woodseaves Staffordshire ST20 0JU
☎ 01785 284495
📠 01785 284877 ✉
sales@batandbottle-wine.
  co.uk
Ben and Emma Robson initially planned to deal exclusively with Mediterranean wines, but have expanded into wines from England, Australia, New Zealand and California. Fizz selection restricted to Champagne from Gardet, Cava from Juvé y Camps and English sparkling wine from Chapel Down.

Berkmann Wine Cellars
12 Brewery Road, London N7 9NH

☎ 020 7609 4711
℻ 020 7607 0018 ✉
postmaster@berkmann.
co.uk
Initially a supplier to London restaurants, but increasingly a general wholesale and mail-order operation, with a very strong list, particularly in Burgundy. The bubblies are relatively few, but high quality. Berkmann Cellars was appointed agent for Deutz in 1998, and has been a long time supporter of Champagne Bruno Paillard.

Berry Bros & Rudd
3 St James's Street,
London SW1A 1EG
☎ 020 7396 9600
℻ 020 7396 9611 ✉
orders@berry-bros.co.uk
www.berry-bros.co.uk *or*
www.bbr.com
A classic range of *grande marque* Champagnes, Berry Bros & Rudd have also been shippers of Champagne Binet since 1887 and all their own-label range are supplied by Binet (which effectively means Germain). Good source for Théophile Roederer.

Bibendum
113 Regents Park Road,
London NW1 8UR
☎ 020 7916 7706
℻ 020 7916 7705 ✉
sales@bibendum-wine.co.uk
www.bibendum-wine.co.uk
Although Bibendum stocks a brilliant range of wines, making it the Oddbins of the independent sector, I have commented in the past about its Champagnes and sparkling wines, which lack the same detailed attention as the rest of the range. Recent additions, however, have started to improve the situation, particularly Bibendum's acquisition of the top-quality Champagne Bruno Paillard agency.

Booths
4 Fishergate, Preston
PR1 3LJ
☎ 01772 251701

℻ 01772 204316
This Yorkshire-based supermarket group of just 24 outlets continues to give the best big national chains a run for their money. Own-label Champagne usually does well in blind tastings, but it was not submitted this year.

Bordeaux Direct
New Aquitaine House,
Exeter Way, Theale,
Reading, Berks RG7 4PL
☎ 0118 903 0903
℻ 0118 903 0130 ✉
dwines@dwines.co.uk
A French wine specialist with a reputation for digging out interesting new finds, Bordeaux Direct is associated with The Sunday Times Wine Club. Its wines fared exceptionally well this year.
🄳 CHAMPAGNE POL D'AMBERT NV BRUT, NM 131-008, DIRECT WINES
Made by Bricout (NM 131 in small type on the label), this wine is currently dominated by perfumed, rich and creamy Chardonnay fruit.
❗ Now–2003 £16.99
🄲 CA'SOLARE MOSCATO SPUMANTE NV DOLCE, DIRECT WINES
Fresh with floral-Moscato aromatics, this fresh and breezy wine tastes truly sweet against other non-designated Moscato. You have to compare against a good Asti to notice the difference.
❗ Now £5.95
🄵 ROCHE LACOUR 1996 BLANC DE BLANCS BRUT, DIRECT WINES
A fine pin-cushion mousse keeps the fruit fresh, crisp and breezy. Hint of almonds.
❗ Now £9.99

The Bottleneck
7/9 Charlotte Street,
Broadstairs, Kent CT10 1LR
☎ 01843 861095
℻ 01843 861095
Proprietors Chris and Lin Beckett have 55 years' wine trade experience between them and have won many awards, including
"Off-Licence of the Year"

1989. They still retain an enthusiasm for wine and enjoy witnessing the many changes in the wine trade, which probably accounts for their selections at The Bottleneck being more New World than Old World.

Bottom's Up
See First Quench

La Bouteille d'Or
Queens Lodge,
Queens Club Gardens,
London W14 9TA
☎ 020 7385 3122
℻ 020 7385 3122 ✉
labouteilledor@newbury.net
Those lucky enough to be on Patricia Norman's mailing list know that she only sells Champagne from a select few quality-minded growers. She can arrange for collection from Calais, saving customers duty and VAT.
🄳 CHAMPAGNE ETIENNE DEFOUR 1995 CUVÉE 2000 BRUT
This Champagne was made by Ellner and exhibits lovely fruit from nose to finish. It might sound a bit picky, but the aftertaste could do with a touch more finesse and with a little time in bottle, it might achieve that.
❗ Now–2003 £12.95

Andrew Bruce
Second Floor, 22 Hans Place, London SW1X 0EP
☎ 020 7225 1982
℻ 020 7225 0366 ✉
abrucewine@compuserve.
com
www.abruce.co.uk
A good source for Ruinart and Pol Roger.

Budgens
Stonefield Way, Ruislip,
Middlesex HA4 0JR
☎ 020 8422 9511
℻ 020 8864 2800
The new buyer here is Christine Sandys, who did such a good job at Cooperative (as opposed to Co-op) superstores. Hopefully Budgens' top brass have learned from their

mistake and will not lumber her with all the responsibility and no staff. In the meantime, Ms Sandys has hacked out some of the deadwood to make room for a new, rationalized range. This resulted in some interesting bargains during the summer, as certain stocks were disposed of.

❽⓪ CHAMPAGNE J. FABRICE NV BRUT RÉSERVE, NM 120, BUDGENS
Fat and tasty, with good acidity and length, but with a peppery edge that will require at least one year in bottle to smooth out. Made by Boizel.
➤ 2001–2002 £13.49

The Burgundy Shuttle
13 Mandeville Courtyard,
142 Battersea Park Road,
London SW11 4NB
☎ 020 7498 0755
📠 020 7498 0724 ✉
peter@burgundyshuttle.
   ltd.uk
In addition to Champagnes Gremillet and Marguet-Bonnerave, this Burgundy specialist stocks two Crémant de Bourgogne, Simonnet-Febvre and Letourneau.

The Butlers Wine Cellar
247 Queens Park Road,
Brighton BN2 2XJ
☎ 01273 698724
📠 01273 622761 ✉
butlerswine.cellar2@cw
   com.net
An eclectic range that majors on Champagnes from a grower called Martial-Couvreur and excellent Italian fizz from Banfi and Bava, plus a number of oddities, including the occasional small lot of mature Champagne.

Anthony Byrne Fine Wines
Unit 1-7 Ramsey Business Park, Stocking Fen Road, Ramsey, Cambridgeshire PE17 1UR
☎ 01487 814555
📠 01487 814962 ✉
The list in general consists of

a fabulous selection of great wines from star producers, which for Champagne includes the UK agency for the excellent Champagne Drappier.

Cave Cru Classé
Unit 13 Leathermarket,
Weston Street, London
SE1 3ER
☎ 020 7378 8579
📠 020 7378 8544 ✉
enquiries@ccc.co.uk
www.cave-cru-classe.com
A specialist in mature vintages of the finest wines in the world, including some of the greatest Champagnes.

The Champagne Company
26 Astwood Mews,
London SW7 4DE
☎ 020 7373 5578
📠 020 7373 4777 ✉
sales@champagnecom
   pany.co.uk
www.champagnecompany.
   co.uk
The Champagne Company sells just one Champagne, Palmer, a cooperative brand I have great respect for. You can buy all the different cuvées and every bottle size.

The Champagne House
28 Longmoore Street,
London SW1V 1JF
☎ 020 7828 4615
📠 020 7828 4615 ✉
This low-profile Champagne specialist for private customers is run by Champagne aficionados Richard and Jenny Freeman.

Andrew Chapman Fine Wines
Freepost (SCE6711),
14 Haywards Road,
Drayton, Oxfordshire
OX14 4LB
☎ 01235 550707
📠 01235 550808 ✉
orders@acfw.co.uk
www.acfw.co.uk
An interesting, hand-picked selection of wines from all over the world, but still pretty thin on the ground when it comes to bubbly.

Charterhouse Wine Emporium
86 Goding Street,
London SE11 5AW
☎ 020 7587 1302
📠 020 7587 0982
Focuses on Georges Gardet and Joseph Perrier, with a few other *grande marque cuvées* and Renard Barbier as the house Champagne.

ChateauNet
www.chateaunet.com
This French-based cyberspace stockist offers just one Champagne, Gaston Perrin, a small grower from Festigny.

ChateauOnline
www.chateauonline.com
Another cyberspace trader, but this one has much more to offer in all categories from inexpensive Champagnes to top-of-the-line, and they are all very well selected too. The number of wines in total has doubled from 700 to 1,400 and these are now sourced from 26 countries, rather than 15. Delivery is throughout the EU. ChateauOnline is also a well-thought-out site, with a good mix of information and a budding forum, although it could do with some reference material, such as an online encyclopedia, atlas and lexicon. This is, however, merely nit-picking. In 1999 ChateauOnline was selected as one of the best 10 e-commerce sites. It operates in French and German as well as English, and is backed up by a staff of 70 with offices in London, Paris and Germany. But above all, the site manager for the UK is Katrina Williams, who in her previous incarnation as Katrina Thom, was the famed Bimbo of Boulogne, as all owners of *The Cross Channel Drinks Guide* will be well aware.

Chateaux Wines
Paddock House,
Upper Tockington Road,
Tockington, Bristol
BS32 4LQ
☎ 01454 613959

FAX 01454 613959 ✉
cheryl.miller@bristol.ac.uk
www.btinternet.com/
~chateauxwines/
A small list with a faithful
following, David and Cheryl
Miller offer the entire range
of Laurent-Perrier as their
personal choice or Bauchet
for those on a budget.

Brian Coad Fine Wines
66 Cole Lane, Stowford
Park, Ivybridge, Devon
PL21 0PN
☎ 01752 896545
FAX 01752 691160 ✉
This is the place to go for the
entire range of Théophile
Roederer, including larger
bottle sizes up to Methuselah.

Connolly's
Arch 13, 220 Livery Street,
Birmingham B3 1EU
☎ 0121 236 9269/3837
FAX 0121 233 2339 ✉
connowine@aol.com
Not a large range, but a well
picked one, Connolly's is
particularly serious about
Champagne and offers some
remarkable prices.

Co-op
New Century House,
Manchester M60 4ES
☎ 0161 834 1212
FAX 0161 827 5117
The Co-op, as distinct from
the Cooperative featured
below, has some 2,500 stores
of varying size and thus a
varying range of products. All
hint of organization and
follow-up seems to have
deserted the Co-op along with
the departure of its head
buyer, Arabella Woodrow
MW. No submissions this
year, and I had to request a
sample of the Aussie-
influenced Spanish fizzy red.
As my old teacher used to say:
can do better!
76 TEMPRANILLO BRUT NV
SPARKLING RED WINE, CWS
*David Kingsbury, an
ex-Rosemount enologist and
former flying-winemaker for
Hugh Ryman, was
commissioned to bring a little
Aussie red-bubble expertise to*

*Spain, where he produced this
raspberry-ripple fizz from
native Tempranillo grapes. Its
sweetish, creamy-oaky fruit
could do with more acidity,
but there is a bit of tannin to
add grip and for £5.49 what
more could you expect?*
❢ Now £5.49

Cooperative
Sandbrook Park, Sandbrook
Way, Rochdale OL11 1SA
☎ 01706 713000/01706
891628
FAX 01706 892195
Some 290 superstores trade
under the Cooperative, rather
than Co-op, banner, and they
represent a completely
separate ownership, although
they all share a hard-core of
Co-op own-label wines
(supplied through CWS, the
Co-operative Wholesale
Society).

Corkscrew Wines
Arch 5, Viaduct Estate,
Carlisle, Cumbria CA2 5BN
☎ 01228 543033
FAX 01228 543033 ✉
wines@corkscrewwines.
demon.co.uk
www.corkscrew-wines.com
An interesting selection of
Champagne and sparkling
wine, including cultish New
World offerings such as
Roederer Estate's Quartet
and Cloudy Bay's Pelorus,
with new offerings this year
from Louis Roederer and
Nyetimber.

Corney & Barrow
12 Helmet Row,
London EC1V 3TD
☎ 020 7251 4051
FAX 020 7608 1373 ✉
adam.brett-smith@corbar.
co.uk
City winemerchant with an
impeccable list, including
various vintages of Dom
Pérignon, the agency for
Salon and Guy de Chassey as
its house Champagne. Apart
from Pelorus the range of
sparkling wine alternatives is
pretty dull, but who in the
City drinks any sparkling
wine except maybe Pelorus?

Cubic World
See King Wines

Rodney Densem Wines
Regent House, Lancaster
Fields, Crewe Gates Farm
Estate, Crewe Cheshire
CW1 6FF
☎ 01270 212200
FAX 01270 212300 ✉
A small but well-chosen list
of Champagnes, plus some
interesting fizz from other
places, such as Argyle Brut
from Oregon, and Green
Point from Australia.

Direct Wine Shipments
5/7 Corporation Square,
Belfast BT1 3AJ
☎ (028) 90 238700
FAX (028) 90 240202 ✉
enquiry@directwine.co.uk
www.directwine.co.uk
Belfast's best winemerchant
offers an excellent range,
including the star-performing
Champagne Vilmart and Miru
Miru sparkling wine.

Drinks Cabin
See First Quench

Drinks Direct
☎ 0800 232221
www.drinks-direct.co.uk
Part of First Quench, Drinks
Direct is a gift service, with a
smallish range of good
Champagne and a few
sparkling wines. Delivery
takes two days and there is a
charge of £5.99 per delivery,
which includes gift-wrapping
up to 12 wines. Also capable
of delivering anywhere in the
world, but this is subject to a
surcharge and the wines will
obviously take longer than
two days to arrive.
See First Quench

Eckington Wines
2 Ravencar Road,
Eckington,
Sheffield S21 4JZ
☎ 01246 433213
FAX 01246 433213 ✉
qandrewloughran@su
panet.com
Andrew Loughran majors on
a Champagne grower called
Soutiran, but also goes in for

several vintages of Dom Pérignon, Dom Pérignon Rosé in magnum and an eclectic smattering of other fizzies, including Didier Cornillon's Clairette de Die (*see Tasting Notes and Scores* for his Méthode Dioise Ancestrale).

Edencroft Fine Wines
8-10 Hospital Street, Nantwich, Cheshire CW5 5RV
☎ 01270 629975
🖷 01270 625302 ✉
edencroftfinewines@ btinternet.com
www.edencroft.com
The full range of Canard Duchêne, Jean Moutardier, Krug and Veuve Clicquot, the latter in a complete range of bottle-sizes.

Eldridge Pope & Co plc
Weymouth Avenue, Dorchester, Dorset DT1 1QT
☎ 01305 251251
🖷 01305 258300 ✉
One of the best and biggest wine lists in the country, Eldridge Pope also owns Reynier London (a separate company to Mark Reynier Fine Wines), a faithful long-term shipper of De Venoge, and stocks all the famous Champagne names. Own-label Champagnes sold under The Chairman's and Reynier labels.

Ben Ellis Wines
Brockham Wine Cellars, Wheelers Lane, Brockham, Surrey RH3 7HJ
☎ 01737 842160
🖷 01737 843210 ✉
ben_ellis@lineone.net
An up-and-coming winemerchant who focuses on Billecart-Salmon in all styles and sizes, but also stocks the non-vintage Brut of Bollinger, Gallimard, Taittinger and Veuve Clicquot, with some splendid prestige *cuvées* in the Fine Wine section. However, the sparkling wine choice could still do with some serious attention.

El Vino Co
Vintage House, 1 Hare Place, Fleet Street, London EC4Y 1BJ
☎ 020 7936 4948
🖷 020 7936 2367 ✉
A small selection of superb *grande marque* Champagne, but an even smaller, much less imaginative range of sparkling wines.

The Fine Champagne Co
64 Linden Gardens, London W4 2EW
☎ 020 8994 4010
🖷 020 8994 7808 ✉
john@hammond-pr.co.uk
Set up in 1998 to sell the grower Champagnes of Bernard Brémont and Mignon & Pierrel.

The Firkin
See First Quench

First Quench
Sefton House, 42 Church Road, Welwyn Garden City, Hertfordshire AL8 6PJ
☎ 01707 385000
🖷 01707 385004 ✉
The country's largest retail drinks group was created when Thresher and Victoria Wine merged to form First Quench, which now includes Bottoms Up, Drinks Cabin, Drinks Direct, The Firkin, Haddows, Home Run, Hutton's, Thresher, Victoria Wine, Victoria Wine Cellars and Wine Rack (*see* separate entries). Needless to say that Bottom's Up and Wine Rack have the best selections, but any Champagne on the combined list can be ordered through any branch of any of its chain. The entire list is impressive, with Alexandre Bonnet and Praisac (made by F. Bonnet) at the cheap end, through Malard for value, to a string of overpriced Dom Pérignon vintages dating back to 1959 at the top end, with virtually every *cuvée* and bottle-size from Bollinger, Charles Heidsieck, Lanson, Laurent-Perrier, Moët, Roederer, Perrier-Jouët, Pol Roger, Pommery, Taittinger and Veuve Clicquot between.

Le Fleming Wines
19 Spenser Road, Harpenden, Hertfordshire AL5 5NW
☎ 01582 760125
🖷 01582 760125 ✉
cherry@lefleming.swin ternet.co.uk
Le Fleming Wines is run by La Cherry Jenkins, who has changed address, but is still living in a madhouse with two dogs the size of horses (I haven't heard from the rugby team). This busy one-woman operation has some stunning wines, but not too many with bubbles in, although most of what she does is well worth buying. Her customers are very lucky indeed, especially since she has recently added Charles Melton Sparkling Shiraz (90 points, *see Tasting Notes and Scores*) to the list.

Forth Wines
Crawford Place, Milnathort, Kinross-shire KY13 7XF
☎ 01577 866001
🖷 01577 866020 ✉
This list contains a number of *grande marque* Champagnes, but the focus remains on Mansard (*see Tasting Notes and Scores*), which is exclusive to Forth Wines. There is a fair selection of other sparkling wines, but most are dependable rather than exciting.

Fortnum & Mason
181 Piccadilly, London W1A 1ER
☎ 020 7734 8040
🖷 020 7437 3278 ✉
info@fortnumandmason. com
www.fortnumandmason.com
As you would expect, there are plenty of famous names and lots of excellent vintages in Fortnum & Mason's Champagne list. You won't get the cheapest prices here, but regular Fortnum & Mason customers are happy to pay a premium for the sort of service they expect and by all accounts receive. Other sparkling wines include some impressive names too: Croser,

Green Point, Graham Beck, Tresor, Pelorus, Quartet and last but not least England's own high-flying Nyetimber.

80 FORTNUM & MASON CHAMPAGNE NV BLANC DE BLANCS, BRUT GRAND CRU *This wine is made by Hostomme in a fresh, light, aperitif style that verges on amylic.*
❗ Now–2002 £19.95

Four Walls Wine Co

1 High Street, Chilgrove, Nr. Chichester, W. Sussex PO18 9HX
☎ 01243 535360
🗎 01243 535418 ✉
fourwallswine@compuserve.com

Although the Four Walls Wine Company supplies and delivers to restaurants and hotels, it also serves private customers, who can collect from their office Monday-Friday 8am–5pm by arrangement or pay for delivery. One of Four Walls' specialities is to locate and supply mature wine for its private customers. Excellent Champagnes include a wide range of *cuvées* and vintages from Bollinger, Cattier (including Clos du Moulin), Gosset, Roederer, Taittinger, Veuve Clicquot, Krug, Cristal and Dom Pérignon, plus Boizel and Canard-Duchêne in the value for money category. With Pelorus, Quartet and Nyetimber representing the sparkling wine alternatives, I think even the fussiest fizz aficionado would find very little here to complain about.

Friarwood

26 New Kings Road, Fulham, London SW6 4ST
☎ 020 7736 2628
🗎 020 7731 0411 ✉
sales@friarwood.com
www.friarwood.com

This upmarket winemerchant is still the best source for Mailly Grand Cru Champagne, in addition to which it now stocks various *grandes marques*, including

Bollinger, Dom Pérignon, Cristal, Krug and Belle Epoque.

Fullers

Griffin Brewery, Chiswick Lane South,Chiswick, London W4 2QB
☎ 020 8996 2000
🗎 020 8995 0230 ✉
www.fullers.co.uk

Recently taken over by Unwins, all Fuller shops should be rebadged by September, but on past experiences of such takeovers I think it prudent to keep Fullers entry in the Guide for another year. The two lists have been rationalized into one, with some wines from both being kept, although not necessarily the best choice in every case.

Gauntleys of Nottingham

4 High Street Exchange Arcade, Nottingham NG1 2ET
☎ 0115 911 0555
🗎 0115 911 0557 ✉
rhone@innotts.uk

The source for Champagne Vilmart, Gauntleys are now starting to import Billecart-Salmon. Like Winston Churchill, Gauntleys are easily satisfied with the best.

Goedhuis & Company

6 Rudolf Place, Miles Street, London SW8 1RP
☎ 020 7793 7900
🗎 020 7793 7170 ✉
goedhuis@btinternet.com
www.goedhuis.com
www.wineuk.com

Three vintages of Krug, one both in bottle and magnum; two vintages of Pol Roger, including the 1990 in magnum, which I would happily kill for (okay, that's a bit of an exaggeration); plus Billecart-Salmon, Laurent-Perrier, Charles Heidsieck, Louis Roederer and Dom Pérignon. If that does not make you phone for a list, then let me get back to the Pol Roger 1990 in magnum. I've tasted this in magnum only once and was blown

away. Goedhuis want £329 for a case of six magnums. That's the equivalent of less than £28 a bottle, but in glorious magnum. That's daylight robbery! You robbing Goedhuis, that is. Or you could buy six magnums of Cristal 1993 for £646 – it's sublime stuff (92 points) – but I know which one I'd buy (after all the Pol Roger 1990 in magnum knocks the spots off the bottle and the bottle jumped from 95 to 96 points this year). Of course you could always buy Krug 1982 in magnum. If I had the money, I'd buy the lot. In the meantime, I think I'll get those magnums of Pol.

Great Grog

Unit 10, West Gorgie Park, Edinburgh EH14 1UT
☎ 0131 444 2332
🗎 0131 444 2552 ✉
great-grog-company@lineone.net
www.greatgrog.com

Great Grog is the creation of Richard Meadows and Martin Thorpe, ex-Oddbins managers with over 15 years' combined experience in the wine trade. Established a little over a year ago, their list aims to combine value for money with eclectic appeal (sounds Oddbinian to me). The best buy here is Champagne Serge Mathieu.

Great Western Wine Company

Wells Road, Bath BA2 3AP
☎ 01225 322800
🗎 01225 442139 ✉
greatwesternwine.co.uk
www.greatwesternwine.co.uk

As a general philosophy the Great Western Wine Company looks for up-and-coming producers whose wines are often not available elsewhere. Most of these wines are from small, individualistic growers, but in the Champagne selection there is just one grower, Jean Moutardier, which is run by Englishman Jonathan Saxby, whose wines normally do very well in the Guide, but were not submitted this year. Great Western also focuses on Joseph Perrier, with the odd *cuvée* from Laurent-Perrier, Taittinger, Roederer and Bollinger.

Greek Wine Centre
46–48 Underdale Road, Shrewsbury, Shropshire SY2 5DT
C 01743 364636
FAX 01743 367960 ✉
greekwines.uk@clara.net
www.greekwines.uk.
    clara.net
The eternally ebullient Jordanis Pertridis stocks all the best Greek wines including Ode Panos and the exciting new arrival on the Greek fizz scene, Villa Amalia (*see Tasting Notes and Scores*).

Growers & Châteaux
Hartland House, Church Street, Reigate, Surrey RH2 OAD
C 01372 374239
FAX 01372 377610 ✉
info@winesite.net
www.winesite.net
Philip and Jane Wharam are agents for Maxims and Bugatti (both made by De Castellane), and import two *grand cru* growers, J.P. Husson from Aÿ and Pierre Callot from Avize, plus Raoul Collet, a small, quality-conscious cooperative based in Aÿ (*see Tasting Notes and Scores*).

Haddows
See First Quench

Hall & Woodhouse
The Brewery, Blandford St. Mary, Dorset DT11 9LS
C 01258 452141
FAX 01258 454700 ✉
admin@hall-woodhouse.
    co.uk
www.breworld.com/badger
    (*brewery only*)
This famous Dorset brewery is better known for its award-winning Tanglefoot Strong Ale than for any wines, but it has a small selection of *grandes marques* and a house

Champagne called Montarlau, plus Mumm Cuvée Napa, Seaview and Lindauer leading what is otherwise a rather lacklustre list of sparkling wine alternatives.

Hall Batson & Co
168 Wroxham Road, Norwich, Norfolk NR7 8DE
C 01603 415115
FAX 01603 484096 ✉
hbwine@paston.co.uk
www.therepertoire.co.uk
A few interesting Champagnes and sparkling wines. House Champagne under the Lanvin label from the same stable as Charles de Cazanove (*see Tasting Notes and Scores*).

Handford-Holland Park
12 Portland Road, London W11 4LA
C 020 7221 9614
FAX 020 7221 9613 ✉
www.handford_wine.demon.
    co.uk
webmaster@handford_wine.
    demon.co.uk
Master of Wine James Handford has a soft spot for Champagnes from Brochet-Hervieux and Soutiran-Pelletier, which he backs up with only the best from Bollinger, Gosset, Roederer and Veuve Clicquot, plus a small, extremely well selected range of sparkling wine alternatives.

Roger Harris Wines
Loke Farm, Weston Longville, Norfolk NR9 5LG
C 01603 880171
FAX 01603 880291 ✉
sales@rhwine.co.uk
www.rhwine.co.uk
The world's foremost Beaujolais specialist focuses on a single grower Champagne, Ruelle Pertois from Moussy.

Harrods
Knightsbridge, London SW1X 7XL
C 020 7730 1234
FAX 020 7225 5823
The world's most famous store lists all the famous

grande marque names, as might be expected, plus a large range of own-label Champagnes, which remains untested by this author.

Harvey Nichols
109–125, Knightsbridge, London SW1 7RJ
C 020 7235 5000
FAX 020 7235 5020 ✉
The most exclusive of top people's shops, Harvey Nichols offers a good range of fizz, with its own-label Champagne supplied by Médot.

The Haslemere Cellar
2 Lower Street, Haslemere, Surrey GU27 2NX
C 01428 645081
FAX 01428 645108 ✉
hcellar@haslemere.com
A traditional wine merchant that selects wines mostly from smaller independent houses and winemakers, who provide quality at sensible prices, according to owner-buyer Richard Royds. Gosset and Gardet are the mainstays.

Haynes Hanson & Clark
25 Eccleston Street, London SW1W 9NP
C 020 7259 0102
FAX 020 7259 0103 ✉
london@hhandc.uk.co
Good value house Champagne under the Pierre Vaudon label (*see* under Union Champagne in *Tasting Notes and Scores*), a quality-focused range of *grandes marques* and a very small but well-selected selection of sparkling wine alternatives.

Hedley Wright
10–11 The Twyford Centre, London Road, Bishops Stortford, Hertfordshire CM23 3YT
C 01279 506512
FAX 01279 657462 ✉
wine@hedleywright.com
www.hedleywright.com
This go-ahead merchant recently merged with Smedley Vintners. The Champagne section leads with Délot, offers George Goulet non-vintage in

six bottle sizes and is so fond of Laurent-Perrier that it also stocks that firm's second label, Lemoine, which is normally restricted to restaurants.

Pierre Henck Wines
283 Tettenhall Road, Wolverhampton WV6 OLE
℡ 01902 751022
FAX 01902 752212 ✉
A small selection of mostly excellent, mostly *grande marque* Champagnes, but the sparkling wine alternatives are in dire need of a bit of imagination.

Charles Hennings Vintners
London House, Lower Street Pulborough Sussex RH20 2BW
℡ 01798 872458/873909
FAX 01798 873163 ✉
chennings@aol.com
A long list of *grandes marques*, with Pelorus heading a small selection of sparkling wine alternatives.

Heyman, Barwell Jones
Barwell House, 24 Fore Street, Ipswich, Suffolk IP4 1JU
℡ 01473 232322
FAX 01473 212237 ✉
sales@heyman.co.uk
www.heyman.co.uk
A select range of *grandes marques* and Duc de Lavigny as house Champagne, but this is the source *par excellence* for Pannier. The range of sparkling wine alternatives is, however, very small and somewhat lacklustre.

Hicks & Don
12 Warminster Road, Westbury, Wiltshire BA13 3PB
℡ 01373 822600
FAX 01373 859009 ✉
mailbox@hicksanddon.co.uk
www.hicksanddon.co.uk
Unfortunately Gosset has been dropped, but the odd *cuvée* of Gardet, Bollinger, Roederer, Joseph Perrier and Pol Roger remain, making a compact selection of good

quality Champagne. However, with just one *cuvée* of Cava and one *cuvée* of English sparkling wine, the alternatives are hardly worth considering.

George Hill
59 Wards End, Loughborough, Leicestershire LE11 3HB
℡ 01509 212717
FAX 01509 236963 ✉
geo-hill-wines@gmtnet.co.uk
www.george-hill.co.uk
A few *grande marque* Champagnes, with a reliable rather than exciting range of sparkling wine alternatives.

Home Run
See First Quench

House of Townend
Red Duster House, York Street, Wincolmlee, Hull HU2 OQX
℡ 01482 326891
FAX 01482 587042 ✉
info@houseoftownend.co.uk
www.houseoftownend.co.uk
A dedicated follower of the grey market, the House of Townend offers an excellent range of *grande marque* and takes delight in sourcing as many of these from legitimate (but unconventional) EU sources where Champagne houses sell their products to importers at a significantly lower price. Gardet is also stocked, the house Champagne is Marquis d'Estrand (made by Ellner) and the sparkling alternatives include top choices such as Argyle and Pelorus.

Hutton's
See First Quench

The International Wine Challenge Online
6–14 Underwood Street, London N17 JQ
℡ 020 7324 2338
iwconline@wilmington.co.uk
The world's largest wine competition features every single award-winning wine with a full description,

approximate price and a list of stockists. There were 304 gold medal fizzies when I last checked.

ItsWine.com
11 Upper Wingbury Courtyard, Wingrave, Aylesbury, Buckinghamshire HP22 4LW
℡ 01296 682600
FAX 01296 682500
info@itswine.com
www.ItsWine.com
ItsWine.com has been selling wine over the Internet since August 1998, which makes it the first web-only wine shop in the UK. Each wine has been selected by a team of experts, including Jonathan Pedley MW and wine writer

> ### ATTENTION UNLISTED STOCKISTS
> It is hoped to build this section into the most comprehensive fizz buyer's reference available in the UK, so if you would like to be included in a future edition, please contact Tom Stevenson at:
>
> tom.stevenson@fizz.worldonline.co.uk
>
> *Warning: Any other unsolicited mail received at this address will be ignored*
>
> Please note that inclusion in this guide involves no charge whatsoever, although stockists are expected to update or correct any factual information given in their profiles below, and those with own-label products are requested to submit tasting samples at their own cost. Stockists in previous editions who have not updated their information have been deleted for the sake of accuracy, but are most welcome to appear in future editions.

Julie Arkell. As far as Champagne is concerned, this includes a few *cuvées* from Drappier, which are an excellent balance between quality and value, and one each from Bollinger, Henriot, Moët and Veuve Clicquot, with Chartogne-Taillet providing the cheapest selection. Overall it's not bad, but could be a lot better, as could the sparkling wine alternatives, which offer little interest beyond Seaview and Lindauer.

Jeroboams

8–12 Brook Street, London W1Y 2BH

☎ 020 7629 7916

℻ 020 7495 3314 ✉

sales@jeroboam.co.uk

www.jeroboam.co.uk

The Jeroboams group includes Laytons (*see further on*), although the four Laytons shops have been rebadged. Jeroboams is famous for its world class range of cheeses, but offers some excellent wines, with a small selection of fizz, including Georges Vesselle and its own-label Champagne.

Michael Jobling Wines

Baltic Chambers,
3–7 Broad Chare,
Newcastle upon Tyne,
Tyne & Wear NE1 3DQ

☎ 0191 261 5298

℻ 0191 261 4543 ✉

www.michaeljoblingwines.
co.uk

There are only two wines that I would not drink on this winemerchant's compact but well-chosen range of Champagnes and alternative fizz.

S.H. Jones & Co

27 High Street, Banbury, Oxon OX16 8EW

☎ 01295 251177

℻ 01295 272352 ✉

This traditional country merchant offers a dozen *grande marque* non-vintage *cuvées*, Gardet and Marquis d'Estrand (made by Ellner) at the inexpensive end, six or seven vintage Champagnes and a good selection of sparkling wine alternatives, with Nyetimber, Pelorus and Quartet topping the bill.

Justerini & Brooks Retail

61 St James's Street,
London SW1A 1LZ

☎ 020 7493 8721

℻ 020 7499 4653 ✉

An excellent range of mostly *grande marque* Champagne, including a number of mature vintage, with Quartet, Pelorus, Green Point and Miru Miru leading the pack of New World fizzies.

King Wines

Upper Slackstead
Farmhouse, 206 Farley Lane
Braishfield, Nr Romsey,
Hampshire SO51 0QL

☎ 01794 843.

℻ 020 7287 8555 ✉

cubicworld.com/wine

This relatively recent venture majors Champagne de Bruyne from the Sézanne, but also sells Laurent-Perrier, Pol Roger and Taittinger. The sparkling wine alternatives are dominated by Castellblanch and obviously need a lot of work on.

❽❽ CHAMPAGNE DE BRUYNE NV CUVÉE ABSOLUE BRUT, SÉZANNE *Fine fruit aromas initially, but they quickly give way to yeast-complexed creamy fruit of some maturity on both nose and palate.*
❗ Now–2002 £18.60

Lay & Wheeler

Gosbecks Park,
117 Gosbecks Road,
Colchester CO2 9JT

☎ 01206 764446

℻ 01206 560002 ✉

laywheeler@ndirect.co.uk

www.layandwheeler.co.uk

The best wine list in the country, with a spectacular range of great Champagnes, including a top-notch house Champagne by Michel Guilleminot (*see Tasting Notes and Scores*) and an excellent selection of sparkling wine alternatives.

Laymont & Shaw

The Old Chapel, Millpool,
Truro, Cornwall TR1 1EX

☎ 01872 270545

℻ 01872 223005 ✉

info@laymont-shaw.co.uk

www.laymont-shaw.co.uk

Juvé y Camps leads the way at this Spanish wine specialist.

Laytons

20 Midland Road,
London NW1 2AD

☎ 020 7388 4567

℻ 020 7383 7419 ✉

sales@laytons.co.uk

www.laytons.co.uk

Although Laytons shops have been rebadged to Jeroboam since its merger with that firm, Laytons the shipper, wholesaler and mail-order winemerchant lives on. The list contains a fascinating collection of 30-odd vintage Champagnes, plus its own-label Champagne, which is much better than last year and almost as good as it was two or three years ago. I was not so enamoured with Laytons' "Extra Aged" Deutz non-vintage, which was a tad too peppery for my liking and much preferred the Deutz Classic Cuvée, but anyone who hankers after the non-vintage as it was prior to the launch of the Classic Cuvée might like to check it out.

❽❸ LAYTONS CHAMPAGNE BRUT RESERVE NV F. BONNET *Extremely fruity now, but should develop violet-vanilla finesse on the finish after a year or so.*
❗ Now–2003 £15.00

Lea & Sandeman

170 Fulham Road
London SW10 9PR

☎ 020 7244 0522

℻ 020 7244 0533

sales@leaandsandeman.
co.uk

An excellent winemerchant with one of the largest and best selections of Champagne in the country.

Lloyd Taylor Wines Ltd

Bute House, Arran Road,
Perth PH1 3DZ

☎ 01738 444994

℻ 01738 447979 ✉

sales@lloyd-taylor-wines.
com

www.lloyd-taylor-wines.com
A small selection of
Champagne and sparkling
wines, with Paul Herard
providing the best value.

Madaboutwine.com

Elsinore House,
77 Fulham Palace Road,
London W6 8JA
☎ 020 8222 9490
℻ 020 8222 9489 ✉
jp@madaboutwine.com
www.madaboutwine.com
Founded originally as The
Rare Wine Cellar in late 1995
by Mark Bedini and Bud
Cuchet, the current owners of
Madaboutwine.com who
launched their cyberspace
wine shop in March 1999. The
object of madaboutwine.com,
according to Bedini and
Cuchet, is "to bring
unparalleled choice and
service across all aspects of
premium wine and associated
products to a world audience
using the best opportunities
that technology and the Web
can offer". What this
translates to in category of
Champagne is a choice
of no fewer than 148
products. That's what I call
mad about wine.

Majestic Wine Warehouse

Majestic House, Units 1 &
2, Otterspool Way, Watford,
Hertfordshire WD2 8HL
☎ 01923 298200
℻ 01923 819105 ✉
www.majestic.co.uk
A chain of 85 wine
warehouses stretching from
Southampton to Glasgow. De
Telmont has long been the
house Champagne, but there
is an excellent selection of
many other very good, well-
priced Champagnes and
sparkling wines. With plenty
of multiple-purchase offers, it
depends what day of the week
it is whether Majestic has the
cheapest prices or Oddbins.

Marks & Spencer

Michael House, 46/47
Baker Street, London W1A
1DN
☎ 020 7268 8580
℻ 020 7268 2674
www.marks-and-spencer.
co.uk
M&S still offers one of the
most underrated own-label
ranges on the market.
86 ASTI NV DOLCE, TOSTI,
ST MICHAEL
*Distinctive hints of mandarin
mingling with Moscato aromas
on the nose and palate of this
first-rate, intensely sweet,
supermarket Asti.*
❗ Now £5.99
82 CHAMPAGNE OUDINOT
NV CUVÉE BRUT, ST
MICHAEL
*Fresh, zippy, sherbety fruit
with a crisp finish.*
❗ Now–2001 £15.99

Mayfair Cellars

Miniver House, 19–20
Garlick Hill, London EC4V
2AL
☎ 020 7329 8899
℻ 020 7329 8800 ✉
sales@mayfaircellars.co.uk
Mayfair Cellars are the agents
for the stunning quality,
beautifully presented
Champagne Jacquesson.

Mills Whitcombe

The Sett, Lower Maescoed,
Hereford HR2 0HS
☎ 01873 860222
℻ 01873 860444
floyd@millswhitcombe.
co.uk
A brand new venture set up
by Floyd Mills and dressage
judge Becky Whitcombe. A
small list with just two
Champagnes, Hostomme and
Pol Roger, the latter of which
is not unexpected since
Floyd's first job in the wine
industry was with that house.

Mitchells Wine Merchants

Vintners House, 354
Meadowhead, Sheffield
S8 7UJ
☎ 0114 274 5587
℻ 0114 274 8481 ✉
John Mitchell is a friendly
Yorkshire winemerchant who
knows what he likes, and in
this case it is Champagne
Montaudon (although Luc

Montaudon did not submit
any samples this year),
although he stocks a large
selection of other brands.

Montrachet Fine Wines

59 Kennington Road,
London SE1 7PZ
☎ 020 7928 1990
℻ 020 7928 3415 ✉
montrachetwine@aol.com
This is one of the best sources
for top quality Burgundy and
German wine, but there are
some nice Champagnes too
(mostly Bollinger, Pol Roger
and Roederer), plus a few
Crémant de Bourgogne.

Morris & Verdin

10 The Leathermarket,
Weston Street, London SE1
3ER
☎ 020 7357 8866
℻ 020 7357 8877 ✉
Jasper Morris MW is a
quality-minded winemerchant
who focuses his attention on
André Jacquart, a grower
Champagne from Le
Mesnil-sur-Oger who, Jasper
is keen to emphasize, has no
connection with the
cooperative Jacquart. There
are also a few *grande marque*
Champagnes on the list,
mostly from Bollinger and Pol
Roger, plus a small selection
of sparkling wine alternatives,
most notably Pelorus.

Morrisons

Junction 41 Industrial
Estate, Carr Gate,
Wakefield, West Yorkshire
WF2 0XF
☎ 01924 870000
℻ 01924 875300
This excellent northern-based
supermarket chain of
100-odd stores has begun to
move south.
74 CAVA BRUT VINTAGE
1996 SANT SADURNÍ
D'ANOIA, MORRISON
*Very malo-dominated, but
there's a seriousness to the
fruit I find appealing.*
❗ Now £5.49

New London Wine

1e Broughton Street,
London SW8 3QJ

C 020 7622 3000
FAX 020 7622 2220
orders@newlondonwine.
    demon.co.uk
With just a handful of
Champagnes and even fewer
sparkling wines of a lacklustre
quality, the fizz section here is
in dire need of some attention.

James Nicholson
27a Killyleagh Street
Crossgar Co Down
N. Ireland BT30 9DG
C (028) 448 30091
FAX (028) 448 30028 ✉
info@jnwine.co.uk
www.jnwine.co.uk
Impeccable quality from
Billecart-Salmon and
Roederer, with Paul Herard
and Medot for value, while
Quartet, Pelorus and Hollick
head up the New World
challenge.

Nickolls & Perks
37 High Street, Stourbridge,
West Midlands DY8 1TA
C 01384 394518
FAX 01384 440786 ✉
sales@nickollsandperks.
    co.uk
www.nickollsandperks.
    co.uk
This list is always
chock-a-block full of great
Champagnes. Currently there
are some 60 products,
including many mature
vintages and small parcels of
even more rare Champagnes.

Nicolas UK
157 Great Portland Street,
London W1N 5HP
C 020 7436 9338
FAX 020 7637 1691
www.nicolas.co.uk
France's premier wine shop
chain now has 18 branches in
London offering a range of
good if predictable *grandes
marques* Champagnes, plus a
number of lesser-known
brands. Being French-owned,
you're going to be sorely
disappointed if you go
looking for anything from the
New World of course.

The Nobody Inn
Doddiscombleigh,
Nr. Exeter, Devon EX6 7PS

C 01647 252394
FAX 01647 252978 ✉
inn.nobody@virgin.net
A country tavern with a wine
list to die for.
80 THE NOBODY INN NV
CHAMPAGNE GARDET, BRUT
RÉSERVE
*Plenty of fruit, but needs a
touch more finesse on the nose
to score higher.*
❗ Now–2001 £14.37

Oddbins
31–33 Weir Road,
Wimbledon, London
SW19 8UG
C 020 8944 4400
FAX 020 8944 4411
www.oddbins.co.uk
It is amazing how Oddbins
can maintain its standard as
the best high street chain
every year without anyone
coming remotely close to
challenging it. Some 250-odd
stores stock one of the most
comprehensive ranges of
Champagnes and sparkling
wines available, and the
Oddbins Fine Wine Stores
boast an even greater
range. Multiple purchase
bargains galore.

**The Oxford Wine
Company**
Standlake Business Park,
Standlake,
Oxon OX13 5DZ
C 01865 301144
FAX 01865 301155 ✉
One of the fastest-growing
independent groups, The
Oxford Wine Company has
three branches and a thriving
wholesale business. House
favourites are Marniquet and
Brugnon, with Veuve
Clicquot heading up a small
selection of *grandes marques*
and its Southern Hemisphere
compatriot leading the New
World fizz.

Pallant Wines
17 High Street, Arundel,
West Sussex BN18 9AD
C 01903 882288
FAX 01903 882801 ✉
contact@pallant-wines.co.uk
A few well-chosen *grandes
marques* supported by a

number of good-value brands
from Marne et Champagne,
Pallant Wines also stocks
Nyetimber, including
Nyetimber's Aurora Cuvée
2000 Blanc de Blancs in
magnum.

**Penistone Court Wine
Cellars**
The Railway Station,
Penistone, Sheffield
S36 6HP
C 01226 766037
FAX 01226 767310 ✉
pcwc@dircon.co.uk
Particularly hot on Pol Roger,
Louis Roederer and Duval-
Leroy, although there are
various *cuvées* from a number
of other quality-conscious
houses.

Philglas & Swiggot
21 Northcote Road,
London SW11 1NG
C 020 7924 4494
FAX 020 7642 1308 ✉
karen@philglasandswiggot.
    co.uk
Although the Champagne
selection is not exactly huge,
owner-buyer Karen Rogers
obviously has a soft spot for
Champagnes of class, with
some nice pickings from
Gosset, Roederer, Paillard
and Krug, not to mention the
value-for-money choice of
Barnaut Grand Cru (85
points). Some pretty exciting
New World stuff too.

Christopher Piper
1 Silver Street, Ottery St
Mary, Devon EX11 1DB
C 01404 814139
FAX 01404 812100 ✉
Christopher Piper exclusively
ships a grower called
Gremillet, who has made some
excellent vintage Champagnes
in the past, and Veuve Fourny,
whose Blanc de Blanc NV
Brut Premier Cru was very
highly rated in the first edition
(88 points), but not submitted
since. Even though the rest of
the Champagne list has been
depleted by the Millennium, it
still offers more choice of
quality and value than most
other merchants.

Planet Wine Ltd
126 Northenden Road,
Sale, Cheshire M33 3HD
☎ 0161 973 1122
FAX 0161 973 2121 ✉
sales@planetwine.co.uk
www.planetwine.co.uk
It might have taken just six
days for God to create the
earth, but it took considerably
longer for Paul Sherlock to
build Planet Wine. However,
it's one of the best and most
interesting sites I've seen, and
it's bursting at the seams with
all the best names and great
vintages.

Terry Platt
Ferndale Road,
Llandudno Junction,
Gwynedd LL31 9NT
☎ 01492 592971
FAX 01492 592196 ✉
plattwines@clara.co.uk
Terry Platt stocks a few
well-selected famous names,
but relies on the excellent
value, expressive wines of
Duval-Leroy to fulfil most
customers' needs. The house
Champagne Edouard
d'Enjoie is also produced by
Duval-Leroy. Argyle has
unfortunately been dropped,
but Pelorus, Quartet and
Shadow Creek now join
Green Point at the head of
the New World section.

Le Pont de la Tour
The Butlers Wharf Building,
36d Shad Thames, Butlers
Wharf, London SE1 2YE
☎ 020 7403 2403
FAX 020 7403 0267 ✉
Dual-function shop and cellar
for the restaurant, Le Pont de
la Tour offers an impressive
selection of Champagne
including Billecart-Salmon,
Bollinger, Dom Pérignon,
Gosset, Krug, Salon and
Taittinger Comtes de
Champagne.

Portland Wine Company
152a Ashley Road,
Hale, Near Altrincham,
Cheshire WA15 9SA
☎ 0161 962 8752
FAX 0161 905 1291 ✉
www.portlandwine.co.uk

House Champagne from
Duval-Leroy, with Drappier
leading the rest of the
Champagne section, including
half a dozen vintages of this
Aube Champagne going back
to 1959, plus loads more
classy stuff.

Quellyn Roberts
21 Watergate Street,
Chester CH1 2LB
☎ 01244 310455
FAX 01244 346704 ✉
Quellyn Roberts offers a good
range of *grande marque*
Champagnes, but obviously
favours Pol Roger,
particularly its non-vintage,
which he sells in quarters,
halves, bottles, magnums,
jeroboams, methuselahs and
even Nebuchadnezzars
(equivalent to 20 bottles).

Raeburn Fine Wines
23 Comely Bank Road,
Edinburgh EH14 1DS
☎ 0131 343 1159
FAX 0131 332 5166 ✉
raeburn@netcomuk.co.uk
www.raeburnfinewines.com
Last year I wrote "One look
at Zubair Mohamed's list and
you know he loves wines. His
fizz section includes just two
I wouldn't – not couldn't –
drink, and I cannot say that
about any other range."
Zubair emailed me "Which
two?"!

Ramsbottom Victuallers
16–18 Market Place,
Ramsbottom, Bury,
Lancashire BL0 9HT
☎ 01706 825070
FAX 01706 822005 ✉
rammy.vics@which.net
As Chris Johnson, the owner
of Ramsbottom Victuallers
and Village Restaurant (BBC
Best Food Shop, Good Food
Guide Greater Manchester
Restaurant of the Year,
Lancashire Life Wine
Merchant of the Year *et al*)
says "We studiously avoid
grandes marques and any other
widely available growers".

Reid Wines
The Mil, Marsh Lane,

Hallatrow, Bristol BS18 5EB
☎ 01761 452645
FAX 01761 453642 ✉
One of the best sources of
old vintage Champagnes and
stockists of Nyetimber,
Britain's world-class sparkling
wine, Reid Wines is, however,
quite useless at sending out
lists to this author, either for
the purpose of what amounts
to free publicity or as an
occasional customer.

Reyniers
See Eldridge Pope

Mark Reynier Fine Wines
See La Réserve

La Reserve
56 Walton Street,
Knightsbridge,
London SW3 1RB
☎ 020 7589 2020
FAX 020 7581 0250 ✉
realwine@la-reserve.co.uk
A small group of shops
owned and run by Mark
Reynier Fine Wines, La
Reserve majors on Pol Roger
and Gosset, with a special
interest in old vintages of
Bollinger, Krug and Dom
Pérignon. House Champagne
under the Charles Leprince
label is made by Beaumont
des Crayères. Also stocks
both the Brut Classic and
Blanc de Blancs from
Nyetimber.

Howard Ripley
35 Eversley Crescent,
London N21 1EL
☎ 020 8360 8904
FAX 020 8351 6564 ✉
What is it about dentists and
wine? I've known a lot of
dentists who have become
fanatical about wine, the most
famous of those who actually
took it far enough to change
professions is, of course,
Robin Yapp. Whereas Yapp
became obsessive with the
Loire, Ripley fell under the
spell of all things Burgundian,
except it would seem Crémant
de Bourgogne. Not that I can
blame him; Burgundy should
be able to produce the most

sumptuous of sparkling wines, but except for the odd fine fizz, which happens so occasionally I assume it must be by accident, this famous French region is bereft of high quality sparkling wines. For this Ripley, it has to be Champagne from Baron Albert (*see Tasting Notes and Scores*), believe it or not. Isn't that just weird?

Roberson Wine Merchant Ltd
348 Kensington High Street, London W14 8NS
C 020 7371 2121
FAX 020 7371 4010 ✉
wines@roberson.co.uk
www.roberson.co.uk
An excellent Champagne list that's as long as your arm, with an awesome selection of fabulous vintages.

The Rogers Wine Co
20 Lower Street, Sproughton, Ipswich,

ATTENTION UNLISTED STOCKISTS

It is hoped to build this section into the most comprehensive fizz buyer's reference available in the UK, so if you would like to be included in a future edition, please contact Tom Stevenson at:

tom.stevenson@ fizz.worldonline.co.uk

Warning: Any other unsolicited mail received at this address will be ignored

Please note that inclusion in this guide involves no charge whatsoever, although stockists are expected to update or correct any factual information given in their profiles below, and those with own-label products are requested to submit tasting samples at their own cost. Stockists in previous editions who have not updated their information have been deleted for the sake of accuracy, but are most welcome to appear in future editions.

Suffolk IP8 3AA
C 01473 748464
FAX 01473 744245 ✉
rogers.co@FSBdial.co.uk
This Francophile winemerchant leads with Barnaut, including the Grand Cru Grande Réserve (85 points), followed by a small selection of rather predictable *grandes marques*.

C.A. Rookes Wine Merchants
7 Western Road Industrial Estate, Stratford upon Avon CV37 0AH
C 01789 297777
FAX 01789 297752
bubbles@carookes.co.uk
www.carookes.co.uk
The best wines here are the full range offerings from Moutardier and Gosset.

Safeway
Safeway House, 6 Millington Road, Hayes, Middlesex UB3 4AY
C 020 8848 8744
FAX 020 8753 1865
A small range of *grandes marques* for a supermarket group with 470 stores, but Albert Etienne is often a bargain, especially in magnum. The choice of sparkling wine alternatives still needs attention.
❸ CHAMPAGNE ALBERT ETIENNE NV BRUT ROSÉ, MASSÉ, SAFEWAY
This rich, tasty Champagne has excellent acidity and will go toasty.
❗ Now–2003 £15.99
❷ CHAMPAGNE ALBERT ETIENNE 1993 SPECIAL CUVÉE BRUT, MASSÉ, SAFEWAY
Firmly structured, but will mellow given time.
❗ Now–2005 £16.99
❿ CHAMPAGNE ALBERT ETIENNE NV BRUT, MASSÉ, SAFEWAY
Although rich and tasty now, and promises to go toasty, there is also an indication that it will become oxidative and aldehydic, so if you have a few bottles tucked away, keep an eye on its progress.

❗ Now–2001 £13.99
❿ ASTI NV DOLCE, PERLINO, SAFEWAY
The soapy character here is merely a youthful phase of Moscato fruit. This should evolve into a more distinctive peachiness.
❗ Now £4.79
❼ CHENIN BRUT NV VIN MOUSSEUX, CCV
After trawling my way through heaps of old-fashioned, unclean and downright dirty sparkling wines from various Loire AOCs, I can do no better than quote from the back-label of this non-AOC fizz: "Modern fresh style of sparkling Chenin". That's what I call truth in labelling.
❗ Now £4.49
❿ CAVA NV BRUT, SEVISA, SAFEWAY
Good basic Cava with nicely focused fruit, fine acidity and a crisp Granny Smith apple finish.
❗ Now £4.99
❼ AUSTRALIAN QUALITY SPARKLING WINE NV BRUT, B. SEPPELT, SAFEWAY
Typical Seppelt lime and lavender fruit.
❗ Now £4.99
❼ LE BARON DE MONCENY NV MERLOT-GAMAY BRUT
Simple fizzy red with Gamay fruit dominating. For those who want a basic barbecue wine, but find Aussie Sparkling Shiraz too sweet and heavy.
Now–2001 £5.00

Sainsbury's
Stamford House, Stamford Street, London SE1 9LL
C 020 7695 6000
FAX 020 7695 7610 ✉
www.sainsburys.co.uk
This supermarket group, which now boasts almost 400 stores, has always been strong on own-label Champagne.
❿ SAINSBURY'S EXTRA DRY CHAMPAGNE NV PREMIER CRU, DUVAL-LEROY MAGNUM
I don't know what pleased me most when the covers came off, the fact that a supermarket Champagne could score 88 points or that it had been

produced by Duval-Leroy. Both I suppose. The difference in actual and potential quality between this wine in a 75cl bottle and a magnum is huge, but then I do not expect that they are precisely the same wine. The magnum is probably a year or so older and its non-vintage blend is almost certainly based on a finer vintage, but do not assume that older means more mature tasting in this case. In fact, this magnum seems fresher and part of that has to do with the floral-finesse of autolysis on the nose. This is a low developer: keep at least another year (if you can keep your hands off it!).
! Now–2004 £27.49
🔵 SAINSBURY'S MILLENNIUM VINTAGE CHAMPAGNE 1995 BRUT GRAND CRU, BOIZEL
Presented in a gold tin with a millennium celebration design. This might be at the high end of supermarket Champagne prices, but I would be very surprised if this is not an early disgorged version of a future release of Joyau de France, which goes for almost twice the price. Any fans of Boizel's prestige cuvée should grab this wine in quantity and, when the 1995 Joyau is eventually released, have fun comparing the development of one against the other for several years to come.
! Now–2007 £19.99
🔵 SAINSBURY'S VINTAGE CHAMPAGNE 1993 BLANC DE BLANCS BRUT, UVCB
Mature, rich, creamy-biscuity fruit for immediate drinking.
! Now £15.99
🔵 SAINSBURY'S EXTRA DRY CHAMPAGNE NV PREMIER CRU, DUVAL-LEROY
Fresh, light and crisp.
! Now–2001 £13.99
🔵 SAINSBURY'S MILLENNIUM CHAMPAGNE NV BRUT GRAND CRU, DUVAL-LEROY
If the label did not say "produced and bottled by Duval-Leroy" I would have sworn that it had merely been

sourced, not made, by that house because the style is much fatter than I expect from its winemaker Hervé Jestin. However, I have no complaints about the quality in terms of supermarket own-label Champagne.
! Now–2002 £16.99
🔵 SAINSBURY'S ASTI NV CASA VINICOLA
Fresh, delicate Moscato aromas with some real richness and sweetness on the finish.
! Now £3.99
🔵 SAINSBURY'S CHAMPAGNE NV DEMI-SEC, NM 120
This fresh, sweet, tasty Demi-Sec was made by Boizel.
! Now–2001 £13.99
🔵 SAINSBURY'S CHAMPAGNE NV BLANC DE NOIRS BRUT, SCAP DES GRAND TERROIRS
Although amylic aromas dominate, they are followed by sweet, ripe Chardonnay fruit.
! Now–2001 £11.99

Sandiway Wine Company
Chester Road, Sandiway, Cheshire CW8 2NH
☎ 01606 882101
FAX 01606 888407 ✉
info@sandiwaywine.com
www.sandiwaywine.u-net.com
A small but well-selected range of Champagne, including three different growers (Dumont, Jacquart and Selosse), plus an interesting choice of sparkling wine alternatives.

Satchells of Burnham Market
North Street, Burnham Market, Norfolk PE31 8HG
☎ 01328 738272
FAX 01328 730727 ✉
An interesting selection of Champagne (Barnaut, Drappier, Montaudon etc), with house Champagne under the Louis Masseran label made by Albert le Brun.

Savage Selection
The Ox House, Market Place, Northleach, Cheltenham Gloucestershire GL54 3EG

☎ 0145 860896
FAX 0145 860996 ✉
savage.selection@virgin.net
Mark Savage has been shipping the top-performing Champagnes of Billecart-Salmon for ages and even has his own, specially selected non-vintage blend (100% Chardonnay exclusively from Vertus, as opposed to a blend of all three varieties).

Scatchard Ltd
38 Vernon Street, Liverpool L2 2AY
☎ 0151 236 6468
FAX 0151 236 7003 ✉
info@scatchard.com
A traditional, proudly independent merchant established in 1959 with a reputation for Spanish wine, which is still very close to their hearts but now a relatively small part of the range. The Champagne selection relies heavily on Nicolas Feuillatte, but also offers André Simon and Paul Herard at the bottom end of the range. However, for 50p more than the Feuillatte you can buy Drappier, which would certainly be my choice. Good though they are, just Moët and Clicquot bolster Feuillatte in the vintage Champagne section, after which there is a compact range of prestige cuvées. Except for Cava, which is well provided for, as might be expected, by the likes of Marqués de Monistrol and Duc de Foix, the sparkling wine alternatives are pretty thin on the ground, with merely Pelorus, Yaldara and Asti Martini.

Sebastopol Wines
Sebastopol Barn, London Road, Blewbury, Oxfordshire OX11 9HB
☎ 01235 850471
FAX 01235 850776 ✉
There still isn't a wine I wouldn't happily drink on this list of impeccably chosen Champagnes and sparkling wines, but don't worry, if I spot one my readers of this Guide will be the first to know.

Selfridges

400 Oxford Street,
London W1A 1AB
C 020 7318 3730
FAX 020 7491 1880 ✉
www.selfridges.com
A large range of Champagne
and sparkling wines, with
some delightful finds for a
department store, such as
Vilmart, Billecart-Salmon and
Jacquesson, with various
parcels of old vintages.

Shaws of Beaumaris

17 Castle Street,
Beaumaris, Isle of Anglesey
LL58 8AP
C 01248 810328
FAX 01248 810328 ✉
This merchant leads with
Gallimard, Veuve Fournay,
Vilmart, Billecart-Salmon and
Bollinger, which can't be bad.
The sparkling wine
alternatives are somewhat
less exciting, but do
include the indestructible
Cray twins.

Andrew Sheepshanks Fine Wines

1 Colebrook Court,
Sloane Avenue,
London SW3 3DJ
C 020 7581 9400
FAX 020 7581 9444 ✉
info@sheepshanks.co.uk
A specialist merchant who
aims to provide "top quality
wines and Champagnes at
wholesale prices".

Edward Sheldon

New Street,
Shipston-on-Stour,
Warwickshire CV36 4EN
C 01608 661409
FAX 01608 663166 ✉
finewine@edward-sheldon.
  co.uk
A small, traditional range of
mostly *grandes marques*, plus
Marquis de Joncry and Abell
& Cie, neither of which I
have encountered, plus
Edward Sheldon's own-label
produced by Marne et
Champagne. Chandon
Argentina is a new addition to
the sparkling wines, but this
section still needs some
attention.

Smedley Vintners

Recently merged with
Hedley Wright.
See Hedley Wright

Somerfield

Somerfield House,
Whitchurch Lane,
Bristol BS14 OTJ
C 0117 935 7080
FAX 0117 978 0629
Another supermarket group
that is having a hard time is
Somerfield's chain of 1400
stores. However, its poor
results have more to do with
the location and presentation
of its stores than the wines it
sells, particularly its
underrated own-label
Champagnes. Somerfield's
own-label Champagnes used
to be poorly presented, but
have now been very tastefully
re-labelled.
❻❺ CHAMPAGNE PRINCE
WILLIAM NV BRUT
PREMIER CRU, UNION
CHAMPAGNE, SOMERFIELD
*A deceptively green tinge on
the nose is followed by an
elegant, exceedingly fruity
flavour with plenty of acidity
and it's all ripe. Those who
have been put off
by the presentation of this
Champagne in the past will be
pleased to know that the new
labelling is classic and
understated, with little hint
of its supermarket origins.*
❗ Now–2002 £13.95
❻❺ CHAMPAGNE PRINCE
WILLIAM MILLENNIUM
CUVÉE 1990 BRUT, MARNE
& CHAMPAGNE,
SOMERFIELD
*On purchase you will find
absolutely bugger all in this
wine to write home to mother
about, but in 12 months time
it will start to blossom into a
full, rich, classically toasty
Champagne.*
▬ 2001–2003 £19.99
❽❹ CHAMPAGNE PRINCE
WILLIAM, BLANC DE NOIRS
NV BRUT RÉSERVE,
ALEXANDRE BONNET,
SOMERFIELD
*Although the amylic aromas
hide the varietal
characteristics, the fruit*

*underneath is certainly nice
enough for a supermarket
Champagne.*
❗ Now–2001 £11.99
❼❷ AUSTRALIAN
CHARDONNAY 1995 BRUT,
B. SEPPELT, SOMERFIELD
*This creamy Chardonnay
tastes as if it's been kept in
tank for two or three years to
preserve freshness prior to
tirage.*
❗ Now £6.99
❼⓿ CAVA NV BLANC DE
BLANCS BRUT,
N.EMB.5584/B, SOMERFIELD
*This is very soft in mousse and
fruit, so should appeal to
regular Cava drinkers,
although its flavour is longer
lasting than that of most
regular soft Cavas.*
❗ Now £5.00

Sommelier Wine Company

23 St. Georges Esplanade,
St. Peter Port, Guernsey,
Channel Islands GY1 2BG
C 01481 721677
FAX 01481 716818
A great list of great wines
with great descriptions and
brilliant prices. A must have!

Frank Stainton Wines

3 Berrys Yard, Finkle Street,
Kendal LA9 4AB
C 01539 731886
FAX 01539 730396
The Champagne range is
an eclectic mix of
penny-savers and the very
best, while Quartet leads
the sparkling wine
alternatives.

John Stephenson

Darwil House, Bradley Hall
Road, Nelson, Lancashire
BB9 8HF
C 01282 614618
FAX 01282 601161 ✉
wbannp@aol.com
This third-generation,
family-run winemerchant has
a small but select choice of
grandes marques, but leads
with the excellent range of
Duval-Leroy and offers
Jacquart for value, with even
cheaper *cuvées* from Lemoine
and Jules Féraud.

Stevens Garnier
47 West Way, Botley,
Oxford OX2 OJF
☎ 01865 263303
FAX 01865 791594 ✉
A good selection of
Champagne, with Gosset and
Roederer scoring highest.

Stratford's Wine Shippers
High Street,
Cockham-on-Thames,
Berkshire SL6 9SQ
☎ 01628 810606
FAX 01628 810605 ✉
stratford@patrol.i-way.co.uk
A small range of good *grandes
marques*.

Swig
206 Haverstock Hill, Belsize
Park, London NW3 2AG
☎ 020 7431 4412
FAX 020 7431 1326
imbibe@swig.co.uk
www.swig.co.uk
Robin Davis used to be the
wine buyer for Conran
Restaurants, so you would
expect Swig to be a slick
operation and that it is, with a
compact list of only the finest
Champagnes. And he offers a
novel service of composing a
wedding present list entirely
of booze. As Robin comments
"Wedding present lists don't
work any more. If you've lived
together first, you've probably
got all the deep fat fryers,
salad bowls and towels you
could possibly want. But
booze? You can never have
too much booze." Even the
process of sorting out this
liquid wedding list sounds
pleasurable, "We have an
initial consultation with the
couple here, over a glass of
Champagne, to discuss their
preferences. Then I'll put
together an appropriate
selection and we invite them
to return for a personalized
tasting. We usually suggest a
fairly wide price bracket, to
suit everyone, and couples
sometimes add the special
Riedel wine glasses to the list."

Tanners Wines
26 Wyle Cop, Shrewsbury,
Shropshire SY1 1XD
☎ 01743 234455
FAX 01743 234501 ✉
sales@tanners-wines.co.uk
www.tanners-wines.co.uk
This country winemerchant
may have an old-world look,
with its oak-beamed décor,
but its information-packed
wine list is up to speed with
some of the best choices of
grande marque Champagnes,
complemented by a number
of reasonably priced grower
Champagnes (Arnould,
Clouet, Geoffroy,
Larmandier) and the grossly
underrated Beaumont des
Crayères cooperative, which
also supplies Tanners
own-label. There is also an
extensive list of small parcels
of fine and rare Champagnes
to make the millennium that
bit special. Quartet, Miru
Miru, Taltarni and Seppelt
Sparkling Shiraz are the pick
from the New World fizz.

Tesco
Tesco House, Delamare
Road, Cheshunt, Waltham
Cross, Herts EN8 9SL
☎ 01992 632222
FAX 01992 658225
webadmin@tesco.e-mail.
com
www.tesco.co.uk
There is no stopping Tesco
from outperforming all the
supermarket groups
financially, and even its
own-label fizz has upstaged
the others this year.
85 TESCO VINTAGE
CHAMPAGNE 1995
COOPERATIVE
UNION-CHAMPAGNE
*This smooth, rich, biscuity
Champagne is ready for
drinking.*
❗ Now–2001 £15.99
83 TESCO ASTI NV SANTO
STEFANO BILBO (L00049)
*Tesco sent me two different
shipments, rather than a
back-up of the wine submitted.
This one has a much smoother,
softer mousse, tinier bubbles,
better cordon retention,
sweeter fruit and more finesse
than EU Lot number L0032.*
❗ Now £3.99

82 TESCO PREMIER CRU
CHAMPAGNE NV BRUT,
COOPERATIVE
UNION-CHAMPAGNE
*The nose could have more
finesse, but the palate packs a
good punch of fruit and the
finish is substantial.*
❗ Now–2002 £12.99
75 TESCO CAVA NV
CASTELLBLANCH (L0093)
*This is distinctly fresher and
crisper than the Tesco Cava
supplied by Mademosa under
EU Lot number L9309, with
tastier fruit and a crisp, almost
tart, finish.*
❗ Now £4.99
75 TESCO ROSÉ CAVA NV
MADEMOSA
*The current cuvée is fresh and
crisp, with clean, well focused
fruit.*
❗ Now–2001 £4.99
75 TESCO VINTAGE CAVA
1995 MADEMOSA (L9284)
*I preferred this shipment to the
previous one (also Mademosa,
but EU Lot number L9201)
because it is fresher with more
vibrant fruitiness on the palate.*
❗ Now £6.99
73 TESCO HUNGARIAN
SPARKLING CHARDONNAY
NV BALATONBOGLÁR
WINERY
*Made by the BB or
Balatonboglár Winery, which
is co-owned by Henkell &
Söhnlein of Sekt infamy, this
creamy-lemony fizz is the
freshest, cleanest and best
Hungarian fizz I've tasted
to date.*
❗ Now £4.99
73 TESCO AUSTRALIAN
SPARKLING WINE NV
CRANSWICK
*Fresh, sweetish, perfumed
fruit nursing a soft mousse.*
❗ Now £4.99
72 TESCO CAVA DEMI-SEC
NV CASTELLBLANCH
*Lemony aromas followed
by fresh, clean fruit with
a sweet finish.*
❗ Now–2001 £4.99

Thresher
See First Quench

Trout Wines
Nether Wallop, Stockbridge,

Hampshire SO20 8EW
C 01264 781472
FAX 01264 781472
A small selection of
non-*grande marque*
Champagnes, of which
Jacquart and Le Brun de
Neuville offer the best value,
plus two sparkling
alternatives.

Turville Valley Wines
The Firs, Potter Row,
Great Missenden,
Buckinghamshire HP16 9LT
C 01494 868818
FAX 01494 868832 ✉
info@turville-valley-wines.
  com
www.turville-valley.com
Christopher Davis claims on
his wine list that Turville
Valley Wines is "The Wine
Trade's Best Kept Secret".
Log into his site and you'll see
"The Web's Best Kept
Secret". Is this just hype?
Well, Turville Valley Wines
acts as a broker with all sorts
of interesting parcels
constantly coming in and
going out. The best and oldest
of these wines end up on
prestigious wine lists at a
multiple of what Christopher
Davis sells them for, but if you
happen by when something
strikes your fancy, you can
come away with a bargain. I
did. I was just checking the
site prior to writing this entry
when I saw four bottles of
Dom Pérignon 1969 going for
a song, so I nabbed them.

**The Ubiquitous Chip
Wine Shop**
12 Ashton Lane, Hillhead,
Glasgow G12 8SJ
C 0141 334 5007
FAX 0141 337 1302 ✉
It's a while since I've been
here, but I hear that it still is
one of the best places to eat
and drink in Glasgow. It is
also the city's best
winemerchant, with a
fabulous list, although its
bubbly was never the most
exciting element in the range.
Things are looking up,
however, with a compact list
of excellent Champagnes. The

Ubiquitous Chip has even got
Pol Roger to produce its
house Extra Dry. Cheaper
Champagne comes from Paul
Herard and there is one
brand called Young &
Saunders, which has me
completely stumped. I'll have
to make another visit, if only
to look at the label!

Uncorked
Exchange Arcade,
Broadgate, London
EC2M 3WA
C 020 7638 5998
FAX 020 7638 6028
drink@uncorked.co.uk
www.uncorked.co.uk
The Champagne selection
here kicks off with Gallimard
and ends up with more
famous names than you can
shake a stick at.

Unwins
Birchwood House, Victoria
Road, Dartford,
Kent DA1 5AJ
C 01322 272711
FAX 01322 294469 ✉
www.unwins.co.uk
Unwins took over Fuller's in
2000, bringing its total
number of shops to just over
460, although some weeding
out of competing locations
can be expected. It's funny to
think that almost 20 years ago
when I compiled the first
edition of The Sunday
Telegraph Good Wine Guide,
the rumour was that Unwins
would soon be taken over.
The notion then was that with
Victoria Wine and Thresher
fighting out a turf war on the
High Street, a family-owned
group like Unwins could not
possibly survive. Well,
Victoria Wine and Thresher
effectively swallowed each
other, Oddbins took the
throne and was subsequently
purchased by Seagram, and
Unwins is not only surviving,
it's thriving.
87 CHAMPAGNE F.
DUCHATEL & CIE NV BRUT
ROSÉ (NM 305)
*Possibly the freshest-tasting
Champagne of all the tastings
this year (well, EU Lot No.*

*L152 was anyway), but it's not
just freshness and fluff, there's
excellent richness of fruit and
splendid finesse considering
the depth of flavour.*
! Now–2002 £15.99
84 CHAMPAGNE F.
DUCHATEL & CIE NV BRUT
(NM 305)
*Packed with fruit on the
palate, but needs 6–12 months
to open up the nose.*
! Now–2002 £11.99
80 CHAMPAGNE F.
DUCHATEL & CIE NV
BLANC DE BLANCS BRUT
(NM 305)
*Fresh, clean and lightly
structured, this wine will pick
up mellow, toasty aromas over
the next 18 months.*
! Now–2002 £15.99

Valvona & Crolla
19 Elm Row,
Edinburgh EH7 4AA
C 0131 556 6066
FAX 0131 556 1668 ✉
sales@valvonacrolla.co.uk
www.valvonacrolla.co.uk
The best place to buy Italian
fizz, and some pretty
good Champagnes too
(Billecart-Salmon, Bollinger,
Dom Pérignon, Krug, Pol
Roger, Louis Roederer, Veuve
Clicquot etc).

Victoria Wine
See First Quench

La Vigneronne
105 Old Brompton Road,
London SW7 3LE
C 020 7589 6113
FAX 020 7581 2983 ✉
A small selection of top
grandes marques, direct
imports from two growers,
Margaine and top-performing
Egly-Ouriet, plus any
mature vintage they happen
to pick up.

Village Wines
Arch 6, Mill Row, High
Street, Bexley,
Kent DA5 1LA
C 01322 558772
FAX 01322 558772 ✉
The Village people lead with
Jean-Pierre Marniquet,
backed up by Veuve Clicquot,

Canard-Duchêne and Bollinger, with Pol Roger in reserve and the odd *cuvée* of Laurent-Perrier.

Villeneuve Wines
1 Venlaw Court,
Peebles EH45 8AE
☎ 01721 722500
📠 01721 729922 ✉
wines@villeneuvewines.
    com
www.villeneuvewines.com
A nice range of great *grande marque* Champagnes, with the occasional mature vintage.
🆖 CHAMPAGNE PRINCESSE DE BAUDRY NV BRUT, PATRICIA BAUDRY
A light, fresh and fruity Champagne with an accent on elegance rather than complexity.
❗ Now–2001 £15.99

Vinceremos
19 New Street,
Leeds LS18 4BH
☎ 0113 205 4545
📠 0113 205 4546 ✉
info@vinceremos.co.uk
www.vinceremos.co.uk
Vinceremos has specialized in organic wines for many years and all the wines it sells, including Champagnes and sparkling wine alternatives, have been certified organically produced. However, their environmentally friendly Champagne, José Ardinat, is new to me.

Vin du Van
Colthups, The Street,
Appledore, Kent
TN26 2BX
☎ 01233 758727
📠 01233 758389 ✉
With a name like Vin du Van, readers would be forgiven for thinking this is some sort of cross-border shopping operation, but the list focuses exclusively on Australian and New Zealand wines. Poor bloody van. Croser tops the Oz fizz list, while Pelorus is the best Kiwi bubbly, but Vin du Van is the source *par excellence* for sparkling reds: Haselgrove Garnet, Cockatoo Ridge, Hollick Merlot,

Seppelt Shiraz, Yalumba Cuvée Two Cabernet, Tatachilla Malbec and the fabulous Charles Melton (90 points). The list is still written by a raving lunatic.

Vintage Roots
Farley Farms, Bridge Farm,
Reading Road, Arborfield,
Berkshire RG2 9HT
☎ 0118 976 1999
📠 0118 976 1998
info@vintageroots.co.uk
info@vintageroots.co.uk
The UK's leading organic wine specialist features Serge Faust, George Laval and Fleury (see *Tasting Notes and Scores*), with Albet i Noya representing Cava and the painful sounding Klaus Knobloch producing an intriguingly named Frizz Rosé Brut in Germany.

The Vintry
Park Farm, Milland, Liphook,
Hampshire GU30 7JT
☎ 01428 741389
📠 01428 741368 ✉
nigel@vintry.co.uk
A group of six like-minded couples in southern England who offer a selection of French-only wines, mostly from English growers or *négociants*. Other members of The Vintry group are located in Gillingham, Dorset; Calne, Wiltshire; Newbury, Berkshire; Richmond, Surrey; and Andover, Hampshire.

Virgin Wines
www.virginwines.com
What isn't Branson into these days? Virgin Wines claim to have 17,500 wines to choose from and that's Virgin On The Ridiculous! It's also not true. There are 15,904. I know because I've counted them, sad person that I am. Still, that's more than any other wine seller anywhere by a factor of almost 10, so who's complaining? There are as many as 762 Champagnes and sparkling wines. These, like all other categories of wine, are divided into recommend-

ations and others. All Virgin Recommended Wines come with the Virgin Customer Promise, which guarantees "great value, and if you don't like these wines, you don't pay – simple as that". All the rest carry the following warning: "These wines are not Virgin Recommended and do not come with the full customer promise. That means that while we do our best to get them to you as soon as possible, we cannot guarantee a delivery time. We cannot guarantee that you will like the wine, because we may not have sampled it." Lots of these non-guaranteed wines are in fact made by the same producers as those that Virgin Wines recommends and many are indeed superior *cuvées*. Obviously the guaranteed wines are either stocked by Virgin or Virgin has a formal arrangement

---

ATTENTION UNLISTED STOCKISTS

It is hoped to build this section into the most comprehensive fizz buyer's reference available in the UK, so if you would like to be included in a future edition, please contact Tom Stevenson at:

tom.stevenson@
fizz.worldonline.co.uk

Warning: Any other unsolicited mail received at this address will be ignored

Please note that inclusion in this guide involves no charge whatsoever, although stockists are expected to update or correct any factual information given in their profiles below, and those with own-label products are requested to submit tasting samples at their own cost. Stockists in previous editions who have not updated their information have been deleted for the sake of accuracy, but are most welcome to appear in future editions.

with their supplier, whereas the others are barely more than a listing of every wine that Virgin can find on the Net or off. This would be fine if Virgin spelt this out, but what I do not like is that consumers are given the distinct impression that they have "17,500 wines to choose from – the largest selection of wines available in the world from one retailer", but if and when they examine the small print, they will discover that Virgin might not even be able to locate any wines beyond its core range of 466 products ("while we do our best to get them to you as soon as possible, we cannot guarantee a delivery time"). This is fair and understandable, given the logistics involved, but Virgin should come clean on its home page about what "the largest selection of wines available in the world" actually consists of. It is after all one of the most obvious ways that both the purveyor and consumer can take advantage of the Internet. However, once consumers understand precisely what Virgin's wine range is, they might also wish to consider other sites, such as Wine Searcher (*see* below). Virgin Wines is, nevertheless, a remarkable site and I know that I shall be using it frequently.

Waitrose
Doncastle Road, Southern Industrial Area, Bracknell, Berks RG12 8YA
☎ 01344 824694
℻ 01344 825255 ✉
www.waitrose.co.uk
This supermarket's large and wonderfully eclectic range of wine is a favourite with many wine enthusiasts, who should be more than pleased with its range of own-brand bubbly, especially Waitrose Cuvée 2000, the highest-scoring own-label Champagne to grace these pages. For those

in Scotland and the north of England who have felt disenfranchised every time a southerner rants on about Waitrose, they can obtain the entire Waitrose range by mail-order through Waitrose Direct ☎ 0800 188881 or ℻ 0800 188882. There are some real beauties you can obtain only through Waitrose Direct. Between editions, for example, Waitrose Direct was offering Lanson 1961 en magnum for £159 and had I noticed before it sold out, I would have purchased some, even though I already have a couple in my cellar. Not only because of its stratospheric quality (I'd have to taste it against other 98 point Champagnes to decide whether I could push the score any higher), but also because it was an absolute steal. This was recently disgorged, just like the ones I selected for a special auction to celebrate the launch of my *Christie's World Encyclopedia of Champagne & Sparkling Wine* back in 1998. At that time a single lot of three magnums went for £650 (plus 10% buyer's premium and 17.5% VAT), which is the equivalent of almost £280 a magnum, and I have to say worth every penny. From Waitrose Direct, however, you could have purchased the same wine from the same provenance for almost half the price! So keep your eyes peeled for these little gems. But don't bother to do this via the Waitrose Direct Website. Not unless you're the sort who likes to watch paint dry, that is. It must be the slowest site in cyberspace, and they've been promising to speed it up for well over a year now.
❽❾ WAITROSE CHAMPAGNE 1990 CUVÉE 2000 BRUT, F. BONNET
For those who might be puzzled, the vintage is found in the small print on the rear of the bottle. This was the best

"Millennium" cuvée offered by any supermarket last year (when it scored 88 points) and was dosaged to come right by 31 December 1999, which it duly did, but has continued to improve throughout the year. This Champagne should remain on splendid form for at least a couple of years, gradually building up its already mature toasty richness, yet remaining fresh and crisp due to heaps of ripe acidity.
❗ Now–2002 £25.00
❽❻ WAITROSE CHAMPAGNE NV BRUT, F. BONNET
There's F. Bonnet and there's F. Bonnet, as anyone who has followed this Guide will know. Well, the toasty-chocolate-coffee aromas mingling in the mature yet fresh fruit of this cuvée tell me that Waitrose has chosen F. Bonnet at its best.
❗ Now–2003 £14.99
❽⓿ WAITROSE CHAMPAGNE NV BLANC DE NOIRS BRUT, ALEXANDRE BONNET
The same producer as Somerfield's blanc de noirs (although Waitrose was the first to source Champagne from Alexandre Bonnet, which is now part of BCC with Boizel, Chanoine, De Venoge and Philipponnat), but this cuvée has no amylic aromas. However, the fruit is not as well-focused, so it's a matter of swings and roundabouts.
❗ Now £11.99
❼❻ WAITROSE CAVA NV BRUT, CASTELLBLANCH
Noticeably more perfumed on the palate than most Cava and not at all like the regular Castellblanch.
❗ Now £4.99
❼❺ WAITROSE SAUMUR NV BRUT, ACKERMAN LAURANCE
Waitrose obviously worked hard to come up with a Saumur of this freshness and elegance.
❗ Now £5.99

Waterloo Wine Co
6 Vine Yard, Borough, London SE1 1QL

☎ 020 7403 7967
📠 020 7357 6976 ✉
sales@waterloowine.co.uk
The UK agents for Le Brun
de Neuville, so it shouldn't be
cheaper anywhere else.

Waters of Coventry
Collins Road, Heathcote,
Warwick CV34 6TF
☎ 01926 888889
📠 01926 887416 ✉
waters@dial.pipex.com
The most exciting change
here is the arrival of
top-performing Champagne
Bonnaire. Although Bonnaire
did not submit any samples
this year, its Blanc de Blancs
scored 90 points in the last
edition. If the current
shipment is just as good, it's a
snip at just over £15 a bottle.

Waverley Direct
Waverley House, Crieff
Road, Perth PH1 2SL
☎ 01738 472019
📠 01738 630338 ✉
customer.enquiries@
   waverley-direct.co.uk
www.waverley-direct.co.uk
A good if predictable range of
grandes marques, the selection
of vintage Champagne being
disappointingly small and
outnumbered two-to-one by
the prestige *cuvées*. Mumm
Cuvée Napa, Shadow Creek,
Green Point, Lindauer and
Graham Beck head up the
sparkling wine alternatives.

Wine&Co
Av. Jean Guillibert,
Zone de Pichaury, 13856
Aix-en-Provence
FRANCE
☎ 0800 169 5043
   or 020 8382 3755
📠 0870 137 5519
   or 0870 169 0627
info@wineandco.com
www.wineandco.com
Predictably this French-based
Internet operation, which has
satellite sites stretching from
the UK to Hong Kong, has
very little fizz from outside
France, and all but one of the
non-French bubblies are from
Domaine Chandon. It will

come as no surprise, then, to
learn that Europ@Web has
invested £16 million in this
venture and that this is the
Internet division of Barnard
Arnault's family holding
company. Bernard Arnault is,
of course, the CEO of
LVMH, which owns Domaine
Chandon. When I searched
the site, I found just 18
Champagnes, which included
the LVMH brands of Moët,
Mercier and Veuve Clicquot.

The Wine Bureau
Cobblers Corner, 58 Tower
Street, Harrogate,
North Yorkshire HG1 1HS
☎ 01423 527772
📠 01423 566330 ✉
sales@winebureau.co.uk
www.winebureau.co.uk
Last year I noted that the
Champagne range might be
small, but it was hard to pick
holes in, with three top class
grandes marques (Gosset,
Roederer and Veuve Clicquot)
supported by two top value
growers (Gallimard and
Fournay), plus Devaux, the
most dynamic cooperative in
the region. In the intervening
12 months Miles Corish has
added Pol Roger to the range,
including the superb Cuvée
Sir Winston Churchill. I had
more criticism for the
sparkling wine alternatives,
which were even thinner on
the ground and although
good, not exactly outstanding,
so it is nice to record changes
here too, most notably
Nyetimber, which is indeed
outstanding.

Wine Cellar
P.O. Box 476, Loushers
Lane, Warrington, Cheshire
WA4 6RQ
☎ 01925 454545
📠 01925 454817 ✉
david.vaughan@parisa.com
www.winecellar.co.uk
A group of 75 wine shops
strung out from Newcastle to
Hove, Wine Cellar is part of
the Parisa group, which also
includes Cellar 5, Berkeley
Wine, Night Vision and

Booze Buster. Some of the
Wine Cellar shops have
licensed café-bars where you
can enjoy any one of the 700
wines on offer for a small
corkage charge. There is a
good, but predictable range
of branded Champagnes,
consisting mostly of *grandes
marques*, with Devaux
for value.

Wine Direct Ltd
18 Rosebery Avenue,
London EC1R 4TD
☎ 0845 066 1122
📠 020 7843 1601 ✉
sales@winedirect.ltd.uk
www.winedirect.ltd.uk
Wine Direct specialises in
next-day-delivery of a good
range of Champagnes (plus
other wines and spirits, of
course) to any part of the UK.
The Champagne range relies
heavily on Ruinart and
Lanson, which is no bad
thing, but there are few
other choices.

Winefinds
Dinton, Salisbury,
Wiltshire SP3 5SR
☎ 01722 716916
📠 01722 716179 ✉
sales@winefinds.co.uk
Every wine offered for sale
has been recommended by a
prestigious blind tasting
panel of independent experts,
including no fewer than ten
Masters of Wine, with Pierre
Moncuit and Jean Moutardier
the result of their
deliberations on Champagne.

Wine Rack
See First Quench

Wine Raks (Scotland)
21 Springfield Road,
Aberdeen AB15 7RJ
☎ 01224 311460
📠 01224 312186 ✉
enq@wineraks.co.uk
www.wineraks.co.uk
An excellent list with lots of
interesting finds from all over
the world, Wine Raks relies
on Aubry & Fils at the
bottom end, moving up to
Cattier (including Clos du

Moulin) and Alfred Gratien, followed by a smattering of quality-minded *grandes marques*. Apparently more sparkling wines are due to be added shortly.

The Winery
4 Clifton Road,
London W9 1SS
☎ 020 7286 6475
📠 020 7286 2733 ✉
dmotion@globalnet.co.uk
This is the sort of merchant that constantly seeks out new wines, rather than those that tend to sit on their butts and rely on their suppliers to do the thinking for them. The Winery exclusively ships Amyot, which was new to me and thus very interesting to taste (I have no contact details for this Champagne, so I have included the recommended *cuvées* below). The Winery also stocks J.P. Robert (as opposed to Alain) and Geoffroy, plus a smallish selection of top *grandes marques*.
🔵 CHAMPAGNE AMYOT NV BRUT ROSÉ, CARTE RUBIS
If you don't mind a touch of sweetness in a Brut Champagne and you like the idea of vanilla-dusted cherries in the fruit, then this is the rosé for you, and I don't mind admitting I was enamoured too.
❗ Now–2001 £15.99
🔵 CHAMPAGNE AMYOT NV BRUT RÉSERVE
Rich and tasty fruit with complex biscuity aromas beginning to push their way through elevated fruit.
❗ Now £16.99
🔵 CHAMPAGNE AMYOT NV BRUT CARTE OR
Elevated fruit for unthinking immediate drinking.
❗ Now £14.99
🔵 CHAMPAGNE AMYOT NV BLANC DE BLANCS
I'd be inclined to rename Amyot Amylic, but there is nice, juicy pineapple fruit underneath and much better acidity than wines of that style normally possess.
❗ Now–2001 £16.99

Winescape
www.winescape.co.uk
A selection of 50-odd Champagnes and sparkling wines, including a number that are very good, but padded out with some that are rather more ordinary.

Wine Searcher
www.wine-searcher.com
This is the best site that I have come across where you can harness the technology of the Internet to track down where specific wines are available and who has the best price. At the time of writing, this site consisted of 172,258 wines available from 358 wine retailers worldwide (98 in the UK). You can restrict your search to specific countries. There were 1,534 Champagnes when I last checked, although many of these would be exactly the same product, of course. The difference merely being price and retailer. That is, after all, the function of this site.

The Wine Society
Gunnels Wood Road,
Stevenage,
Hertfordshire SG1 2BG
☎ 01438 741177
📠 01438 761167 ✉
winesociety@dial.pipex. com
No own-label samples submitted for the second consecutive year.

The Wine Treasury
69-71 Broadway,
London SW8 1SQ
☎ 020 7793 9999
📠 020 7793 8080 ✉
quality@winetreasury.com
www.winetreasury.com
The Wine Treasury has plenty of top-flight wines, but not much in the way of Champagne because proprietor Neville Bleach thinks it's too expensive. I have yet to see this selection blossom into a stunning range of sparkling wine alternatives to Champagne.

Wines of Westhorpe
Marchington,
Staffordshire ST14 8NX
☎ 01283 820285
📠 01283 820631 ✉
wines@westhorpe.co.uk
www.westhorpe.co.uk
The UK source for Törley sparkling wines, for all those homesick Hungarians out there. I think that Wines of Westhorpe have got the message that I'm not exactly fond of Törley fizz, but I thank them for their persistence in sending me samples over the years, for at least I know my opinion is borne of experience, not ignorance. The list has lots of fascinating, super-value classic wine alternatives, but no halfway decent sparkling wine alternatives. One thing that upsets me terribly about a sparkling wine, wherever it comes from, is the use of mushroom-shaped closures made of cheap, nasty, inflexible plastic.

Wright Wine Company
The Old Smithy,
Raikes Road, Skipton,
North Yorkshire BD23 1NP
☎ 01756 700886
📠 01756 798580 ✉
www.wineandwhisky.co.uk
This list offers an excellent balance of good value and great quality Champagnes, with plenty of mature vintage Champagnes for those who might think they've missed out. And there are 200 single malts to choose from, if you're looking for a chaser to your glass of Dom Pérignon!

Peter Wylie Fine Wines
Plymtree Manor, Plymtree,
Cullompton,
Devon EX15 2LE
☎ 01884 277555
📠 01884 277557 ✉
peter@wylie-fine-wines. demon.co.uk
www.wyliefinewines.co.uk
Normally a good source for old vintages, they were somewhat depleted at the time of writing. However, it pays to keep an eye open.

I do and I'm an occasional customer here.

Yapp Brothers
The Old Brewery,
Mere, Wiltshire BA12 6DY
☎ 01747 860423
🖷 01747 860929 ✉
lance@yapp.co.uk
Bruno Paillard has been delisted, which is a pity, and so has Jacquesson, which is extraordinary because but for Yapp Jacquesson would not have got a foot in the UK market door as early as it did. These brands have now been replaced with Dumangin, who makes some nice Champagnes, but not of the class, quality or consistency of either Paillard or Jacquesson. Nevertheless the grower status appeals to Robin Yapp's sense of place and I'm not going to argue with that. Saint Péray is as ever from Jean-Louis Thiers and Clairette de Die from Jean-Pierre Archard, plus various Loire bubblies.

York Wines
Wellington House, Sheriff Hutton, York YO60 6QY
☎ 01347 878716
🖷 01347 878546 ✉
york_wines@lineone.net
www.yorkwines.co.uk
A small, traditional wine importing company specializing in "wines selected for their quality and originality and sold at competitive prices", York Wines takes a pride in providing a first class personal service to all their customers. The range of fizz is very

small indeed, consisting of Loriot and Noirot for Champagne, and Chevaliers de Malte, Château de Brézé, Terrace Road and Darwin's Path as the alternatives.

Young's Wine Direct
Cockpen House,
20-30 Buckhold Road,
Wandsworth,
London SW18 4AP
☎ 020 8875 7007
🖷 020 8875 7009 ✉
wine_direct@youngs.co.uk
www.youngswinedirect.co.uk
The online mail-order arm of Young's, the oldest brewery in the country (it's first brewer, Humphrey Langridge, first brewed beer in 1581, when Elizabeth I was on the throne). The range of Champagne and sparkling wine is relatively small, but it is mostly well selected.
80 COCKBURN & CAMPBELL CHAMPAGNE NV SPECIAL CUVÉE BRUT
What this cuvée lacks in finesse it makes up for with plenty of peachy fruit.
🍷 Now–2001 £12.75

Noel Young Wines
56 High Street,
Trumpington,
Cambridgeshire CB2 2LS
☎ 01223 844744
🖷 01223 844736 ✉
admin@nywines.co.uk
www.nywines.co.uk
Apart from Vilmart, there are no offerings from grower Champagnes this year, but there is plenty of juicy stuff from the likes of Bollinger,

Gosset, Pol Roger and Veuve Clicquot, plus the occasional mature vintages. At the time of writing the latter included Henriot 1959 at £99.50 per bottle and Deutz 1975 at £40 per bottle. Noel Young is also a treasure trove for lovers of Australian fizzy reds, including Hardy's Tintara, Fox Creek Vixen Shiraz-Cabernets, Hollick Merlot, Haselgrove Garnet and the fabulous Charles Melton.

A GUIDE TO WINE AUCTION HOUSES

BUYING AT AUCTION

Although old vintage Champagne is no longer the auction-bargain it used to be, it is still relatively inexpensive compared to Bordeaux. The reason for the disparity in prices fetched is that, unlike Bordeaux, Champagne has never been regarded as an investment. Hundreds of cases of Bordeaux's great classed growths regularly move from cellar to cellar via the auction circuit, but when Champagne appears at auction, it is usually in small mixed lots and bidders are haunted by their uncertain provenance.

Champagne is highly sensitive to changes in storage conditions, making it one of the most awkward wines to buy at auction. Too many mature vintages of Champagne sold at auction are dark in colour, have lost most, if not all, of their fizz and taste like a very old white Burgundy, or even sherry. This keeps auction prices keen and, if you're willing to take the gamble, you can unearth some real treasures for a relatively small outlay.

BUYING TIPS

1. Try to taste all the wines you are interested in. Tasting all your target wines will seldom be possible, because, even for the largest sales, a mere fraction of the lots will be available at the pre-sale tasting. However, satisfying the bidder's palate is worth more than any guarantee of provenance.

2. If you cannot taste the wine, it is wise to bid for only those lots whose provenance is vouched for in unambiguous terms, preferably direct from the producer's cellars.

3. Before the sale, work out how high you are willing to bid and keep strictly to this limit. It is easy to get carried away, but the successful bidder is not always the winner. Only a fool pays over the odds. When working out what your highest bid should be, don't forget to allow for any Buyer's Premium (commonly 10%) and any taxes that might be applicable (17.5% VAT on many UK lots, for example).

4. If you cannot taste the wine, and you are not sure of its provenance, you might still get a bargain. However, the risks are that much greater and you should trim your upper bid limit by at least 20%.

5. Do not be put off bidding for a wine that has an estimate above your upper limit. When lots have no reserve, and fail to achieve the price expected, the auctioneer will be grateful for any bid.

Auction Houses

Contact these firms for their current, scheduled auctions and details of how to obtain a catalogue.

AUSTRALIA

Oddbins Wine Auctions
2 Grenfell Street
Kent Town
South Australia 5067
☎ +61 08 8362 4700
℻ +61 08 8362 3355
Australia's premier wine auctioneers.

UNITED KINGDOM

Bonhams
Dowell Street,
Devon EX14 8LX
☎ 01404 41872
℻ 01404 43137
Head of Wine Department:
Richard Harvey MW.
Founded in 1793, Bonhams is one of the four surviving Georgian auction houses in London. The majority of sales take place at its London salerooms in Knightsbridge and Chelsea, although all wine auctions are conducted at Bath, one of Bonhams' two provincial salerooms. Associated firms are located in the Channel Islands, USA, on Mainland Europe and in the Far East.

Christie's
8 King Street,
St James's,
London SW1Y 6QT
☎ 0171 389 2820
℻ 0171 389 2869
www.christies.com
Head of Wine Department: following the departure of Christopher Burr MW, Thomas Hudson is Head of King Street. Christie's is the world's oldest and largest wine auctioneer, having sold wine by auction since 1766. Most sales are held in

London and New York (in conjunction with the retailer Zachys), with additional sales in Los Angeles, Geneva, Glasgow, Amsterdam, Bordeaux, Hong Kong, and Melbourne. Christie's jumped into the online auction market in early-1999, shortly after Sotheby's.

Philips Auctioneers

1 Old King Street,
Bath BA1 2JT
☎ 01225 310609
℻ 01225 446675
www.philips-auction.com

Founded over 200 years ago in 1796 by Harry Phillips, this auction house has built up a strong reputation both in the UK and abroad, with over 875 sales held each year through its international network of 23 salerooms.

Sotheby's

34-35 New Bond Street
London W1A 2AA
☎ 0171 498 8090
℻ 0171 409 3100
www.sothebys.com
Head of Wine Department: Serena Sutcliffe MW.
Founded in 1744, Sotheby's

is the oldest and largest auction house in the world, although Christie has a longer history of wine sales and a larger turnover in that department. Although most of Sotheby's sales are in London, New York (with Sherry Lehman) and Zurich, the company entered the online auction market in January 1999, and was followed quickly by its rival Christie's. Sotheby's, however, seems determined to keep e-commerce lead, having just signed a deal at the time of writing with Amazon.com, which involves Amazon purchasing one million Sotheby's shares, putting down $10 million on a further million shares, investing $45 million in this old-established auction house. The two companies plan to run a joint auction web site, although Sotheby's will continue with its own online sales.

J. Straker, Chadwick & Sons

Market Street, Chambers,
Abergavenny,
Gwent NP7 5SD

☎ 01873 852624
℻ 01873 857311
Industrious Welsh-based Auction house. While the Big Boys undoubtedly have the cream, some interesting lots pop up here.

UNITED STATES

The Chicago Wine Company

5663 West Howard Street,
Niles,
Illinois 60714
☎ +1 847 647 8789
℻ +1 847 647 7265
tcwc@aol.com

The Chicago Wine Company is widely respected throughout the world, regularly conducting more wine auctions in the USA than all the other auctioneers put together. Sales range from the rarest wines of the finest provenance to the openly daring Caveat Emptor auctions. Catalogues are excellent and free of charge (others charge up to $25) and lots are delivered in complimentary polystyrene containers. Probably the most innovative wine auctions in the world.

Online Auctions

Acker Merrall & Condit

www.finewineauctions.com

Acker Merrall & Condit claim to be "the world's largest Internet Wine Auction To date".

The Wine Auction Gazette

www.wine-auction-gazette.com

This site provides information about wine auctions, prices, auctioneers, vintages and the complete international wine auction calendar.

AuctionVine

www.auctionvine.com
AuctionVine was founded in 1996, when it worked

exclusively with Morrell and Company of New York, but in 1999 decided not to restrict itself to any one merchant. This online auction house offers rare collectible wines from cellars across the USA and Europe. Its site is composed entirely of certified merchants, which AuctionVine claims gives bidders confidence to participate in auctions that they might not have considered in the past. Works in conjunction with Wine.Com below.

The Mid-Atlantic Wine Auction Company

www.netwineauction.com

The Mid-Atlantic Wine Auction Company was founded in 1998 by Hillard Donner, proprietor of Mills Wine and Spirit Mart, Annapolis, Maryland, and auctions off wines from "national and international vineyards of the highest reputation".

Uvine

www.uvine.com
Run by ex-Christie's Head, Christopher Burr MW, Uvine is a universal wine exchange that "allows you to trade fine wine as easily as you would trade stocks and shares". The quality and provenance of every wine is guaranteed. A fee

of 3.5% is charged to both buyer and seller.

Vines Premium Wine Auctioneers

www.vines.netauctions.net.au

Vines Premium Wine Auctioneers have conducted wine auctions in Brisbane and Adelaide for many years in conjunction with other wine auction houses prior to setting up what is claimed to be Australia's premier Internet wine auction site. Allows users to download catalogues.

Winebid

www.winebid.com

Winebid was established in 1996 and now conducts 5 auctions per month in Napa, Chicago, Sydney and London. It is without doubt the most successful online wine auction house of all, with 10,000 registered bidders and combined monthly sales in excess of $1m, making it second only to the traditional wine houses of Sotheby's and Christie's.

WineCommune

www.winecommune.com

WineCommune is a so-called free online wine auction site, connecting wine buyers and wine sellers, both private and retail. Sellers from across the world can post their wines in any number of categories for auctions lasting from one to 14 days. Buyers then log onto WineCommune at their leisure, review the available wine lots, then bid on those that interest them. Reverse auctions are available via a "wanted" section, so you can off-load wines without going to the bother of auctioning them.

Wine Owners

www.wine-owners.com

You can set up a "cellar" of wines you want to sell and allow other members to make "surprise bids" on them, or you can search through other members' cellars for something you want. The seller pays Wine Owners 5% of any accepted price.

Wine Spectator

www.winespectator.com

Wine Auctions is available only to full-access subscribers ($29.95 or $9.95 for a three-month Trial Subscription).

GLOSSARY

Abbreviations: (Fr.) French (Ger.) German (It.) Italian (Sp.) Spanish.

Accessible Easy to drink.

Acidic Some people confuse this term with bitter. Think of lemon juice as acidic, lemon peel as bitter. The right acidity is vital for sparkling wine.

Aftertaste The flavour and aroma left in the mouth after the wine has been swallowed.

Ages gracefully A wine that retains finesse as it matures.

Aggressive The opposite of soft and smooth.

Amylic The peardrop, banana or bubble-gum aromas of amyl or isoamyl acetate, lots of which can be produced if the first fermentation is conducted at a low temperature. An amylic preponderance is not ideal for classic sparkling wine as it overshadows the subtle aromas of autolysis, and may prevent the development of post-disgorgement bottle-aromas. *See Autolysis, Bottle-aromas.*

AOC (Fr.) Appellation d'Origine Contrôlée, the top rung of the French wine quality system. Champagne is unique in that it does not have to indicate that it is an AOC wine on the label: the name Champagne is considered sufficient guarantee.

Appellation Literally a "name", this usually refers to an official geographical-based designation for a wine.

Aroma Some people use the word aroma for grape-derived fragrance, and bouquet for more winey odours, especially when developed in bottle; however the two are synonymous in this book.

Aromatic grape varieties Grapes such as the Gewürztraminer, Muscat and Riesling overwhelm the subtle effects of autolysis, and are thus too aromatic for classic brut sparkling wines, yet often ideal for sweet styles of sparkling wine.

Assemblage (Fr.) The blending of base wines that creates the final *cuvée*.

Asti (It.) A town in Northern Italy that gives its name to a fine sweet sparkling wine.

Atmosphere A measurement of atmospheric pressure. One atmosphere is 15 lbs per square inch (psi). A sparkling wine can be anything up to six atmospheres, or 90 lbs psi. This decreases when the bottle is chilled for serving. A fully sparkling wine of six atmospheres will be just 2.5 atmospheres at 6° C.

Austere A wine that lacks fruit.

Autolysis The breakdown of yeast cells after the second fermentation that creates the inimitable "champagny" character.

Autolytic The smell of a freshly disgorged brut-style fizz. This is not "yeasty" but has an acacia-like flowery finesse.

Balance A harmonious relationship between acids, alcohol, fruit, tannin (only in some red sparkling wines) and other natural elements.

Balthazar Large bottle equivalent to 16 normal-sized 75 cl bottles.

Barrel-fermented Some houses, e.g. Krug, ferment in old, well-used oak barrels. A few others, e.g. Selosse and Vilmart, use new oak, a fashion picked up by a number of New World producers, e.g. Pelorus and Kristone.

Barrique (Fr.) Literally means "barrel", but generically used in English-speaking countries for any small oak cask. Often denotes the use of new oak.

Base wines Fully fermented dry wines that when blended together form the basis of a sparkling wine *cuvée*.

Biscuity A desirable aspect of bouquet found particularly in a well-matured Pinot Noir-dominated Champagne. Some top-quality Chardonnay-dominated wines can also acquire a creamy-biscuitness.

Bitterness Either an unpleasant aspect of a poorly made wine or an expected characteristic of undeveloped, concentrated flavours that should, with maturity, become rich and delicious. See also Acidic.

Blanc de Blancs (Fr.) A white wine made from white grapes.

Blanc de Noirs (Fr.) A white wine made from black grapes.

Blind, blind tasting An objective tasting where the identity of wines is unknown until the taster has made notes and given scores. All competitive tastings are blind.

Blowzy Overblown and exaggerated.

Blush wine Synonym of rosé.

BOB Buyer's Own Brand, under which many retailers and restaurants sell wine.

Body The extract of fruit and alcoholic strength together give an impression of weight in the mouth.

Bottle-age The length of time a wine spends in bottle before it is consumed. A wine that has good bottle-age is one that has sufficient time to mature properly. Bottle-ageing has a mellowing effect.

Bottle-aromas Mellowing aromas created after disgorgement.

Bottle-fermented I use this without discrimination for any sparkling wine that has undergone a second fermentation in bottle, but when seen on a label, it invariably means the wine has been made by the transfer method.

Bouquet *See Aroma.*

Breed The finesse of a wine based on the intrinsic qualities of grape and terroir (growing environment) combined with the irrefutable skill and experience of a great winemaker.

Brut (Fr.) Dry. Literally means "raw" or "bone dry", but in practice there is always some sweetness in a sparkling wine.

Buttery Normally caused by diacetyl, which the food industry uses to make margarine taste more like butter. It is fine in still Chardonnays, but the taste detracts from the finesse of sparkling wines.

Caramel An extreme version of buttery.

Cava (Sp.) The generic appellation for méthode champenoise wines produced in various delimited areas of Spain, mostly in the Penedès region near Barcelona.

Cave, caves (Fr.) Literally cellar, cellars.

Champagne (Fr.) Specifically a sparkling wine produced in the delimited area of Champagne in Northern France.

"Champagne", "Champaña" The appellation for sparkling wine made in Champagne is protected within the EU, but is sometimes used loosely elsewhere, especially in the USA, where it is legal to sell domestically produced "champagne". It is also exploited by the Champenois themselves, who call their South American products Champaña.

Champenois (Fr.) The people of Champagne.

Chardonnay One of the greatest sparkling wine grapes for the classic brut style.

Charmat (Fr.) See Cuve close.

Chef de caves (Fr.) Literally the "cellar manager", but can also mean the winemaker.

Courtier en vins (Fr.) A wine broker who acts as a go-between for growers and producers.

Crayères (Fr.) Chalk-pits in Northern France dug out in Gallo-Roman times.

Creamy Creaminess is most apparent in Chardonnay-based sparkling wines. The sensation, picked up at the back of the throat, is believed to be a combination of the finesse of the mousse (created by the most minuscule of bubbles and their slow release) and a subtle malolactic influence.

Creamy-biscuity See Biscuity.

Creamy-caramel malo A lesser, more acceptable version of caramel.

Crémant (Fr.) A sparkling wine with a gentler mousse than normal.

Cru (Fr.) Literally a "growth", cru normally refers to a vineyard site, although in Champagne it is a term used for an entire village.

Cushiony A beautifully soft, ultra-fine sensation caused by the minuscule bubbles of a first-rate mousse.

Cuve close (Fr.) A method invented by Eugène Charmat of producing sparkling wine through a second fermentation in a sealed vat or tank. Synonymous with Charmat method or tank method.

Cuvée (Fr.) Originally the wine of one cuve or vat, this now refers to a precise blend or specific product, which may be blended from several vats.

Débourbage (Fr.) The settling process that removes bits of skin, pips and so on from the freshly pressed grape juice.

Dégorgement (Fr.) *See Disgorgement.*

Demi-sec (Fr.) Literally "semi-dry", but actually meaning semi-sweet to sweet.

Disgorgement The removal of sediment after the second fermentation.

DOC/DOCG (It.) Denominazione di Origine Controllata/e Garantita. Italian wine quality system based on grape variety and origin. "Garantita" denotes an extra rung of quality.

Dosage (Fr.) The amount of sugar solution added to a sparkling wine after disgorgement.

Doux (Fr.) Literally "sweet", actually very sweet.

Dry straw See Straw.

Easy-drinking Probably not a complex wine, but it slips down easily.

Elevated fruit Synonymous with VA fruitiness.

English aroma A very fresh herbaceous character.

Estery A prickly, ethereal-minerally impression. Esters are essential components of any wine and contribute to its fruitiness, but when estery aromas dominate a wine it is unready and has probably been disgorged too soon.

Explosive A sparkling wine can be literally explosive in the bottle, which is due to defects on the inner surface, or "explosive" in the mouth, which is due to the wine. The latter is often because too much carbonic gas is free (not bound to the wine), although why this sometimes occurs is not fully understood.

Extra-brut Drier than brut, possibly no dosage.

Extra-sec (Fr.) Literally "extra-dry", but usually merely dry to medium dry.

Fat Full in body and extract.

Fixed sulphur Sulphur is added to wine primarily as a preservative, to prevent oxidation. Most of the sulphur molecules fix onto other molecules in the wine, especially the oxygen molecules. Sometimes they combine disastrously with other molecules, creating bad smells. However, the toasty bottle-aroma adored by most Champagne aficionados is also possibly a by-product of fixed sulphur. *See also Free sulphur.*

Flowery Floral aromas are found in young sparkling wines and are the precursors to the fuller, deeper, fruitier aromas of maturity. Specific acacia aromas are found in recently disgorged wines of any age.

Foudre (Fr.) A large wooden cask or vat.

Foxy The highly perfumed character of certain indigenous American grapes. It can be sickly sweet and cloying to other nations' palates.

Free sulphur The acrid odour of free sulphur – smelling like a recently extinguished match – will go away with time in bottle, or a swirl of the glass. *See also Fixed sulphur, Sulphur.*

Frizzante (It.) Semi-sparkling or slightly fizzy: the equivalent of pétillant.

Frizzantino (It.) Very lightly sparkling: the same as perlant.

Fruity Although wine is made from grapes, it will not have a fruity flavour unless the grapes have the correct combination of ripeness and acidity. Simple fruity fizz is fine if it is cheap, but fruit alone is insufficient for a classic sparkling wine.

Full Usually refers to body, e.g. full-bodied. But a wine can be light in body yet full in flavour.

Fully fermented A wine that is allowed to complete its natural course of fermentation and so yield a totally dry wine.

Fully sparkling A wine with a pressure of 5–6 atmospheres.

Grande marque (Fr.) Literally a great or famous brand.

Herbaceous A green-leaf or white-currant characteristic that is usually associated with under-ripeness, particularly with aromatic grape varieties.

Jeroboam Large bottle equivalent to four normal-sized 75 cl bottles.

Lees The sediment that accumulates in a vat or bottle during fermentation.

Light A qualification of body.

Liqueur d'expédition (Fr.) Solution of sugar and wine added to a sparkling wine after disgorgement.

Liqueur de tirage (Fr.) The bottling liqueur – made of wine, yeast and sugar – which induces the mousse.

Magnum Large bottle equivalent to two normal-sized 75 cl bottles, the ideal volume for ageing Champagne.

Malolactic/Malo A biochemical process that turns the hard malic acid of unripe grapes into soft lactic acid and carbonic gas.

Méthode champenoise (Fr.) The process developed by the Champenois that converts a fully fermented still wine into a sparkling wine through the induction of a second fermentation in the same bottle in which it is sold (*see pp10–11*).

Methuselah Large bottle equivalent to eight normal-sized 75 cl bottles.

Mono-cru Champagne made from a single cru.

Mousse The thousands of fine bubbles in a sparkling wine.

Mousseux (Fr.) Sparkling, foaming etc.

Nebuchadnezzar Large bottle equivalent to 20 normal-sized 75 cl bottles.

Négociant (Fr.) Commonly used to describe large wine-producing companies.

Non-dosage (Fr.) A sparkling wine that has received no dosage of liqueur de tirage.

Non-vintage (NV) In theory a blend of at least two different years, but many producers, particularly in Champagne, grade their *cuvées* on selection, often selling a pure vintage *sans année* (without year).

Oaky The aromatic quality picked up from new oak, usually consisting of the creamy-vanilla aroma of vanillin, a natural oak aldehyde and also the principal aromatic component in vanilla pods.

Organic A generic term for wines that are produced with the minimum amount of sulphur, from grapes grown without chemical fertilizers, pesticides or herbicides.

Over-oxidative Verges on oxidised, and infers aldehydic aromas such as the sherry-like acetaldehyde.

Oxidation, oxidized From the moment grapes are pressed or crushed, oxidation sets in. It is an unavoidable part of fermentation and essential to the maturation process: "oxidative" denotes a certain maturity. To say a wine is "oxidized", however, means that it has been subjected to too much oxidation and has an unwanted sherry-like character.

Oxidative A wine that openly demonstrates the character of maturation on the nose or palate. The longer it takes to appear in a wine, the more finesse the wine will have. Too oxidative or over-oxidative verges on oxidised, and infers aldehydic aromas such as the sherry-like acetaldehyde.

Peppery A somewhat incongruous taste associated with sparkling wine. If detected as just a flicker in a young blend, it can add to the wine's future complexity, but be wary of a dominant pepperiness.

Perlant (Fr.) Lightly sparkling.

Perlwein (Ger.) Cheap, semi-sparkling wine made by carbonating a still wine.

Pétillance, pétillant (Fr.) A wine with enough carbonic gas to create a light sparkle.

Pinot Noir (Fr.) Black grape variety used in Champagne.

Récoltant-manipulant (Fr.) A grower who produces Champagne exclusively from his or her own vineyards.

Rehoboam Large bottle equivalent to six normal-sized 75 cl bottles.

Remuage (Fr.) The process whereby the sediment is encouraged down to the neck of the bottle in preparation for disgorgement.

Reserve wines Older wines added to a non-vintage blend to create a sense of maturity.

Rich, richness A balanced wealth of fruit and depth on the palate and finish.

Rooty Usually refers to a certain rooty richness found in Pinot Noir. Not vegetal, which is a negative term.

Rosado (Sp.) Pink.

Rosé (Fr.) Pink.

Saignée (Fr.) The process of drawing off surplus liquid from the press or vat in order to produce a rosé wine from the free-run juice. In cooler wine regions, the remaining mass of grape pulp may be used to make a darker red wine than would normally be possible because of a greater ratio of solids to liquid.

Salmanazar Large bottle equivalent to 12 normal-sized 75 cl bottles.

Sassy Used to describe fruit in a wine that is lively, jaunty, breezy etc.

Sboccatura (It.) Disgorged.

Sec (Fr.) Literally dry, but effectively medium to medium-sweet.

Sekt (Ger.) Sparkling wine produced in Germany, usually by the cuve close method.

Soft An attractive smoothness caused when fruit has the upperhand over acidity. This is very desirable, but a wine that is too soft will lack acidity.

Solera (Sp.) System of continually refreshing an established blend with a small amount of new wine.

Sprightly fruitiness A positive outcome of ultra-fruitiness accentuated by volatile acidity. The term is used in this book instead of "VA fruitiness".

Spumante (It.) Literally just "sparkling", but normally refers to a fully sparkling wine. See Fully sparkling.

Straw Straw-like aromas often blight sparkling wines. Sometimes the aroma is reminiscent of dry straw, other times wet straw, sometimes it is simply straw-like. The aroma possibly comes from the yeast, or rotten grapes, or the reaction of yeast on rotten grapes.

Structure The structure of a wine is based on the balance of its solids (tannin, acidity, sugar, and extract or density of fruit flavour) with the alcohol, and how positively the form feels in the mouth.

Sulphur, SO2 A preservative used primarily to prevent oxidation. See also Free

sulphur, Fixed sulphur.

Tank method Another term for cuve close.

Terpene A terpene character may indicate Riesling in the blend, but is more likely to be due to the base wine being kept unduly long in tank.

Toasty The slow-developing bottle-induced aroma associated with Chardonnay.

Transfer method Decanting under pressure from one size bottle to another, not the ideal of méthode champenoise.

VA Volatile acidity.

VA fruitiness Ultra-fruitiness accentuated by volatile acidity. This can be a positive factor, but VA has such negative connotations that I have used "sprightly fruitiness" instead.

Vanilla *See Oaky.*

Vin de cuvée (Fr.) Made only from the first and therefore the best pressing.

Vin de garde (Fr.) Wine that is capable of great improvement if left to age.

Vintage The harvest or wine of a single year.

Volatile acidity This has a sweet vinegary aroma and if too obvious may be deemed a fault. But a certain amount of VA is essential for fruitiness, and high levels can sometimes be a positive factor. *See Sprightly fruitiness, VA fruitiness.*

Wet straw *See Straw.*

AUTHOR'S ACKNOWLEDGMENTS

I owe my greatest thanks at Dorling Kindersley to Edward Bunting, who has the unenviable task of turning around the editing of this annual publication in next to no time. Other essential personnel behind the scenes who deserve recognition are Sonia Charbonnier, Sally Somers, Kevin Ryan and Nicki Lampon.

The first edition sold over 47,000 copies according to my royalty statement, which was pretty good for a book sneaked out without a launch, so I am literally indebted to Peter Stafford and his sales team, as well as Stefan Reynolds and Sarah Burgess at Special Sales. Since this guide was first published in 1998, it has been translated into German, Italian, Japanese, Norwegian and Danish, with separate English-language editions sold in the USA and Canada. The accumulation of sublicensed editions is the difference between success and failure for any book, thus once more I must thank Anthony Melville and his team for their continuing efforts in this respect.

As ever, my gratitude cannot be properly expressed to the hundreds of producers who at great expense send me samples from all four corners of the wine world, but I remain appreciative, even of those whose wines failed to pass muster (because I hope that a new vintage or a different *cuvée* will qualify in a future edition, so they must not give up hope). My thanks also go to all those who kindly received me during visits for this guide to Champagne, Germany, Franciacorta, Asti, New York, Michigan, New Zealand and Australia. I am greatly obliged to the following, who either organized tastings in the wine areas indicated, set up large centralized tastings in London or orchestrated industry-wide shipments of samples to my tasting facility: Richard Kannemacher (Alsace); Hazel Murphy and Sally Marden (Australia); Madame Martinez (Bordeaux); Nelly Blau Picard (Burgundy); Joe Rollo (California); Françoise Peretti (Champagne); David Wheeler and Jon Leighton (England and Wales); Cathérine Manac'h (France, including liaising with regional representatives); Owen Bird (Franciacorta and Italy generally); Madame Aurousseau (Gaillac); Anne Whitehurst and Ulrike Bahm (Germany); Nico Manessis (Greece); Nicolas Visier (Jura); Christine Behey Molines (Limoux); Claire Duchêne (Loire: Crémant, Anjou and Saumur); Claudine Izabelle (Loire: Crémant, Touraine, Montlouis and Vouvray); David Creighton and Sandra Silfven (Michigan); Scott Osborn and Barbara Adams (New York); Katherine O'Callaghan, Anna Lawrence, Elmira Curin and Anne-Marie McKenzie (New Zealand); Thierry Mellenotte and Jean Gaber (Rhône: Die and St-Péray); Monsieur Bouche (Savoie); Jeff Grier (South Africa); Graham Hines (Wines from Spain); and Steve Burns (Washington state).

Immeasurable thanks to my friend Jeff Porter of Evenlode Press for taking in and forwarding all the wines submitted, and to my wife Pat for logging the wines onto the database and setting up all the blind tastings. Once again my sincere apologies for any omissions.

PICTURE CREDITS

PICTURE RESEARCHERS
Brigitte Arora, Ellen Root

SPECIAL PHOTOGRAPHY AND DESIGN
Andy Crawford, Steve Gorton, Neil Lukas,
Dave Pugh

A special thanks to Bernard Higton for the
initial design and styling.

Dorling Kindersley would like to thank the
following companies for providing items to
be photographed:
**Codorníu, Matthias Deis, Freiherr zu
Knyphausen, Nyetimber, Screwpull
International, Vilmart, Winzersekt
Sprendlingen**

AGENCY PHOTOGRAPHS
t – top; tl – top left; tlc – top left centre; tc –
top centre; trc – top right centre; tr – top
right; cla – centre left above; ca – centre
above; cra – centre right above; cl – centre
left; c – centre; cr – centre right; clb – centre
left below; cb – centre below; crb – centre
right below; bl – bottom left; b – bottom; bc
– bottom centre; bcl – bottom centre left; br
– bottom right; bra – bottom right above; brb
– bottom right below; d – detail

Allsport Adrian Murrell 56t; **Bellavista** 48b;
Guido Berlucchi: 49t, 50b; **Billecart-Salmon**
22t; **Bollinger** 11t, 23t/c/b; **Bouvet-Ladubay**
39b; Ca'del Bosco: 51t; **CBI, London** 11crb;
Cephas Andy Christodolo 2–3; Kevin Judd
59t; Alain Proust 61t, 62t; Mick Rock 13t,
16t, 24t, 27c, 35t, 36br, 37t, 44t, 47b, 55b;
Codorníu 41tr/cl, 43b; **Corbis**: W. Wayne

Lockwood, M. D. 12t; **Culver Pictures** 52t;
Deutsches Weininstitut 46t; **DIAF, Paris**
Jean-Daniel Sudres 1 (insert), 4t, 19t; Daniel
Thierry 6t; **E.T. Archive** 8t, 54t; **Mary Evans
Picture Library** 8b, 9cr/br, 45t, 46c, 47t;
Ferrari Joachim Falco 5c; 48t, 51b; **Freixenet**
40t, 42b, 43t, 40–41b; **Hulton-Getty** 9t;
Gosset 21b, 24bl; **Gramona** 42t; **Charles
Heidsieck** 17, 25cr; De Visu 25t;
**Seppelt/Image Library, State Library of New
South Wales** 58b; **Jackson Estate** 59b;
Jacquesson & Fils 26t/b; **Kobal Collection**
52c; **Krug** 14t, 27t; **Laurent-Perrier** 28t; **Moët
& Chandon** 16c, 20b, 29b; **Pol Roger**
31t/c/b; **Janet Price** 12b, 32b; **Retrograph
Archive, London** Martin Breese 16b, 29t;
Louis Roederer 9bl; Jean-Claude Rouzaud
30t; Michel Jolyot 30b; **Root Stock**,
Ludwigsburg Hendrik Holler 4–5b, 36bl,
38b, 44b, 52–53b, 54b, 56b, 61b, 62b;
Ruinart 18c; *Champagne Ruinart, Rheims*,
Alphonse Mucha @ ADAGP, Paris and
DACS, London 1998 32r; **Salon** 33b; **Scope**
Bernard Galeron 50t; Michel Guillard 22b;
Eric Quentin 20t; **Southcorp Wines Europe**
57bl; **SOPEXA (UK)** 39T; **Topham
Picturepoint** Ulf Berglund 60t; **Veuve
Clicquot Ponsardin** 5t, 11cra/b, 34t/b;
Villiera Estate 63t/b; **Vilmart & Ciel** 35b;
Visual Arts Library Collection Kharbine-
Tapabor 9cl, 18b, 21t, 10, 33t, 55t; **John
Wyand** 64t; **Yalumba** 57br, 58t

Back jacket: **Cephas** Mick Rock top left;
StockFood bottom; **The Image Bank** David
de Lossy top right

Back inside jacket: Jason Bell